Video Production

Seventh Edition

Video Production

Disciplines and Techniques

Thomas D. Burrows

Professor Emeritus

California State University–Northridge

Lynne S. Gross

California State University–Fullerton

Donald N. Wood

California State University–Northridge

Boston, Massachusetts   Burr Ridge, Illinois   Dubuque, Iowa
Madison, Wisconsin   New York, New York   San Francisco, California   St. Louis, Missouri

McGraw-Hill

A Division of The **McGraw·Hill** Companies

VIDEO PRODUCTION: DISCIPLINES AND TECHNIQUES, Seventh Edition

 This book is printed on recycled, acid-free paper containing 10% postconsumer waste.

1 2 3 4 5 6 7 8 9 0 QPD/QPD 9 0 9 8 7

ISBN 0–697–32719–1

Editorial director: *Phil Butcher*
Sponsoring editor: *Marjorie Byers*
Developmental editor: *Valerie Raymond*
Marketing manager: *Carl Leonard*
Project manager: *Peggy J. Selle*
Production supervisor: *Sandy Ludovissy*
Designer: *Lu Ann Schrandt*
Compositor: *Shepherd, Inc.*
Typeface: *10/12 Times Roman*
Printer: *Quebecor Printing Dubuque, Inc.*

Photo image collage: The Image Bank, Television Monitors, RTVE, Madrid, Spain by Luis Castañeda in 1992; The Image Bank, Cinematographer, Marc Romanelli; The Image Bank, TV News Broadcast, Patti McConville.

Library of Congress Card Catalog Number: 97–70089

http://www.mhhe.com

Dedication

To our many students who
have helped make teaching
the most rewarding
of all professions.

About the Authors

Tom Burrows

He now holds the title of Professor Emeritus in the Radio, TV and Film Department at California State University, Northridge. Retirement from full-time teaching has provided him the opportunity to pursue a number of activities relating both to his academic background and to his work as a professional broadcaster. He continues to work with California State University, Northridge, on a number of projects, and he is active in the production division of the Broadcast Education Association. During his earlier career as a producer and director in commercial and public broadcasting, he received the Christopher, Emmy, and Peabody awards. He holds an M.A. degree from the School of Journalism at the University of Southern California.

Lynne Schafer Gross

She has taught television production full-time at a number of United States colleges, including California State University-Fullerton, Pepperdine University, UCLA, Loyola Marymount University, and Long Beach City College. She has also taught production internationally in Estonia, Australia, Guyana, Swaziland, and Malaysia. Her professional experience includes serving as director of programming for Valley Cable TV and producing series for commercial, public, and cable television. She is past President of the Broadcast Education Association and has served as Governor for the Academy of Television Arts and Sciences. Her honors include receiving the BEA's Distinguished Education Service Award and being named a Danforth Associate. She has published ten other books and numerous journal articles.

Donald N. Wood

As professor of radio-TV-film, he has been teaching at California State University, Northridge, since 1970. Professor Wood is the author of *Mass Media and the Individual* and *Designing the Effective Message,* and he is co-author of *Educational Telecommunications.* His most recent book (1996) is *Post-Intellectualism and the Decline of Democracy: The Failure of Reason and Responsibility in the Twentieth Century.*

Contents

Preface

The first edition of this text was written over twenty years ago. Since that time much has changed in the field of television. It has gone from a system that was dominated by three TV networks and some local stations to a structure that includes cable TV, corporate video, direct distribution by satellite, and many computer-based video applications. For this reason, we have changed the title from *Television Production* to *Video Production*. We have also added a chapter on interactive media written by James E. Foust of Bowling Green State University.

Another structural change involves a new chapter on cast and crew. This is near the front of the book to give students information that will be helpful as they begin production exercises.

We have kept chapter 1 as an overview that, among other things, chronicles some of the rapid changes in the video field. Chapter 2 is the new one on cast and crew. Chapters 3 through 11 cover the same equipment as in past editions, but they have all been updated to account for technological changes. We are indebted to Jim Foust for updating chapter 11 and for writing chapter 12, the one dealing with interactive media. Following that are chapters on producing and directing. The final chapter, dealing with field production, also serves as a review of the book. The end material of the book includes a glossary, a bibliography, and appendices that, among other things, include production projects.

Any person who has had access to the best professional equipment over the past several decades cannot help but be very impressed with all that can be achieved today through the use of the new switchers, editing equipment, and computer-generated graphic units. What is also somewhat startling is that the rate of change from year to year is definitely accelerating.

But, while the techniques of television may be changing, the disciplines that serve as the underlying strength of any operation remain much the same. The basic concepts of advance preparation, the constant checking of detail, and the necessity for teamwork assume a position of even more importance as technology becomes more complex. We speak here of a number of attitudes and behaviors involving responsibility, self-control, initiative, and respect for the work of others. These disciplines are, in many ways, the most important part of any university-level production course. The authors firmly believe that these disciplines can be learned only within the structure of production exercises that involve full class participation and the rotation of students within the various crew positions.

As in previous editions, we have presented equipment that in our view serves as an example of the technologies that students work with in their institutions or will work with as they first enter the job market. Some equipment used for illustration will be close to state of the art, but in other cases, we have deliberately shown some older, proven units because they are typical of the technology in general use.

Again, we wish to provide a text that serves as an efficient teaching and learning vehicle for introductory and secondary courses in television production. As always, we welcome suggestions and corrections from our colleagues through our respective universities or the publisher.

We have had the advice and assistance of many colleagues and students in putting this text together. While we cannot single out everybody, we would specifically like to thank Augie Grant for his contributions to the color plates and for his assistance over the years, and Friderika Burrows for her diligent proofreading and helpful suggestions. We also wish to thank those who reviewed this edition of the book. They are:

James L. Crandall, Aims Community College;

John A. Davlin, Hartford Community College;

Roger T. Good, Ohio University;

Michael Korpi, Baylor University;

John Malcolm, SUNY Fredonia;

Tom Streeter, Temple University;

Sandra J. Thompson, University of West Florida; and

Richard Worringham, Radford University.

chapter 1

Introduction to Video Production

I n the various editions of this text there are several goals toward which the authors have worked. We feel it is important that students have some sense of the history of equipment development, and how this progress has influenced program production throughout the first half century of television.

Our primary objective remains the presentation of an accepted body of knowledge that introduces students to the operations underlying multiple-camera video production. Our information ranges from how crew members interact with equipment to the manner in which crews interact with each other under the pressure of a difficult production sequence. We describe components such as an audio console, a camera, and a switcher not only in terms of *what they do*, but also with easily understood descriptions of *how and why they function as they do.* Some of this material is, of necessity, rather technical in nature. Whenever possible, this information is presented in the context of how equipment, when properly operated, can be made to serve specific creative purposes.

Other material deals with the importance of teamwork in a crew situation as well as the importance of one's individual attitude to an assigned task. A related goal is to provide support material that will help to ensure that studio production exercises, involving the entire class, can be carried out in a realistic and efficient manner. Such exercises are important to the process of gaining a firm understanding of video production.

In a broad sense, the material in this text is also written with an awareness that more and more positions in the video production field go far beyond the parameters of traditional video production. As a result, an ever increasing number of employment opportunities require a firm knowledge of both the creative *disciplines* of production and their related operational *technologies.* (See figure 1.1.)

1.1

Aspects of Employment in the Video Industry

By size alone, the electronic mass media have become the most powerful form of communication in America today. Almost all households own radios and television sets; more than 80 percent have VCRs and 69 percent subscribe to cable. The growth of the Internet,

Ken Scott, a visualization supervisor with the Jet Propulsion Lab in California, works to enhance the details of images brought back from the planet Jupiter. It should be noted that the essentials of his workstation are similar to other applications that function by means of a computer platform. Examples would include audio and video editing, interactive video production, and musical composition done through the use of the musical instrument digital interface (MIDI).

CD-ROMs, satellite transmission, and other new technologies almost assure that the influence of these media upon our lives can only increase.

To the outsider, and probably to some of the newer entry-level workers, video production might seem to be an endlessly fascinating combination of glamour and excitement. While it is true that status and income levels are often impressive and that the intensity found in many production situations can make the pulse race, there are other aspects of a video production career that make it very attractive. (See figure 1.2.) Most video professionals feel a definite sense of pride in functioning as a part of a team that creates a product generally valued by our society. Whether one works on a TV news program or on developing an industrial training tape, a number of things about being part of a communications team strongly appeal to intelligent, highly-motivated people. Because the effort requires many different and exacting skills, the process of working together and accomplishing this worthwhile and very viable end product provides a strong sense of continuing inner satisfaction as well as a good deal of mutual respect among colleagues.

Disciplines and Techniques

In the study of media production, it is important for students to develop an early understanding of two differing but related aspects of the creative process. First of all, there are a number of definable *techniques* that apply to elements such as equipment operation, script writing, and team organization. Second, there are some equally important individual *disciplines* that one brings to all aspects of all phases of the production process. Most professionals do not view creativity as the exclusive province of writers, directors, and producers, but extend it into the technical areas as well.

To further define these terms, let's take the example of one camera operator who uses off-air time to

Fast-breaking stories can create a number of last-minute, on-the-air changes in the five o'clock newscast. Those changes are possible because the director has calmly talked through the basic structure of the program with key operating personnel in a session that goes right up to airtime. Note clock.   *Photo courtesy of KABC-TV*

double-check all aspects of focus for upcoming shots, allowing for possible unexpected variables in camera-to-subject distance. Another operator does only a cursory check at several positions of the zoom lens and makes last-second adjustments if changes occur. Both individuals may know the specific *techniques* needed to operate their cameras equally well, but only one will be prepared for the unforeseen surprises that so often occur. To go a step further, let's say that, with prior permission from the director, our camera operator has the discipline to look for special but unplanned shots during a rock concert. One shot he gets is based upon his special technique in using the camera lens and a light source to create a flare effect around a rock performer. Here we have an example of creativity relating to both discipline and technique.

For a professional director, these qualities as exhibited by a highly-motivated crew member are enormously important. They have much to do with the hard-to-define quality of *attitude*. They are what makes "live" and "live-to-tape" sports, news, and

music television possible. This text takes a number of opportunities to extend the idea of self-discipline into the related concept of *teamwork* and to discuss the necessary skills for one to function as a part of a production team. (See figure 1.3.)

The law of averages indicates that, while many students will follow a career in production-based positions, others will gravitate to office jobs such as operations, programming, sales, or management. Whichever is the case, nothing has been wasted. Management decisions constantly revolve around what is done in the studio and how efficiently it is done. People in all facets of the industry, from unit managers and scriptwriters to advertising executives and general managers, will do a better job if they have a good understanding of the production techniques presented here. Today, the need for a good background in studio and field operations also directly relates to the important process of getting that first job. The competition for internships and entry-level jobs at cable companies and independent production houses

Figure 1.3

Field production work puts a certain pressure on both equipment and personnel. Time is always very precious because unforeseen events invariably occur. It is a test of individual skills and teamwork. Interviews such as this may well be the culmination of more than a month of planning and include research, location surveys, and scriptwriting.

is such that it is almost mandatory to have some experience in directing, producing, and writing along with many of the operating skills of lighting, audio, editing, and graphics.

As a video production student, you have entered into a long process of *individual development* that must continue throughout your career. You must be concerned with the *techniques* of knowing precisely how to use all of the equipment as well as developing your own sense of production *discipline* so that others will be able to depend on you with confidence. In fact, one of the most revealing tests of your production capabilities will be to answer this simple question: Do other people really want you on their production team? The attitudinal qualities mentioned above will have much to do with how you answer this question.

Development of a Professional Attitude

When people work together in what sociologists call *task-oriented groups,* ongoing success is very much a matter of what other people think of you (especially those in charge of getting things done). In these circumstances, we are judged by a set of values that are usually summed up under the term *professional attitude.* How do others view your manner of approaching those tasks that fall within your area of responsibility? (See figure 1.4.)

Dependability is probably the most basic virtue in a time-oriented industry like telecommunications. Do you make a conscious effort to be on time, and to be in the sort of physical and mental condition that enables you to give your best effort? Do you handle your equipment with proper care to avoid costly maintenance work? Do you meet deadlines? Do you make an attempt to communicate your suggestions as well as your uncertainties to those in charge? Do you show respect for the work of others and for their operational needs during the production sequence? Finally, and of great importance, have you learned to discipline yourself to remain calm and focused upon your tasks, especially when difficulties begin to

Figure 1.4

Planning sessions are only valuable if all team members work together to share ideas and to put those ideas into operation.

occur? The answers to these and similar questions are what determine how you rank with your peers. For many students, their most important career contacts will go back to the people with whom they worked closely in their production courses. In terms of future employment, it is not so much *who you know* as it is the status of the people *who think well of you*. It therefore behooves all students, beginning on the first day of class, to quietly but confidently start doing those things that go into creating the impression of being one who is articulate, reliable, and skilled. Yes, there are those big talkers who for a while can make an impression without much to back it up, but the realities of production eventually are their undoing.

Attitudes and Self-image

In this process of interpersonal relationships, it is important to keep in mind that others' opinions about us in many ways relate to what we think of ourselves. There has been much discussion recently about how young people need *self-esteem.* A reality, too often ignored, is that people do not simply *get* self-esteem

. . . they must *earn* it. On a production crew, you earn the good opinion of others by consistently doing the sort of job that brings approval and, along with it, that very important sense of self-satisfaction. People know, and the word gets out. Good work does not just happen. It comes from thinking through the things that one must be prepared for in order to function in any given position. (See figure 1.5.)

Do you really understand the signal flow through the audio board or are you planning on figuring it out during the setup period? Where are the tight places in the script when a lot of things happen at once? Do the others working in your area of responsibility really understand their duties, or should you double-check them on equipment and procedures? A few minutes spent in preparation can save a tenfold wasting of precious time during final production.

Competition and Team Functioning

An interesting process of interaction becomes evident as groups of four and five people begin to work

Figure 1.5

For many students, the first experience of working with a well-organized team, and the feelings of reward that are produced by that interaction, serve as an important reason for choosing a career in video production.

together on a project without selecting a specific leader. Such teams quickly find out that it is quite difficult to function properly when everyone tries to have an equal say on all matters. There must be one designated person who has responsibility for final decisions. Those decisions are best made after the leader makes sure there has been an open exchange of ideas and opinions on every aspect of the production. The successful leader maintains the position not only by consistently presenting a good plan of action, but also by acknowledging and adopting other team members' ideas when they are appropriate. Teams usually function best when everyone has a chance to exhibit creative thinking as well as production-related skills. The ability to successfully balance both the competitive and cooperative aspects of human nature within a group is one of the surest tests of good leadership. (See figure 1.6.)

There is another balancing process that can be observed as each new semester begins. A course starts out with a new mix of students. Some are old friends, while others are going through the process of proving themselves. Some of those who have done well in earlier classes tend to take their status for granted. During the normal competitive process of crew performance during production exercises, new people begin to emerge both as leaders and/or as persons with other special production-related talents. It is then that the student who is just coasting along either works extra hard to catch up or suffers the loss of some degree of status. The ability to respond positively in these situations says a lot about a person. In the long run, it is the individual with a firm *ego energy drive*, balanced with an ability for honest *self-evaluation*, who will be sought after not only for school projects, but also throughout a professional career.

Employment Patterns

While many prime time network and cable shows are still produced in large, fully-equipped video studios

Figure 1.6

A three-person editing team combines both technical skill and creative imagination to put all of the diverse elements of a project together into a meaningful whole.

often located on movie lots, an increasing number of programs are done in smaller **production houses,** with or without union sanction. They employ many recently graduated students working at entry-level wages. The reality is that all too often one must trade experience for money during the early years of a media career.

Another negative trend is the employment of most workers on a **daily hire** basis. These workers are not on staff and, even though they may work regularly three or four days a week, they are not eligible for health or other benefits. The result of this **freelance employment** is that many people now make their living working simultaneously in cable, corporate, and broadcast production. The production techniques and equipment are very much the same. Except for the larger unionized broadcasting stations and networks, crew members are often called upon to perform a wide range of engineering tasks such as

audio, lighting, camera, and graphics. Those wishing to direct and produce are selected from these crew positions.

For those about to graduate, the good news is that in many areas of employment, things are expanding at a very healthy rate. Most of those who can survive the difficult early years will find themselves in responsible positions with a fairly secure future. One can take heart in the knowledge that those early career problems facing today's students are not very different from what entry-level people have faced over the past four decades. The oversupply of young people wanting to get into TV production has always existed.

One of the burgeoning areas for jobs today is *corporate video*. Large and small companies produce a variety of material such as orientation tapes for new employees, training tapes for specific jobs, promotion tapes for new products, and video "newsletters" to

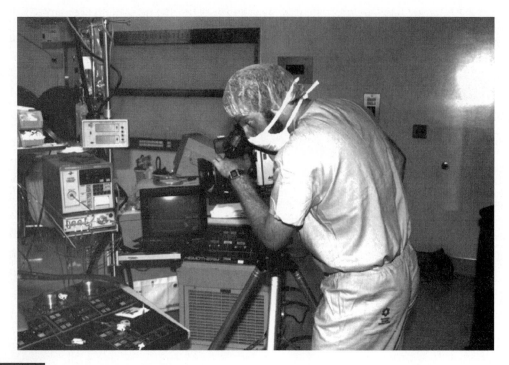

Figure 1.7

Many former broadcasting students have turned internships into fulfilling careers at medical or other types of corporate institutions. *Photo courtesy of Northridge Hospital*

keep employees up-to-date. Sometimes these companies have staff people who use company equipment to produce the material in house, other times they hire freelancers or people who have formed small production houses. In both cases, jobs are created for people with television production skills.

Educational institutions also employ people in media-related jobs. Today, many universities use **Instructional Television Fixed Service (ITFS)** to transmit courses over specially designated channels. At many universities, this service is a part of a media center that also trains instructors in the use of video in their own classrooms.

Interactive video, made possible by the instant access possibilities of **CD-ROM** (compact disc/read-only memory) and other digital technologies, is having an important impact on a variety of aspects of video production from *the Internet* to a large volume of interactive products coming from companies such as *The Disney Studios.*

During the 1980s, the FCC approved the use of commercial *low power television* (LPTV) by educational institutions and other organizations. With a transmission distance of only 15 to 20 miles and the difficulty

of competing with an ever-increasing number of cable channels, its ultimate success remains in question, but it provides excellent entry-level jobs.

One of the largest employers of media people is the government. Local, state, and federal agencies are involved in a myriad of telecommunications projects. The federal government is probably the world's largest television and film producer. Military applications, including the Armed Forces Radio and Television Services, account for worldwide operations—as does the United States Information Agency (USIA) and its worldwide satellite operation, **Worldnet.**

One of the most rapidly expanding areas is in the field of *medical and health services.* More than 80 percent of the 7,000 hospitals in the country use television and related media for patient education, in-service training (staff development), and/or public and community relations. (See figure 1.7.)

Another active field is that of *religious production.* The production level seen on many broadcasts of evangelical groups rivals many network programs. At least five such church bodies operate their own satellite networks.

Figure 1.8

The term "desktop video" denotes a small, compact group of components that can be used to edit sound and video, to create visuals including animation, and increasingly to serve as a part of the production of interactive multimedia sequences. Such equipment serves the communication and training needs of many small corporations. The hybrid unit pictured here features computer control of both videotape and digital disc. *Photo courtesy of Fast Electronic U.S.*

One of the more intriguing applications of video and computer technologies is **desktop video.** A number of manufacturers are now marketing relatively inexpensive but very efficient editing and graphics equipment that enables individuals to do some very effective video production work right in their own home or within a small office space. Many small corporations now have a video production section for training and communication uses. Another growing business area termed **event video** produces videotape recordings of weddings, birthdays, and school yearbooks. (See figure 1.8.)

An idea of the significance and magnitude of all of these various nonbroadcast production operations can be gleaned by simply looking at respective employment figures. According to United States Department of Labor statistics, in 1990 there were well over 200,000 people employed in traditional broadcast operations, including both stations and networks. By contrast, it is estimated that in that same year close to 300,000 people were employed in the nonbroadcast areas discussed earlier including, corporate, educational, interactive, government, and probably others now in the development stage. It is probably safe to say that by the end of the decade one could add another 50 percent to both figures and not be too far off the mark.

1.2

Historical Background

"A people who do not know their own history are bound to repeat its errors." This statement is a paraphrase of an important idea expressed by several philosophers. It serves students as a good reason to get to know something of the history of broadcasting. It is, of course, understandable that some students might find the technical aspects of electronic media growth to be somewhat overwhelming. However, a brief look at what these developments have meant to the viewing public is not only interesting, but also

Figure 1.9

The lack of resolution seen in this kinescope of a late 1950s' KABC-TV program was matched by equally weak recorded audio. The program's live broadcasts were known for excellent camera work and sound.

provides an important background to the study of the techniques and disciplines that make possible today's impressive communication systems.

Early Television

When one of this text's authors was first working in television in the late 1950s, much of daytime programming seen on a major city station was either a "live" network production like *American Bandstand* or, earlier in the day, local kids' shows, cooking programs, or even musical productions that were aired in between reruns of early filmed sitcoms and old movies. Commercials for locally advertised products were usually done from the studio by a "walk-in" announcer with a few slides, maybe some film clips, and usually hand props like a vegetable slicer. Nationally advertised products were broadcast locally as well as on the networks by means of film. Costs of production could be absorbed by repeated usage. One single filmed commercial for a pain relief tablet ran for ten years.

Film in Early Television

Film was also an important part of local news programs, but it was used carefully because of the cost factor. Broadcast footage was shot as a black and white negative. Editors and reporters had to look at this negative film that was projected on the air as a positive picture through the action of a polarity reversal in the *telecine* camera, which was also used to air slides. Sound was recorded on a magnetic strip on the side of the film. Because of the location of the sound pickup head in the projector, editors had to leave an extra second of picture on the film before making an edit. This meant that the audience would often see a moment or so of a speaker's lips continuing to move at an edit outpoint.

The only way to record a "live" program was to use the **kinescope** film process. With few refinements, this was basically a matter of placing a film camera in front of a TV set. (See figure 1.9.) In the late 1950s, many people in the western states were still seeing prime time network studio productions by means of

Figure 1.10

The 1964 political conventions of both parties are thought by many historians to be the first effective use of television for such events. The networks used extensive remote pickups in addition to coverage in the convention halls.

these filmed recordings as they awaited the arrival of coaxial cable in their towns. Programs had to be aired one week late in these areas and, to make things worse, the "kine" caused a noticeable loss of audio and picture quality. The best of these early network programs were either dramatic productions or music variety shows. They were done mostly from New York in the *multiple camera* technique and were watched as they were being done, errors and all.

A few shows were produced in Hollywood using three film cameras running simultaneously for later editing. Compared with today's technology, the mostly black and white programs of the late 1950s and 1960s might seem to be rather primitive, but the audiences loved them. A top network show would occasionally draw over 60 percent of the total viewing audience. It must be kept in mind, however, that on any given evening the three networks together had 90 percent of the total audience. Coverage of national events also gained large audiences. (See figure 1.10.)

To many people, this early period was the "Golden Age of Television." Many others, however, give credit for the success of modern television to the next era centered in the 1970s. During this time, many of the westerns, situation comedies, and movie-of-the-week shows were produced on 35mm film in Hollywood using expensive but high quality film production techniques. The profits were higher because of the improved market for repeat broadcasts of these shows in the U.S. and the growing syndicated markets around the world.

Further complicating the technical side of all of these changes was the fact that by the early 1960s the three networks were going through a process of transition to color. NBC led the way because their parent company, RCA, held many of the patents for color components in cameras and TV sets. CBS had lost money producing color shows to compete with NBC and, for a while, pulled back on subsidizing color programs. ABC, strapped for money at the time, broadcast only color shows produced by the movie studios on 35mm film and did not convert the first of its many multiple camera studios to color until 1966.

The Impact of Recorded and Edited Video

Even as many of television's entertainment programs moved under the control of the film studios in the 1970s, new program techniques were being developed in the areas of sports, news, and public affairs. Most of these changes were made possible with the invention of videotape and the follow-on advances that it made possible. The first **VTR machines**[1] were as tall as the operator and more than 3 feet wide. (See figure 1.11.) They were indeed an impressive piece of equipment in their time. CBS first began to use them in 1956 for delaying the feed of news programs to the western states. It took much of the next decade, however, before videotape was in general use. At first, editing was done with razor blades and plastic adhesive tape. This was quickly replaced by the concept of electronic **transfer editing** that recorded selected segments from a playback machine to an edited master tape on a second machine. By the early 1970s, two developments, now considered the basic essentials of editing, were being put into use. The **helical scan** videotape format permits a slow motion or freeze-frame picture. Each single slanted top-to-bottom scan of the tape produces a viewable complete picture **field,** allowing editors to move a picture back and forth in slow motion as they locate a precise frame for the edit point. The **SMPTE**[2] **time code** provides editors with an accurate address system designating a numbered position for each hour, minute, second, and frame on a tape. It is now only one of several different methods of numbered frame location. This time code information is recorded right on the tape and is an essential factor in all computer-controlled editing.

Portable Video Equipment

Three quarter-inch (and later one half-inch) videotape (packaged into a cassette) gave rise to the small portable video recorders that were a definite boon to what was becoming known as **electronic news**

Figure 1.11

Up until the end of the 1960s, many stations were still using large standing models of video recorders for basic playback and record purposes. To fully appreciate the miniaturization of technology, compare the size of the recording unit pictured to the size of the recording unit inside a camcorder.

gathering (ENG) and **electronic field production (EFP).** Along with new lightweight cameras, movable lights, and a crew of three in a panel truck, they replaced the converted bus, heavy studio cameras, and large videotape recorder on *remote* broadcasts. (See figure 1.12.) For news production there was no waiting for film to be delivered back to the lab to be developed before editing. Small videotape recorders, and later the very portable **camcorder,** definitely changed the way that field production was done. ABC's *Wide World of Sports,* with preproduced video segments inserted into a live broadcast, is possibly the best example of how far field production has

Figure 1.12

This portable electronic news gathering equipment revolutionized news coverage and greatly improved sports programming as well. *Photo courtesy of ABC News*

Figure 1.13

The competitive nature of both news and sports production has meant a never-ending search for ways that allow maximum camera movement while on location. *Photo courtesy of ABC-TV*

come in the past decades. (See figure 1.13.) The equipment improvements described above were always eagerly awaited by those who struggled to get programs produced. In the early 1980s, the pace picked up considerably; a number of new innovations began to compete for dominance.

Recent Digital Innovations

In the previous edition of this text, a number of references were made to the benefits of using newly designed equipment that functions by processing **digital** audio and video signals. Unlike the **analog** signal that resembles the continuous waveforms of natural light and sound, this signal information is actually a very rapid stream of brief "on" and "off" signals which, when encoded in groups, can reproduce all of the essential characteristics of the original analog waveform, such as frequency and wavelength and amplitude. (See figure 3.2.)

The move to the use of digitally compatible equipment, sometimes termed "the digital revolution," had its beginnings almost two decades ago with the impressive computer-generated graphics that added so much to all forms of television in the early 1980s. That technology was made possible by the computer because computer language is digitally-based. Unfortunately, at least some of the brilliance of those early graphics was lost when they had to be transformed back into analog signals for broadcast through the studio facilities of that time.

Figure 1.14

This computer-generated control screen typifies one of many different workscreens that would be used during various aspects of a computer-based editing session. The control process whereby selected source material is moved into position for transfer edit onto a final master tape or disc is done by computer under the operator's control. *Photo courtesy of Fast Electronic U.S.*

Digital Videotape Formats

By the late 1980s, the major companies were producing VTR and VCR machines in a number of competing digital formats that were differentiated by whether the brightness and color signals were combined **(composite)** or separated **(component)** as well as by the size of tape. The large number of formats on the market (labeled D.1, D.2, D.3, etc.) began to cause compatibility problems. Ultimately, most professional video machines of that period had to be designed to convert between analog and digital as well as between composite and component signals.

The introduction of digital recorders was basically an attempt to improve the quality of an edited videotape. Visual special effects, done through the use of videotape, involve making further copies of previously copied tapes as pictorial elements are added to the action. Whereas with analog tape each additional tape "generation" meant a loss of picture quality, the digital multigeneration copies looked as good as the original. With this development the "digital genie" was out of the bottle, and soon a number of other improvements began to appear.

Computer-controlled Editing

The computers that earlier had made possible the impressive graphics were put to work to roll videotape into position for edit transfer. Through the use of a number of display screens, as shown in figure 1.14, an edit controller could be programmed to remember a list of precise segment in and out times on the **EDL (edit decision list).** It could then control the movement of both edit and record tapes during a final automated continuous assembly process.

Figure 1.15

The almost instant access to any part of the hard drive disc is made possible through computer control of the access arm. The signal is either recorded or transmitted by means of a laser beam at the tip of the arm.

Nonlinear Video Editing

As the computer became the standard for edit machine control, the technology of recording digitized information increased its practical limits from megabytes to gigabytes. Sufficient audio and video could now be stored on a hard drive disc, thereby providing a workable edit playback source. (See figure 1.15.) This, in turn, made possible the concept of **non-linear** editing. The computer controls instant access to any point on the playback or edit master disc just as a personal computer can almost instantly find the beginning of a sentence and then add or subtract any amount of copy on a document. The time previously spent rolling tapes back and forth was eliminated.

Once an edit decision list has been created, all planned edits (cuts, dissolves, or special effect transitions) are viewed in a continuous trial sequence that permits changes of varying lengths to be made on a revised edit decision list before final assembly is made.

Video Compression

Further improvements on these impressive achievements are now rapidly arriving on the scene. The next major development in the area of editing and storage is the rapidly developing technology of signal **compression.** This process encodes digital signals in such a way that sound and picture can be reduced to a form that occupies much less "cyberspace" than in its original form whether on disc or tape. Called **bit rate reduction,** it is only possible with a digital signal and is currently being done through the use of several different methods. The best known of these methods operates on the principle that in the thirty frames per second that make up an NTSC (American) television picture, more of the picture stays the same, from frame to frame, than changes with each new frame.

That approach, the **MPEG-2 compression system,**[3] analyzes a group of frames at one time and uses specially designated frames to predict the degree to which parts of the picture will change or stay the same. This analysis process starts with the smallest measurable part of the picture, the **pixel,** and then works with eight by eight blocks of pixels. When one considers that there can be 300,000 or more pixels in an NTSC frame the process can be said to operate on an impressive scale. Because it is compatible with the planned **HDTV (high definition television)** system, the MPEG-2 encoding method (or an improved successor) will probably end up being used in a large number of video applications.

A differing **M-JPEG** compression concept also has supporters because of its current use in nonlinear video editing. It must be kept in mind that the ratio at which digital information can be compressed varies somewhat with which system is being used. A larger degree of variation, however, has to do with a simple tradeoff of a lesser savings in compression for a higher picture quality. MPEG-2, used in conjunction with the HDTV format, would probably be limited to a ratio somewhere between 2 to 1 and 6 to 1. Applications that produce only nonbroadcast "VHS Quality" may eventually be able to achieve a workable 20 or 30 to 1 ratio, depending on equipment.

To carry the new signal forms, equally impressive developments have been made in the area of **fiber optics.** These cables, using frequencies in the spectrum of light, can transmit several times as much information as a standard cable. At present, the technology is expensive, but major equipment manufacturers and some cable systems are already experimenting with its use.

Figure 1.16

The new CamCutter™ camcorder from Avid/Ikegami records its digital signal directly to a disc within the camera itself.
Photo courtesy of Avid Technology, Inc.

Digital Camcorders

The recent marketing of a new generation of digital camcorders by the major companies is very much tied to the ability of these cameras to create a digital video and audio signal that is immediately compressed in the camera and recorded on a relatively small tape cassette (or in one case, to an internal hard drive disc). Some of these new camcorders are digitized versions of older tape transport systems. One is an upgrade of a digital consumer format. Another is "backward compatible" with the S-VHS format. These new digital cameras and camcorders have slightly different tape formats and are not all mutually compatible. They are designed for various levels of the market from semiprofessional to network news.

Some observers feel, however, that for reasons of cost and compatibility, the industry can really only accept one major new format at a time. Which of these camera/tape formats will ultimately be accepted by the industry is difficult to determine at this point. Very possibly we may see a bruising competition among manufacturers or a slowdown of the purchase of new cameras until the predominant format becomes obvious. (See figure 1.16.)

Interactive Video

What may well be the most sweeping new technology to be generated from all of the possibilities afforded by digital signals is that of **interactive multimedia video.** It has origins in earlier audio/video multimedia presentation methods that utilized multiple slide projectors, audio and videotape, and some early attempts at computer control. It soon became obvious that these techniques could be combined with the benefits of operator feedback being used by video games and similar forms of entertainment. For the past several years, there has been an enormous research and development effort to move interactive video beyond its currently successful CD-ROM stage and onto the Internet, cable, and even live television applications.

In 1996 the Directors Guild of America, sensing a possible new direction of entertainment, presented a series of seminars for its members who saw interactive video in their future.

A problem being worked on presently concerns the limits of current hardware and software to reproduce motion pictures at the quality of **NTSC** (National Television Standards Committee) broadcast video. Another problem that will have to be solved before interactive video can live up to its promise is that presently there are multiple standards and methods of assembly, all of which fall under the interactive label. Some methods involve downloading files into the computer. Others involve a CD-ROM with a small amount of material from the disc being permanently downloaded. Distant on-line operations, such as Internet applications, would utilize large digital playback and record machines such as what is described below.

A Convergence of Technologies

When one takes the longer view of electronic media development, however, history tells us that such problems do tend to get solved, and often rather quickly. The earliest equipment used for television was very simple when compared to state-of-the-art equipment just a decade later. In recent times, we have seen inventions, such as the microprocessor, make the miniaturization of video components an important aspect of its development. Now, we are seeing an impressive digital signal, with its interactive capabilities, moving in compressed form over high speed data highways. The inventive process, whereby several electronically-based industries come together to create not only new equipment but also whole new industries, is being termed a "convergence" of technologies.

Originally, television was created out of radio, stage performance, and a few elements of the film industry. Then in what some saw as a slightly backward step, TV was combined with what was basically an older "signal-to-door" telephone technology to produce cable. It is now possible that cable-TV technologies will combine with computerized elements of interactive video into what observers are calling a "killer application" designed to rival the Internet.

High definition television (also known as advanced TV) is one example of a technology that has not stayed on schedule in replacing the NTSC standard in this country and the two other international standards. HDTV was perfected in the early 1990s, but with an analog signal. American and European manufacturers, following up on digital signal developments at the Massachusetts Institute of Technology, were able to delay its adoption until the use of the digital signal could be utilized. However, what had been envisioned as only a short delay has become a series of arguments among nations, manufacturers, and distributors. The problem is that adopting standards for one interest group results in a negative effect for another group. A tentative agreement in late 1996 has raised hopes for HDTV by the year 2000.

Perhaps the most promising example of technological convergence is the large multipurpose, multifunction video storage and delivery channel video file server, known more simply as a **server.** (See figure 9.4.) Although some models have been used at networks and major TV stations since the mid-1990s, the concept is still being developed. This one equipment entity serves as the master recipient of all incoming station video such as programming, news clips, and commercials. Through the use of multiple disc technology and digital compression, there can be almost an unlimited number of inputs at one time.

Simultaneously, other sources of video already in the unit (such as scheduled programming, promos, and newsclips) either for broadcast or editing purposes, are being fed to numerous points in the station's internal network and are available for instantaneous output. These are expensive units and must be able to prove their worth over a period of several years of operation. As with so much of the new equipment, the cost factor is causing great concern in many quarters. The feeling for many people in the industry would seem to be, "the future is suddenly here, and we may not be able to afford it."

Summary

By its nature, the study of video production attracts persons from an increasingly wide range of backgrounds. Within this diversity are the strengths that can do much to assure the future of our nation's communication system. The content of the video industry deals with all aspects of our own lives; people holding conversations, playing games, listening to music, and observing the drama of their lives as mirrored in the form of the video drama.

The programming that the beginning student observes through countless hours of casual viewing may seem deceptively easy. Because of this tendency, the chapter has emphasized that from the first day of class students must seriously begin the process of understanding how the various elements of the media product are brought together in a meaningful whole. They must learn the basic operational techniques and individual disciplines that underlie a successful video product. The ability to creatively blend these elements with the skills of leadership and teamwork has much to do with an individual's employability and long-range career success.

We've tried to provide a long-range view of how attitudes have influenced the development of video production. Today's production has been greatly enhanced by the introduction of signals that have been further encoded into a digital structure. The benefits of this development are that a whole new generation of cameras, recorders, switchers, editing systems, and servers are now gaining wide acceptance.

The material in this chapter has been written as a general overview. Later chapters will present specific details on the equipment and concepts that have been briefly described. In chapter 2, we begin to examine the process through which all of the many elements of video production are brought together.

Footnotes

1. The first videotape machines utilized a reel-to-reel technology borrowed from existing audio equipment. VTR stood for Video Tape Recorder. With the advent of the cassette, first used in the portable three quarter-inch Sony U-matic Recorder, the term VCR came into use.

2. The initials SMPTE stand for The Society of Motion Picture and Television Engineers. It is the pre-eminent organization for those who work to design and to bring about the proper implementation of the technical base that underlies the electronic media.

3. MPEG-2 is the second version of a compression standard developed by the Moving Picture Experts Group. M-JPEG is a motion application of a standard for still pictures developed by the Joint Photographic Experts Group.

chapter 2

Cast and Crew

When television was first being introduced, radio comedian Fred Allen quipped, "Television is the triumph of equipment over people." There are times, (when the camera focus goes out and the computer graphics generator crashes and the audio cable develops a short—all in one day), that cast and crew members may feel that equipment has, indeed, triumphed over them. But as important as equipment is to the production process, it is really the *people* behind and in front of that equipment that are the driving force and the deciding factor regarding the quality of any TV production.

This chapter will give an overview of the duties of the various people involved in production. For the most part, it will discuss the positions and tasks required for studio production where several camera operators frame shots in a **studio** (see figure 2.1) and a bevy of people operate equipment in a nearby **control room** (see figure 2.2). The assumption is that the program is being sent out live over the airwaves or is being recorded from beginning to end with very few, if any, stops. This type of production requires a large crew because many things must be done all at once. Other types of production, such as **field production** or the producing of **interactive** media, can be undertaken with fewer people, because various portions of the programs are constructed in small increments and then joined together after the fact during editing. Although this chapter will make some comparative references to field and interactive productions, these subjects are covered in depth in chapters 12 and 15.

Each crew position covered in this chapter will be discussed in terms of what you would need to do before the actual production process begins, what you do during rehearsal and while the program is being recorded (or aired live), and what you do after production is over. This should give you a general overview of what you should do for your very first production exercise. Because many of these positions are involved with producing or directing or with operating specific pieces of equipment, the chapters that follow will, by nature, give even more detail about the jobs. But this chapter should allow you to get started with production, and then you can hone your skills as you learn more details.

Figure 2.1

A TV studio. The anchors for a newscast sit on the news set that is placed in the studio. Cameras, lights, and microphones are also in the studio. *Photo courtesy of KABC-TV.*

Figure 2.2

A TV control room. While the anchors are reading the news stories from the studio, these people in the control room are making sure that the right picture and sound are broadcast. *Photo courtesy of KABC-TV.*

2.1

Producers

Producers are in charge of the *overall organization* of a production, be it a network comedy, a local station newscast, a cable TV sportscast, a syndicated soap opera, a public broadcasting music concert, an interactive video game, or a corporate training tape. As a producer, you are responsible for seeing that all the elements of a program are in the right place at the right time. Have the actors been cast? Has the fog machine been ordered? Where will the cast and crew eat? Producers often initiate a project and see that it is finished *on-time* and *on-budget* (see chapter 13).

Before Production Begins

Your most intensive work as a producer is accomplished during **preproduction.** This is the period when everything must be carefully planned so that **production** (shooting) and **postproduction** (editing) can progress smoothly. You oversee the script (see section 13.2) and the budget (see section 13.3), make sure all the necessary people have been hired and scheduled (often in conjunction with the director), attend to legal matters, and see that all facilities and equipment are available.

In general, a producer handles logistics of a production while a director makes the creative and aesthetic decisions. But sometimes a producer will be a **hyphenate**—a producer-director. In this case, the producer will handle organization (primarily during preproduction) and then lead the cast and crew through the creative process of production and postproduction.

During Rehearsal and Recording

For most student productions, a producer who is not a hyphenate is present during rehearsal and recording to give the director moral support and to handle any last minute details. On the professional level, a producer's role during rehearsal and recording varies according to the nature of the project, the relationship between the producer and director, and how smoothly things are going. If a drama is shot outside the country, the producer may stay home and not even witness a single day of shooting; if a talk show is taped in the same building where the producer works, it is a good idea for that person to stop in and at least welcome the guests. Producers are usually in the control room during the entire broadcast of a live news program, because so many decisions must be made at the last minute.

When producers and directors work together frequently and harmoniously, the producer comes to trust the director and may never appear on the set. A producer will exert more control if the director's ability is uncertain. Related to this, a director who is still shooting two days after production was to have finished can most assuredly expect a visit from the producer. So can one who is spending money at a rapid clip.

After the Production

The producer's role if a program needs editing has the same variations as the role during production. A producer stationed at some distance from the editing facility who trusts the director may never appear in the editing room, although the producer almost always looks at a rough cut of an edited program and gives opinions as to what needs changes. A student producer will be more involved.

As producer, you should handle the social and legal aftermath of the production. Have the guests been sent thank-you notes? Have the music copyright fees actually been paid?

The producer also oversees the distribution and promotion of the program and evaluates the program and the process so that things can operate more smoothly (or as smoothly) next time.

2.2

Directors

A director has been likened to a symphony conductor. The various crew members are each playing their own "instruments" (camera, audio board, video recorder, etc.), and it is the director who coordinates them and sets the overall pace of the program.

In some situations, especially when the director is a producer-director hyphenate, the director will have helped to shape the script. In many other situations you, as director, will have the script handed to you and will take the production from there.

Before Production Begins

Your first concern should be to determine the *specific purpose* of the script. Ask yourself several questions: What is the objective of the program? How do you want the audience to be different when this program is over? Then you can begin to think in terms of the overall "feel" and image of the program. What kinds of settings, lighting, and graphics would be most effective in this particular *communication* process?

Next, you should check the script for rough timing. Is the length all right or does it need to be cut or lengthened? The script should be put in its final television production format and duplicated for all personnel involved. How many copies do you need?

Once you are completely comfortable with the script, you should be able to start specific *facilities planning.* In the case of a remote coverage of some event, you have to scout the location (often in conjunction with other crew members). In other professional situations, you may have to rent studio facilities. In most academic and training situations, the studio will be assigned to you for a definite period of time. In many institutions—even for training purposes—you will still have to fill out a **facilities request form** (often abbreviated **FACS**) reserving specific equipment or a specific studio and control room (see figure 2.3). Failure to attend to such paperwork carefully at this stage can result in costly problems and misunderstandings later.

In most academic situations, you may not have to be concerned with securing personnel. The technical crew may be assigned from your class or from some other participating class. There may be some occasions, however, when you will be involved in selecting specific individuals for particular crew assignments.

Casting for actors or other performers may also be done on an informal basis in the academic setting. You may work through the drama department, or you may prevail upon your personal friends. In securing such volunteer help, make certain that you have a firm commitment; many a student production has been ruined because some friend or casual acquaintance backed out of a production at the last moment. In professional situations, of course, casting is quite an involved process (see section 13.4).

Next comes the job of pulling the production together. In any kind of major production, the director should plan on holding one or more *production conferences* involving the chief production personnel. (See figure 2.4.) You must now make sure that all the preproduction elements are properly requested and constructed. The lighting and staging plans are developed at this stage. If any special costumes or props have to be ordered or fabricated, they are initiated now. Music and other special audio or video material must be chosen and/or produced.

During the entire preproduction process, you have to be working within a very tight interlocking schedule of *checkpoints* and *deadlines.* Many production elements cannot proceed until other items are taken care of first. The exterior videotape cannot be shot until the costumes arrive. Set pieces cannot be constructed until the set design is completed.

In the midst of this activity, you also must be concerned with preparing your script for the day of production. How are you going to use your cameras? What will be the pacing you want to achieve? In short, what images and sounds do you want to create to achieve your purpose? You should *mark* your copy of the script indicating which cameras you are going to use for which shots and what instructions you are going to give cast and crew (see section 14.1).

During Rehearsal and Recording

The director is *THE* person in charge during rehearsal and recording. During rehearsals (see section 14.1) you must make sure that both the people behind and in front of the camera know what they are to do. Never assume that people can read your mind. Some programs, such as dramas, need extensive rehearsals, because everything must take place in a very precise manner. Other programs, such as talk shows, require less rehearsal. In fact, rehearsing a talk show too thoroughly can ruin its spontaneity, because all the participants will know what everyone else is going to say. For these types of programs, it is often best to discuss only the general topics and the logistical aspects, such as when you will be cutting away for commercials.

After rehearsal, you are ready to start calling shots on your production. No doubt you will feel

```
               FACILITIES REQUEST FORM
                 YOURTOWN UNIVERSITY

Date Facilities Are Needed_____

Time Facilities Are Needed_____
    (Maximum is 4 hours unless special permission has been obtained)

Your Name_____

Address_____

Phone Number(s)_____

Student ID Number_____

FACILITIES REQUESTED
_____Studio
         _____number of cameras needed (maximum=3)
         _____number mics needed (maximum=5 lav, 3 stand, 1 boom)
             Indicate type(s)_____
         _____number of lights being used (maximum=20)
         _____news set
         _____talk show set
         _____other. Specify_____
_____Control Room
         _____audio board
         _____graphics generator
         _____switcher
         _____teleprompter
         _____record VCR
         _____roll-in VCR
         _____other. Specify_____
_____Editing Suite A
         _____U-matic to U-matic system
         _____character generator
         _____audio cassette player
         _____other
_____Editing Suite B
         _____Hi-8 to U-matic SP
         _____graphics generator
         _____CD player
         _____audio cassette player
         _____microphone
         _____other
```

Figure 2.3

A sample facilities request form that might be used by a university.

some anxiety. However, regardless of what might be churning inside, try *not* to let it show. Force yourself to sit back and take a deep breath, let it out slowly, and coolly tell all the crew and the talent that everything will proceed confidently. Remember that the composure or anxiety you communicate to the crew will surely be returned to you.

Your actual commands will depend on the type of production, but usually you must: make sure the tape recorder starts so that the program is recorded; call up the music and graphics needed for the opening credits; make sure the cameras are on shots you are likely to need as the program progresses; call for the proper camera to be on the air at the proper time; bring in prerecorded videotapes or audio material as it is needed; execute the closing credits; and make sure the tape recorder is stopped at the end of the program.

Prior to production, the director holds a conference with the associate director, stage manager, technical director, and lighting director.

During the course of your program, always be *looking ahead* two or three minutes. What possible problems lie ahead? Did the mic boom get repositioned all right? Are the dancers prepared for their entrance? Are the closing credits ready to roll? Usually, it is a good idea to delegate many of these "look ahead" duties to your associate director, but you, as director, have the ultimate responsibility to make sure everything goes as planned.

After the Production

When the program is finished, don't let either talent or crew leave their positions until the VCR operator has played back a bit of the tape to make sure it recorded. Then use the studio address to thank the crew and talent. Assure them that everything went well. Keep your composure until you have a chance to collapse in private. Make certain you and your crew clear the studio and control room of all scripts, notes, props, and everything else connected with your production. Don't expect the next group using the studio to clean up your mess.

If there is any postproduction editing to be accomplished, your job is far from done (see chapter 10, section 10.1). If it is a simple matter of inserting a clean shot to cover the one bad blunder on the air, you may be able to get it done right away. If it is a major postproduction editing job of assembling video pieces from several different sources, it will take quite a bit of scheduling editing sessions.

Associate Directors

The **associate director** (sometimes referred to as the **assistant director** or **AD**)[1] helps the director with various tasks. For this reason, some of the duties the AD is assigned differ from program to program, depending on the philosophy and work style of the director. One director may want you to set up all the on-air camera shots so he or she can concentrate on last minute details, aesthetic decisions, and the actual takes on the air. Other directors want you just to sit nearby to remind them of what is coming up next. (See figure 2.5.)

In virtually every kind of studio operation, however, one of the AD's primary jobs will be that of timing the production. You will time individual

Figure 2.5

The associate director (front) sits next to the director (center) during taping.

segments during rehearsals, get an overall timing of the program, and then be in charge of the pacing of the program—speeding up or stretching as required—during the actual recording.

Before Production Begins

In any major production undertaking, the AD will work with the director well in advance of the actual production period—attending production conferences, working with talent, and assembling props and other materials. You may be in charge of the rest of the crew—checking to make certain that everyone is present and reporting this to the director. In nonunion or corporate productions, you may well be in charge of arranging substitute assignments, thus ensuring that every position is covered.

During Rehearsal and Recording

During the rehearsals, the director will mention various production items that need attention before the actual take. You will jot down the "critique notes," as the director spots problems. Additionally, you should be making notes of similar items that might have escaped the attention of the director. If you notice a major item, such as a missing prop, it should be called to the director's attention before the

rehearsal proceeds. Minor items, such as a distracting shadow on the talent's shoulder, are simply written down to be cleaned up later.

You will be especially concerned with noting all the script changes that are made. If any segments are going to be taped out of order, you should note any **continuity** problems that could arise. For example, if a vase of flowers is needed for the first segment and is removed during the second segment but is needed again for the third segment, you should make a special note to double check that the flowers are returned before the taping of segment three begins.

You may also use the rehearsal period to time as much of the program as possible, including individual segments, tape inserts, and opening and closing elements. All of these will help you with crucial timing that will be needed during the actual production of the program. For example, the final segment of a program might be very crucial to the understanding of the entire program and need to be aired in a specific way. You can time that segment during rehearsal and then **backtime** (count backwards from the end of the program). Thus, you will know exactly when the preceding segment must end so that the final segment can be completed properly. Then during production, you can give time signals to the talent regarding when they should wind up the next to last segment and begin the final segment.

After the rehearsal and before the actual take, it is your job to make certain that the director *follows through* on all production notes that were jotted down during rehearsal. Often, at this point, the director has a meeting with the entire crew to go over what needs to be changed before the program is actually taped or broadcast. This meeting is based largely on your notes.

Next, you must make sure that everybody involved has all script changes marked down. As surely as one person did not get a crucial script change, that omission will lead to an on-the-air mistake. Additionally, you should remind the director of how much time is remaining before videotaping is scheduled to start or before the live program goes on the air.

Just prior to production, you will "read down" the clock, letting the director know how many minutes or seconds until air or until taping is to begin. Once on the air, you should follow the script and remain alert to any and all potential problems—ready to call major troubles to the attention of the director; you must show *initiative* in this regard.

Your primary job, however, is handling *timing*. The AD must ensure that the entire production is the right length. If the program is to be edited, timing all of the segments to be electronically glued together is an important consideration here. You need some way of keeping track of the various timing notes and reminders. The digital clock readouts available in most control rooms are essential, but many ADs also use timing sheets (see section 14.1).

As AD, you are also in charge of making sure the talent receives proper time cues. Either directly or through the director, you will tell the stage manager when to give each time signal to the talent. Time signals are given to the talent in terms of *time remaining*. Thus, as you approach the end of a program, you will have the floor director signal the performer that there are "five minutes remaining," "one minute to go," "thirty seconds left," and so forth.

Also during the production, you will be taking notes for postproduction editing—both those items that the director points out that need to be taken care of (a missed shot, timing that was off a little, an opportunity to insert a reaction shot) and the items that you notice that need to be corrected.

Finally, you must be ready to take over at any time. The AD is literally the standby director. Should the director be unable to complete the program, you will assume responsibility for calling shots, and the production will continue.

After the Production

Once the production is completed, you still have a few obligations. You should help clean up the control room of extra scripts, notes, and other materials, and debrief the director on any errors that occurred during the program.

A crucial postproduction job of the AD in many situations is the final editing session. You may need to set up a schedule with the director for any planned editing. You may simply continue as the director's right-hand assistant in these assignments or, depending upon the nature of the production arrangements, you may be substantially in charge of the postproduction editing session—following the director's instructions, of course.

2.4

Stage Managers

The **stage manager** (also called the **floor manager** or the **floor director**)[2] is the director's key assistant in charge of what is happening in the studio. When you assume this role, your main job is to communicate with the talent. The director is in the control room during the actual production and cannot give instructions directly to the performers who, generally,[3] are not wearing headsets. Therefore, such instructions are relayed by the stage manager, mainly through hand signals, but sometimes with flipcards (see figure 2.6).

Before Production Begins

Prior to actual production, you should attend to the *emotional-physical* needs of the talent. Is the talent physically comfortable? Can you offer a glass of water? Can you get the talent out of the lights for a few minutes? What production mysteries should be explained to the talent?

This last point is important. Because the performers are not tied into the intercom, they are not aware

Figure 2.6

This stage manager is using flipcards to give the talent time cues.

of what is going on most of the time. Explain to the talent why there is a delay (a result of a computer malfunction—not because the talent sat in the wrong chair); explain why the crew is laughing (at the AD's story—not at the talent's clothing). Try to put yourself in the position of the talent—isolated, in the spotlight, and receiving no feedback as to what is going on.

Prior to production, you should also work out with the talent the *technical-production* requirements. What props must be available and where? Where is the talent to stand for the demonstration? What kinds of special cues might be needed? All these details should be considered carefully, so that both you and the talent know what to do during the actual taping.

One inevitable production requirement is the communication of information to the talent through various hand signals and/or flip cards. Prior to rehearsal, you should demonstrate the various hand signals (stand by to start, begin talking, talk to this camera, speed up, thirty seconds to go, cut, and so forth) to the talent and decide exactly what time cues will be given. (See Appendix C.)

In addition to handling talent, the other main job of the stage manager is that of handling all production details on the studio floor. This area includes a variety of concerns: broadly supervising staging and lighting setups;[4] directing studio traffic; distributing scripts to everyone who needs them; making sure props are in their right positions. You must have a great deal of authority, because virtually every other floor position is concerned with the production from only one specific viewpoint. For example, the camera operator, the audio technician, and the lighting director all have their particular perspectives to take care of. Perhaps each of these three will have selected the same spot on the floor to position a camera, a mic boom, and a light stand. It is up to you, working from a broader perspective, to coordinate these needs and decide what goes where.

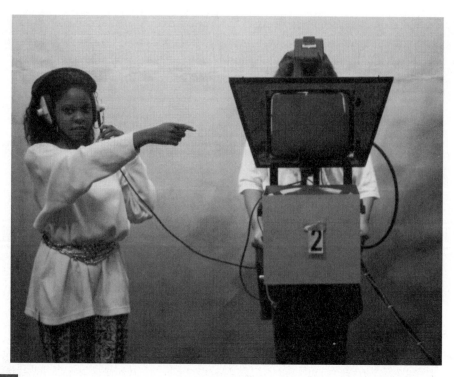

Figure 2.7

During production, the stage manager gives cues to the talent, such as this cue to look at camera 2.

During Rehearsal and Recording

During rehearsal, the stage manager should give the talent hand cues so they can become familiar with them. In doing this, you should always be in a position to be spotted easily by the talent. The performers should never have to turn their heads or search the studio with their eyes to find you. Often it is good to crouch below the camera that the talent should be addressing. You must, however, make sure that you stay out of the way of the camera lens. You are not one of the performers, and you do not want your head or arm to inadvertently pop up in the shot.

During rehearsal, you should also make sure of what your other duties will be. Do you need to move a prop? Do you need to hold up a chart? Do you need to replenish a bowl of fruit?

Once the production begins the stage manager is the primary contact the talent has with the rest of the world—the studio door is shut; the director is in the control room; all lights are focused on the talent who face the cameras alone—except for the support of the stage manager. At this stage, your main job is to give hand cues to the talent and possibly move elements on the set, such as props or charts. (See figure 2.7.) You must remain extra alert for any problems and double-check to ensure that all crew and talent are in their places, executing their cues. In general, you must guarantee that everything for the studio that was worked out during the rehearsal period is executed during production.

After the Production

When the taping is over, the stage manager helps collect props, assists the staging and lighting crew in getting their elements properly stored, and generally polices the studio to see that everything is returned to where it belongs, ready for the next production. After the production, as well as before and during it, you must think of yourself as *the* pivotal individual in charge of the studio—the person who must take the initiative in getting things done.

Figure 2.8

The camera operators practice their shots during setup time.

2.5

Camera Operators

Camera operators are the people who, based on instructions from the director, frame the shots for the program. To do this job, you must understand the operation of the camera thoroughly (see chapters 6 and 7) so that you can physically move the camera while keeping the image steady and in focus. You must pay particular attention to how the camera interacts with the lighting so that the picture is not overexposed or underexposed. In addition, you must have an aesthetic sense so that the pictures are properly composed. The camera operator frames, from a broad panorama, what the viewer will see.

Most studio productions require at least three camera operators who stand behind their cameras and operate them throughout the taping. Some productions use **robotic cameras;** the cameras are located in the studio but have no operators. One person in the control room or on the floor operates all the cameras by handling levers that focus and move the camera parts remotely.

Before Production Begins

Before the production begins, camera operators ready the cameras for operation. Often this involves wheeling the camera out from beside a wall where it is stored, turning it on, taking a cap off the front of the lens, opening and adjusting a number of levers and knobs that allow the camera to move freely, and generally checking to make sure everything is working properly. (See figure 2.8.)

Once all the lighting is set, you often need to make some adjustments to the cameras so that their pictures will be optimized for the lights. Sometimes an engineer in the control room, usually referred to as a **shader** or a **camera control unit (CCU)** operator, assists the camera operators with some of the more technical adjustments for their cameras. For example, this person operates remote controls on the CCU that govern the relationship of the cameras to the lighting.

Figure 2.9

Like many other prompting systems, this on-camera display unit reflects copy from a monitor onto a mirror positioned in front of the camera lens. The camera shoots through the mirror to pick up the talent's image.

During Rehearsal and Recording

Rehearsals are when you find out exactly what will be required and iron out any potential problems. If the program is not rehearsed, you should definitely meet with the director before taping to find out what shots you will be covering. Then during the production, you follow the instructions given by the director over the **headsets.**

You should always try to think ahead to your next shot. Is the talent going to rise, and, if so, have you unlocked the lever that allows you to tilt the camera up? Are you going to need to get out of the way of another camera operator who has to make a wide move? Are there any cables or other obstructions that will get in the way of your own camera move?

After the Production

After the production is over, you should put the cameras away properly. Usually this involves coiling the cable attached to the camera and moving the camera back to where it is stored. You should cap the lens and lock down all levers and knobs. It is not always necessary to turn the camera off. If it is going to be used again within a short period of time, it should be left on, because turning electronics off and on too frequently shortens a camera's life.

2.6
Teleprompter Operators

Teleprompters[5] are mirrors that fit over the front of a camera lens and show the talent the script (see figure 2.9). Usually all the cameras are equipped with a teleprompter so that talent can turn from one camera to another and still see the same script. The viewer does not see this script, but the talent can read it while looking directly at the camera lens. Someone has to control the rate that the script crawls up the teleprompter so that it does not get either ahead of or behind the talent. That someone is the teleprompter operator.

Before Production Begins

Most teleprompters are computerized so that whatever script is written for the program can also be fed into the teleprompter computer without having to be retyped. If the script must be retyped, however, it is your job, as teleprompter operator, to do that before the production begins. Even if the script does not need retyping, you should check it carefully before taping to make sure it is formatted properly and does not contain anything that will confuse the talent (such as stage directions that the on-camera person might accidentally read).

Older teleprompters use paper with the script typed on it. This script is moved past a special camera that sends the image to the screen in front of the talent's cameras. With these you should also check the written copy carefully.

During Rehearsal and Recording

During rehearsal and production, the teleprompter operator (who may be physically located in either the control room or the studio) must position the script properly. Many teleprompters have a variable speed knob that the operator uses to move the computerized copy or the paper on which the script is typed. The words that a performer is reading at the moment should be close to the center of the screen with enough of the upcoming script showing so that there is no chance the talent will need to hesitate.

After the Production

After the production is over, you should delete the script from the computer so that it does not clog up the storage capacity. If a paper-based teleprompter is used, you should throw the paper away or return it to the producer or director.

2.7

Lighting Directors

The **lighting director (LD)** is in charge of seeing that the lights are properly set for the telecast and that any lighting effects needed during the telecast can be executed. Usually this person has a crew that actually places and adjusts the lights while the LD makes sure the overall effect is accomplished. (See figure 2.10.)

Before Production Begins

Most of the work that you do as lighting director takes place well before the taping begins. For a studio shoot, you and your crew members make sure that the proper amount and type of light reach all the studio locations that need it (see chapter 5). For studios that can afford a large number of lighting instruments, this may involve identifying, from the many lights on the **grid** (a series of interconnected pipes that hang just below the ceiling), the lights that are needed and then turning them on. If a studio does not have a large number of lights, then the crew members may have to climb ladders and reposition lights on the grid so that they illuminate the proper areas.

Whether the lights are moved or prepositioned, crew members may have to readjust them slightly so that they cast the best possible illumination. Lights are usually plugged into a **dimmer board** that is used to control the total amount of light hitting the set. As LD, you must make sure that the lights give the proper amount of illumination and the proper emotional feeling.

During Rehearsal and Recording

During rehearsals, you and your crew make whatever adjustments you or the director deem necessary.

During the production, the LD and crew may have nothing to do. If the same lighting is needed throughout the taping, they may actually leave the studio to work on another show. Often for student productions, these people assume other positions during the production. However, if lights need to be dimmed or changed in some other way during production, then at least the lighting director will remain to execute these changes.

After the Production

After the production is over, someone must make sure that all the lights are turned off. If the studio procedures so require, any lights that were moved should be put back where they were.

Figure 2.10

This lighting crew member has climbed a ladder to position a light so that it covers a precise area.

2.8

Audio Operators

Some of the work that is done in connection with audio is undertaken in the studio and some is in the control room. (See chapters 3 and 4.)

Before Production Begins

Someone must select the appropriate microphones and position them in the studio before the production begins. This can involve attaching mics to the talent's clothing, placing mics on some sort of stand or pole, or even hanging mics from the lighting grid. The mics must be connected to receptacles located somewhere in the studio that send the audio signal to the **audio console** in the control room.

Once the mics are positioned and connected, they must be tested to make sure they are working properly. Usually this job involves two **audio operators**, one talking into each mic in the studio and another adjusting it through the audio console in the control room. If only one audio operator is available, the floor manager can talk into the mics. The talent can also talk into the mics (and should in order to set levels), but it is a good idea to make sure the mics are actually working before the talent arrives. You do not want high-priced talent sitting around while you replace a mic battery or trace down a bad cable.

Once the talent is in place, you should make sure each miked person talks as they will during the production and everyone else (including crew) should be quiet so that you can set the volume of the mic as it will be needed during the taping.

Figure 2.11

Working at the audio board, the audio operator combines sounds and adjusts their volume.

If the program is going to contain music, sound effects, or other audio elements, you should also check these out and cue them up before production so that when they are needed during rehearsal or taping, they will come in exactly as the director desires.

During Rehearsal and Recording

During rehearsal and/or production, there may be a need for audio operators in both the studio and control room. If a mic needs to be moved (on a **boom** or other apparatus) during taping, then someone must be in the studio to do this job. If all the mics are attached to talent's clothing, then there is really nothing for a studio audio operator to do. There may be a need for two operators in the control room, however. If a show has complicated audio (and if the control room audio area is large enough), one person can operate the audio console while another starts and stops tape recorders, the CD player, or other equipment. More common, however, is one audio operator handling all the control room audio. (See figure 2.11.)

If you are this person, you should bring in sounds when the director calls for them. Your main job is to make the sound audible and consistent. For example, in most instances you should make sure the music does not drown out what someone is saying, and you should make sure that someone who talks softly can be heard as well as someone with a booming voice.

After the Production

After the production is over, the audio operator(s) should coil the audio cable and put away all the microphones, generally in boxes that are specially made for them. Some microphones have batteries that need to be removed when the mics are not in use. Any CDs or tapes used during production should be stored away or given to the director or producer.

You should put the board in the generally agreed upon configuration for the facility. Because audio boards contain a large number of buttons, knobs, and faders, the audio personnel of a facility should agree on commonly used settings for everything and then set the board that way at the end of each production. An enormous amount of time can be wasted if one operator has a need to turn on a little-used knob and then doesn't turn it off again and the next operator can't figure out what is wrong. This is a particularly common problem in colleges where many students who are just learning the board use it during the course of a day. For this reason, college facility engineers often make drawings of how the board should be set or carefully indicate the desired positions of the various controls.

2.9

Technical Directors

The **technical director (TD)** operates the **switcher,** the piece of equipment that selects which video signal (camera 1, a videotaped segment, camera 2 with graphics over it, etc.) will go out over the airwaves or onto videotape. This piece of equipment can be used simply to **cut** from one picture to another, but most modern switchers are capable of executing a large number of special effects—wipes, swirls, squeezes, etc. (See chapter 8.) Like the audio console, the switcher has a large number of buttons, knobs, and levers, and you must become adept at operating them quickly.

The technical director is also the head technical person for most studio productions. Although the director actually gives the commands to the various equipment operators, the technical director oversees and assists the crew members if they are having trouble executing something the director wants done or if the equipment is malfunctioning.

Before Production Begins

Before the production begins, you, as the technical director are responsible for ensuring that all the equipment will work throughout the production. If one of the monitors is flickering, it is you who decides whether to replace the monitor, try to fix it, or leave it as it is. You also make sure you know about any particularly difficult picture-switching maneuvers the director might want. Often special effects can be partially set up ahead of time so that they are easy to execute when they are needed.

During Rehearsal and Recording

During the rehearsal and recording the TD operates the switcher. As with many other crew members, you

follow the instructions of the director. Usually you sit right next to the director so you can communicate fairly easily (see figure 2.12).

After the Production

After the production, you set the switcher to its normal configuration in the same manner that the audio operator sets the audio board. Usually resetting the switcher involves pushing all the buttons that indicate "black" so that there are no pictures coming through the switcher. You have the responsibility for the technical **strike** of the equipment and, as part of this duty, should note any equipment that needs repair or adjustment and inform the studio engineer.

2.10

Graphics Operators

The **graphics operator** is in charge of the computer system that is used to create words, drawings, and various visual effects. (See chapter 11.) These include such things as opening and closing credits, temperatures used for the weathercasts, short animated sequences used in commercials, statistics for sportscasts, and bar graphs used for corporate productions.

Originally graphics operators were called **character generator** (c.g.) operators, because the early graphic computer systems were only capable of displaying characters, such as letters and numbers. As the sophistication of the equipment has grown, so have the duties of the c.g. operator, so although that term is still used, *graphics operator* or *graphic artist* is becoming commonplace.

Before Production Begins

While the rest of the crew is setting up, you must create the visuals needed for the program. (See figure 2.13.) If these are extensive, you may have to come in a day or two early to create them and store them in the computer or on a floppy disc. If they consist only of opening and closing credits, the job is fairly simple.

Most computer systems are capable of special effects that look very much like those that can be executed with the switcher. The graphics operator, director, and the TD must plan together so each does what is needed to achieve the proper effect. You, as a

Figure 2.12

The technical director (front) sits near the director (center) during taping. On the other side of the director is the associate director.

Figure 2.13

The graphics operator prepares material for broadcast.

graphic artist, should have a good sense of composition and color, because you usually are creating something that will make an aesthetic statement.

During Rehearsal and Recording

During rehearsal and recording you must make sure that the proper graphic is ready when the director wants to display it and that it is displayed in the manner requested—roll, blink, one letter at a time, etc.

As with other positions, you should exhibit the discipline of thinking ahead so everything you are responsible for comes off smoothly.

After the Production

After the production, you should remove at least most of the graphics from the computer so that they do not clog up the hard drive. Some stations or studios use the same graphics over and over. Those graphics are usually stored permanently on the hard drive. It may be that one of the graphics you constructed for a particular program may be something that another program wishes to use with slight modifications. In that case, you should save the graphic in a predetermined file so it can be found easily.

Video Operators

At the present time, the person who plays back and/or records video signals is usually referred to as the *VCR operator* and operates a **videocassette recorder (VCR).** However, devices other than VCRs, such as **video disc** recorders and computer drives, are now being used to record video and audio (see chapter 9), so the term **video operator** is starting to be used.

The video operator is responsible for recording the program being produced. Sometimes even programs that are shown live (such as news or sports) are taped for archival purposes or so the footage can be used in other programs. In addition to recording, the VCR operator often plays back video material that was previously recorded. For example, the video operator may play back a news story that was edited in the early afternoon into a newscast going out live at 6:00 PM.

Before Production Begins

Before the program begins, you, as the video operator, must make sure each playback tape or other recorded material is properly cued up so that, when the director calls for it, the right material will be shown. In line with this, you should also make sure the machine playing back the tape is properly set up so that the signal will go where it is supposed to go. You must also make sure that a blank tape is inserted in the machine that is to record and that all the VCR controls are properly set.

During Rehearsal and Recording

During rehearsal, you are likely to play back tapes but not record the rehearsal itself, although sometimes final dress rehearsals are taped so that material from the tapes can be used if something goes wrong during production. During production you start the record tape when the director so instructs and monitor all the vital signs to make sure the tape is actually recording. You also play back any prerecorded material when it is needed. If a program calls for many roll-ins, you may have an assistant to play back some of the tapes. (See figure 2.14.)

After the Production

After the production is over, you should carefully label the master tape on which the program is recorded. Most studios have a standard labeling system that includes the title and length of the program, the date on which it was recorded, and the name of the director. Usually it is a good idea to label both the tape and the box. You should file the tape in the appropriate place or give it to the appropriate person. The same is true for all the tapes that were rolled into the program.

Editors

The **editor's** job is to piece together different shots or scenes taped in the studio or the field to create a unified piece of work. Sometimes all the editor's work occurs before a production is taped and sometimes it all occurs afterwards. With some of the newer editing systems, editors can even edit while a program is in progress,

Figure 2.14

This video operator readies the tape so that the program can be recorded.

but this is rare. Of course, some shows, such as a live telecast of a telethon, do not require an editor at all.

Before Production Begins

An editor works before a program is taped to piece together material that will be rolled into a production. For example, you may assemble a background piece about an Olympic athlete to include in a magazine show. You usually work alone in a small room called an editing suite (see figure 2.15) that contains all the equipment needed for editing. (See chapter 10.)

Sometimes the director (or a reporter, in the case of news) is also present for editing. Editors who work alone are usually given a script or a list of shots so they have a general idea of what they are to assemble, but they also use their own creativity to present material in an aesthetically pleasing manner.

During Rehearsal and Recording

If editing occurs during production, it is often so that a summary of something that has happened during the course of the telecast can be presented. For example, you might pull together a collage that shows a basketball player sinking six baskets at six different times during the first half. Then the sportscasters could comment on these during half time.

Figure 2.15

The editor, under the guidance of the director, is in the editing suite assembling footage.

After the Production

Most editing, however, occurs after the production has been shot when you place shots in juxtaposition with each other. There may be hours of footage that must be cut down to a 30-minute show. You and the director (and/or associate director) must organize the footage, decide what to use, and assemble it.

Often the editing job is broken down with one or more people editing the picture and several others working on the sound. This is most likely to be the case for dramas and comedies, which often need special audio enhancements such as a laugh track or sound effects. Other editing is much simpler with both sound and picture being edited by the same person. As an editor, you may need to shorten a game show that ran too long, or piece together parts of a variety show taped stop-and-go fashion over the course of an afternoon, or eliminate some dull parts of a talk show.

2.13
Other Positions

A raft of other people are needed for TV production. Sometimes people called *production assistants* undertake all the little jobs that need to be done—distributing scripts to cast and crew, moving flower pots, getting coffee for everyone, etc. For a large unionized production, specialists undertake specific jobs—a *propmaster* places and handles all props, *painters* and *carpenters* are available to touch up sets, *makeup artists* apply makeup to talent, *grips* carry cable and other things. All of these people are usually around before, during, and after production to handle setup, production miscellany, and cleanup on an as-needed basis.

The overall look of a production comes under the province of the **art director, production designer,** and/or **set designer.**[6] These people work to ensure that all the artistic aspects of a program (set pieces, props, graphics, costumes) work together without clashing or giving different psychological messages. Most of this work takes place before the production is begun as does the work of *set builders* and *costume designers*.

Different types of programs require various specialists. *Animal handlers* are needed for shows that feature dogs, monkeys, or more exotic animals. If real plants and flowers are in evidence, *greenspeople* keep them looking fresh. *Teachers* are needed if school-age children make up the cast. A dance program will require a *choreographer*. If the end product of the production is to be an interactive program, *computer programmers* with skills in multimedia programs such as Hypercard will be needed.

People who execute *special effects* have been in great demand in recent years. Even for studio shoots, pyrotechnic effects are used more frequently than in the past, and many shots that used to be shown fairly straight are now enhanced through digital manipulation. Just about every frame of the movie *Babe* underwent manipulation so that the real animals used throughout the movie looked more people-like. The credits include such jobs as Fleece Fabrication Assistant and Feather and Anatomy Designer.

Overall, job classifications are in a state of flux. Technological advances eliminate jobs (e.g., camera operators being eliminated by robotic cameras), but just as quickly other technological advances create new jobs (e.g., digital manipulation). The people most likely to succeed in behind-the-scenes employment are those who have a variety of skills and who are willing to learn new tasks and new equipment.

2.14
Cast

This book, because it is aimed more at the behind-the-scenes aspects of video production, will not dwell on acting techniques, which are covered very well in the many books written on the subject.[7] However, people who are in the television business often have to appear on the screen and certainly, within the classroom setting, producers and directors often call upon their classmates to appear in front of the camera. Therefore, in this chapter, we will give some rudimentary tips on what you should do when you are talent for a TV show.

A distinction is often made between two groups of talent: (1) those who serve essentially as communicators, portraying no role except as a host or reporter; and (2) those in dramatic roles who are portraying some theatrical character. The first category is referred to as **performers,** while the second group is referred to as **actors.** Although the two groups share many characteristics and concerns, it may be helpful to look at them separately in terms of what you need to do when you are in one of these roles.

Television Performers

The category of performer includes announcers, hosts, narrators, reporters, interviewers, demonstrators, panel participants, and the like—talent who are communicating personally with the audience, usually addressing them directly.

You, as a performer, must realize that your primary responsibility is to the audience. Even though millions of people may be watching a particular TV program, television is an intimate medium. It usually is received on a small screen, in the privacy of the home, as a rule by an audience of one or a few people. You will be most successful when you conceive of the audience in that manner—one to four people sitting just a few feet away.

Voice and Eyes

For this reason, a natural conversational speaking voice is best. If you can project the feeling of spontaneity and intimacy in your speaking style, you will be on the way to capturing one of the most sought-after qualities of any television performer—*sincerity.* (As one comedian wisecracked, "If you can fake sincerity, you got it made.")

Just as important as vocal directness is the intimacy of specific visual directness—eye contact with the TV camera. When you are speaking to the audience, you should maintain a direct and personal eye contact with the camera lens at all times, looking straight into the heart of it. This direct eye contact is the secret of maintaining the illusion of an exclusive relationship with each individual member of the audience. By looking directly into the lens, you are directly and personally addressing everyone who is in contact with the television receiver.

In maintaining the illusion of direct eye contact, you must become skilled, of course, in some of the artifice and techniques of the medium. In many productions, the director will cut from one camera shot of the performer to another. You will have to re-establish eye contact with the new camera immediately. One

way to make this transition look as natural as possible is to glance downward—as if glancing at some notes or trying to collect your thoughts—and then immediately establish eye contact with the new camera.

The director should inform you if one camera is being used exclusively for close-ups of some object you are demonstrating or discussing. Then you won't need to worry about ever having to look at that camera, even though it is on the air.

Mannerisms

Because television is such an intimate, close-up medium, any visually- or vocally-distracting mannerism you have will certainly be captured with full impact. Some nervous mannerisms, such as a facial twitch or the unconscious habit of licking lips, may be hard to control. On the other hand, some fidgety distractions, such as playing with a pencil or pulling an earlobe, can be corrected if someone calls them to your attention. Ask for such advice; it will help you come across better on the tube. Besides, many an audio operator has had a few hairs turn gray when a performer thumped his or her fingers on the table next to the desk mic while pondering a weighty question.

Vocal habits and mannerisms can also be distracting. The use of vocalized pauses (saying "um" or "ah") every time there is a second of dead air is a problem many of us share. The ubiquitous "I see" somehow always becomes part of the interviewer's basic vocabulary. Try to avoid these mannerisms.

Handling the Script

Depending upon the specific program, you may be working from a full script or speaking extemporaneously or something in between. Some performers, such as guests on a talk show, may speak spontaneously or *ad lib* with no preparation at all. Many performers think they have to work from a full script—when they probably would be better off working from rough notes. These enable the talent to have enough of a solid outline to speak with confidence; yet, by composing the exact words on the spot, they can add vitality and sincerity that is difficult to achieve with a prepared text.

You can handle fully-scripted material in one of several ways. *Memorization* usually is required only

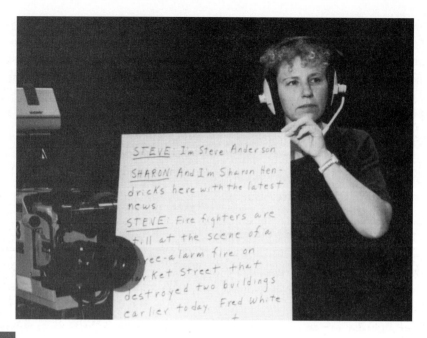

Figure 2.16

This cue card is being held next to the lens so that the talent can see it easily.

for dramatic works and is best left to actors. Seldom can typical television performers deliver memorized copy without sounding artificial and stiff. You are better off reading from a physical script in your hands, from cue cards held next to the camera, or from a prompting device.

Reading directly from a *script* is satisfactory if you are quite familiar with the material and do not have to keep your eyes glued to the script. Some people can handle a script very well, glancing down only occasionally. Others, because of insecurity or nervousness, get completely buried in the script and never establish eye contact. If you do use a script, you should make sure the pages are unstapled so you can slide the pages to the side unobtrusively without creating noise on the microphone. Also, make sure the pages are in the right order before starting the final take.

The difficulties of working with a script can be avoided by using **cue cards,** but they have their own problems. Either you or some crew member will have to transfer the entire script onto large cue sheets. The person holding the cue cards has to be trained to raise each card to keep the exact line being read next to the lens. With a hefty stack of cue cards, holding them can become a very wearisome and demanding assignment.

(See figure 2.16.) Cue cards allow for better eye contact than many performers can muster if they use hand-held scripts, but because they are beside the camera, the performers often appear to be looking slightly off camera.

Cue cards have been largely replaced by the teleprompter (review figure 2.9) which enables you to read the copy while staring directly at the lens. The direct spot on the script can always be positioned directly in front of the lens so that your eyes cannot wander away from the lens.

Other Performing Tips

In order to achieve good camera angles, performers have to work close together. One old television adage is, "If you ain't touching, you ain't close enough." Some performers feel uncomfortable with the close physical proximity they must maintain to other talent. As a result, they will start out in a chair close to the other talent but gradually, during the course of rehearsal and taping, move further and further away. The result is that a gap develops that looks inappropriate in the TV frame. (See figure 2.17.) As a performer, try to get used to this "closeness" and check every once in awhile to make sure you and the other performers are positioned properly.

Figure 2.17

Although these two people are sitting at what is normal distance for ordinary conversation, when the television camera frames both of them, there is an undesirable gap between them. They should sit closer together.

Make sure you know where the microphones and lights are, and don't walk out of the light or out of the range of the sound pickup.

Don't acknowledge the floor manager's hand signals in any way (such as nodding your head), because this will show on camera. You should be aware of where the stage manager is, but it is the stage manager's job to stand where you can easily see him or her.

Don't make any big or sweeping gestures, because the chances are that the camera will be on a fairly tight shot. Similarly, be careful with facial grimaces; there is a likelihood that the camera has a close-up of you.

Whenever you can, help the director prepare for important shots by telegraphing them ahead of time. Say, "Now let's look at the first demonstration . . ." as this will warn the director that you are going to move to the demonstration area. However, don't give direct instructions such as "Now, if I could just get a shot of this wristwatch!"

In a similar vein, if you are going to make a big move, you should lean into it gradually giving the director and the camera operator ample warning. For example, if you are sitting in a chair and are ready to stand and walk over to the demonstration area, place both feet firmly on the floor, lean forward, put your hands on the sides of the chair, and *slowly* lift out of the chair. The camera is then able to follow you smoothly. In general, you should develop a habit of moving slowly as you go from one area of the set to another. This gives the camera operator a good chance of moving along gracefully. (And it always looks fast enough to the viewer.)

If you hold up some object in front of the camera for a close-up, hold your arm tightly against your body to steady the hand. Even better, rest the object on a table or stand so there is no possibility of it moving.

Don't handle microphones, except hand mics, and avoid playing with the mic cords because both can ruin audio. When you are asked to give an audio level, speak as you will speak during the program. Some performers will mumble a relatively weak audio check and then boom out on the air with their best basso profundo. A few will do just the opposite.

Clothing

Usually performers wear their own clothes, not costumes designed by television employees. If you are

Figure 2.18

The fine design on a blouse such as this would be substantially lost once it reaches the home TV set.

going to perform on a program, you should try to find out something about the set so you do not clash with it. If you are going to be sitting in a tan chair, you should not wear a tan shirt or dress because you will disappear. If the set is basically green, don't wear red clothing—unless you want to give the impression of Christmas.

Unless a spectacular, deliberately colorful, dazzling effect is advised, stick to clothing of a *dull saturation*— muted aqua rather than chartreuse, tan rather than brilliant yellow. Brightness and tonal balance also should be considered in terms of the overall emotional effect that is desired. Would dark, somber grays and browns be more or less appropriate than lighter shades and pastels?

Line also is an important design consideration. Vertical lines tend to emphasize tall and slender proportions; horizontal stripes tend to exaggerate weight and mass. Performers who are concerned about appearing too heavy (and television has a tendency to make people appear a little heavier) should be advised to stick to vertical lines.

You should also avoid high contrast and extremes in color brightness. Television cameras have a relatively limited contrast ratio, which makes it difficult for them to handle white shirts against a dark suit. Try also to avoid high contrasts with skin tones. Dark clothes will make a pale person look even more pale; light-colored clothes next to a tanned complexion will make the skin appear darker. Blacks and other dark-skinned performers should be careful of light-colored clothing that would tend to heighten the tonal contrast and wash out facial details in the dark areas.

Generally, finely-detailed patterns should be avoided. Whereas clothing with a rich thick texture will photograph well on television, clothing with a fine pattern usually will not, because it is too busy and distracting and hard to make out once it has gone through the TV scanning process. (See figure 2.18.) Thin stripes, herringbones, and small checks can also create the **moiré effect**—a distracting visual vibration caused by the interference of the clothing pattern and the TV scanning lines.

Figure 2.19

A makeup artist applies final touches to the performer.

One other minor clothing consideration involves **chroma key.** This is an effect wherein talent is taped against a blue background; then the blue is removed and something else, such as a picture of a building, is inserted in its place. (See chapter 8, section 8.4.) The problem is that anything, even a tie, that contains the blue used for the chroma key will disappear, and the background picture will show through. Imagine the effect if you have a scene from the fire keyed in behind you—and we see flames coming through your shirt. Ask if chroma key is going to be used, and, if so, avoid wearing chroma key blue.

Makeup

Many productions (such as public affairs shows) do not require formal makeup. Guests can "come as they are" and look perfectly fine. However, many guests will look better if makeup is used to enhance or correct appearance.

The object of television makeup for performers is to have them look as natural as possible. A good, basic, unobtrusive makeup job should help enhance normal colors (evening up flesh tones, cutting down on the shine of a bald head), minimize any blemishes

or distortions (covering up birthmarks, eliminating bags under the eyes), and emphasize good points. However, with the close-up lens, any exaggerated makeup certainly would be perceived as unnatural.

If you are performing at a TV station, there may be a makeup person available to apply the make-up (see figure 2.19), but often, if you want to wear make-up, you will have to apply your own. Such applications are not all that difficult. Before applying any makeup, clean your face with either a moisturizer for dry skin, or an astringent (such as alcohol or witch hazel) for oily skin. Then apply the *base.* This is the initial covering that is usually applied to the entire face or exposed area being treated (arms and hands and other parts of the body often need makeup treatment). This base is to provide the color foundation upon which all the rest of the makeup will be built.

Next, apply *powder* to help keep the base from smearing. Usually, powder that is a little lighter than the base color is best. You can use *highlights* and *shadows* to emphasize or minimize facial features. Your forehead, nose, cheekbone, and jaw can all be highlighted with lighter shades or de-emphasized with darker tones. Normally, *rouge* is next applied to the cheeks, nose, forehead, and chin as needed to give you a healthy complexion and to counteract the flatness of the base color.

Finally, you should give special attention to those most expressive features of the face—the eyes and the lips. Use specific drawing tools and accessory items as necessary: *lipstick, eye shadow, eyeliner, eyebrow pencil, mascara,* and possibly *false eyelashes.* The extent of the use of these accent items depends upon the need for remodeling and your individual taste.

Hairstyling

Hairstyles with a definite shape or firm silhouette usually compliment the performer more than wispy, fluffy hairdos. You should comb your hair carefully, because backlight will tend to make loose strands stand out. Avoid fancy hair treatments and fresh permanents, because they will make you look unnatural.

Handling all these aspects of performing is part of the overall *discipline* of being in front of the camera.

Television Actors

Many of the observations made regarding television performers apply equally to television actors. Actors, too, must be concerned with their relationship with the audience. They must: talk conversationally as their character would talk; learn to work with scripts; and be aware of the demands of the mics and lights and the hand signals of the stage manager.

However, acting involves special considerations. First, actors have to learn to adjust to the concept of a moving audience perspective. Unlike theater, there is no **proscenium arch;** there is no firm boundary separating the audience from the actors. The audience perspective is switched every time the camera is changed. The viewer can be transported sideways, in or out, or into the mind of the actor. Actors must, therefore, be aware of how their actions will appear from all angles.

Gestures and Voice

As an actor, you must limit sweeping gestures, because you are playing to a camera that is only about 10 feet away. Likewise, you must restrict voice volume level—without losing emotion or intensity—for a pickup point only 3 or 4 feet away. Television is a close-up medium, and actors must play to this intimacy.

Precision

Actors must move very *precisely*, because they must be within the bounds of what the camera is shooting. If the actor's head is tilted at the wrong angle, the framing for a given shot may be off. If a moving actor does not "hit his mark" at exactly the right spot behind the sofa, he may ruin the impact of an emotional close-up. Sometimes directors have actors **cheat to camera.** An actor, in a two-shot for instance, will be directed to turn his or her face slightly toward the camera—rather than looking directly at the other actor straight on. Such *cheating* is not perceived by the viewer, but it does result in more of a head-on shot into the camera.

Television exists generally in a demanding and nonflexible time frame. Most dramatic programs have to be squeezed (or stretched) into given time slots—multiples of a half hour, minus requisite time for commercials. This means that you, as an actor, may need to adjust pacing very precisely, speeding up or slowing down delivery of lines or action. This is especially a major concern with soap operas and situation comedies where there can be little flexibility in timing. It is less of a concern for filmed dramas, however, where the exact timing can be worked out in the editing process by cutting or augmenting silent footage, panoramic long shots, and chase sequences.

Quick Study

Compared to the stage and to theatrical motion pictures, television drama is a quick study medium. Whether working with single-camera or multiple-camera techniques, regular actors in a continuing series must learn up to an hour-long script every week—the equivalent of two feature-length motion pictures every month. For the actor in the hour-long daytime soap opera, the pace is even more demanding—up to an hour of dialogue every day!

Performers and actors are very important to any video production. They are what the home audience sees. All positions are important, however. A mistake by anyone, cast or crew, affects the overall quality of the production.

Summary

Many people are needed for a studio show, because a large number of things must be accomplished at the same time. The *producer*, who may or may not even appear for the taping, is crucial during preproduction when everything is planned. The *director* is the leader in the studio. A director must prepare carefully—analyzing and marking the script, planning facilities, and securing personnel. The director rehearses as appropriate and makes calls during the taping. If editing is required, the director oversees it.

An *AD* assists the director as needed and is particularly responsible for *timing*. The *stage manager* is the director's surrogate in the studio, giving hand signals to the talent.

The *camera operators* frame shots and make sure the camera is set up and put away properly. *Teleprompter operators* control the script as it scrolls in front of the camera lens where the talent can see it. A *lighting director* is in charge of seeing that the set is well-lit before the production begins. *Audio operators* must set up mics in the studio and must combine sounds through the audio board. The *technical director* operates the *switcher* and also serves as the head technical person. The *graphics operator* creates credits and other visual elements and sees that they are put on-air properly. The *video operator* records the program and plays back any needed prerecorded tapes. *Editors* put together material to be inserted in the program and also edit a program after it has been shot. Many other crew members such as *production assistants*, *propmasters*, *greenspeople*, and *choreographers* are needed for certain types of productions.

Talent can be divided into *performers* (who act as themselves) and *actors* (who portray other people). Performers should maintain a *conversational voice* and good *eye contact*, should avoid *mannerisms*, and must learn how to work with a *script*. They are often responsible for their own *clothing, makeup*, and *hairstyling*. Actors must control *gestures* and *voice dynamics*, hit their marks *precisely*, and learn large amounts of script *quickly*.

Footnotes

1. Depending on the actual production setup and the traditional organization of the studio/station, the AD may be labeled either "assistant director" or "associate director." The Directors Guild of America officially refers to the position as "associate director" because the "assistant director" title is traditionally used in the film industry.

2. "Stage manager" is a term brought over from the theater. The first TV term used for this person was "floor manager," but because the person is the director's studio representative, some studios/stations use the term "floor director." "Stage manager" is now probably the most commonly used term, but all three terms are used interchangeably.

3. Sometimes performers are tied into the communication system because they are wearing an earphone for an interrupted feedback system through which the director can communicate with them. News reporters, for example, often wear these when they are in the field so they know when to start talking.

4. In union situations, the stage manager may be restrained from crossing jurisdictional lines, such as giving orders to the lighting crew.

5. *TelePrompter* ™ is a registered trademark of the Teleprompter Corporation. Many companies now produce prompting equipment, but the word teleprompter has stuck, and devices manufactured by other companies are often generically referred to as teleprompters.

6. For most TV shows, the term used for the person who designs the overall look of the show is "art director." "Production designer" is used for highly stylized productions that need a great deal of design coordination—mostly science fiction movies such as *Star Wars* and *Jurassic Park*. The "set designer" just works with the elements of the set, not the overall look.

7. Several books that can be consulted for overall information on acting are: Patrick Tucker, *How to Act for the Camera* (New York: Routledge Press, 1993); John Harrop, *Acting* (New York: Routledge Press, 1992); Brian Adams, *Screen Acting* (Los Angeles: Lone Eagle Press, 1987); and Hayes Gooden, *A Complete Compendium of Acting and Performing in Two Parts* (Sydney: Ensemble Press, 1992).

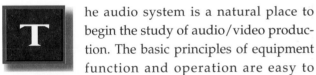

chapter 3

Audio Control Facilities: The Console and Related Components

The audio system is a natural place to begin the study of audio/video production. The basic principles of equipment function and operation are easy to understand, and they provide a convenient frame of reference for the later study of multiple camera video. The concept of how both *disciplines* and *techniques* relate to production can be clearly applied to the field of audio. For example, knowing the steps needed to connect a microphone so that it functions through an audio console is a matter of applying several basic *techniques*. However, the care with which the operator then works to test the quality and loudness parameters of that mic for its eventual use is very much a matter of individual *discipline*.

For many students, their first introduction to a large, multi-channel **audio console** is an impressive, if not somewhat intimidating, experience; however, if each component part of that console is approached in terms of its function within the larger operational scheme, then all of the faders, knobs, lights, and other indicators tend to be more easily understood. The console, along with other external components in the **audio control booth,** is designed to aid the audio operator in accomplishing a number of different control functions.

We begin this introduction to processing audio signals with a simple explanation of how one type of microphone can transform the human voice into an electronic signal. We then follow the path of that signal as it moves through the console where it can be enhanced and/or controlled in several other ways. Some of these control components are used to make sure that basic technical requirements of sound reproduction are met. Other functions are designed to achieve certain creative effects that influence the emotional setting or the informational validity of a production.

Seven Basic Control Functions

The component sections of the console, along with each piece of audio equipment in the control booth and studio, are designed to move, modify, or otherwise control a signal in one or more of the following seven ways: (1) **Transduce:** converting sound waves into electrical energy and back again; (2) **Channel:** routing the signals and sending them wherever necessary; (3) **Mix:** combining two or more sound sources; (4) **Amplify:** increasing (or decreasing) the signal strength; (5) **Shape:** creatively improving or, for other reasons, changing the quality of a sound; (6) **Monitor:** hearing or seeing an indication of the quality and volume of sound sources at various stages of control; and (7) **Record** and **playback:** retaining a sound in permanent electronic form for later use.

While examining this list, many examples of these functions will probably come to mind from your own experience in operating a home entertainment center with recording and playback capabilities. As you apply the previously mentioned characteristics to your unit, you will begin to see that some components perform more than one function. For example, the speaker that *transduces* a signal into listenable sound is obviously also a *monitor*. The bass and treble controls that *shape* the final output of the unit do so by allowing for separate levels of *amplification* for each of those two dimensions of a sound signal.

Keep in mind that the terminology used to define the various components and their functions may vary slightly with time and location. There is, however, a basic structure of functional design common to all audio control rooms. Understanding the essential elements of this structure in your own facility is the necessary prerequisite for successful equipment operation in any production situation.

Transduce

The process through which sound (voices, music, etc.) is converted into an electrical audio signal is referred to as **transducing.** Figure 3.1 shows in simplified form how the transducing elements perform this function in one type of microphone. The tone production of a human voice or musical instrument creates pressure waves in the air molecules. If these waves are produced at a constant rate of 440 **cycles per second,**[1] the result is the musical tone of A above middle C on the piano.

These audible sound pressure waves move through the air and come in contact with the **diaphragm** of the microphone. Their force causes the attached **coil** to vibrate within a part of the permanent **magnet.** When this coil moves within the resulting magnetic field, a small electric current is produced. This signal in its new electronic form not only retains the original **frequency** pattern of 440 oscillations per second, but also the characteristics of wavelength and amplitude.[2] (More information on wave theory is contained in Appendix A.)

The electronic **waveform** at this stage is said to be an **analog** of the original sound pressure wave, since the electronic wave retains essential elements, such as frequency and amplitude, that had characterized the original sound pressure wave.

With the new **digital** playback and recording systems, the signal goes through an additional encoding (and later decoding) stage. Using computer technology, the characteristics of the analog wave are analyzed or **sampled** at numerous points of its structure. The resulting encoded information describing such factors as frequency and amplitude is now in the form of groups or **bytes** of on (1) or off (0) pulses called **bits** as shown in figure 3.2. A commonly used grouping is composed of eight bits. Bytes can be further combined into two- and three-byte groups. A sixteen-bit grouping (two bytes) is often used for recording hi-fi sound on a **digital audiotape (DAT).** The digital signal resists outside interference and therefore retains its quality as it is duplicated or **dubbed** and moved from point to point.

A transduced analog microphone signal can be mixed with digital inputs in newer digital models such as the Yamaha 02R shown in figure 3.3. Whatever its wave structure, this signal will be increased in volume at one or more stages in its journey through the audio control room. Whatever its final destination, it will probably also be heard on a speaker in the audio booth. The speaker is also a *transducer*, something like a

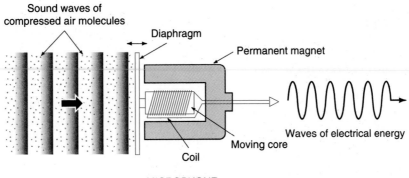

Sound waves of compressed air molecules

Diaphragm

Permanent magnet

Waves of electrical energy

Moving core

Coil

MICROPHONE

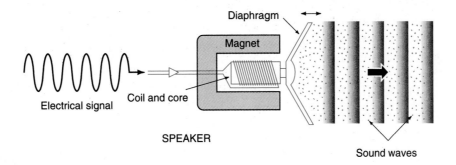

Diaphragm

Magnet

Electrical signal

Coil and core

Sound waves

SPEAKER

Figure 3.1

Transducing element of a dynamic microphone and corresponding speaker elements. When sound waves from a voice or musical instrument strike the diaphragm of the microphone, the waves of compressed air molecules cause the attached coil to vibrate. As the coil moves back and forth within the magnetic field of the permanent magnet, a small fluctuating electric current is produced. This very small current, which will be amplified many times, carries the same information as the original sound waves. At the receiving end, when this minute electrical signal reaches the speaker coil, it produces fluctuations in the magnetic field that then cause the diaphragm of the speaker to vibrate, creating sound waves that reproduce the original sound picked up by the microphone.

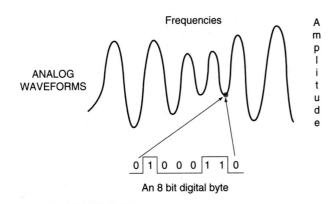

Frequencies

ANALOG WAVEFORMS

A m p l i t u d e

0 1 0 0 0 1 1 0

An 8 bit digital byte

Figure 3.2

The location of this digital byte roughly illustrates that it could be serving as part of a sample of the amplitude of a particular analog wave. It would be one of a large number of samples taken of that wave in the process of converting to a digital signal.

microphone, with the elements, a coil, and a magnet now operating in reverse order. The electrical energy of the signal puts the diaphragm into pulsating motion, pushing against the air molecules. When it moves at a rate of 440 cycles per second, it creates sound pressure waves reproducing the original tone of A above middle C.

Channel

The term **channel** is used as a verb when it refers to the procedure of moving signals from one place to another and as a noun when it describes the actual pathway the signal follows through cables and other equipment from its source to its final destination. Figure 3.4 shows how the audio operator would plan the *sequence of signal flow* of the feed from a studio mic,

Figure 3.3

The Yamaha 02R audio console features sixteen digital and twenty-four analog input channels. The backlit LED displays a number of control settings, and other operational information can be stored for later recall. SMPTE time code automation of motorized faders, comprehensive MIDI functions, and stereo capabilities are among many other features. *Photo courtesy of Yamaha*

going through a **patch bay** connection, into and through the audio console, and then back to the patch bay, where it is available to be fed as program line output to be recorded or even broadcast.

The process starts when a microphone is connected to a cable which is in turn plugged into a studio microphone input. These numbered wall receptacles are located at different points around the studio. This connection might also be made by means of a component called a **snake** that has numbered receptacles for twenty or thirty mic inputs all located together in a box-like component. It is connected to the audio booth by a large multiwire cable. In either case, these permanent lines terminate at the patch bay, where there are similarly numbered receptacles labeled as *mic outputs.* (See figures 3.4 and 3.5.) In addition to a number of other mic outputs, the patch bay will contain outputs from components such as cart machines, CD players, and videotape machines. Usually located just below these output receptacles, another row of input receptacles will lead to the numbered *input channels* within

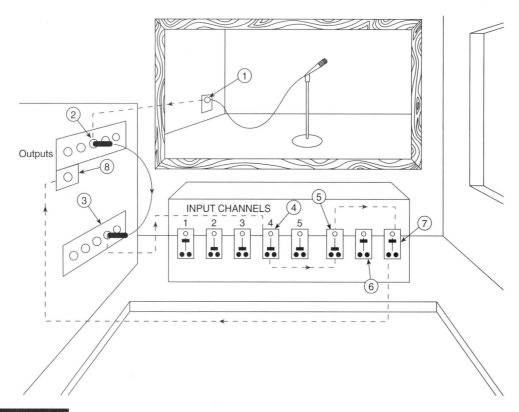

Figure 3.4

Audio signal flow model. (1) Studio microphone wall receptacle input. (2) Patch bay output from studio. (3) Patch bay input to console. (4) Input channel 4. (5 and 6) Group master faders. (7) Master fader for program output. (8) Program-out patch bay receptacle.

the audio console. In figure 3.5, we show "mic 1 output" being connected down and over to "input channel 4" by means of a **patch cord.**

Normalled Connections

We could have patched mic 1 into input channel 5 or into any of the other available input channels, depending upon our *audio setup plan.* However, had we wanted to use input channel 3 (just below the output), we would not have needed to use a patch cord to make the connection into that input channel. Notice the dotted line running from mic 1 to input channel 3 (and the similar dotted lines for the other corresponding vertical pairs). It denotes that in the model patch bay, as on most equipment, a permanent hardwired connection already exists between these two points.

This is called a **normalled** connection because it is *normally* in place. It saves time as the operator does not have to make a patch for the input of equipment constantly in use such as audiotape and videotape recorders and certain basic studio microphones. All normalled connections are designed so that the existing connection is broken (separated) any time a patch cord is placed in either the input or output receptacle. An obvious question arises as to why normalled connections would not always be preferred. The answer is that the sequence of numbers around the studio wall often does not match the way that the audio operator wishes to group mics for easy handling on the console during production.

The Audio Console

With the patch between "mic 1 out" and "input channel 4," we have moved the signal into the audio console (sometimes called *the board*) itself. (See figure 3.6.) Since at this point we are mostly concerned with the concept of *signal flow,* the input channels depicted have been simplified to show only **gain** and **fader** controls for the main feed, along with one gain control used for an **auxiliary send** feed. This *send* feature is a special audio feed that allows a performer in the

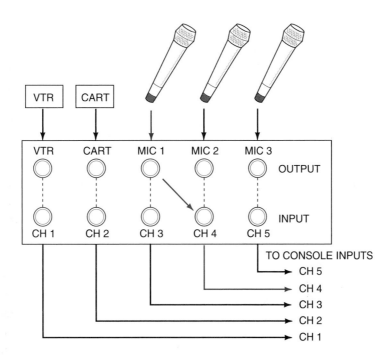

Figure 3.5

Diagram of a simplified patch bay. This diagram shows the configuration of a simplified patch bay. The receptacles on the upper row are source outputs. The receptacle on the lower row are input receptacles leading to numbered input channels at the audio console. Hard-wired (normalled) connections are indicated by a dotted line. A sample signal pathway is shown in color.

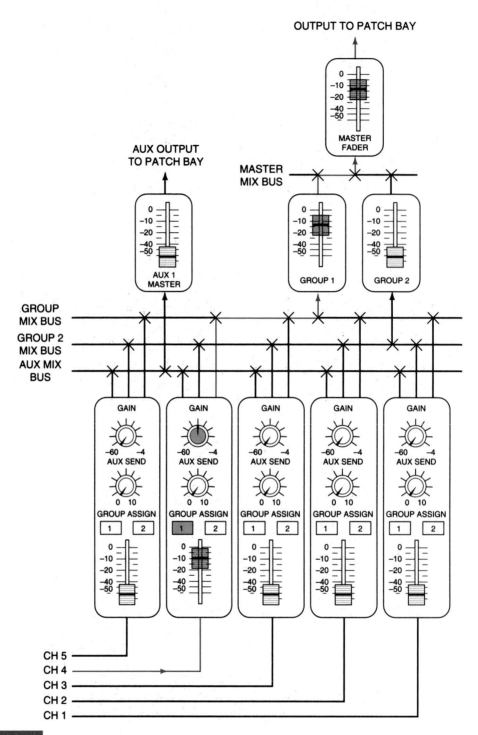

OUTPUT TO PATCH BAY

AUX OUTPUT
TO PATCH BAY

MASTER
MIX BUS

GROUP
MIX BUS

GROUP 2
MIX BUS

AUX MIX
BUS

CH 5
CH 4
CH 3
CH 2
CH 1

Figure 3.6

Signal flow through an audio console. This diagram shows a continuation of the signal flow through an input channel, out to a group fader, and on to the master fader for final volume control.

studio to hear the mixed program output, or even a selected videotape feed, through an earphone during the ongoing production.

We have also included another very important routing device known as a **group assign switch** for each channel. This channeling control allows any input channel to be fed through any of the **group master faders** (also known as **submasters**). These faders in turn feed into a final **master fader** for control of the volume of **program line out.** If the board was designed for stereo, the input channels, group faders, and master faders would work in pairs—along with some special controls (**pan**) to handle the left and right channels of stereo sound.

The capacity of an audio console can be greatly increased by the use of a **routing switcher** that can allow for two or more inputs to be fed into any one input channel. While not included in this simplified depiction, it is usually located just "**downstream**" of the patch bay which is immediately after the signal comes out of the patch bay. Its value is based on the concept that, while some productions will feature a heavy use of prerecorded feeds such as videotapes, carts, or CD material, others will have a heavier emphasis on the use of studio microphones. With the routing switcher, the operator has a choice of *either* a mic *or* a recorded signal being fed into a channel and, in addition, the ability to switch quickly between the two sources without repatching.

The importance of the *input/output* concept cannot be stressed too often. As a signal moves through any system, it is repeatedly going into, through, and out of a series of controls and other components. The *output* of one component becomes the *input* of the next. A thorough knowledge of the *sequence of signal flow* within any system is the key to being able to set up and test audio in any production situation. When trouble occurs, a sequential point-by-point check is the most efficient way to find the button that was not pressed, the fader that was not opened, or the component that is not functioning properly. In later chapters, it will become evident that this same *discipline* has applications to lighting, video, and setting up any video editing/graphics operation.

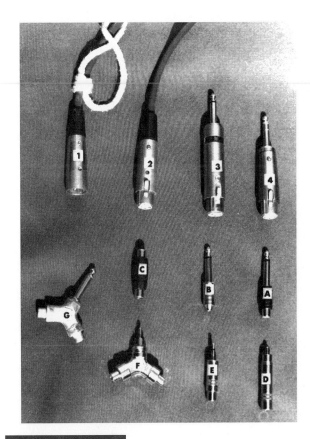

Figure 3.7

Audio connectors and adapters. This figure shows the most commonly used connecting plug types and the adapters that are used to convert an audio signal from one form to another. Caution must always be exercised with the use of this equipment. Not all combinations of levels of impedance with balanced and/or unbalanced signals are possible even though the connections fit. The RCA plugs double as video connectors.

Connecting Plugs and Adapters

The heavy-duty activity that goes with both stringing cables on the studio floor and channeling the signal at the patch bay calls for cables and connectors that are very durable. The male and female *XLR connectors,* as shown in examples 1 and 2 of figure 3.7 (with a rope for tying coils), would be found at either end of a **low-impedance (low-Z)** studio microphone cable. (**Imped-ance** is a measure of resistance to signal flow on a line.) The three-pin connector denotes the presence of what is called a **balanced line.** It is constructed to provide as much protection as possible for the weak mic signal over long distances. Two of the lines carry mic signals that are a mirrored (balanced) version of the other's flow of frequencies. The third wire is a ground line. All three are wrapped in a metal shield and a plastic outer cover. This design provides optimum protection from interference over long distances. The example 3 adapter is designed to do double duty. It converts the low-impedance signal from the mic cable to a high-impedance signal at the male *phone plug* at the top. The signal conversation works in either direction. A similar phone plug design attached to a cable would be used at most patch bays. Example 4 adapts the three-line mic cable into a phone plug. Depending on design, the phone plug could indicate that the adapter is also converting the signal from a balanced line three-wire to an unbalanced line two-wire.

More permanent connections can use smaller plugs and lighter cables as exemplified by the four adapters, examples A, B, D, and E. *Phone Plug* adapter, example A, accepts an *RCA male plug* (example D, below it). Note the presence of the projecting outer shield on the end RCA plug. This projection connects the ground line carried in the metal shielding of the cable. The example B adapter plug accepts what is known as a *male mini-phone plug* (example E, just below). Its shielding also carries the ground line but makes connection in a segmented part of the tip. The RCA and mini-plugs are used with smaller *unbalanced* lines and consist of a single wire with the outer shielding being used for the ground. Unbalanced lines are usually for **high-impedance** signals and have an effective limit of between 10 and 15 feet. (See Amplification below.) The lower ends of examples D and E are designed to accept male phone plugs.

Example C is what is called a *barrel plug.* It accepts RCA plugs at both ends and is used to make extensions to an existing line. The remaining two items in Figure 3.7 are called *splitters.* Each can take either one signal and send it to two destinations or blend two signals together as in the conversion of a stereo signal to a monaural input. Example F adapts two female RCA signals to one male RCA plug. Example G takes the two RCA signals and adapts them to a single phone plug.

Mix

It seems obvious now that the ability to blend and control a number of sound sources and to control separately the volume levels of each would be seen as a primary requisite for any type of audio production. History tells us, however, that early radio studios had only one microphone and that volume control was accomplished by placing people and musicians closer or farther away from that one mic. Fortunately, radio broadcasters in the late 1920s came up with the idea of a common line **mix bus** being fed by several individually-controlled microphones. This concept is the foundation of the structure of the audio console of today.

The basic concept involved in *mixing* several sound sources is not complicated. Take for example an audio operator who, for a segment of a program, has an announcer's voice on one mic (channel 4) and a small orchestra being picked up on a second mic. Because the music tends to rise and fall in volume, the operator will make sure that the voice is always heard above the music by making a series of fader adjustments. If the orchestra were larger and being picked up by four mics, the operator might have a hard time working all of the faders at once. Looking back at figure 3.6, we can see that the solution to the problem would be to use the **group assign switches** to send those channels carrying the music through the group 2 master. Now the operator can control the **balance** between the announcer and the music by using just the two group faders. Individual fader adjustments of individual mic faders would still be possible. The point here is that any of our input channels can be fed to either of the group master faders. The purpose of this arrangement is to allow the operator to group together any number of individual input channels for special purposes. Multiply this simple example and envision twenty-four or even forty-eight input channels controlled by eight to sixteen group masters. Such combinations of multiple microphones call for the use of separate group masters for more precise control over percussion, brass, woodwind, and string sections. The process is known as **submastering,** and it is quite important when handling any large audio operation.

If it is becoming evident that an understanding of signal flow is essential to the mixing function, then it

Modern audio boards feature numerous input channels, each with its own VU meter, and a variety of sound quality controls as well as signal flow options as in this Yamaha MR 1642 Audio Mixing Console.   *Photo courtesy of Yamaha*

will come as no surprise that the functions of *amplifying* and *shaping* are equally related. These functions, along with a necessary ability to *monitor* results, are all interactive aspects of signal control.

Amplify

Large-scale radio broadcasting was only possible after the invention of the vacuum tube with its ability to increase the power of a signal while maintaining its original waveform. Its function has long since been taken over by the transistor and all the other marvels of semiconductor technology that create and control signals of increasing diversity. An audio console must be able to handle them all. The signal produced by the type of mic shown back in figure 3.1 is roughly one-twentieth the strength of the **line level** feed from an amplified source such as a videotape machine. The direct feed from amplified instruments, such as a guitar or an electronic keyboard, may be somewhat lower than line level but still much stronger than the relatively weak signal generated by a microphone. There is also what is known as a *+4dB*[3] level that is used for special high-amplification situations.

Contemporary audio consoles can cope with these varying input levels by having a number of small amplifiers or **preamps** at key points in the console, as well as a number of strategically-placed devices called **pads,** whose function is to absorb or reduce signal strength. To explain how this works, a careful look at an input channel in a professional-level audio console is necessary. Figure 3.8 shows a Yamaha MR 1642 audio mixing console. This type of unit is good in an industrial video studio or an educational institution doing broadcast quality production and class instruction. It is a stereo board with sixteen input channels making it ideal for medium-sized "live-to-tape" productions. It also has a number of features that make it useful for teaching multitrack music recording techniques.

At the top of the **input channel** shown in figure 3.9, we have examples of the controls that deal with varying levels of input. *Control 1* is a **tape switch** that works in conjunction with *control 2*, a **pad switch.** These switches are needed because, on the back of the audio console, each input channel has four different input receptacles. Each is of a different type allowing

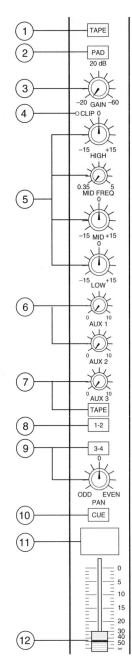

Schematic drawing of an input channel for the Yamaha 1642.

the channel to be matched with signals from microphones of differing impedance or other signals of varying strengths.

In effect, these multiple inputs increase the capability of the board by expanding the capacity of each channel. For example, an input channel can be used for a microphone during the first part of a program and then switched to a videotape feed later when needed. By pressing *control 1* (the tape switch), the videotape signal is brought into the input channel at line level. This is roughly 40 decibels stronger than **microphone level.** If amplified guitars and electronic keyboard instruments are part of the production, then *control 2* (the pad switch) is used to vary the strength of those signals by up to 20 decibels. These inputs are then further adjusted by the use of *control 3* (the gain control) that can adjust levels within a range of 40 decibels (shown as −20 decibels to −60 decibels).

If a microphone (with the usual low-impedance level feed) is being fed into the input channel, then neither the tape nor the pad switches need to be used. Once the proper settings are established, *control 12* (the **channel fader** at the bottom of the input channel) is used to maintain consistent sound levels. *Control 4* (the **clip LED indicator**) is a light-emitting diode monitor that will be discussed along with the monitoring section. It is important to note that the quality of high or low impedance is not a measure of amplification. There is, occasionally, some confusion on this matter, because the unbalanced, single-wire cables that are usually used for high-impedance mics are the same cables that are used for line-level feeds.

Shape

The function of **shaping,** the process of altering the tonal characteristics of the sound, is to a great extent a creative function. A number of subtle but important things can be done to affect the quality of a sound signal. In both a technical and a creative sense, much of the technique and discipline of a trained audio engineer results in the ability to reproduce the same quality and dimension as existed in an original sound pressure wave—replicating the natural sound as we would hear it without electronic intervention. A related goal is that of creating an enhanced version of that original sound so that it sounds like the tone the listener *expects* to hear in a given program situation. The problem of turning natural sound into electronically reproduced sound is that much of what shapes the quality of the sound is strongly affected by the physical conditions of the recording location as well as by the microphones and other audio equipment being used.

The musical notation chart in Appendix B shows the way in which the quality of sound from a musical instrument (or voice) is shaped by the presence of a number of higher frequency **overtones** produced by the instrument in addition to the fundamental note. These tones vibrate at different degrees of loudness according to the resonating qualities of each instrument (timbre). Brass reflects differently than wood. A trumpet has a different sound from a clarinet, because its overtone pattern (as can be seen on an oscilloscope) is very different from that of the clarinet. In addition to this, the sound of a trumpet, as produced in a studio, is further affected by a number of other things such as soundproofing on the walls and cloth material in a cyclorama. These surfaces cause the overtones to be absorbed, and therefore lost, or to be reflected and picked up by the mic. In either case, the result definitely alters the quality of sound picked up by the mic.

The electronic components of the audio system further shape the tone of the original sound. This process starts with the selection of the microphone and continues on through other components of the console. Mics vary greatly in their designed capacity to capture overtones at varying distances and levels of loudness. They should only be used for the purpose for which they were intended. The all-purpose mic designed for an outdoor public-address system is not able to reproduce the subtleties of musical tones required in a commercial recording studio. (See chapter 4.)

Equalizing

For a variety of reasons, including microphone type and the resonance qualities of a studio, a human voice or other instrumental sound may not always produce the tonal quality that is desired. For example, professional singers will complain of day-to-day changes in their voice quality. The Yamaha MR 1642 in the example has audio components designed to help solve such problems by altering the frequency balance of a voice *after* it has been picked up by the mic. In figure 3.9, the four knobs of *control 5* (the *three-band equalizer*) are used primarily to *strengthen* any of those overtone frequencies that make a voice resemble its usual vocal qualities. Going one step further, these same controls

can *reinforce* additional frequencies to create an even more mellow trumpet sound than the one being fed into the mic.

The controls function in three separate frequency ranges—*high, medium,* and *low.* If, for some reason previously mentioned, the trumpet sound is deficient in the higher-level overtone frequencies, these controls can **equalize** the incoming frequencies to produce a tone color that is very close to the quality of the original sound. Since the mid-band of frequencies is the one most important for both voice and instrumental sound reproduction, there is a fourth control knob that allows the operator to "*sweep*" across this range to continually enhance the tone with selected frequencies.

Additional Components

Although not a standard part of this Yamaha mixing console, there are other effect-generating components that are found in many consoles. A **limiter** might be used to cut off levels when they reach a volume that is too strong for equipment to handle without creating distortion. An audio **compressor** can be used to compress the distance between the lowest and highest volume levels, in effect, raising the lowest levels to bring them up close to the loudest levels that the system can handle. (This use of the term compressor predates the current usage where it denotes a process of reducing signal information required for the storage or transmission of a digital video picture.) **Echo** and other **reverberation** devices, often used for musical programs or certain dramatic effects, also fall into this shaping classification.

Monitor

While it is true that certain types of video production do make use of the stop-and-go methods of film, much of the work being done live and on videotape uses the ongoing, multiple-camera style that is the essence of television. For the audio operator who is in a continuous process of amplifying, mixing, and shaping a number of sound sources, this requires constant awareness of the status of the signals going through the audio console. Fortunately, a basic understanding of the components that provide this important feedback of information is not difficult to achieve.

But, as with the other elements of a large audio console, the skillful use of this equipment should be looked upon as a never-ending study.

The most important of these components is the primary audio monitor or **program speaker** in the audio booth. Its obvious function is to provide the operator with a high-quality reproduction of the sound being fed out over the **program line** as the final mix of all combined sound sources. In a live broadcast situation, there might also be a separate **air monitor** to pick up and check the quality of the actual transmitted signal.

In larger productions, one may need the ability to monitor separately any of the single sound sources from among the ten, twenty, or even more channels that are being mixed for transmission or recording. This is done by means of a preview or **cue channel.** Each input channel and each group master channel will have a **cue button** (see figure 3–9, *control 10*) which, when pressed, will send that channel's output into a common line. At this point, the signal becomes a part of a totally separate sound system with its own amplification, gain control, and speaker. The operator can select either one single mic or a group master for audition purposes while the full orchestra is playing. Of necessity, these selected cue channel feeds would be heard on their own speakers in the booth.

The VU Meter

The **volume unit (VU) meter** provides visual description of volume levels and the degrees of difference among the ongoing level changes. Some VU meters, such as the one in figure 3.10, have a needle-sized pointer that is in constant motion as it indicates differing intensities of volume. On newer equipment, the VU meter often consists of a vertical column of **light emitting diodes (LED).** The effect is a bar of light that grows and shrinks (usually vertically) to indicate ongoing changes in volume level.

In spite of the marvelous structure of the human ear, even highly-trained personnel are not always able to discern differences in volume accurately enough to exert the precise control necessary for controlling amplified electronic signals. This is often critical, because there is a point of amplitude at which the shaping and amplifying components lose their ability to process the signal properly. As the amplification of

Figure 3.10

Volume unit (VU) meter. The traditional VU meter provides a depiction of continuing peaks and low points of an audio source. Higher decibel readings hold the possibility of signal distortion as indicated by a red line. The parallel percentage of modulation scale (shown here) is often seen on older equipment. On many consoles, such as the Yamaha 1642, there are individual meters for each channel as well as for the final line out feed.

the signal is increased beyond this point, not all frequencies are equally amplified, and the sound becomes distorted. When levels drop below an acceptable minimum, they are not processed by the system and are lost.

On audio consoles comparable to the Yamaha MR 1642, there is a VU meter for each group master channel as well as one for the final program feed. For stereo applications, both left and right group and master faders would have VU meters. Most of the newer audio consoles have a VU meter for each input channel.

The VU meter readout uses a **decibel (dB)** scale. Slightly to the right of the top of the arc is *zero point*. The zero does not signify a lack of volume; rather, it indicates the point where the signal is at its *optimum* level. All differences in signal strength are measured from this point either in **plus decibels** (to the right) or **minus decibels** (to the left). As you can see in figure 3.10, the range of measurement goes down as far as −20 dB and only up to 2 or 3 dB on the plus side. Keep in mind

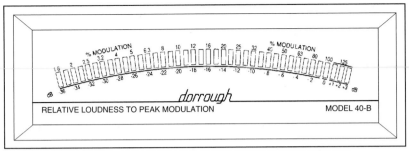

DORROUGH RELATIVE LOUDNESS TO PEAK MODULATION METER, Model 40-B

Figure 3.11

The Dorrough Loudness Meter uses LED bar graphs to indicate sound activity at lower dB levels in addition to peak volumes.   *Drawing courtesy of Dorrough Industries*

that the decibel is not an absolute unit such as an ounce or a foot. Decibel readings indicate a *ratio* of the strength of one signal as compared to another or to the amount of variation occurring in a signal at continuing points in time.

It must be noted that the traditional type of VU meter shows only the peaks of the loudest sound being heard, but not the continuity of sounds at lower volumes. There is no indication, for example, of what the rest of an orchestra is doing during a loud trumpet solo. New types of monitors are solving that problem. Figure 3.11 shows a *loudness monitor* that utilizes a display of small LED bar graphs at each different decibel level. The persistent illumination of groups of these bar graphs indicates the nature of continuing sound activity at lower volume levels. Peaks in the volume levels are simultaneously displayed to the right of the scale.

As an operational introduction to the meaning of differing decibels, two basic rules and some simple example numbers may provide a basis of understanding. *1. For every 3 dB increase (or decrease), the power (wattage) of a signal has been doubled (or halved).* If 1 watt of power is used to produce a "0" level calibration point of volume, then 2 watts of power will produce a 3 dB level and 4 watts will produce a 6 dB level. This measurement of power as applied to an electrical signal is not to be confused with any measure of relative loudness. The following rule applies to that factor. *2. The doubling or halving of loudness represents a plus or minus change of 10 dB.* Thus, it would take a 10 dB increase to make the sound on a speaker twice as loud

to the average listener. The perception of loudness does, however, vary somewhat with each individual listener.[4]

In most operational applications, the audio operator adjusts the fader knobs to have the needle oscillate between a point in the area of –2 or –3 dB swinging up to the optimum "0" point. Ideally the needle is always made to **peak** (reach the high-point of its swing) at the "0" position. This process of using the fader or other gain control to maintain a consistent level of volume is called **riding gain.**

During the preproduction setup period for any program, audio inputs from all sources must be checked and noted so that uniform levels of volume can be maintained during production. The audio operator *sets mic levels* by having each performer speak into the microphone in a normal voice. The operator then sets the channel fader at the zero (optimum) position and adjusts the gain knob to get the VU meter to peak at "0." Similarly, all prerecorded audio sources such as CDs, carts, and videotapes are checked for their signal levels. All these procedures will be covered in some detail in chapter 4. As we shall see, the concept of the "0" dB optimum level is very important in calibrating the levels of all feeds to and from the audio console.

Other Monitoring Capabilities

One small but important type of monitor is to be found in figure 3.9 at *control 4.* In this case, it is the **clip LED** (light-emitting diode) **indicator** that shows that the #3 *gain control* has been properly set. It is designed to show an optimum audio level by continuously flashing. If it is constantly on or consistently off, it means that the levels most likely need to be adjusted.

Previously mentioned was the *auxiliary send* feature, located at the midpoint of the input channel shown in figure 3.9. One of its main purposes is to provide on-the-air talent with a small monitor (earphone) in the ear, with an audio monitor for selected feeds. This earphone monitor setup is referred to as an **interrupted feedback (IFB) system.** The volume knob, *control 6* in figure 3.9, could be used to provide studio talent with either instructions from the director on the intercom or program sound from a field reporter. *Control 7* would be used to send the news anchor sound from a videotape insert.

Two final controls complete the structure of our example input channel. *Controls 8 and 9*, as shown in figure 3.9, are the *group assign switches* that send the output of the input channel to the group master faders. On this model, they are in a stereo configuration and would work in conjunction with the pan control, used for balancing L and R channels, located just below them.

Playback and Record

Most of the audio equipment used to **record** programming is also designed to be used for **playback** purposes. While the preliminary setup procedures may be much the same for both operations, the operational *disciplines* and *techniques* used during actual production are rather different. An important part of the early setup procedure is that of making sure that the audio line output from the console is properly patched to its ultimate destination. In a class production situation, this would probably be a videotape machine, but it could be a transmitter or a cart machine being used to record inserts for a later production.

After the patching process is accomplished, the next priority for the audio operator during any recording session is that of "getting the sound right." Is the mic quality appropriate? Is there proper balance between voice and music? Is the stereo balance right? (Here the concern is with the techniques needed to produce tonal fidelity and a consistency of

volume.) On the other hand, the ability to efficiently feed sound inserts from tape or other sources combines both the disciplines of alertness with the techniques such as the labeling of tape machine faders on the console for ease of operation. When a number of such things are employed, the operator is in a position to respond quickly to the director's commands. This is especially important when a program is only semiscripted and the inevitable changes begin to occur during production.

Sources of Production Audio

In preparing for even the simplest program, the person in charge of audio should always develop a definite plan of operations. In thinking through how resources will be used, it is often convenient to organize such things as patching and the setup of the audio console in terms of the various sources of the audio. In the traditional studio, the majority of sound inputs will be microphones, prerecorded cartridges, or compact discs. As we shall see later in the chapter, there could even be digital inputs that come directly from the instrument into the console, eliminating the distortion of a speaker fed through a mic.

Microphones

The microphone comes in a wide variety of types and sizes, designed for a multitude of specialized purposes. The main purpose of any microphone, that of accurately reproducing sound in an electronic form, could be seen as a process that would lead manufacturers to a very standardized design. Such is not the case. The constantly improving technology of microphone pickup characteristics has led to a greatly-improved quality of recorded sound, but often with a related increase in the cost factor. This specialization also has a self-limiting aspect. The expensive, delicate boom mic that is used to record a symphony orchestra wouldn't last five minutes in the hands of a "rap" music performer, where it is as much a prop as it is a device to pick up sound. Outdoors at a ball game, the director is not so much concerned about a full frequency response as the ability of a mic to do a

Figure 3.12

Audio cartridge player designed to access nine different carts on three different channels.

dependable job of picking up crowd noise in wind and rain. The degree to which a mic can accurately reproduce sound is also related to its distance to the source of the sound. Mics that can pick up sound at distances measured in yards usually must sacrifice some degree of quality as the distance is increased. The volume may be increased to compensate for the lower level of sound, but what is being amplified is a sound that no longer contains all of the frequencies heard in the original sound. By becoming aware of the different microphone classifications and characteristics in the following chapter, the audio operator will be able to select the most appropriate microphone for each application. Which microphones should be used for talk shows? drama? musical productions? What kinds of mics are best suited for outdoor as opposed to studio productions? Which microphones are used for picking up sound from a great distance? What if the microphone must be concealed or hidden? These are just a few of the considerations that an audio operator must consider.

Prerecorded Sound Sources

For the most part, the audio operator will think of prerecorded sound used in a production situation as coming from one of several basic sources: the videotape soundtrack, audiotape units for both cassettes and cartridges, CD players, or even possibly one of the newer digital audio delivery systems (see below). Reel-to-reel tape, 12-inch vinyl discs, and film sound may occasionally be used when dealing with older

library sources. Most professionals prefer to copy (**dub**) these older formats over to cartridge or a digital system for production use.

Videotape Audio Tracks

Many types of productions will have videotape inserts, in which short, previously-recorded tape segments are incorporated into the body of the program being assembled. The insert videotape machines are usually located in a separate area along with computer graphics and camera control equipment. This is the **master control room** mentioned in chapter 2. The videotape machine operator in this area is responsible for making the connections that send the audio from the machine on an assigned line. The audio operator then patches it through a fader position on the console for mixing.

Audio Tapes

Naturally, all playback and record equipment used exclusively for audio is located in the sound booth. Until the advent of the CD, the audio **cart machine** had been the workhorse of most audio control rooms. Figure 3.12 shows a typical three-channel cart machine. Since there are no variations in tape speed, track configuration, or reel size, they were a big improvement over vinyl discs. At the conclusion of a segment, the **cartridge** automatically rolls on to any subsequent **cue** point and comes to a stop. This means that each tape may be programmed to contain one or several cue points which saves the operator from having to change

Figure 3.13

The CD (compact disc) player has become a standard audio playback unit in most radio and TV stations because of its crisp digital sound and its ease of cuing. Station KLOS uses a bank of three units and controllers to enable the operator to play back one CD, to have a second unit cued up in the standby mode, while previewing a third CD.   *Photo courtesy of KLOS-FM*

cartridges during a very busy production. Perhaps its biggest virtue is that the technology used to record on cartridge is inexpensive and available at most learning institutions. For these reasons, cart machines are still an integral part of many audio operations. The smaller **cassette** tape recorders are also used for video production. They are harder to cue than cart tapes, because most units are not designed to stop at cue points, but they are frequently used for background music or other material that does not need to be tightly cued.

Compact Discs

The **CD player** has found a secure spot in most modern audio booths. Digital signal and control technology has produced equipment with the highest sound fidelity coupled with a number of benefits. The laser acquisition system permits cue points to be held indefinitely in the *pause* position with no wear to the disc. A precise minutes and seconds read-out allows the disc to be easily programmed for sequential cue points with almost instantaneous access to each when needed. When several units are "ganged" together (see figure 3.13), there is an almost unlimited source of quickly presented program sound feeds. Complete libraries of sound effects and stock musical selections have been released on CDs. The compact size of the disc offers a great improvement in storage and handling.

Musical Instrument Digital Interface

An example of equipment that could be considered as a sound source external to the audio board would be one or more keyboard instruments used as a part of studio production. The digitally-based control system of these instruments is known as **musical instrument digital interface (MIDI).** The term refers to the *protocol* that governs the digitized information used to control a synthesizer. A wide range of tonal sounds and rhythmic effects can be generated through the use of such an instrument. It is able to analyze (*sample*) the timbre of any traditional musical instrument such as a trumpet, determine its overtone structure (Appendix B), and then digitally reproduce a close copy of that sound in all ranges of its keyboard. With some equipment, a melodic series of notes can be recorded and played back so that additional notes can be added to produce the sound of an entire string or woodwind section. Through the use of another component called a *drum machine,* an entire rhythm section can be created to provide the beat for a band. Many of the orchestral sound tracks heard on television and film are constructed in this fashion.

The application of this technology to a video production class is that students from a school's music department can become part of a class production.

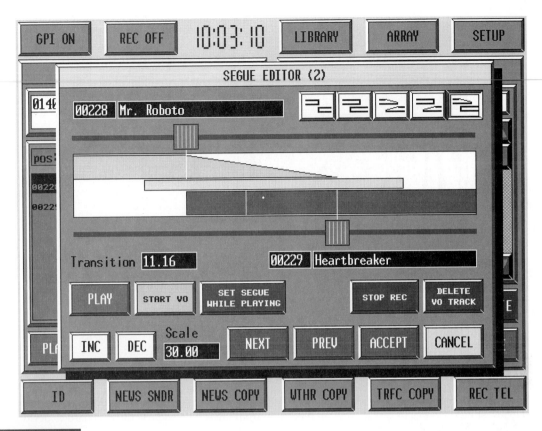

Figure 3.14

Segues and crossfade transitions can be modified and auditioned just prior to execution using the segue editor application of the DADpro Digital Audio Delivery System. *Illustration courtesy of ENCO Systems*

One person at a synthesizer can create backup music for a vocalist as a part of a variety show. Incidental music for a drama can also be composed and performed to the completed video.

The newer digital consoles, such as the Yamaha 02R shown in figure 3.3, have MIDI IN, THRU, and OUT terminals. If such technology is not yet available in your facility, then it would be worthwhile simply to put a mic in front of a synthesizer speaker and get the experience of working with the musician and the possibilities of the instrument.

Digital Audio Delivery Systems

Multipurpose digital audio delivery systems that were originally designed for radio broadcasting are beginning to find favor with audio operators doing video production. In its newest configuration, the Enco DADpro workstation combines editing and numerous other preproduction functions with computer control of preset feeds of stored music, sound effects, and other insert materials. Its operation is supported on Pentium/PCI hardware. Overlapped segue transitions between events are edited through the use of the Segue Editor Screen seen in figure 3.14. More than ten other control panels display a number of additional control and delivery features, including lists of all available insert pieces by name and number. For broadcasting applications, the DAD486x provides additional features such as script display. The workstation can be programmed to receive satellite feeds of news and commercials which can then be programmed for broadcast within minutes. (See figure 3.15.) In addition to the "live-assist" mode in which a disc jockey keeps final control, there is also provision for automated broadcasting using satellite feeds. The automated option includes such features as a rotation of commercial spots or other broadcast elements.

Figure 3.15

This photo shows how the computer has been combined with the new digital audio technology for preproduction work as well as radio broadcasting purposes. A disc jockey can read copy from the screen and use the keyboard to perform numerous production transitions.   *Photo courtesy of ENCO Systems*

Summary

As an introduction to the audio system, we have been concerned more with *technical* functions than with *creative* functions. The seven *basic control functions* are *transducing, channeling, mixing, amplifying, shaping, monitoring,* and *recording for* playback. These control functions were traced through the *audio signal flow* pattern—typically from studio *microphone input,* through the *patch bay,* into the *audio console,* through an *input channel,* through the volume control or *potentiometer/fader,* into a *submaster* channel, through the *master* potentiometer, out the board through the *line out,* and back to the program-out position on the patch bay.

The *microphone* remains the basic ingredient in audio production along with some of the established *audiotape* technology such as the *cartridge* and *cassette.* Playbacks from *videotape* are often integrated into productions, and the *CD* has become widely used. The newer *digitally-based audio equipment* is impressive and will make it possible for an operator to handle increasingly complex assignments with enhanced precision.

It must be kept in mind, however, that technology itself can never replace training in terms of *technique* or preparation as it relates to *discipline.* In chapter 4, we will go into more detail on how microphones and playback equipment are used during the production sequence.

Footnotes

1. The term cycles per second (cps) is used as the basic unit of measure for sound pressure waves and, in the past, for electromagnetic waves. In recent years, engineering terminology has for the most part replaced the term cycles per second with the term hertz (abbreviated Hz), in honor of Heinrich Hertz who first demonstrated the existence of electromagnetic waves.

2. Actually, the tone A above middle C at the frequency of 440 cps in our example is only the fundamental tone. It is by far the most prominent of many tones that are simultaneously produced when a voice or an instrument is sounded. The other

tones that are much softer in volume and occur at higher frequencies are called "overtones" or "harmonics." Their presence and relative volume are what produce the distinctive quality of any individual voice or instrument. To reproduce any single complete tone accurately, all these resultant frequencies must be picked up and simultaneously transduced into the electrical signal. A more complete explanation of the overtone series is presented in Appendix B.

3. dB is the abbreviation for the term decibel which is used to measure the loudness of sound. A more complete description of its use is found later in the chapter in the section dealing with the VU meter. A decibel is actually one-tenth of a larger unit, the Bel, named for Alexander Graham Bell of telephone fame.

4. Davis, Gary, and Ralph Jones. *The Sound Reinforcement Handbook,* Milwaukee: Leonard/Yamaha, 1987.

chapter 4

Fundamentals of Audio Production for Video

The seven basic control functions presented in the previous chapter serve an important function in that they can provide an understanding of *how* signals are changed in their structure, combined with other signals, and otherwise enhanced as they move through the console and related components. In this chapter, we will examine some of the reasons having to do with *why* audio production goals necessitate numerous control and adjustment procedures. We will see that it is largely a matter of the very nature of those signals, first as sound pressure waves in the air, and then as transduced analog waveforms. The emphasis will be on *why* one type of microphone will have definite advantages when used in one set of circumstances, but have limitations in another. The chapter will also serve as an introduction to the mechanics of production—the skills that enable one to follow instructions on a split-second basis or to act on one's own initiative so that all elements of planning occur at the required time. The material is designed to prepare students to work together on an audio production exercise and, thus, provides the opportunity to put material presented thus far into practical use.

4.1

Primary Considerations Relating to Microphone Response

As illustrated in Appendix B, the differing combinations of **overtone** frequencies that resonate along with any single **fundamental** tone are what give various musical instruments their individual tonal qualities. While these overtones (also known as **harmonics**) are produced at much *lower amplitudes* (loudness) than the fundamental tone, they are very definitely picked up by the human ear. What we as humans hear ranges from a low rumble at 20 **cycles per second (hertz)** up to a possible high of 20,000 cycles per second. The ultimate quality of any microphone is

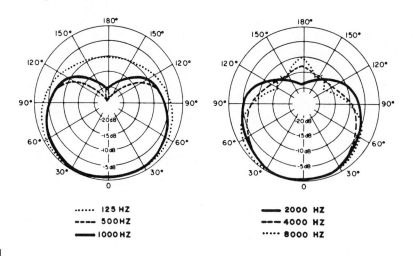

.... 125 HZ
---- 500 HZ
—— 1000 HZ

—— 2000 HZ
--- 4000 HZ
.... 8000 HZ

Figure 4.1

The different lines in these two polar pattern projections show the directional sensitivity of the Shure SM 58 mic at six different frequencies. The heart shape traced by the lines indicates a cardioid pickup pattern with least receptivity at the rear of the mic. *Pattern courtesy of Shure Bros. Inc.*

judged by the accuracy with which it is able to transduce these sound pressure waves, especially those in the higher frequency ranges.

The importance of overtones is best exemplified by comparing the sound on AM radio with FM radio and compact discs. AM radio has a top limit of only 7,500 hertz **(Hz)** and, for a variety of reasons, many stations do not even take full advantage of this potential. Music has always been much more impressive on FM, because it has the ability to reproduce frequencies up to 15,000 Hz. This additional area of the sound spectrum is what contributes so much to sound fidelity. Under ideal circumstances, the compact disc technology, with its digital signal and a number of other component improvements, is able to encompass almost the entire range of our hearing. The result is consistently impressive sound reproduction. Television sound is an FM signal with the potential of transmitting up to 15,000 Hz. While many stations are equipped to transmit these upper frequencies and do so in stereo, the program producers often do not opt to spend the money on hi-fidelity stereo sound for their shows.

Keeping in mind that an electronic signal is a complex combination of a great number of fundamental and overtone frequencies, imagine a 100-piece symphony orchestra, each instrument producing not only a fundamental tone, but also ten or more related over-

tone frequencies. It is truly impressive that a relatively small number of specially-designed and properly-placed microphones can transduce the majority of those frequencies necessary to produce a professional recording of the orchestra.

Pickup Patterns

In most professional circumstances, a priority is usually given to the fidelity factor. Each mic has its own set of **specifications (specs)** in printed form available at the time of purchase. In addition to matters of structure and levels of power output, there is always important information relating to what a microphone's **frequency response** will be in a given set of circumstances. Simple graphic charts are possibly the most useful part of this information. One is the **polar pickup pattern** that depicts the *directional* sensitivity of the mic at several different frequency levels. Figure 4.1 shows the actual pattern for the SM 58 professional mic manufactured by Shure Bros., Inc. that is pictured in figure 4.2. The directional sensitivity is shown as dotted or continuous lines. The heart shape traced by the lines on the diagram classifies it as having a **cardioid** pickup pattern with a decreasing response to sounds coming from the rear of the mic. All such patterns are only

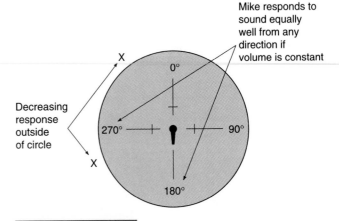

The SM 58 mic is well known in professional circles as an all-purpose hand/stand mic with a dynamic transducing element. *Photo courtesy of Shure Bros. Inc.*

Omnidirectional microphone pickup pattern. The omnidirectional mic picks up sound equally well from all directions.

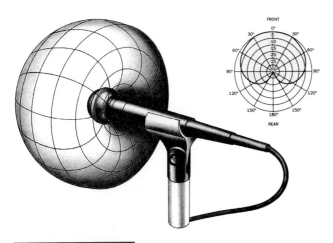

All pickup patterns are actually a 3D sphere as depicted in this cardioid type. *Illustration courtesy of Shure Bros. Inc.*

2D depictions of an actual sphere, as shown more clearly in figure 4.3.

While the "0" degree point may be placed at either the top or bottom of the circle's outer ring, the front of the mic is always oriented directly toward that "0" degree point. Do not be confused by the minus dB numbers (a measure of less volume) that get larger closer to the mic in the center of the circles. The –dB numbers denote the declining decibel level for each smaller circle. Note how the heart-shaped response pattern develops when the response lines come into the larger –dB numbers at the rear of the microphone's

position. As stated above, it is this position directly behind the mic that pickup is least effective.

With high quality microphones, the information presented in a pickup pattern is often also expressed in terms of the distance between the sound source and the microphone. The important point to keep in mind when using pickup patterns is that, while some sounds coming from outside the pickup pattern may be transduced and amplified, they will not be picked up with the correct balance of all the different frequencies. The result is an **off-mic** distortion of the original sound usually caused by a substantial loss of higher frequencies.

The whole idea of **directional response** is one of an awareness that, while one mic may include sounds from side angles, for instance, another will not. The selection of a specific mic would then revolve around whether or not "background sound" was wanted along with the announcer's voice.

The **omnidirectional** pattern seen in figure 4.4 produces an equal response to sound from all directions. Obvious advantages in this pattern include its ability to pick up a large number of people, often including an audience. The pattern for some omnidirectional mics might receive good quality sound from all directions, but then have a sharp dropoff at a distance of four feet. This could be very desirable in some types of outdoor production.

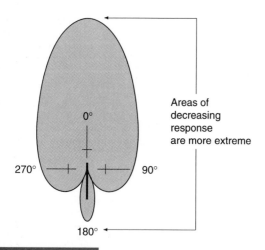

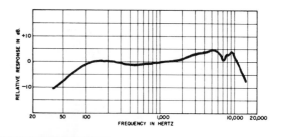

Figure 4.7

The frequency response chart gives the audio operator an accurate and quick indication of how a mic will perform at all frequency levels.

Figure 4.5

Highly directional microphone pickup pattern. The highly directional microphone is designed to pick up sound in a narrow response pattern from relatively long distances.

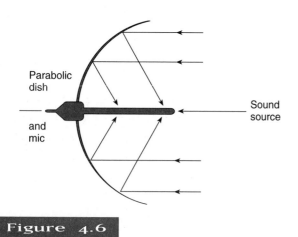

Figure 4.6

The parabolic dish increases the range of a shotgun directional microphone by focusing sound sources into the transducing element.

(See figure 4.6.) This equipment is often used at sporting events and other outdoor occasions.

Equally important pickup information is expressed by the **frequency response chart.** This linear graph shows how consistent the mic is in transducing frequencies at all the various points of the hearing spectrum. Many professional mics have what is called a "flat" response with more or less a straight line representing frequencies in the 50 to 15,000 Hz range. Figure 4.7 shows a mic frequency response chart with what is called a "shaped" response. It has increasing strength in the middle and higher frequencies, and then a rather rapid decline after 10,000 Hz. This chart would represent a typical professional mic used more for voice applications than for the recording of classical music. Such a mic would help compensate for the fact that a lower and louder male voice has the effect of sounding closer to a mic than a female voice.

Transducing Elements

Since the invention of the first microphones, a number of transducing elements have been used to accomplish the delicate matter of turning sound pressure waves into an electronic waveform. Carbon granules and foil ribbons as well as ceramic and crystal elements have been used. Most microphones in use today are of two basic types. The classic mic described at the beginning of chapter 3 is called a **dynamic microphone.** It uses the basic **coil** and **magnet** combination found in all electric engines. This structure makes it able to tolerate rough handling as

The opposite effect is achieved through the use of a highly directional pickup pattern found in the specialized long-distance **shotgun** mics. (See figure 4.5.) This mic often presents a trade-off involving some loss of quality for the ability to get a fairly good pickup at a distance of 20 feet. To further increase their sensitivity, these mics are often used in conjunction with a **parabolic dish** that collects and concentrates an even more distant audio source and reflects this focused audio beam directly into the microphone.

well as temperature and humidity extremes. The majority of microphones in use are of this type.

Like the dynamic mic, the **condenser microphone** has a movable diaphragm to receive sound waves. Its difference lies in its use of an electrically-charged **backplate** just behind the diaphragm. The two elements form what is called a **capacitor,** enabling the unit to generate voltage in response to sound wave pressure. This structure not only produces very high quality sound, but also allows the unit to be as small as a clip-on lapel mic. While a dynamic mic can generate its own charge, this condenser unit must have a source of electricity to function. Batteries are located in the handle, or, with a **wireless mic,** they may be part of the portable unit that transmits the signal from the performer to a receiving station. Another solution to the need for power is accomplished by the use of what is called **phantom power.** In this case, the power is a small current sent to the mic through its cable from a controlling component in the audio console. Condenser microphones that have a permanently charged backplate are another option.

Microphone Usage Categories

No single all-purpose microphone has ever been designed, although some come much closer than others. Even the most expensive mic would have limitations in some situations. Instead, manufacturers provide a wide variety of models, each of which may combine a number of qualities suited to differing needs. So rather than presenting a long, unwieldy list of microphones by category, we shall simply classify the types of instruments generally found in teaching institutions. This introduction to the classification process will enable students to feel comfortable with microphones starting with the first hands-on exercises in the studio. We, therefore, suggest the following three broad practical categories: (1) hand and/or stand mics, (2) limited-movement mics, and (3) attached personal mics.

These categories are obviously very general, designed simply to aid the student in thinking about the different ways in which microphones can be positioned and used—keeping in mind the positive qualities and limiting factors of each grouping. Also, note that these are not mutually exclusive categories; there is obvious overlap. Many mics could fit into two of the groups.

Hand and/or Stand Mics

The most versatile group of mics are most likely the medium-sized, elongated instruments designed to work best at a range of 6 inches to 3 feet from a speaker or musical performer. Although a few require a fixed mount, most are structured to fit into a holder on a desk (for a news program or panel show) or in a floor mic stand (for a performer). The same microphone is used as a hand-held mic for an on-location news event or for spontaneous interviews with members of an audience. This category can overlap both the stationary and mobile distinctions. For example, a performer begins a number by using a mic stand (stationary), then removes the mic from the holder, and then concludes the number using it as a hand mic (mobile). (See figure 4.2.)

Resistance to the rugged handling of a rock or rap performer is an important quality for such a mic. Most microphones in this category are the *dynamic* types utilizing the coil and magnet transducer. Many such instruments have a **pop filter** (a plastic foam ball placed over the top of the mic) that minimizes the plosive effect of sounds such as *T, K,* and *P.* Such a mic is even more useful if it is designed to function in the outdoor conditions of news and sports remotes. These instruments require a fairly wide angle of sound acceptance and are usually either *omnidirectional* or *cardioid* in their pickup pattern.

Limited-Movement Mics

This category encompasses several different microphone applications from stationary, fixed-position uses to a considerable amount of movement on large **perambulator booms.** Generally, microphones in this category are larger than those intended to be hand-held. Almost always, mics in this grouping are not intended to be seen by the audience. As off-camera mics, they are required to have good pickup qualities at relatively moderate to long distances.

Figure 4.8

Two or more large studio perambulator booms usually are used to cover a drama or other program where hand mics cannot be used. *Photo courtesy of KCET-TV, Los Angeles*

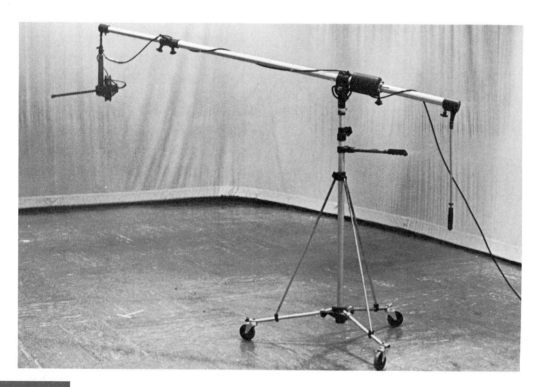

Figure 4.9

A giraffe (tripod) microphone boom.

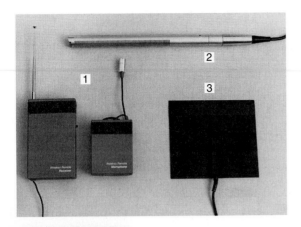

Figure 4.10

Three very different methods of picking up sound. (1) A lapel mic used in conjunction with wireless transmission and receiver units; (2) A highly-directional long distance "shotgun" mic; and (3) A pressure response, surface mount mic.

The label "**boom mic**" can cover a wide variety of applications. The big boom, or *perambulator* (see figure 4.8), is a large three-wheeled movable platform that holds the boom operator and has a long counter-weighted boom arm that can be extended and tilted, while the microphone itself can be rotated in almost a full circle. It is a large cumbersome piece of equipment requiring two operators—one dolly pusher and one mic manipulator—and is effective only in spacious studios. Perambulators are often used in pairs, for example, to cover guests on a talk show such as *The Tonight Show.*

The smaller boom, similar to that in figure 4.9, is the **giraffe**—a counter-weighted boom arm supported by a tripod on casters that can be operated by one person. Although not as flexible as the big boom, the giraffe can be moved more easily and takes up much less floor space. Even though it is thought of as a movable boom, the giraffe is usually stationed in a fixed position for an entire production.

Finally, consider the use of the **fishpole**—literally a small, lightweight pole to which the mic is attached. The operator hand-holds the pole to continually get the best audio position in any changing scene or situation. These are quite often used in the video coverage for an impromptu appearance of a celebrity or politician.

Most production situations calling for boom, dolly, or even fishpole mics utilize some variation of a highly-directional type of mic. As mentioned earlier, the long distance *shotgun* mics have found an important place in the world of outdoor video production. News and sports programs, as well as all *reality-based* productions in the early 1990s, were greatly enhanced by the very effective use of these mics in conjunction with the parabolic dish. While earlier models had a limited range of frequency response, some of the newer, more expensive, top-of-the-line models have produced impressive sound quality and are used in outdoor stage and concert work. (See example 2 in figure 4.10.)

The limited-movement category has recently been expanded to include some very different adaptations of mic structure. One of the most successful is the **surface-mount mic.** Also known as a **PZM™** mic, it is shown in example 3 of figure 4.10. They have a flat base with angled sides and are designed to be placed on a large table, floor, or even ceiling. The operating concept is based on the principle of physics claiming that sound pressure waves are intensified as they gather and move along a flat surface. These mics are best used on a desk or table-top. When used on a floor, they can pick up a lot of unwanted vibration.

Attached Personal Mics

Television created the necessity for an unobtrusive instrument that could move with the performer. The **lavaliere** (suspended by a cord around the neck) and the **lapel mic** (clipped inside the clothing or to a tie or lapel) are the result. Most early lavaliere models were effective omnidirectional mics, although they were limited to the frequency range of the human voice. Later models filtered out unwanted noise caused by clothing rubbing against the mic. The more recent lapel models have a frequency response more than adequate for instrumental pickup.

The problems caused by mic cords have resulted in the development of the **RF** (radio frequency) or *wireless* microphone shown example 1 of figure 4.10. A miniature transmitter—either a part of the mic itself or in a concealed pack—sends an FM signal to a portable receiver that can be placed as far as several hundred feet from the performer. Although these systems have obvious advantages for television production, a propensity for dead spots in the transmission pattern and some limitations in frequency range have been the major limitations to their use. Recent progress with sophisticated receivers, however, has eliminated many of the problems. Most live stage concerts and musical videos have made the wireless mic almost indispensable in contemporary production. A recent variation of the **RF mic** has been the **headset** mike as used in some rock concerts and other outdoor performances. It gives the performer total freedom of both arms for that all-important body movement.

4.2

Factors Governing Production Use of Microphones

The process of achieving an optimum quality of sound in any given situation rests upon the ability of the chief audio engineer to have developed a previously established concept of just what the sound quality goals are for the final mixed sound in a given situation. For example, there is a certain *country western sound* that is known to the professional recording engineers who work in this field. It involves a very distinctive quality of tone from the singer's voice as well as some very definite levels of amplification among guitars and rhythm instruments. The field of jazz has another very different "sound" that is essential to a successful recording and ultimate sales of albums. Those wishing to pursue a career in any phase of musical audio production should start early to be in the sort of working situations that will allow them to hear and work with this concept of a "sound profile goal."

Producing a sound mix that is appropriate to the established production goals is really just an extension of three basic considerations: (1) selection of the correct microphone using the polar pattern and other technical information that establishes parameters of mic use; (2) proper placement of the mic, again based upon application of the known features and limitations of the mike; and (3) careful application during production of such factors as balance, perspective, and a consistency of amplification levels.

Microphone Selection

When selecting the proper microphone, first define the audio job to be done. For example, the task of picking up a well-tuned concert grand piano. Mics should be selected on the basis of their known positive and negative qualities. Lavalieres designed primarily for the human voice and older long-distance shotgun mics are not able to pick up all of the true tonal quality of the piano. However, any of several condenser mics placed either inside or underneath the instrument can do this satisfactorily. As with the pickup of most musical instruments, the source-to-mic distance is crucial.

If one is concerned with recording a pop vocal personality, it is best to take into consideration whether or not the singer wants to use a microphone as part of the performance—as a hand prop. If the singer does, you would want to use a fairly rugged dynamic mic. If, however, the production calls for an off-camera boom mic, then a full-frequency condenser microphone might be used, especially if fidelity to the musical quality is uppermost.

When producing a news program or panel discussion, the full-frequency range of a condenser is probably not as important as on a musical production. Depending upon the "look" of the production, you may decide on either a dynamic desk mic, lavalieres, or mic booms.

Suppose you are to handle a remote assignment covering a parade or sporting event. You would probably want a rugged, relatively sensitive cardioid dynamic mic for the narrator/announcer (to allow him or her to work closely to the mic, cutting out as much background noise as possible) coupled with a highly directional shotgun mic to pick up selected crowd or parade sounds as desired. The first task, however, is always the same: define the job to be done in terms of frequency response needed, appropriate pickup pattern, and the amount of physical abuse to which the microphone will likely be subjected.

In selecting microphones correctly for a particular audio pickup, one must be aware of two critical considerations. One is *aesthetic* and the other is *acoustical*. In a dramatic production, the mic must not be seen as part of the picture. Usually, directional long-distance pickup mics mounted on movable booms are used. In some cases, wireless equipment may be used. On the other hand, if you are working in a news, public affairs, or sports situation, the use of a hand mic is accepted by the audience—as is an occasional camera shot that reveals an operator holding a shotgun mic mounted in a parabolic dish. Sometimes one must compromise between aesthetic and acoustical needs. In the telecast of a symphony performance, for instance, the quality of sound is very important. A number of mics must be placed relatively close to the musicians to assure proper balance and timbre. This is especially true of string and woodwind instruments. A sensitive, unobtrusive, microphone located on a small stand is now generally accepted by the audience.

Microphone Placement

Several important basic rules apply to the placement of microphones in all situations. These rules seem so obvious to those who work with sound reinforcement and recording that they are sometimes overlooked in a general discussion of operating procedures. Since this textbook is concerned with basics, this is the perfect place for them to be set forth.

1. Place microphones as close to a desired sound source as is practically possible. The very nature of the transducing element in a mic is such that proximity must be given priority. If a mic is too close and distortion results, the mic can always be moved farther away. Quality loss from too distant a position, however, may never be noticed unless the closer position is tried first.

2. If studio audio monitors are needed as a part of a production, be sure that microphones are not aimed in their direction. The audio **feedback** effect of a high-pitched squealing sound is caused when a microphone is aimed at a speaker and picks up output that is then fed through the amplifying system. This creates a circular monitor-mic-amplifier-monitor situation with the amplification being escalated and distorted with each cycle. When recorded sound is to be used behind a person talking or singing on a live studio mic, careful testing of safe levels is required prior to production. With any public address system the speakers should always be placed *in front* of the microphones.

3. Observe instructions relating to directionality and source-to-mic distance patterns to avoid picking up unwanted ambient sound that is present in almost all situations. Outside traffic, building machinery, and even air conditioning may not be noticeable during setup in a busy studio, but often greatly detract from an otherwise efficient production.

4. Avoid a placement situation where two nearby microphones pick up the same sound source. When signals from each mic get to the audio console, the similar waveforms tend to cancel each other out. This is called a **phasing** problem. The "**three-to-one rule**" states that if two singers (or other performers) are standing side-by-side, each working at a distance of *1 foot* from their respective mics, then the two mics must be at least *3 feet* apart. If source-to-mic distance is increased, mic separation must similarly be increased. A further application is that if a person wearing a lavaliere mic walks over to a standing mic, one of the mics must be turned down. These considerations are part of a much larger area of study of how the length and construction of cable (**timing**) and the overlapping of pickup by two mics can have serious effects on the signals being mixed in the console.

These general rules, along with the other *disciplines* and *techniques* discussed below, should serve to remind students that the operations needed to utilize all the seven basic control functions require careful planning along with a sense of respect for the equipment and the manner of its use. The right mic, used with the best of intentions, cannot do the job if the realities of the specific mic pickup pattern have been disregarded. A microphone that works well at one location may be inadequate in a slightly different position. Sound, especially the higher frequencies, diminishes in loudness (amplitude) very rapidly as it passes through the air. This loss directly relates to the amount of energy it takes to propel the pressure waves through the air molecules.

The rate at which sound volume diminishes with distance is scientifically described by what is known as the **inverse square law.** Although this text is not the proper place to attempt to describe all the principles of physics involved, the operating concept is easily understood: *as microphone-to-source distance is doubled, the loudness is reduced to one-fourth of its previous strength*. Therefore, if you have an audio source (voice) giving you a constant level of sound at a distance of 1 foot from a microphone, and then you move the mic back to a distance of 2 feet, the strength of the sound pressure (loudness) hitting the microphone will be only one-quarter of what it was when the mic was 1 foot from the source. If you again double the distance and place the microphone 4 feet from the source, it will again reduce the loudness level to one-quarter of what it was at 2 feet. The level is now one-sixteenth of what it had been at a distance of 1 foot. When working with relatively short source-to-mic positions, any distance change can be critical.

Putting this principle into simple operational terms, suppose you have checked the sound level of a performer speaking 1 foot away from a desk mic. Once the program starts that person then decides to lean back just 1 foot to be more comfortable. You have lost close to 75 percent of that person's volume! On the other hand, if you have a performer working 10 feet from a long-distance directional microphone, and that person moves 1 foot backward, there will not be much of a noticeable difference, because the performer has only increased the distance by a factor of one-tenth.

In addition to the above *source-to-mic distance* effect, it is equally important to consider the *source-to-mic direction* factor. This refers to the degree to which the main source of projected sound of a voice or musical instrument is in a straight-line path to the primary receiving area of the mic. Sound waves do not curve around corners. When sound is reflected by several angled surfaces, there is a definite loss in both volume and quality.

Let us take as an example two actors playing a dramatic scene. As in any conversation, they would normally face more toward each other than toward the "audience" area. The audio operator must work closely with the director to determine the various speaking positions of the actors as they move about the set. Untrained people often make an error in this situation. They decide to place a one-directional mic in the camera area in an attempt to pick up both

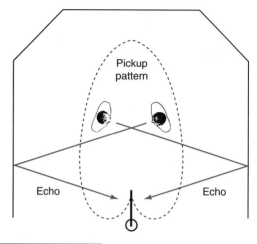

Figure 4.11

Incorrect placement of directional mic between two performers. Although the two actors are standing "in the pattern" of the directional mic, their voices will be picked up with a hollow "off-mic" quality because they are not facing toward the mic; they are directing their voices away from the microphone.

voices. (See figure 4.11.) The actors would seem to be within the pickup pattern of the directional mic. One must keep in mind, however, that each sound source has a *projection* pattern that is somewhat similar to the pickup pattern of a microphone. With the human voice, the shape of the mouth and lips tend to focus the strongest pressure waves in a relatively narrow channel to the front as represented in figure 4.12.

This illustration shows why mics placed at a side angle (60 or more degrees from the straight-ahead direction of the sound pressure waves) result in a considerable drop-off in audio level. If you attempt to turn up the amplification to compensate for this loss, you will also begin to hear the reflected (echo) sound waves coming back from the set and walls of the studio. The result is an *"off-mic"* distortion of the original sound. While these reflected echoes are always a part of any sound pickup and contribute to the effect of natural room "presence," they should be heard only in their original proportion to the primary sound waves and not become the primary source itself.

The proper placement of microphones for a two-person conversation is shown in figure 4.13. Using two mics, the audio operator positions one mic directly in the path of each voice to pick up the best

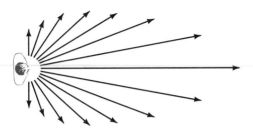

Figure 4.12

The sound pressure waves of the human voice begin to decline in intensity beyond a 45 degree angle from those projected directly to the front of the speaker.

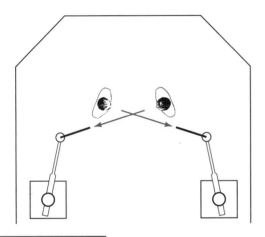

Figure 4.13

Correct placement of directional mics. To achieve optimum audio pickup from two actors facing each other, it is necessary to use two directional microphones—a separate mic placed directly in the vocal path of each actor.

and most direct voice quality. If the two persons move about the set during the conversation, the perambulator dolly is necessary. The boom arm is extendable, and the angle of the mic can be changed to keep the proper distance and mic direction in relation to the actors.

Determining the correct distance from a source to a microphone starts with a check of the polar pickup pattern provided by the manufacturer. Ultimately it is also a matter of knowing what to listen for in the shape of the sound being picked up by the mic. A professional may work for years to gain a knowledge of just how the voice or other tonality should sound given the "specs" of the mic and the natural quality of the source. Depending upon the type of microphone

and the audio quality desired, the optimum speaking distance may be anywhere from a few inches to several feet. A typical shotgun directional mic might give fairly good audio pickup as far away as 15 or more feet, while the average hand mic works best at about 12 inches.

With so many variables, the factor of experience becomes more and more important. From the student's first opportunities to work with the sound system, it is important to begin to keep mental or, even better, written notes on how different mics respond in differing production situations. One needn't be a musician to develop a trained ear and the other disciplines necessary to successful audio work.

Balance and Perspective

In establishing the overall quality of sound in a production, the audio director must always consider how each individual sound is being heard in relation to all the other sounds that make up the ongoing audio **mix**. No frequency response chart, polar pattern, or VU meter can replace the human ear in determining the proper combination of sounds for a program.

Keeping in mind that each individual sound relates to all the other sounds in the mix, one seeks the right proportions (**balance**) of volume from the different sources. Are the musical instruments balanced? Is there too much piano for the vocal group? Are all the panelists being heard at the same level? Can a proper balance be achieved simply by adjusting volume levels with the faders, or is the quality of sound such that microphone placement should be altered?

This last question leads into the area of audio **perspective**—an especially important concept in dramatic audio. Actors must all appear to have an audio **presence** that matches the subconscious perception of "distance" between the viewer and sound source on the screen. While this sometimes can be a matter of relative volume of a source, it more often has to do with vocal *quality*. In an intimate love scene, each subjective close-up shot puts the viewer in a visual perspective of one of the lovers. From this perspective, the sound that would be heard would usually be characterized by a soft and low voice quality. Were one lover to get up and walk to a distant door, the voice quality would become entirely different, possibly diminishing slightly in volume as the person approaching the door is seen from over the shoulder of the other.

While the skills necessary to create these types of artistic effects are obviously developed over long periods of time, they are not beyond the abilities of beginning students, at least in an experimental, training sense. Students should be encouraged to work toward these more subtle uses of the audio vocabulary. Most will find they are usually rewarded by the results of trying the very things that they have seen on television and in the movies over thousands of hours of viewing time.

Stereo Considerations

The current competitive nature of the broadcast and cable markets has had the fortunate effect of an increasing use of **stereophonic sound** in much of the available programming. For many productions, the increased costs are easily affordable when put in the perspective of million dollar plus budgets for one hour of prime time television. While true professional stereo involves some complicated elements, very effective results can be obtained through some rather practical methods. In its simplest configuration, stereo audio pickup requires two microphones or a single unit containing elements for both a left channel and a right channel.

The simplest setup would be the **spaced (split-pair) mic** setup shown at the top of figure 4.14. In this configuration, two mics are placed parallel to each other facing into the set—roughly analogous to the placement of stereo speakers at one's home. Cardioid or omnidirectional mics can be used. Since most of the rules about mic placement similarly apply to stereo, the mics should be anywhere from 3 to 10 feet apart depending upon source distance.

A second and usually more effective technique is the **X-Y (crossed-pairs) mic** placement. This is known as a *coincident* microphone technique. It involves placing two cardioid microphones like crossed swords, forming (as seen from above) a perfect X and Y axis (see figure 4.14, center). The angle actually can be anywhere from 60 to 120 degrees, depending on the specific production requirements—the wider the angle, the greater the apparent stereo separation.

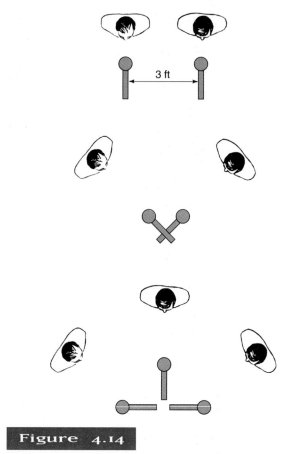

Figure 4.14

Three basic stereo microphone patterns. *Top,* the split-pair setup works only if the microphones are at least 3 feet apart and are receiving somewhat different sound inputs. *Middle,* the X-Y (crossed pairs) is a simple but effective approach in that it allows the mic angle to be changed easily to suit the situation. *Bottom,* the M-S (mid-side) setup is a more complex approach in that it requires balancing the center mic with the two side mics.

A third configuration, also a *coincident* pattern, is the **M-S (mid-side) mic** technique. This involves three microphones arranged somewhat like an inverted "T" forming two 90-degree angles (see figure 4.14, bottom). This is a more technically sophisticated setup in that it requires a transformer matrix or mixer. The matrix decoder can then combine the middle mic (M) with the two side mics (S) separately to form the two complementary stereo channels. Although it involves more electronic juggling, the result can be very effective, because the audio technician can often manipulate spatial perspectives and stereo effects without having to move either microphones or audio sources. Another variation of this technique involves only two mics, one of which is a bi-directional mic (separate pickups from two sides) and the other a cardioid pattern. Here again, there is some complicated mixing and separating of channels requiring some equipment that is not always available.

As with the creative uses of sound presence and perspective mentioned earlier, students should be encouraged to experiment with these other components in terms of their creative use and just how they can fit into the many possibilities offered by the larger concepts of audio production. It is through this sort of process that one can make some early decisions as to how difficult or feasible any desired audio effect really is.

4·3

Phases of Audio for Video Production

After the initial planning sessions that are extremely important to the success of all types of production, most of the studio and other equipment-related work taking place for a video production can be broken down into one of four categories: (1) preproduction; (2) studio setup and technical preparation; (3) primary program assembly period; and (4) postproduction. While these terms may have somewhat different application within various types of production, they serve as a convenient framework for organizing production work.

Preproduction

The preproduction phase involves the tape editing or studio production of complicated inserts that could cause trouble during later program assembly. Usually this involves using an announcer and recorded sources of music or effects. It would certainly include opening and closing segments that come at what is often a rather vulnerable time for the crew in terms of fatigue and nervous tension. This period could also be used for connecting and testing additional pieces of equipment as well as testing special effects, but usually does not include any work that would call for the presence of performers. The effectiveness of this phase is very often an indication of the strength (or lack thereof) of those in leadership positions. It is here

that many of the intangible elements of operational discipline come into play. Are crew members clear on their duties in the next phase, when the time allotted for setup usually cannot be expanded to meet unforeseen needs? At this point there is time to "get it right." Such preproduction work at the networks and production houses is increasingly being done at digital audio workstations such as those described at the end of chapter 3.

Studio Setup and Technical Preparation

For most productions, both large and small, the **setup** period is usually scheduled on the same day leading directly into full crew studio production. However, with large operations, such as a network football game, there might be a two- or even three-day setup period prior to game day.

Regardless of the production's size, there are a number of steps that directly relate to the efficiency of the final assembly process. During this period, the audio assistants must be extra alert to carefully follow the instructions of the primary audio operator as to which studio mic inputs are to be used and where those mics are to be set. In addition, it must be fully coordinated with the stage manager who is getting tables, chairs, and other facilities in place. This entire process is an important introduction to the concept of how *cooperation* and *responsibility* function within the chain of command.

To go a step further, let's say that the director wants to get certain tonal qualities from the band. Having the larger view of the set design and camera positions, he or she will make general suggestions to the stage manager and the chief audio operator while referring to the *stage plot*. They can then work together to come up with the best arrangement for all concerned.

To accomplish any sort of efficiency, the chief audio operator (sometimes called the audio director) should have at least one assistant always in the booth and one or more on the floor to set up and test mics. The assistant can help with patching and other duties, leaving the person in charge free to talk to the director or solve other problems. The second assistant can also be drawing up a chart with mic positions, patch bay cable positions, and console fader

Figure 4.15

This KABC-TV news audio booth gives the operator separate video monitors for cameras, remotes, video cassettes, and other possible picture/sound sources. Note patch bay at right. *Photo courtesy of KABC-TV*

inputs. When troubles strike, this sort of paperwork can be immeasurably important. It should be noted that in many studios the person operating the console does not have a window and can only keep track of action on the floor by means of monitors as shown in figure 4.15.

Once each microphone has been connected, it should be tested and checked off as being in operating condition. Later, when the performers are all in place, there must be an additional test of audio **voice levels** for each performer. The audio engineer must have the stage manager's help in ascertaining that all performers are in the same positions that they will occupy during the program and that they are speaking at the voice level that will be used during the performance. Many operators use small pieces of tape to mark those locations. All too often in beginning student exercises one hears the audio operator say "have him speak louder," or "have her move closer to the mic." There are two reasons why this is a very wrong approach. First, the person (especially one who is seated) who moves into the mic or speaks louder dur-

ing the test will probably lean during the show to the more natural position. Also, the loudness of voice quality will probably return to its normal level. In this situation, the operator is using the VU meter incorrectly and is not really getting a valid voice level test. During this setup time, much of the effort is dependent upon the crew's ability to interact with one another.

Production Communication

The efficient use of several studio communication systems is almost as important during setup work as during the actual program assembly period. The most used of these is the **intercom** system, sometimes still referred to as the **PL** or **private line.** It is, in essence, a closed-circuit audio network that connects all primary production and engineering personnel by standard headsets that have earpieces with attached mics that are held in place by steel braces. Technically, any crew member with a headset can talk to anyone else with a similar unit. In practice, the audio director and the technical director make heavy use of

Figure 4.16

The successful use of the intercommunication system both before and during production is not only essential for the director but also for lighting, audio, and assistant director duties.   *Photo courtesy of KABC-TV*

the system during setup time, but it is the director who is heard most of the time during a production. (See figure 4.16.)

A **double headset system** with intercom on one headset and program audio on the other is sometimes used by personnel working in the studio. This is invaluable for a single boom operator who is picking up dialogue among three people. The operator can directly monitor audio quality such as *balance* and *perspective* being picked up while adjusting the boom position.

In some large network productions, separate intercom networks may be set up for engineering and production personnel. Thus, the audio operator and technical director can work on a problem during a production without interfering with the director and floor crew.

In many live news and sports productions, there is an adjunct system called the **interrupted feedback**

or **IFB** line. On-camera talent wears an unseen **earphone** that carries the output of the program line. When the director needs to give instructions to the talent, a button is pressed and his or her voice interrupts line audio. Its value is obvious for live newscasts during which new instructions must be given to the talent.

The **studio address (SA),** or **studio talkback** system, occupies yet a different position in the production communication system. The SA talkback microphone in the control room (usually, there is also one for the audio operator) enables the director to activate a special studio speaker so that he or she can talk to everyone in the studio, regardless of whether or not they are wearing PL headsets. Most studios also have the talkback feature with a mic hanging in the studio so that anyone in the studio, including lighting crews up on ladders, can be heard in the control rooms. Obviously, this system can only be used prior to production, during breaks, or while a videotape is being fed into the production. The SA speaker automatically cuts out the regular program microphone input to guard against any unintentional feedback that could overload the audio system.

During the setup period, it is a good practice to divide the two main communication systems so that the audio team has full use of the intercom system and the lighting crew uses the studio address sound system. This ensures that the two groups do not overlap their messages. In most productions, the audio crew usually has the larger volume of communication. It is also true that the lighting director usually splits his or her time between the studio floor and the video control room to observe the effects of lighting as viewed on the camera monitors. The director, who also uses the video control booth as a main working area, shares the studio address system with the lighting director for those messages that go to the stage manager.[1]

An important discipline (especially for directors) is that of knowing how to use the studio address system during both the setup and program assembly. By its very nature, the system has a loud and irritating quality unless used with care. In day-long setup and production sessions, these qualities begin to get in the way of the message itself. At this point, the director can use the intercom system and have messages relayed by the stage manager.[1]

Primary Program Assembly Period

The actual program production phase can be accomplished using any one of several structures. Program type and budget usually have a big part in this determination. TV's original technique of a continuous "live" sequence still continues to be used for much of today's news and sports programming. On shows where it is possible, a similar "live-to-tape" approach is used that allows for interruptions if problems occur, but the plan is to do an entire program in one continuous take. Early evening game shows often do five programs in one day. The daytime "talk shows" also use this method to good advantage. There is an actual "live feel" to these programs that is very important to their success.

The daytime "soap operas" use a variation of this system that takes advantage of a planned stop-and-go technique. An entire 3- to 5-minute scene is run with shots from three cameras being edited through the switcher. Boom mics are used to pick up sound. Usually, it is only at the end of scene that the tape stops rolling. At this point, the director does any audio or video "pickup" for post-production corrections. Most other dramatic and situation comedy shows seen on TV are shot on film using the single-camera film technique. However, on most shows, the film is then transferred to videotape or a digital hard drive for post-production editing to put the scenes in order and to add titles and credits. It is also at this point that multiple track audio editing for music and effects takes place.

Voice Command Procedures

The correct use of voice commands by the director is one of the most important factors in the success of productions that use any one of the several continuous sequence types of assembly. Much of this system originated in tank and airplane crew communication with each other. Early live television saw the utility of a system that separated all commands into two distinct phases—preparation and execution. The *commands of execution* are those cues that directly affect what goes out over the line monitor. "Fade-in music" or "Cue-the-announcer" call for an immediate action at a precise point in time.

For a crew member or performer to respond with this immediate action, however, adequate preparation time is required to be mentally ready and physically prepared to perform some action or equipment operation. For this reason, all commands of execution must be preceded at some point by a related *command of preparation*. Figure 4.17 shows how the commands fit into the time frame of the production sequence for a simple audio exercise. The commands and their timing are shown for the first paragraph of a longer radio commercial written to be performed as a "round-robin" production exercise by all members of the class. A complete script is found in Appendix D.1.

The term "*stand by . . .* music, announcer, cartridge" etc., is probably the most functional preparatory command for our present needs. It alerts the

TIME	DIRECTOR COMMANDS		
-:10	Stand by music & announcer		
:00	Music up full	MUSIC:	UP FULL 10 SEC. AND UNDER
:05	Stand by music under & annc.		
:10	Music under, cue announcer	ANNC:	THE INTEGRATED SOUND CORPORATION IS PLEASED TO PRESENT ITS NEWEST HOME STUDIO COMPLETE SOUND SYSTEM FEATURING A CD PLAYER, DIGITAL TUNER, TURNTABLE AND CASSETTE DECK ALL HEARD ON SKEAKERS WITH 120
:25	Stand by music up full		WATTS OF POWER FOR EACH STEREO CHANNEL. THESE COMPONENTS FEATURE A REMOTE CONTOLL FOR CONVENIENCE.
:30	Music up full and stand by announcer	MUSIC:	UP FULL 5 SEC. AND UNDER.
:30	Music under, cue announcer	ANNC:	DO YOUR OWN HIGH QUALITY DUBBING FROM RADIO, CD OR TURNTABLE USING METAL OR NORMAL AUDIO TAPE. THE FIVE-BAND GRAPHIC EQUALIZER LETS YOU SHAPE THE SOUND TO YOUR TASTE.
:45	Stand by music up full		SPEAKERS EACH HAVE A TWELVE INCH WOOFER, A FIVE INCH MIDRANGE AND A THREE INCH TWEETER.

Figure 4.17

This example shows how each of the director's commands is given at a precise point in time during the ongoing production sequence. Each command requiring some action by a crew member would be given slightly ahead of its actual execution to allow for the normal reaction time of an equipment operator.

audio operator—and all other personnel—to listen carefully for the subsequent command of execution that can take several forms. The object of the command of preparation itself can become the first word of the command of execution as shown in figure 4.17, *"music up full."* The verb *"cue"* is quite often used as the first word followed by a reinforcement of the object of the command of preparation involved, such as *"cue announcer"* or *"cue music, cartridge"* (if two music sources were being used). A *"segue,"* is a transition that temporarily blends two sound sources. A *"crossfade"* is a transition that fades out one source very briefly before fading in the other source up to full volume. Complete voice command procedures can get complicated, but they all are built upon these basic structures. Commands involving video will be discussed in conjunction with the explanation of video switching procedures in chapter 7. Once this basic structure is understood, other commands can be used using other terms.

Most successful television directors work to develop a calm, articulate manner when using the intercom. Whenever possible, they speak in a very casual style and even use a bit of humor. Those not used to being on the intercom net should not be misled by this apparent easygoing banter. It is designed to mask the intensity and ongoing pressure under which the director and all key members of the crew are working. Good directors know that to betray anxiety is to risk losing the confidence of the crew. Inexperienced directors who speak in loud and commanding voices are very hard to put up with on a long-term basis. Crew members listen much more carefully when the director's voice is calm and assuring. All directorial commands, whether they are for preparation or execution, must be delivered with practical consideration of the realities of the production. To request that the audio operator do too many things in too short a time is to invite a series of problems. Once an operator falls behind in a sequence, there can be a "domino effect," which can put a whole series of production elements at risk. The wise director knows what is possible and what is not.

Since most of the operational commands, as well as a considerable amount of general information, is coming *from* the director, the crew must always maintain the *discipline* that the director has first priority at all times. Professional crew members are quick to learn the intercom style of a director. With this style in mind and an understanding of the basic sequence of the production, they know when it is safe to talk and when it is not. Often the director specifically asks crew members for information that is needed for a quick decision. Crew members must remain alert and respond rapidly.

Hand and Arm Signals

It must be emphasized at this point that all of the director's commands to the talent and also to stage hands who do not have headsets must be relayed by hand signals through the stage manager. The only exception to this would be the use of an interrupted feedback unit as described earlier.

The total intercommunication system is further extended to the performing talent during the production by the hand and arm signals of the stage manager. This is the pantomime system, by which different directions can be given to persons while on camera without vocalizing any commands, and thereby possibly getting those directions unintentionally picked up as part of the program audio. (See Appendix C for illustrations of basic hand and arm signals.)

Postproduction

There is a wide range of production activity that takes place after all camera work in the studio has been completed. It can be as simple as the "sweetening session," where short delays are eliminated, bits of applause added, and segments tightened to make the program come out on time. Game shows are very careful in this regard. The work is usually done by the associate director who has kept careful notes during taping. The daytime "soaps" use the multiple-camera technique to shoot 3- to 5-minute segments without interruption. If there have been minor problems, the director will then go back and do audio or video "pickups" for later editing. Many of these production methods have evolved over the years from the days of network radio. They have endured because they function well in a wide range of circumstances.

A Full Participation Audio Exercise

With all of the above in mind, the class is now ready to put all of this information to practical use by engaging in a studio production exercise that gives each class member a chance to function one time in all ten crew and talent positions. Figure 4.17 shows the beginning of the script and shows all commands as they are used. (Except for *"fade the music."*) The full script is Appendix D.1 but without the commands to the left. Even though this is an audio exercise, we suggest that one crew member open up a camera and provide the director and assistant with what is known as an "information shot." This serves two purposes. First, it gives the director some contact with the floor, and second, it provides a small introduction to the camera for everyone. Since each exercise only uses a crew of about ten people, we suggest that the other half of the class spend the time receiving introductory information on lighting from a teaching assistant.

At first glance, this script may look like a rather simple application of what has been learned by the class up until now. However, the key positions of head audio operator, stage manager, and director will quickly be seen as being more than a little difficult to perform for the first time. It is designed as a "no threat" introduction to the idea of how a team works together within the time disciplines of a continuous production sequence. The script as presented in the Appendix can also serve merely as a guideline for another version of a similar exercise that reflects other forms of today's radio.

Summary

As part of the *technical* requirements for audio production, it is important to know the basics of microphone design in terms of *pickup patterns, transducing elements, frequency response,* and differences of *impedance* in both cables and microphones. It is also important to know whether the mic will be *hand-held* or on a *stand,* require *limited movement,* or be *attached* to a person. These factors in turn affect a number of creative considerations. The audio director must be concerned with the way microphones are used—*selection* and *placement* of the mics, and audio *balance* and *perspective.* Moving into *stereo* production may add a few complications to the usual problems, but it also adds another dimension that reflects audio of the future. The audio operator will find that the examples presented in the previous chapter dealing with seven basic control functions will aid in the operation of various other sources of prerecorded sound in the audio booth, such as cart machines and CD players.

Since most types of video production follow a somewhat standard procedure in structuring the work effort, it is important that the commonly used four phases, *preproduction, setup, program assembly,* and *postproduction,* be understood so that they may be applied to future production work done in the studio. The relatively simple audio production exercise found in Appendix D.1 provides just such a beginning opportunity.

Footnote

1. The terms "stage manager," "floor manager," and "floor director" are used interchangeably in this text. Used in different parts of the country by different kinds of production centers, they all refer to the chief crew member on the floor—the director's surrogate in the studio production area.

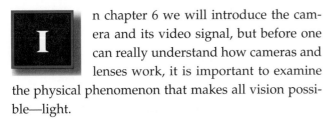

chapter 5

TV Lighting: Equipment and Techniques

I n chapter 6 we will introduce the camera and its video signal, but before one can really understand how cameras and lenses work, it is important to examine the physical phenomenon that makes all vision possible—light.

5.1

Types of Light: Incident and Reflected

Light exists in the form of waves that move at the speed of 186,000 feet per second. Variations in frequency of those waves account for what many living creatures perceive as differences in color. Visible light is part of a much larger electromagnetic spectrum that also includes X-rays and all frequencies of the broadcast band. (See Appendix A.) All light that comes to our eyes is one of two different forms of the same basic light energy. When it comes *directly* from a

source, such as the sun or a light bulb, it is called **incident light.** As important as this light is, it conveys little beyond the fact that we are looking at a car headlight or a neon sign, for example.

Our ability to see is largely the result of **reflected light** that has first come in contact with some material surface before it enters our field of vision. In this process it has been changed, and this now *reflected light* can tell us much about such things as an object's color and structure. As children, we constantly reinforced our developing visual sense by touching the objects in our immediate vicinity. We were, in effect, programming our computer-like brains so that we could "believe our eyes" and, looking out on the world, we began to *know* that things were hard, soft, red, curved, or maybe wet.

The reflected light from all of these diverse surfaces comes to our eyes in differing intensities depending upon the position of the incident light source as it relates to the physical structures that we are viewing. Our brain learns to translate variations of light and shadow into the concept of shape and texture. Take for example the instructor's desk in a classroom. The desktop dimensions are defined for us by the uniform intensity of the light reflected from all points of its hard, smooth surface. The light reflected from the side of the desk is of a different intensity, possibly in a shadow. This tells us that these side surfaces are at a different angle from the top and indeed are the sides of the desk. Other features, such as the drawer handles and the legs, are defined by the shadows that the light source "molds" around them.

Reflected light also tells us much about the *texture* of a surface. The even, shiny quality of light reflected from the desktop denotes a hard, uniform surface. Cloth is much more light absorbent. We can perceive the texture of heavy cloth material by the many tiny shadows created by the design of the weave.

Illumination for video production is an art that involves the proper use of lighting equipment to control the light that is reflected *from* the subject *into* the camera lens. It is the way in which we shape and control this reflected light that determines what the TV camera perceives as a picture, and the result creates somewhat of an illusion of three dimensions on the viewing surface of a picture tube.

5.2

Lighting Objectives: General and Particular

When the **lighting director (LD)** designs the lighting plan for any type of video production, two interacting concerns must be addressed. On one hand, important considerations grow out of specific *artistic needs* of the program. On the other hand, the LD knows that those creative aspects of lighting must coordinate with the larger context of a plan for *general illumination* based on the technical needs of the camera system.

The lighting plan starts with the need for all performers to be lit in a way that allows their features and person to be adequately portrayed in all locations of the set. Is there a consistency of light on all background locations of the set? Are there consistent light levels for performers as they face into multiple camera directions from varying set locations? There can

be no dark circles under eyes or other feature distortions, unless such are intended as a part of the performer's role as in the case of a drama for example. The lighting for the set must be appropriate to the general atmosphere as required by the nature of the production. Lighting for a dramatic love scene is different from that of a situation comedy. Even the most basic lighting concepts relate directly to important aesthetic considerations.

An actor in a daytime soap opera may go through most of the day with fairly basic lighting, but for a certain scene, there may be special needs for that actor at a specific moment in the drama. This could include a moment in the story that requires lighting that adds greatly to the performer's features and to a segment of the set. Such considerations are not necessarily limited to drama. Some of the most successful quiz programs will use what appears as very general illumination of the host and participants, but in the final playoff rounds of competition, there will be a dramatic change. Suddenly the background will grow darker and the key lights on the participants will be from a steeper angle that is almost directly above them. The host's light will get very intense. Most of the audience will not be consciously aware of the changes but will feel the increased tension, aided by a talented lighting director.

Contrast Ratio

The human eye can accept a **contrast ratio** of up to 100 to 1. In other words, within your range of vision, the brightest element can be 100 times brighter than the darkest element. The eye allows you to see both. A conservative but safe figure for the television camera would approach a ratio of 30 to 1. This means that the brightest area of a picture should not be more than thirty times as bright as the darkest area. This disparity obviously means that some care must be taken in designing lighting that falls within the safe parameters of the camera tube or CCD chip. (See chapter 7, section 7.2.)

As an example, take an evenly-lit living room scene on a wide shot. The colors are correctly balanced and the detail of the picture is clear. A performer wearing a white coat enters and, by mistake, steps into a brightly lit area of the set. This sends much more light into the camera lens than was expected, and several rather drastic things immediately happen to the picture. The camera's **automatic gain control (AGC)** reacts to the introduction of the very bright area by decreasing the intensity of the rest of the picture. Without changing either the lighting or the camera controls, the right three-quarters of the picture will suddenly become much darker. The colors will have a muddy tone and the set details will be obscured. The raincoat will be an out-of-focus blur and the person's face will be a dark spot. Stated in simple terms, the acceptable range of contrast between the brightest and darkest elements of the picture has been greatly exceeded. The light level that was previously sufficient for a picture has been "compressed" and distorted by the introduction of an overpowering amount of light. If the white coat had been necessary to the story, a lighting plan could have been devised that would minimize light to the performer's entrance area, but still allow for a small light to cover the performer's face from the closeup camera angle.

An error commonly occurs as students are learning balanced lighting techniques. For example, consider a picture in which the faces appear to be slightly darker than the background. In an attempt to solve the problem, the novice LD adds more light to the set. If this light, aimed toward the dark faces, also falls on an already too brightly lit background, the problem has actually been made worse. As this additional light illuminates the background, the camera's *automatic gain control* reacts as described above and attempts to compensate for the generally brighter video, and that adjustment darkens the entire picture. The faces remain dark in relationship to the brighter background. The solution to the problem is to use equipment, described later in the chapter, that provides additional light on the faces, while blocking the light falling on the background. Another part of the solution could be to change the angle from which the light falls upon the subjects. A higher angle would put light harmlessly on the floor.

Light Meters

While it may be surprising to some that the human eye is much *less* sensitive than the video camera in detecting light intensity *differences,* a few simple tests

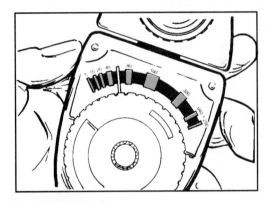

The photo above shows a digital readout of footcandle levels. The photo (below) shows an older type of meter, originally used for film photography, with a movable needle that points to various footcandle readings on a scale. *Photo courtesy of Minolta.*

with a **light meter** quickly show why all video lighting uses this piece of equipment. Using the **footcandle (fc)** as a unit of measurement, the meter visually indicates the intensity of light coming from the direction in which the meter is pointed.[1] Some light meters have an analog footcandle scale with a needle that indicates the number of footcandles being registered. Other light meters give a digital readout of the number of footcandles. (See figure 5.1.)

During the lighting setup time, the LD constantly uses the light meter to check for balanced light within the set as well as those special locations. We can find

 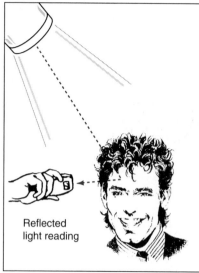

Figure 5.2

Incident and reflected light readings. An incident light meter reading indicates the amount of light energy that is falling on a subject or larger surface from one general direction, possibly a single source. A reflected light reading indicates the amount of light energy being reflected from that subject or surface directly toward the camera lens.

out how much *incident* (source) light is falling upon a subject by holding the meter very near to the camera subject and pointing it directly toward the light source. This incident light measure tells us how much light *arrives* at a given point, but it by no means tells the LD all that must be known to light for the camera. (See figure 5.2.)

The second, and possibly more important, method of measuring light intensity within the set is achieved by the *reflected* light reading. It indicates how much light is reflected *from* the surface areas of subjects *into* the camera lens. For this reflected light reading, the meter is pointed directly at the subject *from the perspective of the camera*. The meter should be held close to the subject, but care must be taken to avoid casting any sort of a shadow on the subject.

As could be expected, the two methods of measuring light produce quite different intensity readings. Reflected light loses much of its strength in the process of being reflected, and the reflecting ability varies considerably. The two different meter readings are generally used for different purposes. In the primary stages of setting up a lighting pattern, one looks for more general levels of intensity and area coverage as generated by the main source lights. The LD first

adjusts the primary strengths of individual lighting instruments, and then again uses the meter from different points in the set to find reflected *hot spots* where overlapping projection patterns have caused the intensity to exceed the average level. These readings, however, still do not tell the whole story.

With regard to the more subtle aspects of lighting, we work with the reflective qualities of the texture and color of a surface. While only reduced amounts of the original source light are reflected back to the cameras, this is the light that really matters. A light green knitted dress might reflect 30 to 40 percent of the illumination falling upon it, whereas a black knitted dress might reflect less than 10 percent. A white vinyl jacket, on the other hand, might reflect well over 90 percent. Different elements of the set may also produce large variations in the amount of reflected light bounced back to the camera.

These reflected light readings tell the LD when the contrast ratio for a given camera has been exceeded. For example, if the brightest spot at which the camera aims is 600 footcandles and the darkest spot in the picture is 20 footcandles, the ratio is 30 to 1; the camera probably will not handle it too well. If, on the other hand, the brightest spot is 450 footcandles and the

Figure 5.3

The dimmer board allows a light or group of mutually connected lights to be gradually increased or decreased in power from full strength to total darkness. It is used in conjunction with a patch bay (shown in figure 5.28) that connects power cables to all lighting instruments for final control.

darkest is 30 footcandles, the contrast ratio is 15 to 1. Under the right circumstances, this could be acceptable. Whenever the contrast ratio is too great, either the bright hot spots must be toned down or the darker areas must have more light.

While the preliminary work of establishing overall light levels is best determined by a direct incident light meter reading, contrast ratios are best determined by a comparison of reflected light from the brightest and darkest elements in the picture. Divide the brightest reflected light reading by the darkest reading to determine your contrast ratio. As important as the light meter is during this process, it is still vital that the lighting director continually check shots on camera through a reliable viewing monitor. Some of the problems so discovered may also have to be corrected by additional camera adjustments, as will be discussed in the next chapter. (See color plate D.)

Color Temperature

An additional factor must always be considered when working with both natural and artificial lighting for video production. It concerns the variations in the color quality of light as affected by the time of day, the reflective characteristics of sky light, and the nature of artificial light being used. Many fluorescent bulbs give off more of a bluish light compared to the reddish light given off by the tungsten bulb used in the home. This is the phenomenon of **color temperature,** and it is measured on a scale of **Kelvin (K)** degrees. What is being measured is neither heat nor brightness, but the *frequency* of the lightwave. One rule of thumb to remember is that the redder the light source, the lower the Kelvin temperature frequency; the bluer a source, the higher the Kelvin temperature. (See Appendix A.) Most studio lights registers about 3,200 degrees Kelvin and have a slight red tint. Outdoor light for most of the day register about 5,000 degrees Kelvin and is quite blue. Not surprisingly, red sunrises and sunsets go down to about 2,000 degrees Kelvin.

If a light is connected through a dimmer board (see figure 5.3) that allows for gradual changes in applied voltage, the light wave frequency and color temperature will decrease as the light voltage is decreased. Thus, a lighting element that produces a white light when operated at full intensity of 3,200 K will gradually begin to produce an increasingly reddish tint as voltage is decreased. Increased voltage results in a bluish white tint. This distortion is not readily perceived by the naked eye, but the camera is very sensitive to any drop in color temperature over a few hundred degrees Kelvin. As a result, most lights are connected through a lighting patch bay (further explained in section 5.6), and only those used as part of a special effect fadeout are connected through the dimmer.

Shooting in an outdoor setting where sunlight becomes a major source of illumination necessitates an added awareness of Kelvin temperature. Depending upon haze and cloud conditions, outdoor color temperature readings can range anywhere from *2,000 degrees Kelvin to over 10,000 degrees Kelvin*. In these situations, video cameras must be adjusted for the abundance of bluish light by changing the built-in color temperature filter and/or by resetting the white balance. (See chapter 6, section 6.5.) The main problems with outdoor shooting occur when the sun moves across the sky or when weather conditions change. Scenes shot during late afternoon or sunset will have a much lower color temperature than scenes shot around midday and, therefore, may not edit well together. The same is true when clouds suddenly cover the sun.

5.3
Lighting Objectives: Creative Purposes

As a creative or artistic factor in video production, lighting can be said to have four main purposes: (1) to define the shape and texture of physical form and, by extension, to create a sense of depth and perspective within the elements of the set or location; (2) to imitate the quality of light that is characteristic of a situation or setting in reality; (3) to establish and enhance the psychological mood of a performance or setting; and (4) to focus attention upon a single performer or aspect of the production and, thereby, to separate that subject from any feeling of relationship with setting or location.

While this last concept usually has a specialized application, the other three purposes should be thought of as principles that can be simultaneously applied within a given production situation. The same light that gives shape to a person's features can also provide mood, and at the same time, relate to the setting itself (for example, a beam of sunlight coming through a window and falling on a woman's face). At first glance, it might seem that some of these purposes apply only to dramatic productions. This is not necessarily true. These principles apply to all types of programs, from game shows to live news remote transmissions.

Shape, Texture, and Perspective

When a light source is placed right next to a camera, the light waves reflected back into the lens will be of a generally uniform quality. This effect is *flat lighting*, because the illumination has "filled" the hollows and curves that are the distinguishing features of the subject. When the light source is moved so that the beam comes from an angle, the resulting shadows "etch" the features so that the eye can perceive depth and texture. The camera system functions best when there is an exaggeration of contrasting light values within the video picture. The art of creating the illusion of depth on a flat video tube is largely a matter of accentuating the illumination patterns that influence our normal process of vision.

The experienced lighting director knows that often the manipulation of shadows, rather than direct illumination, most effectively adds form and texture to any object. Light coming from the side or below an object will throw shadows in certain shape-defining ways. Extreme side lighting (at right angles to the camera position) will emphasize textural quality by exaggerating shadows, making any object look more textured than it would otherwise appear.

The heightened sense of perspective necessary to the video picture is simply an application of this basic concept in the context of the entire set. Performers and foreground objects can be separated from the background when the angle and intensity of the light beam are adjusted to create a slight "highlight" effect.

Reality

Light operates on our conditioned responses in other equally important ways. We all have tuned in to the middle of a television play and watched a series of

Figure 5.4

Sinister lighting effect. Lighting from unusual angles or sources can give unnatural or symbolic effects; for example, lighting from a low angle usually results in a foreboding, sinister appearance.

close-up shots. Either consciously or unconsciously, we are soon aware of being indoors or outdoors and of the time of day by the quality of light on the actor's face. It is probably outdoors and near noontime if the light is relatively bright and if there are definite shadows under the actor's eyebrows, nose, and chin. If the scene has been shot inside a studio, the *imitation of reality* is a product of the lighting.

Other specific shadow and lighting effects suggest certain kinds of realistic situations. Shadows of venetian blinds or prison bars cast on the rear wall of a set help to suggest a particular locale. Other *off-camera* lighting effects help to pinpoint a setting: a low-angle flickering light indicates a campfire or fireplace; a continually flashing red light indicates the presence of an emergency vehicle. Other effects help to carry forth the dramatic narrative: a shaft of light coming from under the door of a previously unoccupied room indicates the presence of an intruder; a flashlight probing around a darkened room helps reveal evidence of a burglary in progress.

Mood

Similarly, the psychological *mood* of a performance or production can be reinforced by the quality of light

and its abundance or absence. Comedy is bright; therefore, **high-key lighting** is used to give an intense overall illumination with a fully-lit background. Situation comedies, game shows, and big musical numbers in a variety show rely on this kind of lighting to establish a light-hearted mood.

Conversely, tragedy or fear are communicated when the area surrounding an actor is dark or dimly lit. **Low-key lighting** refers to selective illumination that highlights only special elements of a scene. Usually the background is dark, and extreme lighting angles are used. Specific dramatic moods may be reinforced by special effects—a flashing neon sign outside a sparsely furnished hotel room suggests a seedy part of town; lightning flashes create an eerie mood; source light from a low angle gives a character a sinister, unnatural appearance. (See figure 5.4.)

Focus of Attention

When a high contrast exists between the light on a subject and the light on the background area, the eye is drawn to the subject. The most obvious example is the use of a **follow spot** on a performer in a musical or variety show. Another variation of this technique is **limbo lighting,** where the subject is placed "in limbo"

Figure 5.5

Typical cameo lighting: figure against a dark background.

Figure 5.6

Representative silhouette lighting: dark figures against a light background.

against a softly lit cyclorama or some other nondescriptive, neutral background.

Another way to achieve focus of attention is with **cameo lighting**—the performer is lit, but the background is completely dark. (See figure 5.5.) A **silhouette** effect—with the performers kept in darkness, but outlined against a brightly-lit background—may be desired for a dance routine or other special situation. (See figure 5.6.) A single shaft of light may be used to accent a contestant in the suspenseful climax of a game show. The host of a documentary may be

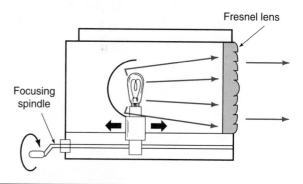

Figure 5.7

Focusing mechanism of the Fresnel spotlight. By turning the focusing handle or spindle, the bulb-reflector unit can be moved toward the lens or back to the rear of the housing. When in the forward position, the spotlight beam is "spread" to cover a relatively wide area. When moved to the rear of the housing, the beam is more narrowly focused, or "pinned," on a smaller area.

accented with a strong back or side light. Subtle lighting highlights may be used in many other dramatic and nondramatic settings to control focus of attention.

So, above and beyond the necessity of using enough **base light** for basic illumination, the lighting director must also plan creative lighting to: add shape, texture, and perspective; heighten the illusion of reality; create and enhance a specific mood; and focus attention.

5.4
Types of Lighting Instruments

A visit to a commercial supplier of theatrical and television lighting equipment can be a dazzling experience in every sense of the word. Hundreds of highly specialized pieces of equipment are on display or in the catalogs. One sees a range of instruments designed for the largest studio set as well as the newest lightweight portable gear for EFP and ENG uses. In section 5.5, we will examine the basic studio lighting techniques to establish a foundation for all video illumination. These principles will be adapted to small format and EFP production in chapter 15.

Our understanding of lighting technique is made easier because most lighting instruments fall into one of two basic categories—the controlled-beam

spotlight and the diffused-beam **floodlight.** (Many lighting professionals use the term *hardlight* to refer to a spotlight, distinguishing it from the "soft" light of a floodlight.)

Controlled-beam Spotlights

The classic controlled-beam instrument illustrated in figure 5.7 is the workhorse of studio lighting. This spotlight is used whenever a highly directional beam of light needs also to be shaped and focused. Its chief characteristic is the ability to throw a variable-sized spot of light on an area or performer. It is commonly referred to as a **Fresnel** (pronounced without the *s*), although each manufacturer will have a different name for it.[2]

This type of lamp generates intense heat, but it has a special structure of indented lens rings to help dissipate the heat. Another distinguishing feature is the movable assembly that allows the illuminating unit (bulb and reflector) to move back-and-forth between the front and rear of the instrument. With the bulb in the rear "**pinned**" position, the light rays focus in a narrow beam of high intensity, perhaps spreading no more than 10 degrees. As the bulb moves forward in the housing, the beam becomes "**spread**" and its intensity is diminished. In its full-forward spread position, the beam forms approximately a 60-degree angle.

The models of spotlights most generally used range from 500 watts to 10,000 watts. In a 2,000-watt instrument (commonly called a "junior"), a spotted (pinned) light produces an intensity of 600 footcandles when measured at a distance of 25 feet. In the fully-flooded (spread) position, the intensity of the same instrument drops to roughly 60 footcandles, but the light now covers an area six times larger in circumference. Fresnel spots are also classified by the diameter of the lenses. The most common studio sizes would have lenses ranging from 10 to 16 inches, and smaller field models would feature 6- and 8-inch sizes.

Some newer lights are designed to be fully adjustable from the floor with a *light pole.* (See both photos of figure 5.8.) To make adjustments, knobs located on either side of the yoke and on the lower assembly are engaged by a connector on the end of a matching pole. The light can be spotted and flooded, adjusted up and down, and moved sideways or

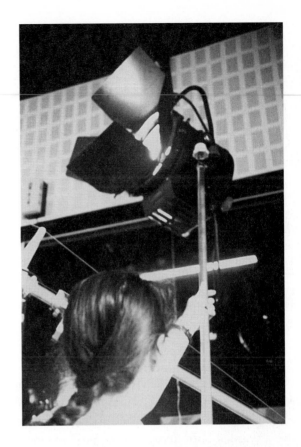

Figure 5.8

Fresnel light. Both of these Fresnel lamps are equipped to adjust focus as well as vertical and horizontal movement by means of a pole that fits into receptacles on the instrument. The four barn door beam controls can similarly be moved into required positions. *Photo courtesy of Strand Lighting*

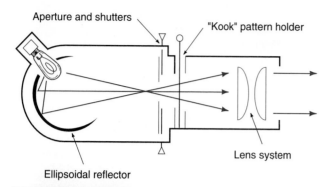

Aperture and shutters

"Kook" pattern holder

Ellipsoidal reflector

Lens system

Figure 5.9

Lens system of the ellipsoidal spotlight. Light rays are reflected from the fixed reflector and focused through the aperture. At this point, the shutters can be adjusted to shape the beam of light precisely, or cucalorus patterns may be inserted to project hard-edged shadow designs through the lens system.

back-and-forth without the crew member climbing a ladder. The same pole can adjust the four movable panels extending from the front of the instrument. These are called **barn doors** and are used to block off selected areas of the projecting light beam.

The **ellipsoidal,** or **leko,** spotlight diagramed in figure 5.9 gains its name from the curved, fixed reflecting mirror at the back of the unit. By means of the tube shape and focusing lens, it projects an intense directional beam that is well-defined at its edge. It is rarely used for lighting people. The beam can be further shaped by movable metal shutters (also known as *cutters*) located inside the lamp housing, behind the lens. At this point, where all the reflected light rays are in sharp focus, there is also a place to insert a patterned metal design cutout. The shadow of this **cucalorus** or **cookie** or **kook** is then projected to add visual interest to large, plain background surfaces. Some common kook patterns include prison bars, arabesques and Moorish motifs (see figure 5.10), venetian blinds, crosses, squares and other geometric designs, and cloud patterns.

Several other varieties of fixed-beam spotlights exist. One popular type is much like an auto headlight, with the lens, bulb, and reflector built together as a single unit. This **internal reflector spotlight** is commonly used as a portable light source for news and similar work done on location.

Figure 5.10

Left: ellipsoidal spotlight. *Right:* example of a shadow pattern cast by a "cookie" inserted in a leko (ellipsoidal) spotlight. *(Left) Photo courtesy of Strand Lighting*

Another type of portable spotlight is the **external reflector** model—a highly efficient quartz lamp in a small housing with no lens. Although not as controllable and precise as a Fresnel spot, this model is lightweight, easily moved (often with a clip-on attachment or a lightweight tripod), and more than adequate for most remote lighting assignments.

Floodlights

When we examine the specific techniques of lighting in section 5.5, we will see that the effects of the focused-beam spotlight are balanced by the use of softer light from a different angle. The purpose of this light source is to soften and, thereby, control the

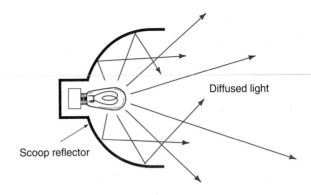

Figure 5.11

The scoop is a common source of fill light. Using either quartz or incandescent elements, the 14-inch and 16-inch diameters are the popular sizes for most television studio applications. Drawing indicates the diffused pattern of reflected light rays.
Photo courtesy of Strand Lighting

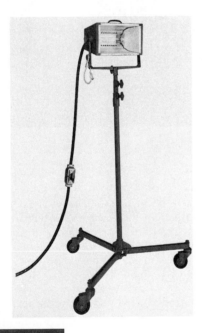

Figure 5.12

The *pan* shape of the reflector or the *broad* beam provided is the source of the name that describes this lighting instrument. *Left*, pan mounted on a floor stand; *right*, ColorTran 1-K broad with barn doors. *(Left) Photo courtesy of Mole Richardson (Right) Photo courtesy of Colortran.*

shadows that are created by the angle of the focused spotlight. When a number of floodlights are used in a set, the effect is a soft, diffused light that eases the harshness of the shadows. To help achieve the effect of a large source area of light and the resultant easing of shadows, the floodlight does not use a lens. It will use a diffusing reflector that has the effect of spreading out the source. It may use a soft-light bulb with no exposed filament at all, and it may use a **scrim**—a soft, spun-glass filter or other translucent piece of

material in a rigid frame attached to the front of the instrument.

The classic model for a floodlight is the one-half hollow globe structure known as a **scoop** (see figure 5.11). Its large reflecting area is made of a light-diffusing material that spreads the illumination in a nonfocused scattered pattern. Floodlights built in a rectangular shape are known as **pans** or **broads** (see figure 5.12). Some have controls that allow adjustment of the degree of spread. Their square shape makes

Figure 5.13

Strip lights.

Figure 5.14

Super-softlights. Left: In this 8K super-softlight, there is no direct light from the eight 1,000-watt quartz bulbs; all light is reflected by the large, curved surface. Right: The Lowel Softlight 1500 has two bulbs that bounce light off the canvas reflector impregnated with foil for a diffused light. These provide an easily placed source of fill light.   *(Left) Photo courtesy of Mole Richardson (Right) Photo courtesy of Lowel-Light*

possible the additional use of blocking devices known as **barn doors.** Another type of floodlight is the **softlight.** It is constructed with the bulb positioned so that the light is reflected off the back of the lamp housing before leaving the housing; the reflection material diffuses the light intensity coming from the bulb. A 2,000-watt floodlight will have a pattern of illumination that is more than twice the area of a 2,000-watt Fresnel spotlight in the maximum spread position.

When a series of pans are constructed in a continuous side-by-side row, they are called **strip lights.** They are used frequently with colored **gels** in lighting the background **cyclorama** (**cyc**, pronounced "sike") or other large set surfaces (see figure 5.13). Each individual lamp will typically be from 500 to 1,000 watts.

For larger studio productions, huge multibulb instruments, such as those pictured in figure 5.14, may be used. Such an 8,000-watt "super-softlight" may be mounted either on a floor stand or hung from a lighting grid. The eight 1,000-watt bulbs can be separately controlled to produce a variety of intensity levels. The bulbs are positioned so that only diffused light is sent out from the large reflector.

Today, most spotlights and floodlights are designed to use the **quartz** bulb. The term "quartz" is applied to a variety of quartz-iodine, tungsten-halogen, and similar illumination sources that have largely replaced the incandescent bulb. Its advantages are that it is smaller, longer lasting, more efficient (producing more illumination per watt), and does not darken with carbon deposits as it gets older. It does, however, tend

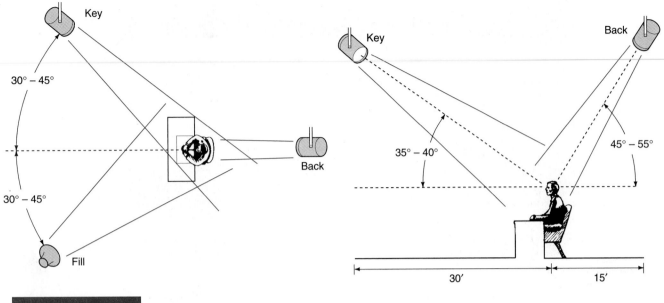

Three-point lighting. The key light and fill light should normally be placed approximately 30 to 45 degrees from a line drawn straight in front of the talent (with the fill being more directly in front of the talent). The back light is always behind the talent at a steeper angle than the key or fill lights.

to lose some of its Kelvin temperature as it ages, producing a slightly yellowish light.

This brief review of lighting instruments barely suggests the scope and variety of available equipment. In the past decade, leading manufacturers have developed a whole new generation of highly efficient, lightweight, and portable lighting systems. This section has been presented to provide a practical background for an understanding of the principles on which all stage, film, and television lighting is based.

5.5
Fundamental Lighting Concepts

As noted in section 5.3, creative lighting is largely a matter of careful control over the effects of light and shadow. The manipulation of these two factors permits the camera to create an illusion of depth on the viewing screen.

Three-point Lighting

The specific techniques through which these effects are accomplished can be easily understood by exam-

ining the classic lighting setup borrowed from motion pictures. It is known as **three-point lighting,** because it involves the use of three different light sources—the **key light,** the **fill light,** and the **backlight.** Each has a separate effect upon the subject being lit, because the three lights differ in relative angle or direction (or apparent source), level of intensity, and the degree to which they are either focused or diffused. Taken together, the cumulative effect is that of a balanced and an aesthetic unity—what Rembrandt called a "golden triangle" of light. Figure 5.15 illustrates how the three sources are used in a typical situation. The effect of three-point lighting is very natural, often occurring in our usual surroundings. By modifying one or another of its three sources, it can be made to achieve the *creative purposes* of form and texture, reality, mood, and focus of attention.

It is important, however, to keep in mind that our three-point lighting model was most recently perfected as an ideal for film production where a *single* camera shoots the subject or subjects from only one angle. Each shot is separately set up and lit. The ways that this underlying concept must be modified to apply to multiple-camera, continuous-action video

Figure 5.16

Subject with key light only.

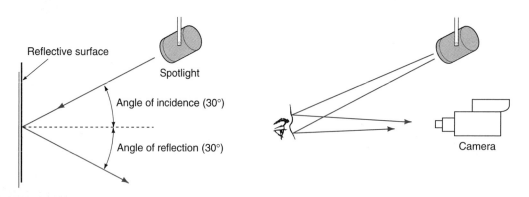

Figure 5.17

Angles of incidence and reflection. Basic laws of optics tell us that the angle at which the rays of light hit a flat reflective surface (angle of incidence) will equal the angle at which the reflected rays (angle of reflection) bounce away from the surface. Depending on the angle, a reflective surface such as metal or the talent's shiny forehead may send an unwanted glare or highlight back into the camera.

production are discussed throughout the rest of this section. (Single-camera EFP video production, of course, can come closer to the filmic model of separate setups with balanced three-point lighting carefully plotted for each shot; see chapter 15.)

Key Light

The most important illumination in any lighting plan is the **key light.** It is the apparent source of the light hitting the talent and provides the majority of the light that is reflected back into the camera lens. (See figure 5.16.) Almost invariably, a spotlight is used

for the key light; its strength and directional beam emphasize the contrast of light and shadow, defining the shape and texture of the subject. It is the use of the key light that brings out the features of the face and illuminates that most dramatic feature, the eye itself.

While more extreme angles can produce special dramatic effects, the optimum result is achieved by placing the key off to one side of the subject's face, coming in at an angle between 30 and 35 degrees. (If the key light is placed directly in front of the talent, the result is a flat, washed-out appearance with no

Figure 5.18

Subject with fill light only.

shadows, no sculpting, or molding of the face.) The height of the key will depend to some extent upon the talent's facial contours. It should be placed high enough to produce a slight shadow under the chin and nose, yet low enough to get the light directly into the eye socket itself. (If the talent has deep-set eyes and the key light is at too steep an angle, the result is simply two dark shadows under the eyebrows.) A good rule of thumb is that the key should normally be placed at a 35- to 40-degree angle above the subject's vision line.

In setting all lights—but especially the key—you must consider carefully the angle of light hitting the subject as it relates to the light intensity being reflected back into the camera lens. In terms of the basic laws of optics, *the angle of incidence equals the angle of reflection;* or, reflected light bounces off a flat surface at the same angle as the incoming light hits the surface.

If you have a light source projecting a beam perfectly perpendicular to a flat surface, that beam would reflect directly back upon itself. However, if you raise the light source to create a 30-degree angle above the perpendicular, as in figure 5.17, the reflected beam will bounce back downward at a corresponding angle of 30 degrees. If the subject being

lit has a rough texture or an uneven surface, the reflected light will be diffused and this angle is not important. However, if you are lighting a smooth and relatively polished surface (such as vinyl or polished metal), this angle can become very critical.

Applying this principle to the way light is reflected from the subject's face, you can see how the relatively smooth (and sometimes oily) surfaces of the forehead and nose can create shiny, highly reflective "hot" spots as light is bounced back directly into the camera lens. This same effect may occur many times within a large set with various angles and planes. Similarly, productions using studio graphics or photographs mounted on cards may have trouble with reflected glare—unless a dull matte surface is used or the cards are properly angled to reflect the light away from the camera lens.

Fill Light

In order to "fill in" on the dark side of the face or object being lit, some sort of **fill light** is needed. It should come in at an angle on the side opposite from the key. Ordinarily, a floodlight (such as a scoop or broad) would be used, although a spotlight in its *flooded* position can often be effective. In any case, a soft diffused light is desired. (See figures 5.18 and

Figure 5.19

Subject with balanced key and fill lighting.

Figure 5.20

Subject with backlight only.

5.19.) Fill light is used simply to soften the shadows and give some illumination to the less illuminated side of the face or other object. Fill light should not be as strong or directional as key light; it should not compete in creating shadows or countering the shaping qualities of the key.

Backlight

As the name implies, **backlight** comes from behind and above the subject. (Not to be confused with *background light*, discussed below.) A spotlight is virtually always used so that the light can be directed and focused like the key. The backlight falls upon the subject, and as a result, accentuates such features as hair, shoulders, and top surfaces of set elements. (See figures 5.20 and 5.21.) This highlighting effect separates the talent from the background, adding to the illusion of depth within the total picture. Without adequate backlight, the subject appears flat and tends to blend in with the background, as in figure 5.16.

Backlight requirements will vary with the background and some important items relating to the subject. Hair color and texture are especially crucial. For example, blondes require relatively little backlight.

Figure 5.21

Subject with balanced three-point lighting (key, fill, and backlight).

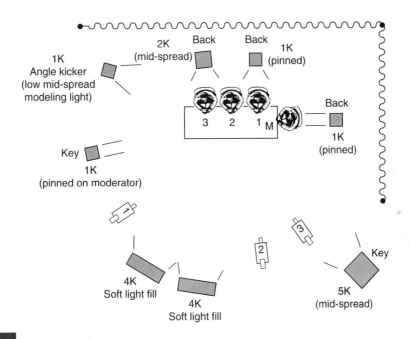

Figure 5.22

"Plan A" lighting plot. Modified three-point lighting plan designed for participants primarily addressing the audience.

Their natural hair color separates them from the background. On the other hand, darker tightly-curled hair generally needs extra backlight, because it does not reflect light well. The effect of different material in a person's clothes must also be observed. There is one rather specialized kind of backlight known as a **kicker.** Its illumination comes over the camera left shoulder of the subject(s) as shown in figure 5.22. Because it is used with a relatively high intensity, it also functions somewhat as a key light. It can work on the side of the face without really disturbing the basic three-point effect.

Auxiliary Light Sources

One of the most important additional illumination sources is the **set light** or **background light** (not to be confused with the *backlight*). This is the major source of lighting for the cyclorama or background set behind the performers. In addition, to helping fill in the overall picture (basic illumination), background lighting can give form and texture to the setting, provide a sense of reality, or suggest mood (creative functions). Colored gels on a plain cyclorama can help establish mood in a production. Sometimes the background is hard to control, because the background tends to catch the wash of a lot of other lights being used for other purposes. As mentioned earlier, there can suddenly be too much light if the lighting director has not kept an eye on the set as lights are being turned on.

In one function or another, most types of lighting instruments can be used appropriately for background lighting. Floodlights (scoops or strip lights) are often used for general illumination of a cyclorama or flat space. Spotlights can be used to highlight certain areas or present dramatic lighting effects (for example, strong diagonal slashes of light or selected low-key elements). And, of course, the ellipsoidal spot can be used with a variety of cucalorus patterns for various shadow effects.

Other special lighting effects depend upon careful background lighting. A good *silhouette* demands an evenly lit background, balanced from top to bottom as well as from side to side. A good *cameo* effect, on the other hand, requires a complete lack of any light hitting the background; front lighting must be carefully controlled to make certain that no spill is reflected onto the set behind the talent.

Actually, in any moderately complicated lighting setup, the illumination is coming from many directions and angles. In addition, the subjects—the persons being lit—will be moving within the set. The concept of key, back, and fill lights should be used as a guide, not as a rigid set of rules. Auxiliary lighting and special effects will be added as needed for certain creative purposes. The important consideration is that the lighting director be in total control of the *direction, intensity, quality* (harsh shadows or diffused), and *color* (if applicable) of light falling upon performers and set.

Multiple-camera Lighting

As previously mentioned, the concept of three-point lighting was developed for the motion picture single-camera technique—always concerned with lighting from the viewpoint of the camera. With this approach, every shot has its own lighting setup.

When the subject and camera move, the lighting changes. Detailed care can be taken to sculpt the face and other features of the subject with the key light, blended with back and fill lights.

With television's multiple-camera formats and continuous-action productions, lighting directors have found it difficult to adhere to classic three-point lighting. In the talk show format, for example, the host or hostess moves to people in the audience, and the cameras must shoot from many angles. The solution to this situation is to create an overall *wash* of illumination throughout the entire set. Many soft fill lights (fewer keys) are used from all possible camera angles. The result is called *"flat"* lighting, because the faces take on more of a flat look as differentiated from the *"shaped"* effect of shadows created by a strong key. It is a workable solution to a common lighting problem.

Some situation comedies shot with electronic multiple-camera techniques have had substantial success in overlaying the three-point lighting within a flat-lit set. Working together, the TV director and lighting director select points within the scene where the actors will remain in place for a period of time. In these spots, careful three-point lighting can be used for close-ups. When portions of the scene contain physical movement, the action is picked up by the cameras on wider shots (see chapter 7, section 7.2), so the flat lighting will not matter as much. Close-ups are kept to a minimum in the areas lit by flat lighting. It is a compromise, but it works fairly well.

Daytime serials ("the soaps") that crank out an hour a day of multiple-camera production are hard-pressed to spend much time on subtle lighting, but using the previous technique, they manage to achieve an overall satisfactory lighting effect. Since productions of all types operate within tight budget constraints, lighting directors never have all the time and crew they need to do a perfect job. They simply do the best they can with what resources they have. But in all video production, three-point lighting—with its potential for texture, depth, modeling, perspective, and focus—remains the standard against which all lighting work is measured.

Two Lighting Approaches

To examine some multiple-camera lighting problems, as well as their solutions, let us look at the example of

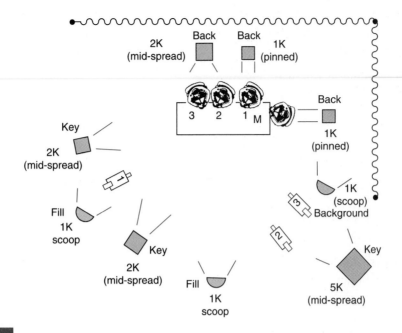

Figure 5.23

"Plan B" lighting plot. When the shape of a discussion is such that participants are turning side to side for discussion, cameras 1 and 3 must move to appropriate angles. At this point, cross-key lighting is used in "Plan B" so that faces are well lit from those side angles.

a four-person discussion program such as the one suggested by the "Frame of Reference" script in Appendix D-2. The participants are seated in an "L" shape with the host on the camera-right side. This arrangement allows the host to keep eye contact with the three guests while leading the discussion.

If the three guests speak to the host or straight out to an audience area behind the camera 2 location, and the host addresses the viewers by means of camera 1, then we can use the "Plan A" lighting plot as shown in figure 5.22. In this illustration, the key light is provided by the 5-kilowatt Fresnel spotlight that is spread to cover all four participants. Its angle will create slight shadows on the faces of the three guests. It should be tilted so that its light also falls on the cyclorama in the background. Fill light is provided by the two 4-kilowatt *softlights* (see figure 5.14) from the camera left side. This is basically an application of the *three-point lighting* technique.

One possible problem may occur when guests 1 and 2 occasionally turn to their right to speak to guest 3 (on the camera left side)—they would have only fill light on their faces from the angle of camera 1. This problem can be solved by placing a spotlight *kicker* from over their right shoulders to provide a "model-

ing" effect from the camera 1 angle. To do its job properly, this controlled beam light should be hung somewhat lower than the two backlights. The host is covered by a pinned spot from a slightly different angle from the camera 1 shooting perspective. This gives the host's face some shape and definition. The host's fill light comes from the two *softlights*.

The back lights are located as indicated on the lighting plot. (See figure 5.22.) Whenever possible, their intensity should be adjusted to take into account the different amounts of back light needed, for example, by blondes as opposed to brunettes. Differences in light or dark clothing around the shoulder area may also require back light adjustments. Light falling on the cyclorama must be checked to be sure that its brightness and color are the same behind all camera shots. Problems can be solved by placing additional scoops or broads to fill any dark spots on the cyc.

However, if the guests for the most part will be constantly turning to speak to each other and to the host during the course of the discussion, then the "Plan B" lighting arrangement (see figure 5.23) would be more appropriate. It utilizes a **cross-key** lighting technique, so named because the multiple key lights are aimed onto the set from different directions. Their beams *cross* each other as they light their respective subject areas.

The lighting must be done in this way, because both guests 1 and 2 will at times be facing to their extreme right or left as they talk to their fellow panelists and the host. Note that cameras 2 and 3 have been moved farther to the right and camera 1 more to the left in order to be shooting faces at less than a 30-degree angle from a straight-on position. A well-lit camera shot showing the eyes and other facial movements then tells us much about an individual.

It should be noted that figures 5.22 and 5.23 are not exactly drawn to scale. Both the key and the fill lights would be half again as far away. The back lights would be placed about as they are drawn in relation to the guests. As mentioned earlier, all lights, and especially the *key lights*, should be sufficiently distant from the subjects and at a low enough angle to eliminate any possibility of dark areas around the eyes and unflattering shadows under the nose and chin.

Balanced Lighting Ratios

The first step a lighting director must take to create a three-point lighting pattern is to decide on the relative strengths of each light source. There are some basic guidelines that should be used in making preliminary plans. Figure 5.24 shows the suggested ratio of key, back, and fill lighting that can be applied in most basic lighting situations as a preliminary to later adjustments. The footcandle figures represent incident meter readings that would be made from the point where incident light strikes the subject.

During the lighting setup period, a definite sequence of activity should be followed by the lighting director and the crew. Working from light "Plan B," the LD would first turn on the 5K light and adjust it on all three guests, over the shoulder of the host, and on as much of the background as possible. An *incident* light reading from the position of the three guests at this point should be just under 200 footcandles. (Remember, the dimmer is not primarily used to adjust brightness.) Spread and pin the pattern to lessen or increase the brightness. Then, the other two 2K lamps should be similarly adjusted. These three *key*

Light	Footcandles	Relative Strength
Key	150 fc.	Reference point of 1
Fill	75 fc.	½ of key
Back	225–300 fc.	1½ to 2 times key
Background	75–115 fc.	½ to ¾ of key

Figure 5.24

This suggested ratio among key, back, and fill as well as background incident light strengths is intended only as an initial structure to facilitate the setup process. It would need to be modified by later reflected light readings as well as constant checking through the camera.

lights should be adjusted to add up to about 200 footcandles on all performers from all three camera directions. An all too common mistake among those doing projects for the first time is to turn on all of the lights at once and then try to adjust. The result is confusion.

Second, the *fill lights* should be turned on so that they both soften facial shadows and, at the same time, help out the background lighting. Check on-camera to see if more background light is needed making sure that intensity is the same behind all camera shots. Spread Fresnels can sometimes do the job even better than scoops or pans. The last lamps to be adjusted are the *back lights*. They will not add much to the accumulative general illumination of the set because of their downward angle, but they are important and must be set with the help of a camera.

As soon as the actual guests are present and can sit in their assigned positions, it is wise to check closeup shots on camera to see if the shots match. If there are problems, then take some *reflected* light readings from faces to see if natural skin tones are markedly different and adjust with the application of powder. In the "Plan B" light plot some adjustment could be made with the middle 2K Fresnel lamp. At this point, the LD should walk around the set and take a number of incident readings, both from guest positions as they face into all cameras and along the background of the set. Guest faces should be receiving about 225 footcandles and the background wall should be at about 115 footcandles, possibly more depending on its reflective texture. What one is looking for is a consistency of light.

Economy of Lighting

Frugality in the use of lighting instruments is an important consideration. Good lighting technique is often as much a matter of knowing when to take out or soften lights as it is of knowing how to add lights to a set. The modeling and texturing effects of a few well-placed key lights are easily wiped out by adding too many lights from too many directions. Newer cameras that require less light are making it increasingly possible to capture the subtle effect of natural light that we are all used to seeing.

Lighting Setup Procedures

Having looked at some of the basic television lighting requirements and concepts, we are ready to consider the actual techniques and procedures involved in lighting a television setting. Several of these aspects also involve practice and discipline in the execution of specific lighting functions in, for example, the precise preparation and use of lighting plans and plots and in careful observance of all safety precautions.

Mounting Lighting Instruments

Our first concern should be with the way the lights are actually mounted or supported. How are they to be positioned and held in place? Basically, there are two ways—by *hanging* them from above on the grid or by mounting them on a *floor stand*.

Hanging Mounts

Every television studio is equipped with a **lighting grid** for mounting lights above the staging area. It is comprised of pipes and supporting mechanisms that place the lighting instruments in a position to produce a proper angle of illumination, while leaving the studio floor uncluttered for camera and talent movement, microphone placement, and various set elements. Most studios have a pipe grid or **batten** system upon which the lights are actually sus-

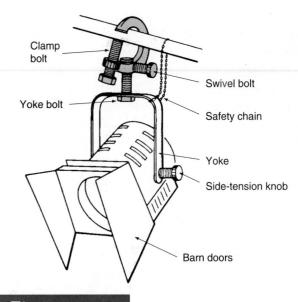

Figure 5.25

The C-clamp is the most common type of lamp hanging device. It is held in place on the pipe by tightening the clamp bolt against the pipe. There are three additional control bolts. At the bottom of the clamp unit there is the important yolk bolt that connects the yoke to the light itself. This bolt (Y-bolt or yolk bolt) should never be loosened. Instead, the swivel bolt should be loosened to allow for left and right lateral movement of the lamp. The two side-tension knobs are used for the vertical movement. A steel safety chain is used as illustrated or sometimes connected directly to the lamp housing.

pended. The pipe grid is a rigid permanent arrangement of pipes several feet beneath the studio ceiling. A movable batten system raises or lowers the pipes by a counterweight system so that lights can easily be worked on from the studio floor. Lamps are connected to the grid by a **C-clamp**. (See figure 5.25.) The clamp is always used in conjunction with an additional steel **safety chain** that prevents the light from falling should there be any accidental disconnection of the clamp. Whenever possible, the hanging of lamps should be considered as a permanent placement. While lights can be moved when necessary, the effort is strenuous, and there is always a degree of danger involved, especially with students. With a well-designed permanent grid, the lighting director can save much time by planning the best use of existing positions in the form of a **light plot,** shown in simple form in figures 5.22 and 5.23.

sonnel to climb up to various working positions in relation to the light, as shown in figure 5.26.

Floor Stands

In many kinds of studio arrangements, the suspended lights often have to be supplemented by lights mounted on floor stands. Although too many floor stands tend to clutter the studio floor and get in the way of other production elements, they do represent a certain degree of flexibility and simplicity of setup. Sometimes there are positions where it is simply impossible to position a light except on a floor stand.

Floor stands for studio use are usually mounted on a heavy metal base for stability. They come in a variety of weights and sizes capable of handling many different types of lighting instruments. Of course, for location productions (wherever supplemental lighting is needed), the portable floor stand is indispensable.

Lighting Control Factors

The video camera system is extremely sensitive. Optimum performance is possible only when illumination is kept within certain carefully prescribed limits. To achieve the artistic and technical purposes of lighting, the lighting director must work within four separate yet interrelated parameters:

1. The level of intensity
2. The degree of focus or diffusion
3. The shape of the projected beam
4. The color quality

After the initial setup is completed, the lighting director, working with the director and camera operators, makes a continuing series of adjustments throughout the rehearsal period and prior to the final take. A number of mechanical and electronic controls are utilized during this process.

Intensity

We have already briefly described the way that the beam from a Fresnel lamp can be spread to lessen its intensity and, at the same time, cover a much wider area. Remember that the *fully spread* beam has roughly one-tenth the intensity of a completely *pinned* beam. But whether a beam is focused or diffused,

Figure 5.26

High-tech it may not be, but this type of wooden ladder, with one alert person to stabilize it, provides a quick and efficient way to trim lights.

With this plot, the actual work involves aiming the lamp, adjusting the light intensity, as well as shaping the beam by means of the barn doors. All of these efforts come under the title of **trimming**. With most equipment, most of these efforts are done at the height of the grid. Some of this work can be done with a connecting pole mentioned earlier in the chapter. In most studios, the majority of the work is done with a movable *lighting ladder* that allows lighting per-

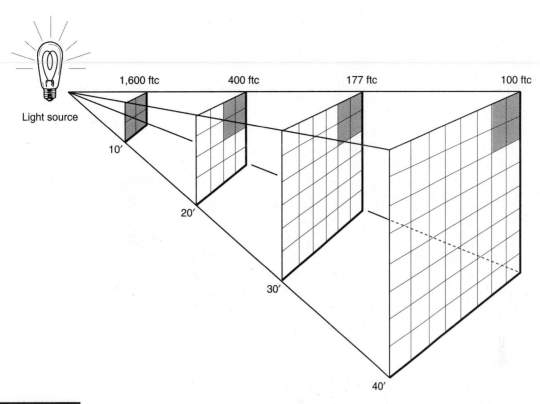

1,600 ftc   400 ftc   177 ftc   100 ftc

Light source

10′

20′

30′

40′

Figure 5.27

Inverse square law as applied to television lighting.

another factor has important implications in terms of intensity. Although it is not easily apparent to the naked eye, variations in the distance between a source light and the subject create large differences in intensity.

The same **inverse square law,** which in section 4.3 informed us about critical microphone-to-source distances, also applies to illumination. As shown in figure 5.27, the strength from a light source is reduced to one-quarter of its previous strength as the source-to-subject distance is doubled (and, of course, the strength is multiplied by four as the distance is cut in half). It is actually a matter of an increasing surface being covered by the same amount of light energy. As a result, the power to illuminate diminishes. A light that produces 1,600 footcandles at a distance of 10 feet is reduced to only 400 footcandles at 20 feet as it covers four times the area.

In terms of a practical field production example, let us assume that a *clip-on* spotlight attached to a camera working 10 feet from a subject produces a reading of 100 footcandles (exactly one-tenth of the figure reading illustrated in figure 5.27). Should the subject move away to a distance of 20 feet, the light level is now 40 footcandles. This may not be adequate for professional purposes, because the very process of zooming into the subject even further reduces the amount of light coming through the lens. (See chapter 6, section 6.5.)

On the other hand, in a studio situation where we are working with much stronger illumination and with the talent at greater distances from the lights, a change of even 10 feet in the source-to-subject distance should be noted but is not critical. It would probably only need a minor change of the brightness control.

Located some distance from the actual lighting instruments—either in a corner of the studio or a separate control room—is the patching and control equipment that, in any kind of sizable studio operation, is centered around a *patch bay* with a dimmer

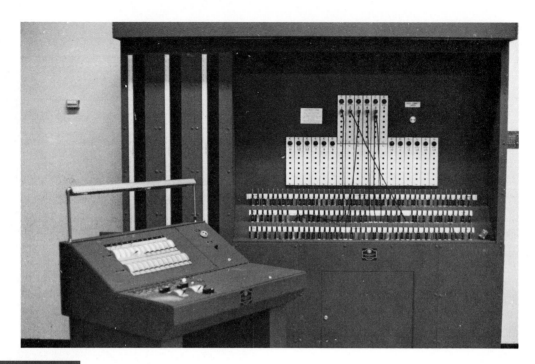

Figure 5.28

A patch bay. A patch bay is the connecting point between a power source, numbered switches, and the cables that run through the grid to all lighting instruments. It also may be used in conjunction with a dimmer board that can provide gradual increments of more or less power to selected lines.   *Photo courtesy of KCET, Los Angeles*

board nearby. (See figure 5.28.) Although this equipment will vary in size and capacity, it all functions on the same general principles. The *patch bay* serves to connect numbered lights on the grid with similarly numbered cables for connection to switches in the control area creating a **nondimmer circuit.** For rapid control of a group of lights, the cables for a number of lights can be brought through one **dimmer circuit** (above) at the dimmer board. As mentioned earlier, the majority of lights would go through nondimmer circuits, because any lessening of power light causes a drop in color temperature that in turn produces a reddish tone to the light source.

Focus and Diffusion

Diffused light is created and controlled in several ways to keep it in its proper perspective in relation to the focused key light. The primary control factor is that of adjusting intensity through some of the methods described previously. Placement is also very important. The best diffused light is achieved by using several instruments placed at differing angles.

Several devices are also important to the lighting director's toolbox. The most commonly used pieces of equipment for these purposes are either attached to the front of the instrument or mounted in front of it. A *scrim* is a wire mesh, shaped to fit the front of the lighting instrument. (See figure 5.29.) It works by scattering the beam and cutting back on intensity. Scrims are used to soften a spread Fresnel light. To further soften scoops, pans, and broads, a cloth-like opaque filter made out of spun and pressed fiberglass is used. Available in three thicknesses, it greatly cuts down on the intensity and projects a soft, almost shadowless light.

Shape

If lighting directors had to work with only the large raw beam projected by most instruments, their work would be difficult indeed. One of the main difficulties is controlling the overlap of multiple light sources. Fortunately, there are a number of shaping devices that are used to modify and block parts of the beam. These can produce high-intensity hot spots. The most common solution to this problem is achieved through

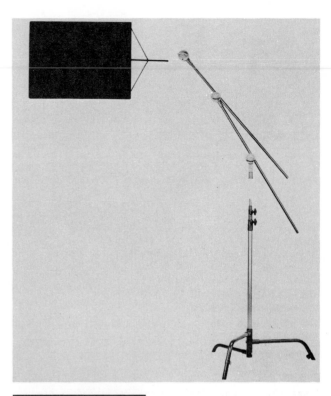

Figure 5.30

A beam control "flag." Flags are used to block the light on specific areas of the performer or set. With their stands and extension arms, they provide an important final control over illumination and can provide a sharp line of shadow.
Photo courtesy of Mole Richardson

the use of *barn door* shutters that, as mentioned earlier, are attached to the front of a spotlight. (See figure 5.8.) Used in pairs or sets of four, these hinged plates can provide an adjustable edge to the beam. By moving the shutters, both the height and width of the projected light can be limited. Most assemblies can be rotated to provide maximum adjustment. In a leko or ellipsoidal lamp, the movable shutters are inside the instrument (adjusted with outside handles) to provide an even greater definition to the projected pattern. (See figure 5.10.)

Sometimes the lighting director needs to create a small area of reduced intensity *within* a projected beam. For this a **flag** is used. Flags are rectangles of varying size made either of metal or of frames covered with black cloth. They can be hung from the lighting grid or mounted on a floor stand in a position to block out light to a specific area. (See figure 5.30.) One use, for example, is to cast a slight shadow on the forehead and on top of the head of a person with thinning hair who otherwise might appear almost bald under the bright lights of a close-up shot.

Occasionally, an added amount of light must be pinpointed at a particular area of the set. If barn doors cannot project quite as precise a pattern as needed, a **top hat** can be used to do the job. Inserted in the same frame designed to hold the barn doors, the top hat, a circle that ranges in diameter from 4 to 12 inches, can reduce the spotlight's beam to a smaller, clearly defined circle without increasing the intensity of the spot.

The *cucalorus* (*cookie* or *kook*) is a cutout design that, when placed in front of a spot, projects a pattern upon a cyclorama or large set surface. Ellipsoidal spotlights are designed so that smaller metal kooks can be inserted into the instrument housing by means of a "dipstick." (See figure 5.10.)

Color

There are occasions when a set or other production location is simply too dull and drab for attractive pictures with sufficient color contrast. It may be that more "warmth" from red-brown earth tones is

Figure 5.31

Gel holder on a scoop. Frames that hold a gel filter in place are designed for all types of floods and spotlights. *Photo courtesy of Mole Richardson*

Figure 5.32

In implementing the original lighting plot, the lighting director works closely with the director to assure that camera angles on faces and elements of the set can take full advantage of light placement. *Photo courtesy of Dina Fisher*

needed. Or possibly the "cool" effect of green and blue is desired. To solve this problem, variously colored *gels* are used to add color to the setting and occasionally to the performers' clothes and flesh tones. The gel is a thin transparent celluloid material and is available in a wide variety of colors. The gels can be cut to fit a specially-designed holder that slides into the same frame that is intended to hold the barn doors on a spotlight. (See figure 5.31.)

In using gels, the lighting director must work carefully with both the video control operator and the makeup artist. The effect of projecting three or four different colors onto a set can be subtle, but must be carefully controlled. Since the camera system tends to pick up and accentuate red, one should be especially cautious with its use. Because most normal makeup is in the reddish range, too much light through a red gel will greatly exaggerate flesh tones. A green gel, on the other hand, has an unflattering effect on most people—especially on those with darker complexions.

One of the most effective applications for gels is to use them with strip lights to color a cyclorama. A wide variety of color combinations and effects are possible. A continually changing dawn effect, for example, can be created with the background shifting from a deep violet, through various reds and pinks, to a light blue during the shooting of a scene.

5·7

Preproduction Planning

Newscasts, as well as talk programs and game shows make very few changes in their lighting on a day-to-day basis. A new production or one with continuing changes in set, such as a soap opera, usually schedule their lighting period to run right up to the beginning of the main camera and sound production time. Woe be unto the lighting director whose work runs over into this period causing a delay in its conclusion. In professional studios both large and small, the performers, engineering, crew, and equipment are scheduled very tightly. Any extension of studio time becomes prohibitively expensive.

It is, therefore, incumbent upon the lighting director to be very sure that planning the lighting design is done with the utmost care. First, there must be a session with the director (and possibly the producer) in which the lighting needs are carefully detailed. Only after this is completed can the lighting director start the process of drawing up the **light plot** that will serve as the basis for both the setup period and operations during the camera production phase. (See figure 5.32.) With some additions and instructions, figures 5.22 and 5.23 could both serve as the basis of a light plot for a simple discussion program.

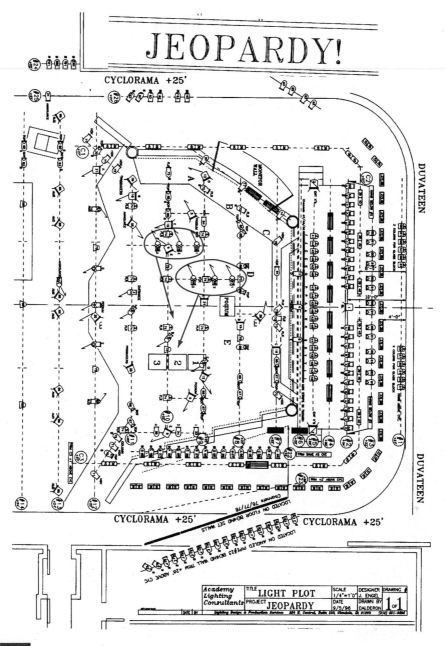

JEOPARDY!

Figure 5.33

Light plot for the Jeopardy! **television program.** A relatively large number of lighting instruments are needed for a large-scale television program such as **Jeopardy!,** which features numerous lighting changes and special effects. As can be seen in color plate A, much of the effectiveness of the set is the result of the lighting design.

Figure 5.33 shows the light plot for the set of the nationally syndicated TV program *Jeopardy!*. (See the *Jeopardy!* set shown in color plate A.) It provides an insight into what is needed to achieve the numerous lighting changes and special effects seen during the show. When a new set was installed in the fall of 1996, Lighting designer Jeffrey Engel was commis-

sioned to create an entirely new lighting scheme to be implemented for each show by the regular LD, Vince Cilurzo. Those who know the program will recognize the podium for Alex Trebek in the center of the set. Looking carefully, one can find his keys and back-light. Contestant podiums 1, 2, and 3 are to his left (camera right). As indicated, two different sets of key lights are strategically located for these positions. For most of the program, contestants are lit by keys directly in front of them. (See corresponding numbers on lamps.) When the show reaches the point of *Final Jeopardy!,* the second trio of keys is used. When aimed correctly for the production, they strike the participants from a 30-degree angle, giving the faces a more sculpted look. Light on the background panels is also reduced and changed in color. These two factors help to create a sense of added tension.

It may not seem possible, but all of the remaining lights provide some function, either generally illuminating the set or providing the flashing lights at the show's conclusion. In this plot, lights are shown in their positions on each grid, but not exactly as they will be aimed. Those lights shown with a tail and check mark indicate that they are hung from a device that drops them 3 or 4 feet lower from the grid. Accompanying any light plot is always a key that indicates the type and strength of each light as well as the use of floor stands, grids, and other information. There would be several more pages of paperwork that work accompany a plot as complicated as this one.

In the Sony Studio (Culver City near L.A.), where the show is produced, each light is on a computer-controlled dimmer. The power of the processor for each light is nearly that of a 1980s home computer. Such computer-controlled lights can be observed in large stage productions, where the lights projection patterns move in addition to changing color and focus. It all happens on the command of a computer program.

5.8

Safety Precautions and Disciplines

Safety is the responsibility of everybody connected with a television production. Any unsafe situation can be avoided by using common sense and observing basic precautions. Part of the *discipline* of television production is the habit and attitude of *thinking safety.* Every crew member, whether or not part of the lighting team, should be disciplined to think always in terms of avoiding or correcting hazardous conditions.

When working in a studio, you should always "think overhead." Are all lights, mounts, and other equipment securely fastened? When heavy equipment is moved or repositioned overhead, is everybody warned and the area below cleared out? In addition, crew members should "think electrically." Is all equipment turned off before moving or inspecting it? Is the circuit turned off before it is plugged into an instrument? Everyone should also "think hardware." Has the item of equipment been thoroughly checked out and is it ready for use? Has everything been connected? Tightened? Tested?

Whenever a lighting assistant is moving or trimming lights, at least one person should steady the ladder from below. The person on the ladder should always carry a wrench (secured by a band or tie around the wrist to prevent dropping it on persons or equipment below) to tighten any lamps that may have become loose from excessive turning. When making any adjustment on any lighting instrument, the safety chain must always remain fastened, securing the light to the pipe or grid.

When changing the direction of a light, always loosen the thumb screw (swivel bolt) *first.* Do not mistake it for the bolt holding the lamp hanger to the clamp—loosening that bolt will detach the lamp from the lighting grid.

When moving a light (clamp, hanger, and housing), always make certain that there are no people or equipment below the working area. Be certain the power to the lamp is off. Just because no light is being emitted does not mean there is no power coming through the cord. Damaged lights, burned-out bulbs, and short circuits are all potential dangers. Again, be sure the power is off at the lamp's new location before plugging it into the grid outlet or load circuit. When moving an instrument from one location to another, the safety chain is always the last item to be unfastened, and it is the first thing to be hooked up when the instrument is repositioned.

In professional studios lighting instruments are rarely moved. A basic pattern of lights is established, and the LD has a plot showing where each light is located. There is a deliberate oversupply of instruments on the grid, much more than is needed for any single production. If a light goes out during a production, the LD can replace its function very quickly, and the audience is usually unaware that any difficulty occurred. Moving a light is also unwise from a finan-

This photo of the set for the nationally syndicated **Jeopardy!** program actually shows only one of a number of different lighting effects that are used within various phases of the program. Every one of the lights shown in figure 5.33 is used during the program to illuminate the set as well as to enhance the mood and pace of the program.

PLATE B

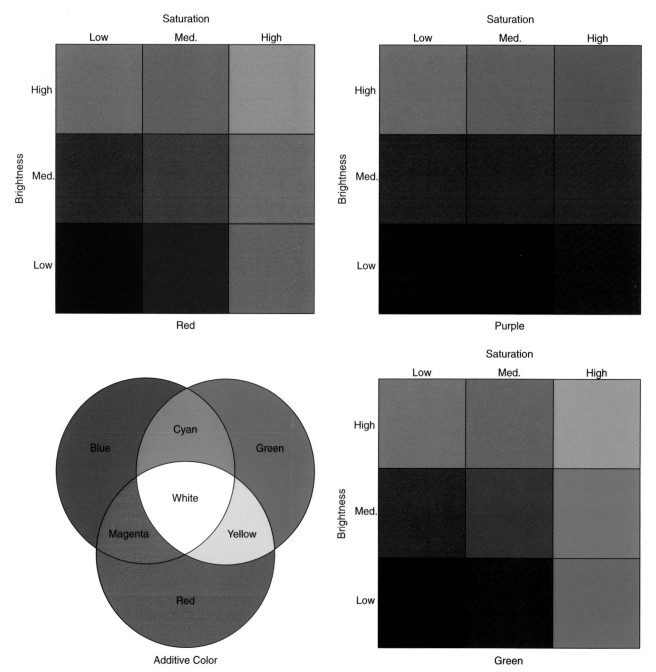

Additive color

Where any two of the three primary colors (red, green, blue) overlap, they form a secondary color—cyan (green-blue), magenta (blue-red), or yellow (red-green). Combinations of varying intensities of the three primary colors can produce all possible hues. When all three primary colors are combined in the specific proportions of 59 percent green, 30 percent red, and 11 percent blue, the result is a pure white.

The properties of color: hue, brightness and saturation

Each of these three boxes illustrate nine variations of one color that can result when the factors of brightness and saturation are varied in different combinations. With computer controlled graphics units, two or more colors can be mixed together with these innumerable gradations of saturation and brightness to produce (theoretically) close to one million individual color combinations.

PLATE C

Which monitor is adjusted correctly?

The monitor looks as if it is adjusted correctly, but the vectorscope to the right shows that this color signal is out of adjustment. (The points on the green display are outside of the boxes etched on the overlay.) The phase of the color signal should first be adjusted (by a competent technician or engineer), and then the monitor should be adjusted so that it will reproduce the color signal *faithfully.*

In this case, the vectorscope shows that the signal is accurate, therefore the monitor is out of adjustment. This usually happens when the monitor is adjusted by someone trying to make a bad signal look better. The picture on the monitor should be corrected by a component technician or engineer.

PLATE D

Typical video problems

The pictures on the right illustrate a number of video problems that should be watched for in every production. The top picture is getting too much light, as indicated by the "blooming" of the white shirt. This can be corrected by adjusting the lighting or adjusting the iris on the camera. While the white shirt makes the problem worse, it is also visible in the white patches on both faces. The middle picture shows the opposite problem—the scene is too dark. This may be due to improper lighting or incorrect iris setting on the camera, but it could also be caused by a low "pedestal" (black level) setting on the camera. (When the pedestal is too low, darker areas lose all detail and look completely black.) The bottom picture has color problems that could be due to (1) a camera that was not correctly "white-balanced," (2) a playback of a tape that is "out of phase" with the switcher, or (3) an improper monitor adjustment. To correct the picture, first check the white balance (for a camera) or the phase—using color bars and a vectorscope (for a tape machine). As a last resort, have a technician use a properly calibrated reference signal to adjust the monitor. Remember—do not adjust a monitor just because it does not look right!

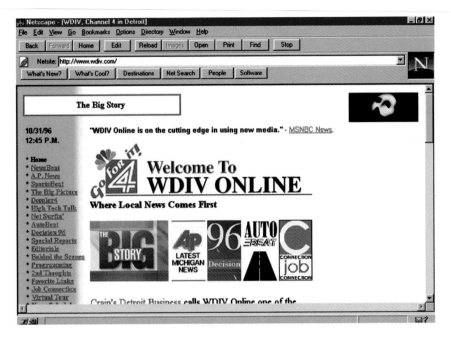

(a)

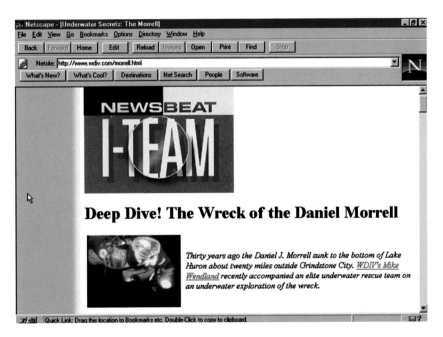

(b)

World Wide Web (WWW) users can access a wide variety of information on the Internet. Here are some sample pages from television station WDIV's site. The main page, often called a Home Page (a), leads users to other content, including additional information about news stories (b), biographies of news anchors (c), and general information about the station (d). Screens courtesy of WDIV-TV

Continued

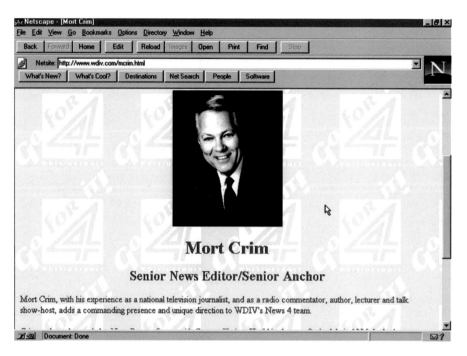

(c)

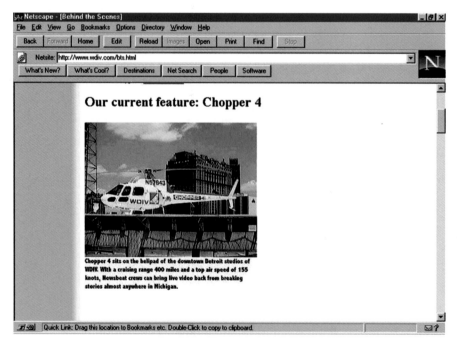

(d)

cial standpoint. Rough handling, whether it takes place during movement or even during adjustment, greatly cuts down on the usable life of the bulb and/or lighting element.

When focusing lights, never look directly into a light. A light that measures 200 footcandles at 30 feet may approach 100,000 footcandles at the source. Studio lights are bright enough to permanently damage or even blind the naked eye.

A 2,000-watt lamp creates a dangerous amount of heat. After being on for only a few minutes, most studio lamps are hot enough to cause serious burns. Most studio lamps have handles—use them! Lighting technicians should also be furnished with heavy-duty, heat-retardant gloves. Use them! Special caution must be used when adjusting barn doors, as they are directly in the path of the light source at only a few inches and absorb a large amount of heat.

Make sure never to touch the surface of a quartz bulb with your bare fingers (even when the bulb is cold). Always use gloves or some other cloth between your hand and the globe. Quartz lamps generate tremendous amounts of heat, and even a small amount of finger oil or acid on the face of the globe will interact chemically to weaken the glass envelope and hasten discoloration.

Summary

As with audio considerations, lighting directors must be concerned with both technical needs and creative purposes. In addition to establishing the correct amount of *general illumination* (usually determined by an *incident light* meter reading), the LD must also work within an acceptable *contrast ratio* (established by *reflected light* meter readings) and maintain the correct *color temperature* (3,000 to 3,400 degrees *Kelvin*).

The creative lighting objectives include *perspective,* molding *shape* and *texture,* establishing a feeling of *reality* (or nonreality), creating a *mood* or emotional setting, and *focusing attention*. All these functions are accomplished with *spotlights* that have a highly directional focused beam and/or with *floodlights* that give off a nondirectional diffused light.

Lighting a typical subject involves standard *three-point* lighting (*key* light, *fill* light, and *back* light). *Auxiliary sources* such as a *kicker* or *background light* may also be incorporated. When working with *multiple-camera lighting,* certain modifications and compromises in the ideal three-point lighting concept must be accepted—such as *cross-key* lighting.

As a starting point, lighting directors use a *basic ratio,* with the back light strongest, then the key light, with the fill being the weakest source. Complete studio lighting procedures also include knowledge of various *mounting devices* and, most importantly, various approaches to *lighting control* (intensity, focus and diffusion, shaping the beam, and color control). Finally, the concern should be with essential *safety precautions* and the discipline of thorough *preproduction planning*.

All the lighting considerations, of course, are but a means of creating the picture that will be picked up by the camera and its lens system. Camera/lens structure and camera operations are discussed in the next two chapters.

Footnotes

1. One footcandle (fc) is the amount of light that falls upon a surface placed at a distance of 1 foot from an established theoretical source approximating the brightness of one candle.

2. The lens generally used in the instrument has a series of raised concentric rings on the outer face that help to dissipate the tremendous heat buildup in the enclosed structure. Augustin-Jean Fresnel was a nineteenth-century scientist who did important research into the nature of light.

chapter 6

Camera Structure and Lens Design

T his chapter begins an examination of the video system. It is usually referred to as the **camera chain,** because a large number of components shape and in other ways influence the video signal as it makes its way through this complex system. It should come as no surprise that over the past several decades the video part of television has changed more than the audio part. From both a technical and creative standpoint, the pictures we now see as a part of cable and broadcast television are very impressive. What we will see within the next decade may be truly amazing.

6.1
Video Signal Flow and Control Functions

Just as we discussed the audio system in terms of audio signal flow, so also it would be helpful to think in terms of the *video signal flow* for the visual part of television production. The same *seven basic control functions* introduced in chapter 3, section 3.2, apply equally to the video system. In a simplified

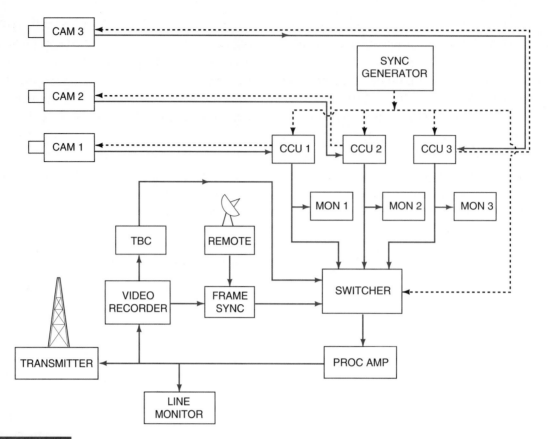

Figure 6.1

Simplified diagram of the video signal flow. A portion of the synchronizing ("sync") pulse (dotted line) is sent out from the sync generator to each camera control unit (CCU) and on to each camera—keeping all cameras in perfect synchronization. The complete sync pulse is also sent to the switcher. Simultaneously, the picture information (solid line) flows from each camera to the CCU, where the video signal can be shaped and altered. The signal is then channeled into the switcher, with the picture information also being displayed on the video monitor for each camera. (In the diagram, from the CCU on through the rest of the system, the solid line represents the complete video signal—color and brightness plus sync pulse; the dotted line is omitted for simplicity's sake.) From the switcher, the composite signal can be sent through a process amplifier, to the line monitor, to a video recorder, and/or to the transmitter after audio is added. A video recorder also can be used, of course, as a picture source—sending its recorded program material through the time-base corrector (TBC) and on to the switcher or to the transmitter. Remote sources (satellite feeds, microwave links) can also serve as inputs to the switcher, flowing through the frame synchronizer that conforms the sync pulse with the other composite signals.

form, figure 6.1 illustrates the basic units in the video signal flow.

The Seven Basic Control Functions

The first step, *transducing,* is accomplished by the camera which receives physical energy in the form of light waves and transforms them into electrical energy in the form of video signals. Unlike the relatively simple microphone, the video camera must have an entire support system of additional equip-

ment, because it takes roughly 600 times more signal to produce a video picture than sound.

Live camera and recorded feeds are *channeled* through the video **switcher** which is much more than just a routing device. It can *mix* picture inputs and also *shape* them in terms of both color and design. Camera signals first shaped by the **camera control unit** (**CCU**) are then further enhanced by switcher-controlled digital effects or graphics units that make pictures whirl, twist, and explode in combination with two or more other video sources. As digital cameras are brought into use, all lines from the camera will be of the *fiber optic* variety that carry very large bandwidth in a very narrow cable.

The *amplification* of the video signal may occur at several different points in the flow of the signal by **distribution amplifiers (DAs).** Amplification is necessitated by cable distance and other factors that require the balancing of signal strengths. Our simplified diagram (see figure 6.1) does not attempt to show all the points where distribution amplifiers are placed throughout the system.

As with amplification, *monitoring* takes place at several different points within the system. In any regular studio production, the camera operators, like VCR and audio operators, must have monitors to provide the informational feedback needed to control their equipment. In the video control room, the numerous monitors are crucial to the producer, director, LD, and AD to perform their duties. In this same area or in master control, there may be several technically-oriented monitors and scopes used for camera control. Learning how to get maximum use from these visual displays is an important attribute for all members of the television production team.

The rush to exploit the benefits of the digital signal, starting in the middle 1990s, has meant that camera signals are now *recorded* for *playback* on digital *hard drive* recorders as well as on digital videotape machines. The newer VCRs have been designed to input and output a variety of digital component and composite signal varieties. This proliferation of tape formats has had more of an effect on camcorder design than on the traditional studio camera; however, in preparation for the future, some of the newer studio cameras have an optional capacity to export both a digital and an analog signal.

Control Components

The processing video signal is much more complex than the audio signal. It takes roughly 600 times as much "information" to produce a video signal as to produce sound within the same time frame. As a result, the picture is vulnerable to a number of disruptive influences within the system itself.

Many of the difficulties arising from the use of analog video will be solved or at least reduced by the use of the digital signal throughout the entire flow and control system. Complete digital replacement of studio system equipment will depend very much upon the commercial demands of the different levels of production organizations. Because most educational institutions will, unfortunately, be among the last to accomplish this changeover, the current edition of the text will again present a general background on the video system in terms of the analog signal. The new digital tape formats and how they will affect picture acquisition, transfer, editing, and storage will be covered in chapters 9 and 10.

Synchronizing Generator

To coordinate the functioning of all components in the video system, the **"sync" generator** creates a series of timing pulses that lock all elements of the video signal together at every production stage: switching, recording, editing, transmission, and reception. This sync pulse has often been called a system of *electronic sprocket holes* that keeps everything coordinated in a lock-step pattern. The timing pulse is based upon the basic 60-cycle alternating current used in the United States and in many other countries using the NTSC television systems.[1]

Process Amplifier

The **proc amp** takes the video signal from the switcher—color, brightness, and synchronizing information—and then stabilizes the levels, amplifies the signal, and removes unwanted elements or **noise.**

Time Base Corrector

Video signals from videotape recorders often have synchronizing pulses that have deteriorated or been slightly altered during the recording and playback process. The **time base corrector (TBC)** takes these signals, encodes them into a digital form, and then reconstructs an enhanced synchronizing signal for playback and editing purposes.

Frame Synchronizer

An increasingly necessary piece of equipment, the **frame synchronizer,** takes video sources from outside of the studio sync system (satellite signals) or from videotape playback units, compares their sync pulses

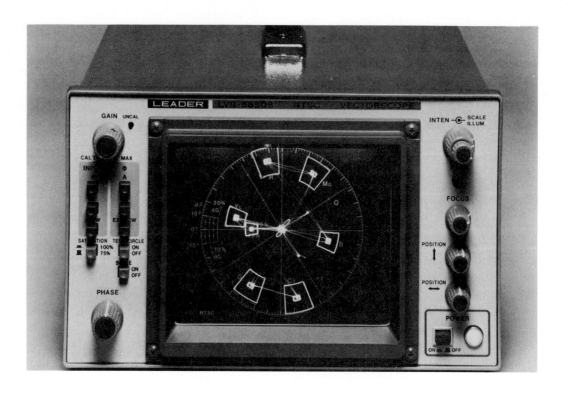

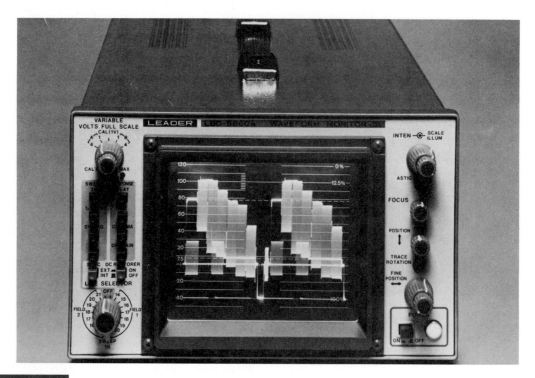

Figure 6.2

The waveform monitor (top) is used for analyzing and adjusting the luminance portion of an analog picture. The vertical bars indicate differing ranges of color brightness. The display on the vectorscope (bottom) provides information on the status of both hue and saturation levels of an analog color signal. Positioning of the light spots within the boxes indicates correct adjustment of the three primary and three complimentary colors. *©1996 by Tektronix*

These two waveform monitor displays are among several that are used to show the status of a digital video signal. Note references to such factors as time, voltage, sample, and field.

with studio sync, and adjusts the differences between the two. The signals are put through a digitalized phase prior to output. Satellite and other out-of-studio feeds can thereby be coordinated through the studio switcher.

Color Bar Generator

This component sends a standardized pattern of vertical colored bars through the switcher. This monitor display (see color plate C) calibrates the color values and adjustments on all cameras, video recorders, and monitors. The **color bars** are also recorded at the beginning of a video recording so that the playback machine can be matched to the color levels set at the time of the recording.

Waveform Monitor

The display on the analog **waveform monitor,** shown on the top in figure 6.2, indicates the relative brightness of the primary and complimentary colors in the signal. The vertical bars help the operator adjust for the proper amount of contrast between the brightest and darkest elements in the picture. Note the very different displays used for the digital waveform (see figure 6.3).

Vectorscope

The display produced on the **vectorscope,** on the bottom of figure 6.2, provides a visual indication of the

accuracy and intensity of the color portion of the video signal. It shows the individual levels for the proper adjustment of the three **primary colors**—red, green, and blue—as well as the three **complementary colors**—yellow, cyan, and magenta. (Video uses an **additive** system in that yellow is not a primary color but is instead derived by combining green and red.) These ongoing adjustments are crucial to the consistency of a color picture. Color plates C and D show problems that can occur when signals and monitors are out of calibration.

Those well-meaning novices who "fix" bad pictures by adjusting the program line monitor are the source of many problems at educational institutions. Trained personnel continually maintain these monitors at the proper color levels through the relatively simple use of the color bar generator. Considerably more time is spent in adjusting the cameras by means of the waveform monitor and vectorscope. With VCR output, a time-base corrector is also involved. Once this work has been done, monitors must be left alone. But then along comes a *"video dodo"* who, unbeknownst to anyone, starts to mess with the monitor. The person in charge of video, who does not know that this has been done, may be asked for last-minute changes in camera or VCR settings based upon how the program monitor looks. All too often the result is a poorly balanced picture replacing the good one that could have been recorded.

The Color Video System

While one must acknowledge the impressive graphics now being produced by digital computer technology, for most applications the camera is still the centerpiece of video production. Throughout much of television history, the heart of the camera was the **pickup tube**—that miraculous variation of the cathode-ray tube that transforms (transduces) frequencies of visual light into electronic signals. In recent years, however, an offshoot of the computer chip, the **charged-coupled device (CCD),** has almost completely replaced the tube in both professional and consumer-level cameras.

At the receiving end of the television system—the home TV set—the **cathode-ray tube** is still the primary element in the *display* of all video pictures; however, many portable TV sets utilize a newer **liquid crystal display** (LCD) screen technology.

Three Attributes of Video Color

To do its job, the camera must first separate incoming light into the three primary colors (above) by means of a **beam splitter,** made up of a glass prism and reflective mirrors. The prism is all-important whether the camera has three tubes, three CCD chips, or one CCD chip with red, green, and blue filters. The three CCD chips themselves are identical in structure. They are labeled red, green, or blue only, because the beam splitter separates the three colors and directs just one designated color to each chip. To function properly, the camera must be sensitive to the three factors that affect color as humans see it: the color tint itself **(hue);** the vividness of that color **(saturation);** and its relative brightness **(luminance).**

Hue

Color plate A indicates the three *primary colors* and shows how any two of them can be combined (in the overlapping areas) to produce the three additional *complementary colors—cyan* (a turquoise formed from blue and green), *magenta* (blending red and blue), and *yellow* (the combination of red and green). These primary and complementary colors are the basic pure hues seen when a prism breaks up white light into its constituent **wavelengths** (every hue has its distinctive **frequency** and wavelength), or when we marvel at a rainbow (which essentially is millions of droplets of water acting as tiny prisms to create the vivid primary and complementary colors—ranging from violet to red[2]).

It has been known for centuries that a prism separates white light into its spectrum of constituent colors. Conversely, when light waves of all three primary colors are added together in a proportion that relates to the color sensitivity of the human eye (59 percent green, 30 percent red, and 11 percent blue), the resulting effect is *white.* Sometimes thought of as the absence of color, white is actually the *presence of all colors.* The proportions are a bit off, but one can get the idea from color plate A. If one still has trouble accepting this on faith, prove it by looking carefully at the individual grains of sand that make up a white sandy beach. The variety of colors that we are used to seeing in our daily lives result from the reflected combination of these primary colors.

As the proportions among the hues being combined are varied, an enormous range of colors becomes possible. For example, when red and green are added together, a range of pure hues from red to orange to yellow to green can be created. As the third primary color, blue, is added, a wide variety of browns, tans, mahoganies, beiges, ochers, maroons, sepias, and so forth is achieved. Computer graphics programs have an almost infinite ability to mix ultrafine gradations of color and, as a result, can create literally millions of different hues.

The concept may be hard to accept at first, but when we see a television picture containing what appear to be numerous colors, we are actually seeing the result of a continuous mixing process. In figure 6.4, we see how over 300,000 **pixels** (points of light) of red, green, and blue, are made to glow at varying degrees of brightness 30 times a second. Each is part of a series of rapidly changing combinations of those primary colors that produces the effect of a myriad of shades in the eye of the viewer.

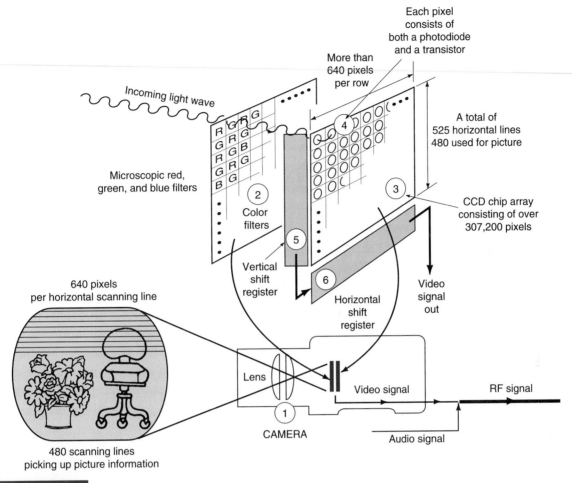

Figure 6.4

Cameras with only a single charged-coupled device (CCD) chip can produce a normal color image through the use of filters placed between the lens and the chip. After the incoming image travels through the lens (1), it passes through a color filter consisting of a checkerboard pattern of red, green, and blue filter elements (2). The filtered color images are then focused on the 2D image-sensing CCD chip located immediately behind the filter (3); therefore, there is a tiny red, green, or blue filter in front of each pixel on the chip. The precise alignment of these microscopic filters and corresponding pixels is crucial for a clear picture. Each pixel (4) consists of a photodiode (which generates an infinitesimal electric current in proportion to the amount of light hitting it) and a transistor (which stores the current for a tiny fraction of a second). When a trigger impulse is generated by the vertical shift register (5) (sixty times every second), the stored charge in each photodiode is transmitted along each row in sequence to the horizontal shift register (6). The information in the horizontal shift register is then shifted out and becomes one scan line of the video signal. This video information, along with the horizontal and vertical sync pulses, is now the video line output. For broadcast it is combined with the audio signal.

The calibration of these color values is accomplished by means of the *vectorscope*. Its clock-like readout has a point of light for each of the six primary and complementary colors. Each of these points of light must be in a precise location within a circular pattern for that color to be at its proper value. In figure 6.2 (bottom), the red response is displayed just to the left of the 12 o'clock position, blue is at 4 o'clock, and green is located at 7 o'clock. The three complementary colors are displayed in between these locations.

If the indication for one (or more) of these colors is outside of the marked parameter, then that color and any shade derived in part from that primary or complimentary color will not be seen in its intended hue on a monitor.

Saturation

The intensity or vividness of a color is described in terms of its *saturation*. If we are dealing strictly with a red hue, then the intensity of that red can range from a highly saturated *vivid* red, as shown in the lower right square of color plate B, to the less saturated *pastel* red shown in the upper right square. The pastel red is achieved by diluting the color with white. Another effect is achieved by diluting the vivid red with grey, producing more of a brown tone as seen in the lower left corner.

As other hues are blended together, other color combinations result. Red and green hues combined in varying proportions with different amounts of white produce yellows. If increasing amounts of grey are used to dilute the saturation of the red and green factors in this yellow, a series of golden brown tones will result. Just as the saturation effect can be controlled on a scale leading to white, grey is on a scale of increasing darkness leading to black. Together, the *hue* and *saturation* portions of a video picture are termed the **chrominance** signal.

On the vectorscope, the gradations of saturation are indicated by the position of the points of light, but in a different plane. The greatest color saturation is indicated when the point of light is closest to the outer edge of the circle. As saturation is decreased and diluted by white, the light spot moves closer to the center of the circle.

Luminance

It is really not possible to describe how hue and saturation interact to produce color without including the influence that the *luminance* (brightness) factor has upon the color picture. The illumination of a subject by a light source and the resultant reflection of light from that subject into the camera starts a complex process. The picture focused through the lens is comprised of a number of colors in varying degrees of brightness as reflected from all surfaces of the subject. Important information about the subject's shape and texture are made evident through the contrast of light and shadow in the luminance aspect of the image. It gives the picture a structure and creates whatever illusion of depth exists on the flat screen.

Keep in mind that luminance is generated by a response in voltage to the various brightness levels that make up the incoming picture. It relates to, but must not be confused with, the increase and decrease of video **gain** which is a matter of adding (or reducing) brightness of an entire picture through an amplification of the video signal. This adjustment is part of the process through which color and brightness levels are controlled. The proper adjustment of video gain is important in ensuring that all cameras match each other within the variations of camera angle, set, and lighting conditions. In section 6.3, the way the lens also influences this complex combination of factors will be examined.

The differing bright and dark portions of the video picture are seen on the waveform monitor display as bar-like columns that change their structure as the picture changes shape. (See figure 6.2.) The highest point on the screen indicates the brightest part of the picture. If this registers above the "100" mark, the signal may be too strong and become distorted. It is also important to observe carefully the lowest part of the display that represents the brightness level of the darkest part of the picture. It is called the **pedestal,** and its adjustment is important to ensure that the darker portions of the picture do not lose their detail and become black blobs.

Characteristics of the Video Signal

Originally all video signals combined the color (chrominance) and brightness (luminance) signals into one feed that was channeled into a single cable. It became known as **composite** video. In the late 1980s, professional videotape formats, such as **Betacam,** were introduced that separated these two video signals and became known as **component** video. S-VHS and Hi8 used a different approach to separate chrominance and luminance with such success that they moved from being consumer formats to use in some professional situations. Starting with the **M-II** format, more and more digital signals have used *two* chroma channels in addition to the luminance signal. The move to the digital signal has been even more impressive, because it took advantage of these earlier advances in picture quality and then added digital picture stability.

The new Panasonic AQ 20D camera is a prime example of a whole new generation of cameras that could lead to new methods of sports and other outdoor production venues. It operates in low light levels and its signal can be carried over 12 miles on a fiber optic cable with virtually no loss in quality.

The Panasonic portable AQ 20D, shown in figure 6.5, is not a camcorder, and while it may outwardly resemble some cameras seen fifteen years ago, it is definitely different. The "specs" tell the story. Designed for use at large-scale live sports events, its signal can be sent over twelve miles on a fiber optics cable without noticeable smearing or other quality loss. Much of its setup is done with the touch of a finger. Its three CCD picture operates well in extremely low light. A base station at the end of the fiber optic line can convert the signal to any one of several field applications. There is also a similar model, the AQ 225, that has all of the same attributes but is designed for more permanent locations.

The CCD Scanning Process

In a *three-chip CCD camera*, a *beam splitter* separates the focused beam of the lens into three images consisting of the red, green, and blue parts of the picture. Figure 6.4 shows how a color camera can function with only one CCD chip roughly the size of a postage stamp. Small as it is, the one in our example contains 307,200 pixels. This is a number common to many cameras. In the NTSC picture format, there are 525 horizontal scanning lines from the top to the bottom of the tube. But, because not all are used for picture purposes, our example will have a figure of 480 of those horizontal lines dedicated to picture use. To achieve a 3 by 4 aspect ratio, there would have to be 640 pixels per horizontal line.

In front of each of the 307,200 pixels, a red, green, or blue filter is placed so that lightwaves of each of the three colors act upon a corresponding color pixel. The brightness and color information from each individual pixel are transformed into a minute electrical charge, depending upon the amount of light falling on the pixel. This infinitesimal electrical charge is passed on in an incredibly precise and rapid sequential pattern—one that resembles the way the electron beam scans the image target in the traditional camera pickup tube.[3]

This sequence of picture information is gathered by *vertical and horizontal shift registers* at the left side and bottom of the CCD chip. After the picture/electrical information from the first line is scanned from left to right, the current is momentarily turned off by a **blanking pulse** and pulled back to the left side of the chip by the **horizontal synchronization pulse.** Then the information on the *third* horizontal line of pixels is scanned. Sequentially, the process is repeated as all of the *odd-numbered* lines on the CCD chip are scanned. It takes one-sixtieth of a second to scan all of the odd-numbered lines (1-3-5-7 . . . down to . . . 479). This top-to-bottom half picture is termed a **field.** Because only half of the lines have been scanned (picking up information from only half of the pixels on the chip), this field represents only half of the total video picture.

Now a **vertical synchronization pulse** repositions the vertical and horizontal shift registers to start the scanning process all over again. This time, the *even-numbered* lines on the CCD chip are scanned to produce another "half-picture" field. These two fields, first the odd then the even-numbered lines, added together comprise a total picture that is referred to as a **frame.** Thus, thirty of these full frames are produced every second. The basic pattern of this scanning process is similar to that of your eyes reading across a line of type on a page and then jumping back to the left side of the page and starting on the next lower line—525 lines per page, thirty pages per second!.

It is the transistor part of the pixel, with its ability to store and then quickly move small electronic signals, that allows the vertical and horizontal shift registers to gather the total signal of the multitude of pixels—thirty times per second. This generates the

Figure 6.6

The large scale integration device (LSID) chip (inset) with the Hitachi SK-2600 camera processes the digital signal. It is an example of miniaturization of components. Its 600,000 pixel CCD unit provides a very high 900 TV line resolution figure.
Photos courtesy of Hitachi

chrominance and luminance signals as well as the vertical and horizontal sync pulses that are so important to picture stability. All this electrical information is amplified and in other ways modulated within the camera to produce either the composite or component video signal. The resulting electrical message is the electronic signal that has just begun its long and complicated path.

Another important part of the recent improvement in camera technology has been that of miniaturization. The Hitachi digital SK-2600 camera, shown in figure 6.6, contains a *large-scale integration device* (LSID) that provides 13-bit digital processing of the signal (see inset). It replaces three to four analog component boards needed for older cameras.

The Receiver Picture Tube

Just as the radio speaker resembles the microphone, the TV set's picture tube mirrors the older technology of the camera pickup tube. By extension of the same analogy, it can be said that the display tubes of the future will probably relate more and more to the CCD and LED (light-emitting diode) technologies.

As the camera picks up the picture—and during the subsequent channeling, mixing, shaping, amplifying, and monitoring—the signal remains in a "pure" line *video* format. Switchers, studio monitors, recorders, and editors all process this line level signal. For the picture to be transmitted, however, the audio signal must be added, and then the video and audio information must be converted to a **radio frequency (RF)** signal. It is this RF signal that can then be modulated onto a **carrier wave** that can be broadcast on a radio frequency in the **electromagnetic spectrum.**

The first task of the home TV set is to strip off the audio signal. Next, it **demodulates** the picture information. Then the red, green, and blue guns in the receiver tube each shoot out a stream of electrons. This electron beam, like the scanning beam in the older camera pickup tubes, is controlled by a ring of magnets that deflects and controls the beam to reproduce the left-to-right and top-to-bottom scanning pattern in the camera.

In most TV sets, the electron beams pass through a **masking plate** that focuses the electrons as they strike the designated phosphor pixels on the inside glass of the picture tube. This inner coating can be either in the form of triad groups of red, green, and blue dots or in the form of tiny vertical phosphorescent strips of the same colors.

It is the control information on the synchronizing pulse (including the horizontal and vertical blanking intervals) that guarantees a synchronized scanning rate of sixty fields (thirty frames) per second. This control over the electron beams in the TV receiver tube reproduces the video picture essentially as it was originally picked up by the camera tube.

Like the image picked up by the camera, the picture displayed on the receiver screen never actually exists as a single completed frame. The TV frame does not have a discrete existence the way a frame of motion picture film does. What we have is the linear tracing of a point of light moving at an incredible rate of speed. At any given microsecond, one "half-picture" field is always at some stage of the continual scanning process.

Because of the phenomenon of **persistence of vision** ("visual lag"), the brain perceives this incredibly rapid series of light flashes as a moving picture. The human eye retains images for a split second after the image has been removed. If about fifteen or more separate images per second are flashed before the eye, human perception will cause them to blend together, thus creating the illusion of motion. This persistence of vision is what makes simulated moving pictures possible—on celluloid film as well as on the face of a television tube.

Lens Characteristics

Working in conjunction with the CCD image sensor, possibly the most crucial element in the whole pictorial process is the lens. Very little can be done if an improperly focused picture is presented to the beam splitter (or directly onto the CCD chip in single chip cameras). A good lens can help the cheapest camera, but an inferior lens can turn the best professional camera into blurred trash.

Within five years of its introduction in the late 1950s, the **zoom lens** became standard equipment on virtually all studio television cameras. For most video production, this will likely remain true in the future. Indeed, most television production students will prob-

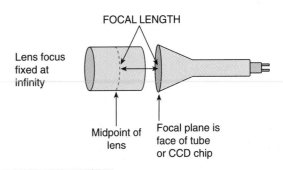

Figure 6.7

The focal length of a lens is measured from the center of the lens to the point where the subject image is in focus on the surface of a CCD chip, a frame of film, or a video tube as shown in the illustration.

ably never see a **fixed-focal-length lens** on a television camera. The zoom lens by virtue of its numerous lens elements can quickly become any one of a wide range of focal length lens types. This very technology prohibits it from being quite as optically perfect as a fixed-focal-length lens designed for one specified magnification. As a result, some feel that high definition television,[4] with its potential for much clearer pictures, may set the stage for a return to fixed-length lenses for single-camera-film-style shoots.

Most factors that characterize the zoom lens are based upon the optical principles underlying the traditional fixed-focal-length lens. Such characteristics as **focal length, focus, f-stop,** and **depth of field** are simpler to understand if the example of a nonzoom, fixed-focal-length lens is used. It is much easier to comprehend the concept of **long lens** compression of a picture or how a **short lens** (wide angle) gives a greater depth of field, if one visualizes the actual length and angle of the lens. We will, therefore, use these lenses as a reference point and return to the zoom for further consideration in section 6.4.

Focal Length

The *focal length* of a lens is measured from the optical center point of the lens (when it is focused at infinity) to a point where the image is in focus. This **focal plane** can be the film in a movie or still camera, a single CCD camera chip, or the face of the pickup tube in an electronic camera, as shown in figure 6.7. Focal length is measured in either millimeters or inches (25.4 millimeters being equal to 1 inch).

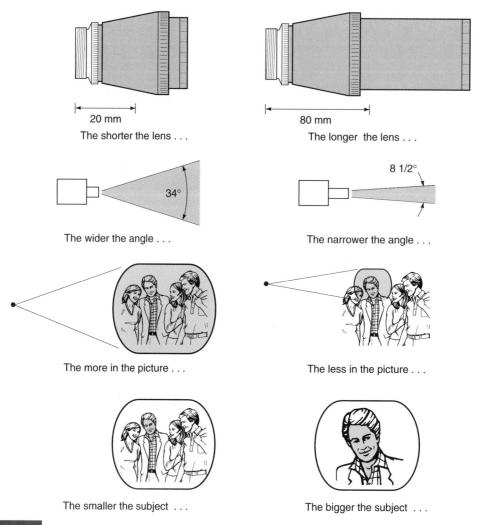

20 mm
The shorter the lens . . .

80 mm
The longer the lens . . .

34°
The wider the angle . . .

8 1/2°
The narrower the angle . . .

The more in the picture . . .

The less in the picture . . .

The smaller the subject . . .

The bigger the subject . . .

Figure 6.8

The relationship between focal length of a lens and the horizontal angle of view through that lens.

Lenses of differing lengths are used primarily so that differing amounts of a scene can be included in the picture when shot from the same position. *The longer a lens is, the narrower its viewing angle will be, the less you will be able to fit into the picture,* and therefore, *the more magnified individual subjects will be.* Conversely, a short focal-length lens will give you a wider viewing angle, thereby allowing you to fit more into the picture, but individual subjects will appear smaller than normal. This *law of lenses* is illustrated in figure 6.8. Long lenses, therefore, can be used to obtain closer views of objects. A long **telephoto lens** can get a relatively close-up view of an object from a great distance. On the other hand, a **short lens** (wide

angle) will tend to increase distance and make things look farther away than they are. This fact can lead to distance distortion.

A long lens (or a long-lens setting on a zoom lens) will *compress* distance. Two objects that are far apart from each other and at a great distance from the camera will be brought closer to the camera with a long lens and, consequently, will seemingly be brought closer to each other. A common example is the baseball shot of the pitcher and batter as seen with an exceptionally long telephoto lens from center field. Although the pitcher and batter are about 60 feet apart, the camera is perhaps 400 feet away. Thus, the two players are brought much closer to the camera,

Figure 6.9

In the picture on the left, the zoomed-in lens approximates a 54mm high magnification fixed-focal-length lens. Note the optical compression even though the children are 9 feet apart. The picture on the right approximates a 9mm lens. The children are still 9 feet apart, but the effect of the wide-angle lens shows the actual separation. To approximate the girl's position in the earlier picture, the camera was moved much closer to her.

Lens Length	Viewpoint
10 mm	Extreme wide angle
25 mm	Wide angle
40 mm	Normal
100mm	Narrow angle
200 mm	Extreme narrow angle (telephoto)

Figure 6.10

Sample measurements of fixed-focal-length lenses.
Traditional studio lenses were in the 40mm to 100mm range. For reference, remember that 25.4 millimeters is equal to 1 inch.

and consequently, the distance between them is apparently compressed. On the home screen, they may look as if they are only 10 or 15 feet apart.

As seen in figure 6.9, the zoomed-in setting produces the illusion of distance reduction. In both shots, the young man was standing 9 feet behind his sister. The picture on the right was shot at the zoomed-out position after the camera had been moved closer to the girl to keep her at the same position in the frame. The 6-to-1 zoom used was listed in the camera "spec" as being the equivalent of a 9mm lens in the zoomed-out position.

Figure 6.10 lists the horizontal viewing angles of lenses that were used on the last studio fixed-length cameras several decades ago. This chart, along with a review of figure 6.8, should provide some idea of how different degrees of magnification affect the picture. Now, look at two additional variables that interact to have an even more significant influence upon picture quality.

The F-stop Aperture

As mentioned in the discussion of contrast ranges in chapter 5, the television camera has a relatively narrow range of light tolerance as compared to the human eye. At the front of all camera lenses is an adjustable **iris** that opens or closes the **aperture** by moving a **diaphragm** in and out. This opening is necessary so that the amount of light coming into the camera can be kept within acceptable limits. It does not affect the size of the picture the lens will pick up.

With zoom lenses, the iris can usually be operated with manual or automatic control. Students must understand the following principles in order to comprehend how manual operation of the f-stop can affect the picture quality. As will be explained, many production situations exist where the camera operator will want to override the **automatic iris control** and adjust the iris manually for a variety of creative reasons.

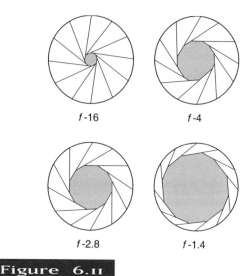

Figure 6.11

Diagrams of various f-stop openings. The basic rule to remember with iris changes is the higher the f-stop number, the smaller the opening. Each marked position on the lens represents one full f-stop, and each time the stop is changed one position, the light going into the camera is doubled or cut in half.

The various sizes of aperture openings are identified by different f-stop numbers. The first rule to remember in working with f-stops is very simple, once you get it straight. *The lower the f-stop number, the larger the lens opening,* and *the higher the f-stop number, the smaller the lens opening* (see figure 6.11). For instance, f-22 is typically the smallest aperture found on most television lenses. The widest opening could be f-2.8, depending upon the structure of the lens. In between, the numbers would range through 4, 5.6, 8, 11, and 16. The change from one stop to another represents a doubling or the cutting in half of the amount of light being allowed to come into the camera. It is a precise measurement, hence the need for some decimal figures.

The most obvious application of the f-stop is to enable camera operators to adjust to varying light sources. If working under very poor lighting conditions with no option for increasing the amount of light, it might be advisable to open up to f-4. On the other hand, if working under extremely bright conditions (perhaps outdoors on a sunny day), you might want to "stop down" to f-11 or f-16. The *stop down* term that actually means *closing up* the iris to a *higher*

number may take a little "getting used to," but it's the accepted phrase.

One word of warning about f-stop adjustments should be stated at this point. Generally speaking, the camera operator should not routinely think of the f-stop as a means of compensating for bad lighting. The f-stops, together with the various electronic camera controls, are often established for a given lighting situation by a trained studio technician and should only be changed after consultation. Bad lighting or uneven lighting should be handled by correcting the lighting, not by tampering with the camera adjustments. Increasingly, cameras in educational institutions are being set up with all cameras in the **automatic iris control** setting. Again this setting should only be changed with the knowledge of some responsible engineer, because all other camera controls have been coordinated with this setting. Overriding the automatic iris control may be a desirable creative effect, but the changeover should be tested and planned in advance.

Depth of Field

The final factor in consideration of camera focus has to do with determining the location of an area of consistently good focus within any picture. This so-called *depth of field* refers to *the distance between the nearest point at which objects are in focus, and the farthest point at which objects are in focus.* In a typical shot, objects close to the camera will be out of focus and objects too far away may be out of focus. Making sure that we can predict the location of this middle ground, where objects are in focus, is important in the production planning process.

Three different factors interrelate to determine the depth of field: *the f-stop* (the smaller the lens opening—only possible with adequate light—the greater the depth of field); *the distance from the subject to the camera* (the greater the camera-to-subject distance, the greater the depth of field); and *the focal length of the lens* (the shorter the lens, the greater the depth of field). Figure 6.12 illustrates these three variables in terms of fixed-focal-length lenses. While the same basic rules apply for zoom lenses, there is less flexibility.

The best way to increase the depth of field in a studio shot is simply to add considerable light and to

The depth of field of a lens can be increased by altering any one of three different variables:

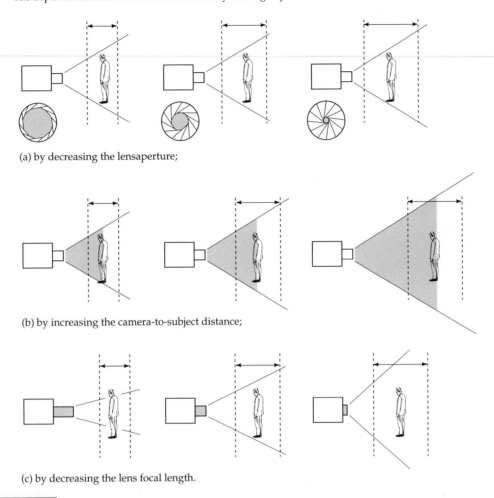

(a) by decreasing the lensaperture;

(b) by increasing the camera-to-subject distance;

(c) by decreasing the lens focal length.

Figure 6.12

Depth of field. The depth of field of a lens can be increased by altering any one of three different variables: (a) by decreasing the lens aperture, (b) by increasing the camera-to-subject distance, (c) by decreasing the lens focal length.

stop down the lens. This allows the shot to remain the same, which would not be the case if attempts were made to change the focal length with a zoom movement or to change the camera-to-subject distance. However, in some situations the desired effect is that of *decreasing* the depth of field, where backgrounds are deliberately out of focus. This is easier in a studio situation than on an outdoor location, where sunlight is hard to control.

Occasionally, for dramatic effect, the director may want the camera operator to **pull focus** to shift a shallow depth of field from a foreground object to the background, or vice versa. This also can be accomplished with a wide-open aperture. For example, the

director may want to open on a tight close-up shot of a half-empty glass close to the camera with the background out-of-focus; the camera operator could then change the focus (without otherwise altering the shot at all) to focus on the figure lying on the sofa, while the foreground glass goes blurry.

Production Use of the Zoom

The development of the *zoom* lens has allowed camera operators and directors to achieve rapid and continuous adjustment of the focal length of the lens and,

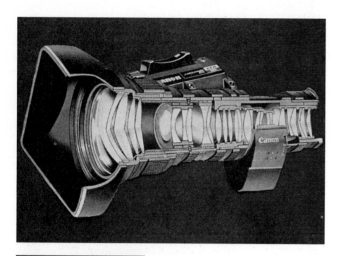

Figure 6.13

Cutaway illustration of movable lenses and gears in a 14-to-1 ratio zoom lens. *Photo courtesy of Canon*

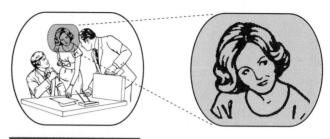

Figure 6.14

Range of a zoom lens. These two views represent the extreme focal lengths of a 10-to-1 zoom lens: *left*, zoomed "out" to the shortest focal length (widest angle); *right*, zoomed "in" to the longest focal length (narrowest angle).

consequently, to control precisely the size and framing of shots. It has greatly changed the way directors approached visual continuity. In addition to giving the director and camera operator a wider range of lens lengths that are immediately available, the zoom lens also facilitates very smooth on-the-air movement. Its imaginative use was the foundation on which the incredibly successful era of network sports coverage starting in the 1970s was built.

An optical as well as mechanical marvel, the variable-focal-length zoom lens is essentially an arrangement of gears and optical elements that allows the operator to shift these lens elements—moving them back-and-forth in relation to each other. (See figure 6.13.) This achieves varying focal lengths by changing the theoretical center point of the lens. Zoom lenses will vary greatly with price and manufacturer. Those lenses designed for professional and industrial levels all share some of the same basic characteristics.

Lens Ratio

For most production situations, a 10-to-1 magnification ratio is common. On a typical lens this would result in focal lengths possibly ranging from 10.5mm at the wide-angle position to 105mm at the *zoomed-in*

high-magnification or "long-lens" position. Figure 6.14 provides some indication of the range of shots available with a 10-to-1 **zoom ratio** lens. Consumer camcorders are often equipped with a 6-to-1 zoom lens with a still very adequate 9mm to 54mm range. For sporting events and other outdoor public events production, professional cameras with zoom ratios of 30-to-1 and greater are not uncommon. The Canon J55X 9B IE "Super" field zoom lens (see figure 6.15) can change its effective focal length from 9mm to 500mm and, with the use of an **extender,** can double those figures from 18mm to 1,000mm. Weighing 37 pounds, it is almost 22 inches long, roughly 10 inches high and 10 inches wide. It is a common lens for platform cameras at large sporting events.

Movement Control

Virtually all zoom lenses will have a motor-driven zoom mechanism. Less expensive models may have only one or two speeds. This does not give much artistic control over the effect to be achieved. Therefore, professional lenses will usually have *variable-speed* controls. Generally, professional zoom lenses will also provide an optional manual zoom control lever for those times when only the human touch will suffice. It should be noted, however, that serious damage will result if the manual lever is engaged while the power zoom control is in operation.

It is this ability to obtain smooth, on-the-air zoom movement that gives the director production flexibil-

Figure 6.15

Canon J55X 9B IE "SUPER" field zoom lens. This 55-to-1 zoom lens is one of the largest field production zoom lenses in professional use today. When it is zoomed in, its picture is fifty-five times larger than when it is zoomed out. It is almost 22 inches long, roughly 10 inches high, and 10 inches wide, and is used extensively for sporting events and similar large area outdoor work.   *Photo courtesy of Canon*

ity when using zoom lenses. It is possible to *tighten up* a shot, going smoothly from a **wide shot** to a **medium shot** to a **close-up** at variable speeds. The best zoom work usually goes unnoticed, because it does not call attention to itself. The movement of a zoom produces a visual effect that is similar to what was seen through a fixed-focal-length lens when the camera was moved toward a subject during a shot. As mentioned previously, however, the lens characteristics produce very different relationships of subjects in the picture. These differences are discussed in chapter 7, section 7.1.

Focus

On all zoom lenses, the focus control is the slip ring located farthest toward the front of the lens (see figure 6.16). This ring is usually adjusted by remote control when cameras are set up for studio use. Staying in focus can be a problem with zoom lenses. As cameras are moved to different positions on the studio floor, there is

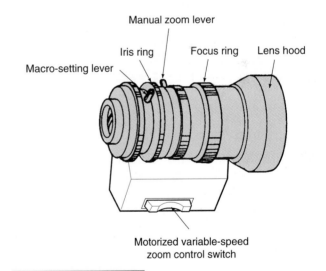

Figure 6.16

Portable camera zoom lens. In addition to the motorized variable-speed zoom control switch, adjustments on the lens include the macro lens setting, the iris (f-stop) setting, the manual zoom lever, and the focus ring.

a constantly changing distance relationship between the camera and the various subjects. Each change necessitates checking to be sure that the lens is set for a "zoomed-in" close-up shot—before it is needed. If it is not set, the operator coming from an in-focus wide shot may zoom into an out-of-focus close-up.

To preset a focus, zoom in all the way to the tightest shot possible and then adjust the focus. This is called **front focus.** Next, zoom back slowly and check to make sure the subject is in focus throughout the entire length of the zoom. In most cases it will remain focused, unless the close shot being attempted is too near to the camera. If this is the case, repositioning and repeating the procedure should solve the problem. The other alternative is simply to remember when to stop the zoom out.

Macro Lens

This special adjustment has become a standard focusing feature of most newer zoom lens units (see figure 6.16). In the **macro** position, one can take extreme close-ups of printed material or small objects at distances of 2 inches or less from the lens. The procedure will vary with individual equipment, but the rather sensitive process of such delicate focusing is usually handled by adjusting the manual zoom lever and not the focus ring.

6.5

Picture Quality Controls

Teaching institutions that have professional or industrial-level cameras possess sophisticated equipment having a number of controls that make high-quality pictures possible. Misuse of those controls can greatly diminish picture quality and even cause permanent damage. Each class should establish a definite policy as to which controls on the camera (or CCU) are for student adjustment and which are to be handled only by the instructor or trained staff personnel.

Those controls relating to zoom operation described earlier would normally fall within the realm of student control. Such controls should be checked for correct settings as part of camera setup. On the camera itself, however, there are several controls that may need to be designated for use by students at a later time in the class term as a part of the planned curriculum.

Color Temperature Conversion Filters

Professional cameras designed for both studio and field use usually have some sort of a built-in **filter** system to compensate for Kelvin temperature differences between indoor and outdoor lighting. Usually located in front of the beam splitter, this filter component is an integral part of the camera system. Many industrial and educational cameras have a rotating disc of four filters for different lighting conditions: (1) iodine lamp and sunrise and sunset; (2) bright outdoor; (3) cloudy or rainy; and (4) white fluorescent. It is interesting that sunrise and sunset have a color temperature that is very similar to artificial quartz-iodine light. This has to do with the angle of the light rays and the filtering effect of the atmosphere at those times of day.

Most professional cameras have what are known as **neutral density** filters that are designed to limit brightness, but do not adjust color. The ND #1 allows one-half the light to pass through. An ND #2 and ND #3 allow one-quarter and one-eighth, respectively. Other filters are used to create a fuzzy effect or the often-used star effect, which radiates from bright spots on the screen.

White Balance

Possibly the most important control on the camera is the one that establishes the correct color balance by using a pure white reference card. In a studio situation where all illumination is produced by lights having a consistent 3,200 degrees Kelvin temperature, it is possible to do most production work with the **white balance** switch at the factory established *preset* position. If, however, a camera is to be used for field production, where Kelvin temperatures are constantly changing, the white balance procedure must be understood and used at every change in lighting condition.

The alternate white balance switch position on most cameras is labeled *auto*, which simply means that the camera will automatically accomplish the necessary adjustment process. In this mode, with a white card filling the lens image, the camera color system senses any excess of either red or blue light and, within a few seconds, adjusts accordingly. The white card serves as a neutral reference point so that the camera can judge the balance between red and blue coming from the light source. To get the proper adjustment for flesh tones, the white card must be placed exactly where the subject's face will be for the shot. In field work, where a change in the camera-to-subject angle may introduce a new light source, a new balance adjustment may be necessary. Also, when shooting on location, lighting conditions will change throughout the day (the sun changes color when it descends; cloud covers vary) and occasional white balance adjustments will be necessary.

Video Output Level Selector

Many cameras have an **automatic gain control (AGC)** that automatically adjusts video levels to compensate for differing light conditions. Other cameras have a **video output control** that allows the operator to adjust to some degree for low light levels. The "0 dB" position is established by the manufacturer as the standard level of video output for the camera under prescribed lighting conditions. The video output control increases the decibels so that the camera can function at lower light levels than at the 0 dB position. The term **decibel (dB)** has been borrowed and slightly altered from its audio derivation; however, as with audio, each 6-dB increase means that the amplified signal is doubled. This control should never be thought of as a way to make a poorly lit picture better. All it can do is make the poor picture look a little brighter.

Viewfinder Visual Indicators and Controls

On some cameras the **tally lights** that tell both the operator and the talent/subject that the camera is feeding the switcher will also light up to indicate that the white balance adjustment in the camera has been completed. On those cameras designed for field use, several **warning lights** may indicate *low battery power, insufficient lighting,* or an *abnormally high setting of the gain control knob,* which causes excessive battery drain.

It should also be noted that the *brightness* and *contrast* controls are only for the viewfinder adjustment; *they do not have any effect on the video output of the camera.* Operators who are unaware of this basic fact can be a menace to any proper camera setup procedure. Such uninformed operators may take one look at their incorrectly adjusted viewfinder picture and assume that the camera settings are wrong and need adjustment. Then they proceed to mess up a perfectly good camera output by changing the f-stop, filter setting, and gain controls. The viewfinder controls—like the camera controls themselves—should be adjusted only while the operator is in headset contact with the person (usually the instructor or technical director) who is in charge of camera setup in the video control center.

Iris

As covered in section 6.3, the iris (f-stop) position has an important relationship to picture focus. If incorrectly set, it can greatly affect the quality of color in the picture. In a studio situation, where light values are fairly constant, settings will stay within a narrow range. Operating instructions for each camera will usually provide optimum **lux**[5] or **footcandle** levels as related to an f-stop setting. For example, on many lenses an f-4 setting would be proper for a 200 footcandle reading. Many cameras have an automatic iris control that reacts to incoming light and continually adjusts the f-stop as light values change. Some manufacturers provide a *temporary automatic* feature that allows the lens to hold any f-stop position set by the automatic sensor.

Other Controls

Some cameras have several additional control units that, while not necessarily complicated, are best suited to an individualized-study approach. Such items as the **fade time control,** the **negative/positive selector,** and the **phase control** selector all have clearly marked "0" or neutral positions. The beginning student should be made aware of these *off* positions and make sure that such controls are in the safe neutral position for normal camera operations.

Modern video cameras have incorporated numerous other internal monitoring systems, feedback

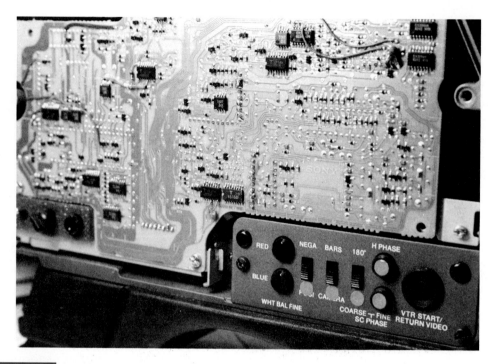

Figure 6.17

This view of one of the circuit boards of an older analog camera gives some insight into the sort of care that is imperative in its use.

circuits, and computer-based controls. Figure 6.17 shows the electronic complexity of some of the inner workings of a small studio. An awareness of the fragile nature of these circuit boards should help the novice camera operator appreciate the need to treat these instruments with care.

Summary

As with audio and lighting considerations, an examination of the technical side of the camera operation capabilities reveals that much must be considered before the production uses of the instrument can be seriously considered. The sections in the chapter dealing with the camera image-sensing devices (*CCD chip* or *pickup tube*), the *receiver picture tube,* the lens characteristics, and the *zoom lens* are concerned largely with technical matters.

The *video signal flow* can be seen as parallel to the audio signal flow. The same functions apply to both audio and video control: *transducing, channeling, mixing, amplifying, shaping, recording* (and playback), and *monitoring.* Additional sophisticated *control compo-*nents are added to the video system—*sync generator, proc amp, time-base corrector, frame synchronizer, color bar generator, waveform monitor,* and *vectorscope.*

The color video system is concerned with accurately rendering three color components—*hue, saturation,* and *brightness.* The transducing function is identified largely with the *CCD* chip. Concepts important to the formation of the video signal are *composite* video, *component* video, *analog* processing, *digital* processing, and *scanning.*

The three-chip color camera splits the incoming light into the three *primary colors* of red, green, and blue—each one being channeled to its own image sensor creating both a *luminance* and *chrominance* signal. The receiver picture tube, which can be thought of as a mirrored version of the old camera pickup tube, also has clear similarities to the newer CCD technology in that it is driven by the same *synchronization pulse* that keeps the production-distribution-reception system locked together.

Mechanical and optical considerations of the *fixed-focal-length lens* include *focal length, focusing characteristics, f-stop lens aperture,* and *depth of field.* While the *zoom lens* has several advantages pertaining to flexibility in selecting focal length and facilitating smooth movement, it also has a few drawbacks relating to focusing characteristics. Operating considerations of the zoom lens include *lens ratio, movement control, focusing, macro-lens setting,* and *iris control.*

Several other camera controls that students should be familiar with, although they would not necessarily be authorized to make such adjustments without explicit approval and supervision, are: *color temperature filters, white balance, video output level,* and *viewfinder picture adjustments,* among others.

Footnotes

1. In 1941, the FCC adopted the NTSC television system with the 525-line, 30-frame format described in this chapter. It presently remains in use in much of North and South America. Two other systems, PAL and SECAM, are used in other parts of the world.

2. As indicated in Appendix A, red, the lowest visible color in the electromagnetic spectrum, has a wavelength of 6,500 angstroms (each angstrom is one ten-millionth of a millimeter). Violet is the shortest wavelength we can see, with a wavelength as short as 4,000 angstroms.

3. In the tube-type camera, the light image falling on the face of the pickup tube charges individual pixels on a "target" located at the front of the tube. The electrical charge on these pixels is then "read" by a beam of electrons that are being shot from an electron gun at the rear of the tube. This beam is pulled side-to-side and up-and-down the face of the tube by magnets. As the beam scans back-and-forth across the pickup tube, it creates the electrical current that becomes the video signal.

4. Over the past decade and one half, numerous conferences were held in an attempt to agree on an international standard for the new high definition picture. At this writing, there seemed to be only a few items that were holding up final agreement.

5. The "lux" measurement is based upon an amount of candlelight falling upon an object from the distance of 1 meter. While not completely accurate, footcandle readings are often multiplied by ten to get a rough lux measurement (e.g., 40 fc = 400 lux).

chapter 7

Camera Function and Operation

I n the previous chapter, we examined many of the technical aspects of the creation of the video picture by the camera. In this chapter, we will study various ways through which the electronic potential of the camera can be shaped and controlled by the operator to achieve the creative purposes of the director.

7.1

Operational Control of the Camera

Efficient use of the camera depends upon several primary factors that interact with one another during any studio production sequence. The first of these is simply the *position* of the camera in its relationship to a subject (or multiple subjects in wide-angle shots). The camera reveals the front, side, or top of the elements in the picture according to where it is placed. A second factor involves changing the *direction* in which the camera is aimed to reveal different subjects.

There can also be a continuing change in the *point of view* of the camera as it is moved to reveal different aspects of a subject or sequence of subjects. This movement can also involve changes in the *elevation* of the camera, especially for artistic effect. The effectiveness of these operations is very dependent upon the hardware that provides movement and support for the camera.

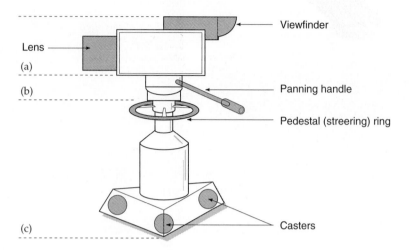

Lens

(a)

(b)

Viewfinder

Panning handle

Pedestal (streering) ring

(c)

Casters

Figure 7.1

Three basic parts of the camera. (a) The video components of the **camera** itself including the lens, viewfinder, and tube or CCD; (b) the **mounting head** with the panning handle that controls camera movement; and (c) the **camera mount** that is the transport and support mechanism for the entire unit.

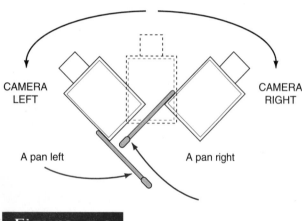

CAMERA
LEFT

CAMERA
RIGHT

A pan left

A pan right

Figure 7.2

Camera panning. To pan the camera in a given direction, the panning handle must be moved in the opposite direction. Thus, in order to execute a "pan left," the camera operator has to move the panning handle to the right.

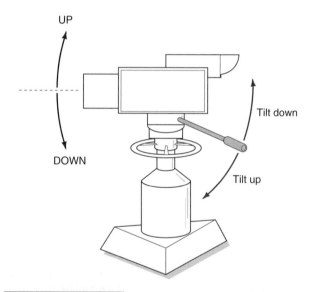

UP

DOWN

Tilt down

Tilt up

Figure 7.3

Camera tilting. In tilting the camera up or down, the camera head is pivoted through the use of the pan handle. Several different cam and cradle mechanisms can be used for this assembly.

Camera Head Movement

Figure 7.1 shows the basic parts of a studio camera unit, including: (a) the video components of the **camera** itself; (b) the mounting **head** containing the equipment used for movement of the camera; and (c) the **camera mount** that controls floor movement of the entire unit.

Shot changes involving vertical and horizontal camera movement are fundamental to video produc-

tion. When these kinds of movements are continuous "on the air" moves, they require a skilled operator and a suitable mounting head with which to execute them. A horizontal movement to the left or to the right is known as a **pan.** (See figure 7.2.) When told to "pan right," the operator moves the camera lens in the

Figure 7.4

Camera mounted on a cam head assembly with an adjustable tripod.   *Photo courtesy of Panasonic*

direction of his or her right hand. This is the reverse of stage movements that are given from the standpoint of the performer looking out toward an audience.

Up-and-down movements of the camera are called **tilts.** The lens end of the camera is moved up or down to view elements at different elevations of the set. (See figure 7.3.) Both movements are accomplished by exerting pressure on the **pan handle** that projects from the right rear of the camera. Zoom and focus controls are usually located on this pan handle. In the mounting head area, there is a coupling device such as a **cam** or **cradle** assembly that is important to a smoothness of motion, especially in a tilting action. (See figure 7.4.)

Camera Mounts

Any change of camera position, whether done as a continuing movement or simply for the purposes of changing the framing of a shot, is accomplished through some movement of the camera mount. Of the four types of camera and lens movements mentioned in this chapter's introductory paragraph, the last two—camera elevation and camera position— are both dependent upon the camera mount. The simplest and least expensive camera mount is the **tripod.** This three-legged stand is usually fastened to a dolly base consisting of three casters. The casters can either rotate freely, which facilitates quick and easy

Panasonic's new digital studio camera operates with the support of the compressed air pedestal mount. The ring is used to turn the wheels for changes of direction.
Photo courtesy of Panasonic

Figure 7.6

A large truck-mounted crane used for Olympic coverage. Such equipment is now commonplace for any large-scale outdoor concert, parade, or sporting event. *Photo courtesy of ABC Sports*

The **pedestal** mount shown supporting the new digital Panasonic AQ 225 (figure 7.5) has been the standard for studio production since the beginning of television. Its design helped camera operators move smoothly from point to point on the studio floor at a time when there were no zoom lenses. Its distinctive feature is the central pedestal that can be raised or lowered by an assist of counterweights or air pressure. It also has a steering ring that controls all three casters in a synchronized manner so that smooth, on-the-air camera movements across the studio floor can be achieved. This ease and steadiness in camera movement have made the studio pedestal a "must" in any big studio production.

When more pronounced changes of position and elevation are called for, they are accomplished through the use of mounts, such as the motorized **crane** mount (shown in figure 7.6), as a part of an Olympics telecast, and the **crab dolly** (shown in chapter 1, figure 1.13). With the crane, considerable differences in camera position are possible, because there is a separate driver for the motorized base. Inherited from the film industry, the *crane* is the largest and most flexible type of camera mount and comes in a variety of sizes. The camera itself is mounted on a boom arm that can be moved vertically

movement of the camera in all directions, or can be locked into a nonmovable position, resulting in a steady camera unit for straight-line movement.

The field model tripod, illustrated in figure 7.4, has a crank-operated elevation adjustment that can be used to raise and lower the camera—although not smoothly enough to be used on the air. Many tripods have no adjustment for height other than the laborious process of mechanically adjusting the spread of the tripod legs. Thus, there is no way to achieve any elevation change during an actual production. The tripod, however, is lightweight, and most models are readily collapsible. This makes the tripod a desirable camera mount for most remote productions.

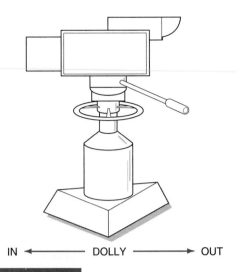

IN ◀—— DOLLY ——▶ OUT

Figure 7.7

Camera dollying. In a dolly movement, the camera is simply moved closer to or farther from the subject.

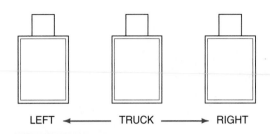

LEFT ◀—— TRUCK ——▶ RIGHT

Figure 7.8

Camera trucking. In a trucking movement, the camera and mount are moved laterally without any adjustment of the camera mounting head.

or laterally without moving the crane base. Depending upon the model, the length of the arm extension is 10 to 15 feet for studio models and much more for a few special field units. For everything from rock concerts to Olympic coverage, the moving crane shot has become an indispensable part of the visual language of television.

The *crab dolly*, named for the ability of the base to move quickly in any direction, is usually used in a studio, but it can be adapted for outdoor use and mounted on tracks for smooth travel movement. Another holdover from the film studios, it allows the camera to be moved from floor level to over 6 feet high. Newer models usually have power units for both movement and elevation.

Camera Mount Movements

Any discussion of camera moves must begin with the understanding that the basic terms denote movement that takes place *while the camera is providing the selected picture feed*. A director does not usually use these terms to tell the operator how to get into position. With some exceptions, the commands of preparation are usually a description of the shot or moves that will be needed on the program. One of the most obvious changes in picture framing is accomplished by

moving the camera closer to or farther away from the subject. This is referred to as **dollying** the camera, and it produces a **dolly** shot. (See figure 7.7.) While the zoom lens may have reduced the use of *dolly-in* and *dolly-out shots*, this move still has its uses. As pointed out in figure 6.9, there is a definite difference in the way the zoom lens in a wide-angle mode sees two subjects separated by 10 feet or so, and the way those two subjects are seen with the lens in the high magnification mode. Directors should experiment with the variables of lens **focal length** and **camera-to-source distance.** One interesting move is to dolly in on a very wide shot and then continue the move toward the subject with the zoom for maximum effect.

Lateral movement of the camera and its mount is known as **trucking.** A change of picture is accomplished as the camera *trucks right* or *trucks left*, because the camera moves sideways without panning to the right or left. (See figure 7.8.) In the field, dollying and trucking movements normally cannot be attempted unless special tracks have been laid down to facilitate smooth, level movement. Usually, such movements are set up only for ambitious productions like high budget dramatic programs or major sporting events.

A **follow shot** can use both the trucking and dollying techniques. In it a camera moves with the subject and maintains a constant distance from it, while the background is seen to move past in a constantly changing panoramic sequence. An **arc** shot is another variation of a trucking movement. The camera circles

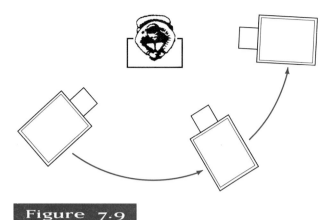

Figure 7.9

Camera arcing. This move is accomplished mainly by a maneuver of the camera mount as the camera arcs around, keeping the lens pointed at the subject. The move is much easier to make with a crab dolly than with a tripod or pedestal mount.

around the stationary subject to reveal different aspects of the subject. It is especially effective on facial features that have been well-sculpted by a **key light.** (See figure 7.9.) The crab dolly is recommended for this and the other moves listed above.

In larger studios where the crane mounts or crab dollies are used, other effective movements are also possible. **Craning,** or **booming** (up or down), involves raising or lowering the crane or boom arm. The effect is similar to a pedestal movement, except that much greater vertical distances can be covered. The **crab** shot is an improvement on a trucking shot because of the presence of a separate driver and four coordinated wheels that turn together; the angle of movement can be easily changed mid-course into a number of different directions.

One different kind of motion is the **arm move.** With a large crane, the boom arm or crane can be moved left, right, up, or down or any continuing combination of these, while the base remains stationary. With both the crane and the crab mounts, the camera operator retains control over the angle and tilt of the camera throughout all these moves.

An older move that is still used involves studio camera pedestals that were designed to facilitate a slight change in camera height. In this case, the word "pedestal" is used as a command verb as the camera operator is asked to *pedestal up* or *pedestal down.* (See

figure 7.10.) Because these pedestal moves are limited to less than 3 feet at best, this effect is usually reserved for the crab dolly that extends from floor level to a height of more than 6 feet on most models. It should be noted that all these movements are difficult to accomplish when a zoom lens is at a position of high magnification (narrow angle). The slightest unsteadiness during the camera movement is exaggerated, because the **long lens,** while magnifying the subject, is also magnifying the shaky camera movement. To a lesser extent, the same problem is apparent with panning and tilting movements.

Hand-held Cameras

For out-of-studio production work, increasing use is being made of hand-held cameras. The shoulder-supported professional units, as well as the consumer-oriented palm-sized camcorders, have popularized an informal and candid approach to production.

With amateurs, such hand-held camera work often results in poorly framed pictures, unsteady shots, and jerky camera movements (wobbly pans and shaky tilts) that may only be appropriate for small market news coverage and submission to *America's Funniest Home Videos.* When used by professionals, the hand-held camera is considered indispensable for "reality-based" television and is used for both symphony and rock concerts. It has long been recognized for its contribution to news, sports, and public affairs productions.

Sophisticated gyroscopically-balanced systems are often used to steady hand-held cameras for ambitious professional EFP programs or film shoots. These systems are just becoming available for smaller-scale and amateur productions.

Robotic Camera Control

As a result of the rising costs of video production, the use of remotely-controlled cameras in news, public affairs, and sports programs is on the rise. The cameras shown in figure 7.11 are part of a group of three that are operated from the studio floor by one individual who is on a headset with the director. Most of the moves and zoom changes have been programmed into a computer. Final control is with the operator.

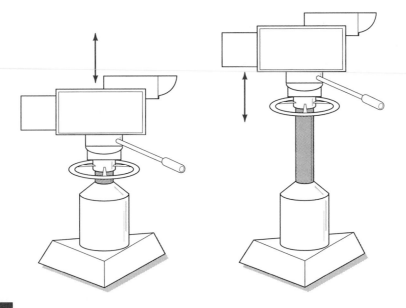

Figure 7.10

Camera pedestaling. In a pedestal movement, the entire camera and mounting head are moved straight up or down by a system of counterweights or compressed air.

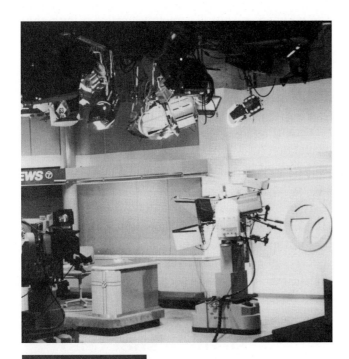

Figure 7.11

These Sony BVP 357 cameras are mounted on a robotics pedestal. They are part of a three unmanned camera system used in the production of the KABC-TV newscast. Three cameras are under the computerized remote control of an operator located in the studio.   *Photo courtesy of KABC-TV*

For example, a camera can be programmed to execute a shot involving a specific person, the location of the pedestal on the floor, and the framing of the zoom lens. "Joe, box shot left" describes the news anchor (to set pedestal position) and the framing of a shot that permits insertion of second video picture to left of the performer. A final one-touch control makes this all happen.

7.2

Camera Viewpoints

The video camera is used to place the viewer in one or more of three different psychological perspectives as a part of the visual program presentation. These methods are usually represented as the following viewpoints: *reportorial, objective* or *subjective.*

Reportorial (Presentational) Perspective

This viewpoint is used when a presenter or reporter is speaking directly to the audience through the camera. The speaker establishes eye contact with the camera and talks directly to the lens. This approach is most often seen in newscasts, corporate training programs, instructional TV lessons, some variety acts (for example, stand-up comedians), some political talks, demonstration programs, and so forth. Camera work in this situation usually calls for a relatively close shot of the speaker—unless he or she has something to display or demonstrate for the camera. Basically, the camera work is simply to give the viewer a reasonably comfortable look at the person speaking.

Objective Perspective

The easiest way to visualize this use of television is to imagine the camera as an eavesdropper. The camera is standing back, taking an objective look at what is going on. No one is addressing the camera directly; the camera is only observing the action. This type of camera work constitutes the bulk of what we see on television. It includes virtually all drama, most variety and musical performances, talk shows and game shows (except when the host or announcer is directly addressing the audience through the camera), sporting events, and similar productions.

Camera techniques vary tremendously for objective production. A wide variety of panoramic shots, quick reaction shots, leisure camera movements, and rapid camera transitions are required for various formats. Virtually all techniques discussed in the remaining chapters are applicable to objective camera work.

Subjective Perspective

This particular camera use takes on special meaning when applied to dramatic productions. It refers to those occasional moments when the playwright/director wants to place the viewer in the position of an actor. The camera actually becomes a participant in the drama. It interacts with other players, and it views the world from the individual perspective of the character it represents. The camera, as the actor's eyes, is in the front seat of the car for the chase sequence; it is in the boxing ring, squaring off against the champion; it is trapped in the burning building, flames licking at the lens. The subjective camera is a specialized technique. Used with care and discretion, it can have substantial impact.

These three perspectives are intermingled in many video productions. The newscast mixes reportorial and objective perspectives as the newscaster turns from the camera to interview an in-studio guest. Television drama mixes objective with subjective techniques, and a touch of the reportorial-presentational is used as an actor turns to make a comment directly to the audience.[1] The talk show jumps back-and-forth as the host and guests turn from their conversation with each other to talk directly to the viewer. When the camera operator is aware of these varying perspectives—and the production effects appropriate for each one—it is much easier to achieve good camera work.

7·3
Field of View

The camera operator should be familiar with the various terms designating the size of the shot desired, or the **field of view.** Generally most television shots can be related to three basic categories and one subtype. They are shown in figure 7.12.

The Wide Shot

The wide-angle shot is sometimes called a **long shot (LS)** in that its perspective is far enough away from a person that the entire body and quite a bit of the surroundings are included. Often, the facial features of a performer are not exactly distinguishable at this distance. By its production use, it is also known as an **establishing shot** when used in the beginning of a production (or segment), because it relates those people involved in a program not only to each other, but also to the setting and circumstances of that program. In drama and in other applications, these wider shots are also necessary whenever people move from one part of the set to another. It can be used as a closing shot to signal a pulling back from the action—out of the drama—as it comes to a close. The wide shot could thus be said to communicate an *objective* view of the scene or situation.

The Medium Shot (MS)

These shot designations are to some degree relative to their use and the artistic concepts of the director. What is a long shot for one dramatic segment could be considered a medium shot in another situation. For the most part, however, a medium shot of a person includes most of the body or perhaps even two peo-

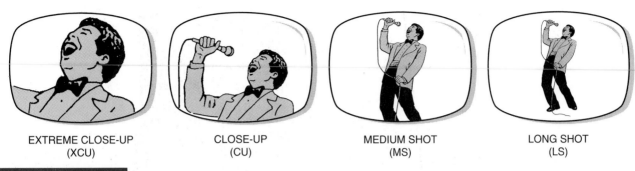

| EXTREME CLOSE-UP (XCU) | CLOSE-UP (CU) | MEDIUM SHOT (MS) | LONG SHOT (LS) |

Figure 7.12

Basic television shots. In addition to these basic shots, many other designations and modifications are possible, such as the "extreme long shot," the "medium long shot," and the "medium close-up."

ple. The **medium shot (MS)** is probably the basic shot in standard television production. It is used to convey much of the dialogue in drama and most of the action in talk shows, game shows, variety programs, and many other studio productions. Medium shots are designed to include gestures but not position moves. Depending upon their use, they could be either *objective* or *subjective* in what they communicate.

The Close-up (CU)

The close-up shot—with its sense of physical intimacy—can probe the individual and personal aspects of what a program is communicating. It is designed to be *subjective*. The eyes and facial expressions provide important insight into the full meaning of a person's words. In many dramatic situations (as well as in many reportorial-presentational circumstances), the close-up is the only way to get insight into the emotional state of a person or performer. A close-up shot may, of course, be used to view objects other than a person. It may be a close-up of some item that has importance to the narrative of a drama. In a commercial, it may be the product that is examined in more detail.

The close-up is usually defined as a shot consisting of the subject's head and top of shoulders. The **extreme close-up** (ECU or XCU) showing less than a person's full face (see figure 7.12) is most often used to intensify the emotion of a dramatic situation or musical performance. When these shots are used carefully, they can add the right artistic effect at the right moment.

Many programs obviously call for a wider range of shots, or fields of view, than these three categories.

Many times a director will want to establish a panoramic scene or cover the sweep of action with a very wide shot. If characters are so far away that they are hardly identifiable as specific individuals, the shot can be labeled an **extreme long shot** (**ELS** or **XLS**).

The process of alternating between the long shot and close-up segments of a program is possibly the most important element in the communicative language of both film and television. This basic principle was discovered by pioneers such as Edwin Porter and D.W. Griffith during the early days of the motion picture. They realized that by moving the camera into a closer position, they could accomplish what is automatically done by the eye and the mind. While the scope of human vision is almost 180 degrees, we immediately isolate and particularize the focus of our attention to a single person or object when the brain is motivated by a stimulus such as motion or sound. Cutting from a wide-angle to a close-up camera shot is much the same process, except that the distance factor is greatly reduced by lens magnification.

7.4

Picture Composition

Much has been written on the subject of picture composition and the related concepts that deal with the cumulative effect of a series of picture images. As in motion picture, the main concern of television is usually the human element. Sets, props, and graphic arts have an important auxiliary function, but it is people we watch—the movements of their bodies and the expressions on their faces. When one considers the

WRONG   WRONG   CORRECT

Figure 7.13

Correct headroom framing. Although it is largely a matter of subjective judgment and artistic "feel," it is important that the camera operator *always be aware* of the headroom on every shot. Too much headroom is as bad as too little.

viewer sitting at some distance from a 19-inch or 25-inch screen, the positioning of those faces and bodies assumes a critical importance.

As we discuss the following elements of framing, headroom, lead room, depth composition, angle of elevation, balance, and movement, keep in mind that the various "rules" that have evolved as part of the grammar of the medium should be considered *guidelines.* As with any artistic effort, there is always room for a new approach if it truly communicates to an audience. For the person who is just beginning to learn the disciplines of creative activity, the lessons passed on by more experienced people have much value. Once the rules have been mastered, they can be modified or even ignored as long as the creative person does so with a full understanding of the basic purposes of those guidelines.

Framing

Television directors (borrowing from the older traditions of their film cousins) have developed a simple terminology to describe the basic dimension of a shot to the camera operator. The scope of a shot is described in terms of that portion of the body that is to be cut off by the bottom edge of the picture. Thus a *full shot, thigh shot* or *chest shot* quickly communicates the desired framing of a person or persons in the picture.

Equally useful are the terms *single, two-shot,* or *three-shot*, which describe the number of people to be included in the shot. Other descriptive labels have evolved to specify certain kinds of desired shots. For example, an **over-the-shoulder shot (O/S)** might be called for in a situation when two people are facing

each other in a conversation (such as a dramatic scene or an interview program). This is a shot favoring one person (who generally is facing the camera) framed by the back of the head and shoulder of the person whose back is to the camera.

Headroom

An important discipline for all camera operators is to consistently maintain an adequate amount of **headroom.** This term refers to the space between the top of a subject's head and the top of the frame. When this distance is not observed, the results can be somewhat distracting. (See figure 7.13.)

It is especially important that headroom distance be uniform among all cameras on any production. A helpful guide for shot consistency is to place the eyes of subjects at the point of an imaginary line approximately one-third of the way down from the top of the picture. In close-up shots, the framing is best with the eyes slightly below the line; in wider shots, they should be slightly above the line. (See figure 7.14.)

There is a very good technical reason why headroom distance is carefully watched by camera operators and directors. Due to several factors, most home television sets lose up to 10 or 15 percent of the picture area at the outer edge. As a result, framing that would appear to be adequate on the studio monitor will actually result in a **cropping** of heads on the home receiver.

Lead Room

When speakers or performers directly address the camera (reportorial perspective), they generally are centered in the frame, unless a foreground object or

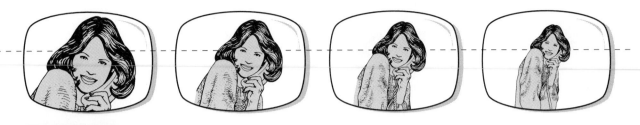

Figure 7.14

Correct headroom on different-sized shots. As a general rule—with many exceptions—the longer a shot is, the more headroom it should have.

BAD   BETTER   BEST

Figure 7.15

Proper lead room or "talk space." The camera operator should always intuitively give additional space in the direction that the talent is looking.

BAD   CORRECT

Figure 7.16

Proper lead room for a moving subject. Whenever a person is moving across the screen, the camera operator should visually anticipate the flow of movement allowing the viewer to see where the subject is going.

over-the-shoulder visual effect is to be included in the frame. When a subject in a close-up shot is speaking to another with head turned toward that person, the framing is much more attractive if there is an added amount of **lead room** (talk space) in the side of the frame to which the person has turned. (See figure 7.15.) By the same token, a distracting, crowded effect is created if the framing is such that the face of the subject is placed too close to the frame edge. The concept of lead room applies even more strongly to moving subjects. If a person is moving laterally across the screen, it is important to allow lead space in front of the person. Lead the talent; do not follow. (See figure 7.16.)

Depth Composition

The video message is transmitted by means of a 2D medium. To simulate some feeling of depth, the

Figure 7.17

Depth staging. The over-the-shoulder shot (*left*) generally presents a more dynamic, interesting, and aesthetically pleasing picture than the flat double-profile two-shot (*right*). By shooting the person behind the desk from an angle (*left*), a more inviting and vigorous effect can be achieved than with a formal head-on flat shot (*right*).

director has a number of options that involve lighting, camera work, the set, and the placement of performers. One method is to make sure that the performers are separated from the set in the background both by their physical positions and by the constructive use of lighting. In this situation, it is important to portray something familiar like the interior of a room or office to provide a feeling of scale or perspective. If a plain or abstract background is used, the viewer has no yardstick against which to gauge the distance from the subject to background.

Foreground objects can add significantly to the feeling of depth. By framing some nearby objects off to one side of the picture or along the bottom of the picture, the subject in the background is placed in greater relief. Care must be taken though not to force an unnatural effect for its own sake, as this will undoubtedly appear contrived to the viewer.

Whenever possible, depth composition can be achieved with the arrangement (**blocking**) of talent. If several people appear in a scene, try to arrange them so that some are closer to the camera than others. Nothing is deadlier than three or four people stretched out in a straight line, all equidistant from the camera. In a two-shot, an over-the-shoulder shot as a rule is preferred to a flat two-shot of a double profile. (See figure 7.17.)

A feeling of depth can also be achieved by careful use of angles. If a shot calls for someone to sit behind a desk, the camera can get a much more interesting shot by trucking right or left and shooting the desk and subject from an angle. (Of course, the dramatic context might call for a formal head-on shot of a character such as a judge or stern employer.)

Angle of Elevation

For most conventional composition, one wants the camera to shoot at an angle relatively level to the subject. Generally speaking, try to place the camera lens at eye level with the talent. This is fairly normal when the talent is standing. When seated, however, this means that you must pedestal down so the camera is as low as the talent. To achieve this level angle, most "talk sets" (news programs, interviews, discussion shows, talk shows) will be staged on a raised platform or **riser.** (See figure 7.18.)

If you cannot avoid shooting down into an interview or discussion set, the steep angle can be minimized somewhat by using a longer lens setting and dollying back away from the set. The farther back you can get, the less steep the angle will be. The "working newsroom" set between and behind the two "anchor" delivery sets shown in figure 7.18, is an example of how this would work.

There are times when, for dramatic effect, you will not want to be shooting the talent at a level angle. To portray an actor as being overwhelmed, submissive, or downtrodden, you will shoot the actor from a higher elevation. Shooting from a high angle implies control and dominance over the individual. On the other hand, if you want to give a character power and authority, you should shoot that actor from a low angle. By placing the viewer in the lowered position, you endow the character with force and strength.

Figure 7.18

This news set is staged on a platform to bring the newscasters up to camera-eye level. *Photo courtesy of KNBC, Los Angeles*

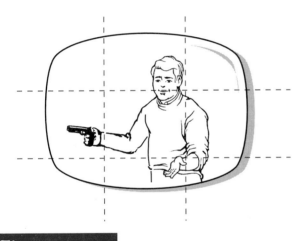

Figure 7.19

Asymmetrical balance and the rule of thirds. Note how the two main focal points—the face and the hand holding the gun—are located at the intersections of the thirds.

Balance

Many beginning camera operators try to achieve a pleasing composition by striving for **symmetrical balance.** They try to place the most important element directly in the center of the picture and/or try to balance picture components with equal elements equidistant from the center. This kind of mechanical or symmetrical balancing can lead to very stiff, dull, formal pictures.

A more dynamic kind of composition is **asymmetrical balance,** wherein a lightweight object some distance from the center of the picture can balance a heavier object closer to the center (similar to a seesaw with a light person at the end of the board balancing a heavier person seated close to the center).

Another way to avoid centralization of picture elements is to think in terms of the **rule of thirds.** Imagine the television screen divided horizontally and vertically into thirds. If major pictorial elements are placed at the points where the lines intersect, the result is a more pleasing balance than if perfect symmetry is achieved. (See figure 7.19.)

Movement of the Camera Position while the Shot Is Being Used

A final consideration of picture composition is the temporal and fluid quality of the medium. Since an important element of television is *movement* of one kind or another, pictures rarely remain static for any period of time. While the zoom lens has largely replaced in-and-out pedestal moves while feeding a live shot, arcing and trucking shots are still occasionally used. On a discussion program, as a panel member who has previously been speaking to the person on camera left turns to the person on the right, it is very natural for the camera to pan right for a new two-shot. In a large musical or dramatic production, the set and other background elements must be taken into consideration. For these reasons, proper composition involves a constant process of adjustment and an exercise of discretion in achieving balance and proportion.

7.5
Production Techniques

At this point, the beginning camera operator should feel ready to start working with the cameras. A few words about some operating procedures—especially some safety precautions—should be mentioned first.

Standard Procedures

The following are several basic standard procedures that every camera operator should observe when a camera feed is needed for technical reasons, or a rehearsal or final production is about to begin.

1. Put on the headset and contact the control room.
2. Remove the lens cap only when clearly instructed to do so.
3. Check the operating condition of the camera tilt and pan controls making sure to check the spring balance of the pan controls. Also check the compressed air unit that allows for raising and lowering the camera along with the turning control of the wheels. If a field tripod is attached to a separate wheel unit, be sure that all connections are tight.
4. Act to guard the **coaxial cable** for the camera. It consists of numerous individual strands of fine wire. Unnecessary pressure can break them.
5. After the production, reverse these procedures. Put the camera in its proper location and wrap the cable in a neat figure-eight pattern.

The process of developing all the above actions into the regular disciplines of production activity is an important step toward professionalism.

Operating Hints

Aside from these rules, several other operational disciplines and techniques will help you in most studio situations. Check to see exactly what procedures are followed in your studio.

Camera Setup

Even before you are ready to set up the camera, see if you can help with other studio preparations. Can you be of assistance during the early stages of lighting and staging setup? In union studios, of course, this is not allowed; but in many university, corporate, and educational closed-circuit operations, all crew members are expected to assist in all positions. Always be ready to help out wherever needed. This is part of the discipline of a successful team member.

Check out all connections, locks, adjustments, and controls on the camera. Make sure everything is in working order. Do not try to adjust the specific camera controls (except for focus and viewfinder adjustments) without explicit guidance or permission from the person who has adjusted the brightness and color balance. (See chapter 6, section 6.5.) Check the f-stop to be sure that it conforms with what has been established by the technicians.

Many camera mounting heads have adjustments that will apply a variable amount of drag or resistance to the pan and tilt controls. Depending upon the explicit production requirements, you may want the pan and tilt controls rather loose and free, or you may want them tightened up. Adjust them accordingly. (See figure 7.20.)

Rehearsals

In general, do not abuse the **PL intercom** (see chapter 4, section 4.3). Quite a few production positions will be using the same line. Use it for speaking only when absolutely necessary and develop the ability to *listen* carefully. Directors and others who give instructions should develop the habit of clearly stating key information *one time* when they have everyone's attention. It saves endless repetition of the same information, especially while the setup period is in progress.

During the early technical or blocking rehearsal, familiarize yourself as thoroughly as possible with the production and your role in it. Make certain you have floor assistance wherever and whenever you need

Figure 7.20

The efficient use of the setup and rehearsal time is the mark of a motivated camera operator. Thinking through the sequence of shots and checking out framing always provide that extra edge during the production itself.

it—someone to handle any graphics, someone to pull the cable in a difficult move. If you are working with a boom or crane camera, make sure you coordinate all moves with the camera assistants. Rehearse all dolly and trucking moves as well as pedestal changes. Make sure that helpers can provide plenty of cable for all moves. Practice all zoom transitions and related focus considerations. If you have been provided with a **shot sheet** (a list of your camera shots), use it to think through the sequence of production.

The efficiency of the final production time is dependent upon the care exercised by the camera operators during setup and rehearsal periods. Even the latest "state-of-the-art" camera is of little value in the hands of an untrained and/or unmotivated person; however, when controlled by a caring, responsible operator, today's cameras become instruments of true creativity.

On-the-Air Production

In general, be extra alert. Be prepared for anything. Anticipate problems. (The camera cable may tangle; the zoom lens may go out of focus; the camera may get caught in a microphone cable.) Assume nothing. Television professionals have always had a phrase to describe this potential for things going awry at exactly the worst moment. Called *Murphy's Law*, it states, "Anything that can go wrong, probably will go wrong." It is really their way of reminding themselves to be constantly alert for the unexpected and prepared to solve problems quickly.

Prepare and anticipate all of your moves. Check the focus and if necessary preset your lens every time you get on a new long shot. If camera-to-subject distance changes significantly between shots, focus throughout the zoom move may not be maintained. Make certain that you are zoomed out to a sufficiently wide-angle position before attempting any camera moves (such as dolly, truck, or arc). Even slight movements of the camera head are very noticeable when the zoom is in a highly-magnified position. If you are using a free-wheeling tripod, be certain the casters are set, all pointing in the correct position, before trying any camera mount moves.

Always be ready for your next shot. Use your shot sheet if the director is working from one; otherwise, anticipate your next shot based upon the rehearsal. Every camera should be equipped with **tally lights** on the front of the camera (for the talent) and in the viewfinder (for the camera operator). These indicator lights signal that the camera is on the air or a part of a two-camera visual combination. Watch your tally light; break to your next shot as soon as you are off the air—but not before.

If you are shooting a spontaneous, unrehearsed, or a semi-scripted program, do all you can to help the director. Try to anticipate shots the director may need. Quite often directors will ask the camera operators to "hunt" for a shot of opportunity in an ad-lib situation. Do not, however, *ever* presume to tell a director what shot to take. In some panel or interview programs, the director will have good reasons for you not to move from your basic shot. That shot may be the constant cover shot around which other camera shots are able to be quickly changed. Stay with an assigned shot until other instructions are given.

Watch the talent for signs that will telegraph any moves on his or her part. When the talent leans forward, shifts feet, or looks toward the next set element, it may mean a shift to or from your camera. If you are to do a follow shot, be ready to move with the first step or the rising from a chair. Again, anticipate, be alert, and enjoy.

Summary

Camera movements include those facilitated by the camera head and those facilitated by the camera mount. A *cradle* or *cam* head is used for *panning* and *tilting.* Various camera mounts—*tripods, pedestals, cranes,* and *crab-dollies*—are used for movements such as *dollies, trucks, arcs, cranes, booms, crabs, arm moves,* and *pedestals.* Sometimes cameras are *hand-held* or moved by *robotic* camera controls.

Three different camera perspectives can be employed: *reportorial (presentational)* (the camera is addressed directly); *objective* (the camera is an eavesdropper); and *subjective* (the camera is an actor).

The field of view of a camera can be thought of as consisting of *wide shots, medium shots,* and *close-ups*—with quite a few variations and combinations. In determining picture composition, shots are labeled descriptively such as *full shot, thigh shot, chest shot, single, two-shot, three-shot,* and *over-the-shoulder shot.*

Headroom and *lead room* (talk space) are two important *framing* considerations. The illusion of *depth* in a television picture can be enhanced with proper background considerations, foreground objects, *blocking* of talent, and use of staging angles. All successful directors quickly come to realize that picture composition assumes an important role in the visual vocabulary of video.

Footnotes

1. The impact of mixing various camera perspectives can be quite striking and original, as in "It's Garry Shandling's Show," where the host/actor frequently breaks the proscenium arch to talk directly to the audience.

chapter 8

Operation of the Special Effects Generating Switcher

A number of complex and impressive components are found in the modern video production center. One piece of equipment that fits this description more than most is the **switcher.** It goes back to the very beginning of television; and, while retaining all of its original functions, it has constantly been redesigned to greatly enhance its operational capabilities. The video switcher's functions are much like those of the audio console. First and foremost, it is an *editing device* developed to facilitate the time-ordered *sequencing of inputs* within a live or live-to-tape video production. To do this, the switcher serves a *channeling* or routing function as it selects a video source from all the available inputs, such as cameras, videotape machines, remote feeds, character generators, and computer-generated graphics. The switcher functions as a *mix-ing component* that can combine two or more picture sources by means of **superimpositions, key** effects, **wipe** transitions, and other **special effects.**

To achieve these special effects, the switcher must also function as a *shaping device* that can alter not only the color and luminance quality of a picture, but also visual shape and design. It is in this realm, through the use of **digital video effects (DVE)** that the switcher becomes a **special effects generator (SEG).** Some of these units are termed "smart switchers," because they allow the operator to preprogram effects such as dissolves, wipes, tumbling cubes, flipping pages, and shrinking inserts. Effects that include timed transitions—such as an exact two and one-half second (seventy-five frame) wipe—can be similarly programmed into the switcher's microprocessor for later execution. The syndicated program *Entertainment*

Entertainment Tonight technical director Wayne Parsons working on the Grass Valley 300 SEG/Switcher at Paramount studios in Hollywood. *Photo courtesy of* Entertainment Tonight

Tonight has been noted for its creative use of such effects mixing photos of major performers in cleverly designed visual packages. (See figure 8.1.)

Similarly impressive effects are accomplished with switcher/SEG units that are found in **postproduction editing** facilities. Here, great amounts of time, talent, and money are lavished upon special animated effects that emphasize the creative use of animation and color. In commercials that cost hundreds of thousands of dollars, much of the cost pays for ever more sophisticated equipment and for the salaries of those who can productively operate it. In major *postproduction houses*, the special effects generating switcher is the primary creative control factor among a number of other edit-related components found within very sophisticated editing suites. (See figure 8.2.)

Many educational institutions find that budgetary restrictions make it difficult to keep up with such state-of-the-art equipment. Schools and small-scale video operations are more likely to have much more modest equipment. It is, therefore, important to keep in mind that with the switcher, as with many other components, there are a few basic principles of

design, function, and operation that are common to all units—no matter how simple or complex the construction. Once these essential principles are understood, one can more confidently approach the task of operating the large, impressive switcher units found in professional studios. Once you know what you are looking for, the process of understanding machine function is greatly simplified. For example, the concept of video signal flow, as presented in chapter 5, section 5.1, is integral to understanding how the switcher serves as a channeling device. It is suggested that, before proceeding, you review chapter 6, sections 6.1 and 6.2, which provide a background for understanding the nature of the color signal that switchers control.

8.1

Basic Principles of Video Switching

The fundamental elements of any switching device are represented in figure 8.3. Each of the two or more rows of buttons on the board is known as a switching

The digital switcher shown here at Hollywood Digital, a West Coast postproduction house, is the central unit among a number of components used in the final assembly of major television and cable productions.   *Photo courtesy of Hollywood Digital*

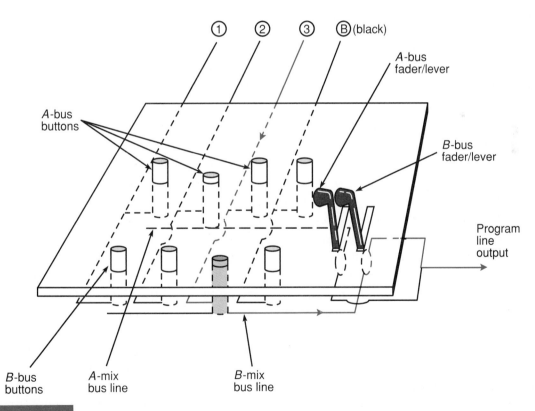

Cutaway schematic drawing of a two-bus switcher. On the *A* bus, camera 2 is punched into the mix-bus line. On the *B* bus, camera 3 is punched into the mix-bus line. Thus, with the fader arms in the down position (activating the *B* bus), camera 3 is providing the program line output. If the fader arms were to be moved into the up position (activating the *A* bus), camera 2 would then provide the program line output.

bank or bus.[1] Each button on a bank is, in effect, the temporary termination point of a video cable coming from a picture source such as a camera or a video recorder. The two or more rows are usually identical in terms of the positions assigned to the different picture sources. In figure 8.3, there is a position for each of three cameras and also a button for the **black** (fully synchronized) picture signal.

In the two-row example, the top row would be designated as the *A* bank, and the lower row as the *B* bank. Only one signal source per bus can be pressed down for connection at a time. The buttons are mutually canceling, so that when one button is pushed, that action releases the previously depressed button. Therefore, each bus can have just one camera signal punched into it at any given moment.

For a camera picture from camera 3 to be sent out on the **program line,** two conditions must be met. First of all, place both fader levers in the lower, *B* bank position. Each *individual* fader is designed to send full signal strength when it is in position nearest to its assigned bank and will send an increasingly weaker signal as it is moved away from that position. Second, press the camera 3 button on the *B* bank. By doing so, the incoming picture source, camera 3, is directly connected to the *B* bus line under the button row. As shown in figure 8.3, this leads through the fader control area and out on the program line.

In this configuration of the two levers connected and together at the *B* bank, any button pressed on the *A* bank would have no effect on the line output, because the *A*-bus fader is in its deactivated position. With camera 3 pressed on the *B* bank, you will see the picture from that camera on the line monitor. If you want to replace the camera 3 picture with the picture from camera 1, you would perform a camera **cut** (a **take**) by pressing the camera 1 button on the same *B* bank. With no loss of synchronization, you will see an instantaneous change of picture on the program line from camera 3 to camera 1.

8.2

Fades, Dissolves, and Superimpositions

From its earliest film beginnings, the moving picture art has always made use of the gradual transition between pictures known as the **dissolve.** Related techniques include **fades** to and from black, as well as *superimpositions.*

Fades from Black

During the process of channeling, mixing, and shaping, the switcher must at all times be able to maintain the waveform and synchronization information of the various signals, so that its final *program output*, whether broadcast or recorded, can ultimately produce a picture on the home receiving set. The "sync" generator, shown in figure 6.1, is the source of a system-wide signal that keeps all studio equipment together as the timing factor which controls when each picture frame is to begin. Its function is essential when two or more pictures are blended together in one way or another. A gradual fade from "black" on one bank to a full picture signal on the opposite bank is a primary example of the correct functioning of the synchronization principal.

Most video programs begin with a one- or two-second "fade-in" from black to the first picture. (An instantaneous *take* from black to picture would seem very abrupt.) Figure 8.4 shows how the *technical director* prepares a simple two-bank switcher for an initial fade-in.[2] This follows the director's command, "Prepare to fade from black to camera 1." (See section 8.5 for a discussion of preparation and execution commands.) With both faders locked together in the lower *B*-bank position, the "black" button is pressed on the *B* bank and camera 1 is pressed on the *A* bank. At this point, the program line monitor would show a "blank" screen. At the command, "Fade from black to camera 1" or "Fade in camera 1," the technical director gradually moves the interlocked fader arms from the lower to the upper position, gradually reducing the strength of the *B*-bus signal and simultaneously increasing the *A*-bus signal with camera 1 "punched up" on it. On the monitor, we will see the camera 1 picture gradually fade in and come up to full strength. At this point, if the director asks for an instantaneous cut (take) to camera 2 or camera 3, it is accomplished by pressing the designated button on the *A* bank.

Dissolves

If, for any one of a number of dramatic or aesthetic reasons, the director wants to get to the next shot by momentarily blending the images of two cameras in a

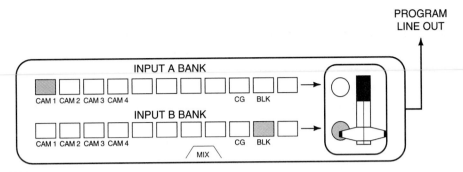

INPUT A BANK

CAM 1 CAM 2 CAM 3 CAM 4   CG   BLK

INPUT B BANK

CAM 1 CAM 2 CAM 3 CAM 4   CG   BLK

MIX

Figure 8.4

Simple television switcher. This figure shows how the two mix banks on a simple switcher would be set up to execute a dissolve from black (or fade-up from black) to camera 1. The red tinted buttons indicate which input selector buttons would be pressed. "Black" is punched up on the *B* bank, and camera 1 is punched up on the *A* bank. The small red light just to the left of the fader lever in the *B*-bank position serves as a reminder of which bus is feeding the program line. As the fader arms are raised from the *B* bank to the *A* bank, the *A* bus will be activated and camera 1 will gradually be faded in and appear on the line monitor.

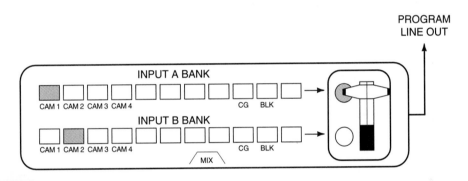

PROGRAM
LINE OUT

INPUT A BANK

CAM 1 CAM 2 CAM 3 CAM 4   CG   BLK

INPUT B BANK

CAM 1 CAM 2 CAM 3 CAM 4   CG   BLK

MIX

Figure 8.5

A dissolve on a two-bank switcher. As a continuation of the switching sequence started in figure 8.4, the switcher is shown here as it would be set up for the next transition—a dissolve to camera 2. The camera 1 selector button is still punched up on the *A* bank (from the fade-in executed in figure 8.4) and is feeding camera 1 as the line output—since the fader arms have activated the *A* bank at this point. Punch up camera 2 on the deactivated *B* bank ("black" was previously punched up for the initial fade-in), and you are ready for your dissolve from camera 1 to camera 2. Simply pull the fader arms down from the *A*-bank position to the *B*-bank position, and you have dissolved from camera 1 to camera 2.

transition, the dissolve is used. Assuming that the switcher is set as shown in figure 8.5 (with camera 1 punched up on the *A* bank), camera 1 is on the line, because both levers (locked together) are in the *up* position, so that all the video signal is coming through the *A* bus (camera 1). When the director gives the preparatory command, "Prepare a dissolve to camera 2," the technical director will prepare the switcher by punching up camera 2 on the *B* bank. There is, of course, no change in the picture on the

line monitor, because all the signal is coming through the *A* bus (where camera 1 is punched up).

When the director gives the command, "Dissolve to camera 2," you move the interlocked fader levers downward, which activates the *B* bus while deactivating the *A* bus—thus decreasing the video signal from camera 1 on the *A* bank at the same rate that you are adding power to the picture (camera 2) on the *B* bank. When both faders are at the bottom position—fully activating the *B* bus and cutting out the *A* bus—you see only camera 2. But for a brief period, you had the two camera pictures overlapping during the *dissolve* transition.

It should be noted that for years motion picture directors, working in the dramatic idiom only, used what was termed the *lap dissolve* to denote the passage of time or a change in physical location from one scene to the next. With the advent of television with program forms such as music, news, and sports, the dissolve is also often used as a way of aesthetically *connecting* two visual ideas.

Superimpositions

If the director wishes to blend two images together and hold them in combination for a specific period of time, the result is termed a superimposition or, more often, a **super.** A superimposition is really nothing more than a dissolve that has been halted at midpoint. With both the *A*- and *B*-bank levers locked together at the halfway point—and different cameras punched up on the two banks—the switcher is simultaneously feeding 50 percent of the picture from the *A* bank and 50 percent from the *B* bank. The result is a "blended" picture with two half-strength, ghostlike images seen at the same time.

A good example of when to use such a super may be in a musical production—for example, a vocalist accompanying herself on the guitar. At a point dictated by the nature and tempo of the music, the director will have a wide shot on camera 1; then, telling the camera 1 operator to slowly pan left (moving the performer to the right half of the frame), a close-up shot of the singer's face, from camera 3, is supered in the left half of the frame.

If one or both of the camera shots in a super seems to be relatively weak in terms of brightness, it is possible to press a release button on the handle of the faders and separate the *A* and *B* levers. Each fader can then be adjusted individually to enhance its brightness level. This process is called *splitting the faders.* Since both pictures are only at half-strength when two pictures are *in super,* an obvious question might be, "Why not split the faders on all supers, activating both buses all the way, and have the full value of both pictures?" The best answer is that the resulting two-picture video level will often exceed what the video control system can handle. The effect is usually

a *blooming* (or white domination) of the brightness scale of the picture. To achieve the best balance of the two pictures, ideally, the TD should have a chance to note the needed levels during a rehearsal period; however, because this is not always possible in live programs, we begin to see the inadequacy of our simple two-bank switching system.

There is one other transitional effect that the basic two-bank switcher is able to accomplish *after* the superimposition has been set up as the output of the switcher. Called an **undercut,** it is a matter of *retaining* one of the picture sources making up the super and *changing* the second picture by means of a simple camera cut procedure. As an example, let's say that we wish to start a program with the lettering of the opening title originating from the character generator (position 5 on the *B* bank) *in super* with a still picture being shot by *camera 1* (on the *A* bank). After the initial fade-in from black to camera 1 (on the *A* bank), you would then super the character generator (on the *B* bank) over camera 1 by moving both of the faders to the halfway point. Next, the director wants to replace the still picture (on camera 1) with a wide shot of the studio (which is on camera 2) but still leave the title supered. To accomplish this undercut, you would simply push the camera 2 button on the *A* bank—without moving the fader arms—and the studio shot (on camera 2) replaces the camera 1 shot *in super* with the title. It should be noted that the undercut works equally well with a very different two-source effect called a *key* that will be covered later in the chapter.

Fade Outs

At the end of the program—or at the end of a major segment—the usual transition is a fade to black. The normal method of fading out is to use the black position on the inactivated bus as another camera source and dissolve to it. For instance, in figure 8.5, if the director called for a fade to black, you would first have to punch up "black" on the *B* bus. Then, on command, you would move both faders down to the *B*-bus position.

If, however, there are two picture sources *in super* (both faders together at the midpoint position), a fade to black must be achieved by simultaneously moving each fader toward the bus that has had a black synch signal activated and away from the bank with the pic-

The Grass Valley Model 100 switcher has produced considerable flexibility with its deceptively simple design. *Photo courtesy of Grass Valley Group, Inc.*

ture source. This is another application of the *split fader* technique described above. In effect, both buses have now been inactivated—no program signal is coming through on either bank—and we have black on the screen. (If, however, you have gone the wrong direction with both faders, you will then have two very bright pictures on the screen.) Another method of getting to black is to first fade out one of the two signals, and then fade that bank to black.

Background to Development

The visual transitions just described are exactly those that were available to directors during television's formative years in the 1950s. The top network shows, from what is often called "The Golden Age of Television," did not have their creativity limited by what would today be considered a rather primitive switcher. The technical directors of this earlier period knew very well what improvements were needed and were at the forefront of improvements. Supered titles were always a problem, because there was no way to preview them in advance. Except for the super, there was no way to combine elements of two pictures at full strength or to show two sources on a split screen. There was no way to combine more than two pictures at once, so a later generation of switchers was pro-

duced with an impressive array of special effects that not only solved these problems, but also greatly enhanced the "visual vocabulary" of television.

The term *special effects generator (SEG)*, truly describes the functions and capabilities of the modern switching unit. Along with the basic cuts, dissolves, and supers, the simplest SEG can create, for example, *two- and three-source keys, chroma key effects,* and *pattern wipes* that are very impressive—although somewhat complicated from an operational standpoint for the beginning student. (See section 8.4.)

If one approaches the SEG/switcher to understand the *functional logic* that goes into the creation of each individual effect, then the unit is not nearly so intimidating. Always try to picture the underlying video signal flow, and the basic operations should be much easier to follow. In other words, one should look for certain *patterns of operation* that apply to a number of different production functions. For example, whether you are doing a camera cut, dissolve, or wipe, you must first make certain that the correct camera or other picture source has been selected on the proper switcher bank. Only then can you proceed with the specific operations that will accomplish the desired effect.

The Grass Valley Group Model 100 Production Switcher, as shown in figure 8.6 (along with the

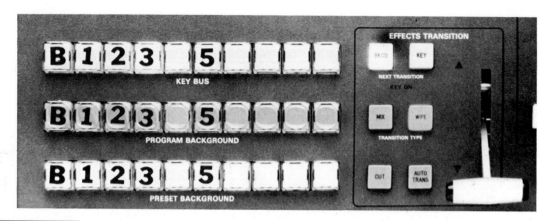

Figure 8.7

Operating buses of the GVG 100 switcher. The "transition control section" is comprised of the individual buttons on each bank for input selection and the fader arms for dissolves and effects. *Photo courtesy of Grass Valley Group, Inc.*

newer model 110), is used in well over 5,000 production facilities throughout the world. With a price range and functional complexity designed for the medium-sized operation, it is perhaps the best known of all switchers used in industrial and educational institutions. Both models have found favor as editing switchers in postproduction houses. With its impressive special effects capability and other electronic picture control components, it has many of the features found in larger and more expensive units. Therefore, we shall use the GVG Model 100 as an example to show operational techniques that students will be using as they move into professional video activity of all types.

8.3
Operational Techniques for Transitional Effects

Having previously outlined some of the general switcher operations in terms of fader bars, which always correspond to a specific *A* bank or *B* bank, we must now modify that generalization because on many of the newer switchers, such as the GVG models 100 and 110, this is not the case. In the following example of the dissolve, the fader arms could be placed in either the upper or lower position prior to the beginning of the move. It would not matter at that point—as long as other buttons were preset properly.

The Concept of Program and Preset Banks

A careful look at figure 8.7 shows that there are two lower switching buses (sometimes called *crosspoint buses*). These are labeled **program bus** and **preset bus.** (We shall, for the moment, ignore the additional *background* aspect of their function. We shall also, for the moment, ignore the *key bus* directly above.) The main concept in this arrangement is that the upper *program* bank (the middle of the three buses) is *always* the bank that provides the source of the picture that is the *line output of the switcher*. It follows, then, that the *preset* bank is where you press the button for the camera picture that will be the *next line output* following the completed transition.

Using the GVG Model 100, let us follow an example of a simple dissolve from camera 1 to camera 2. We would first go to the transition section shown at the right-hand side of figure 8.7 and press the *mix* button just above *transition type,* because with a dissolve we will be mixing two signals together. We also press the *background (bkgd)* button above the *next transition* section of the effects transition group of controls. (We will look at this in more detail later.) Next, with the fader lever in the *upper* position, the *camera 1* button is pressed on the upper *program* bank and the *camera 2* button is pressed on the lower *preset bank.* The camera 1 button on the program bank will glow brightly with what is called *high tally;* this reinforces what our program monitor tells us—that we are feed-

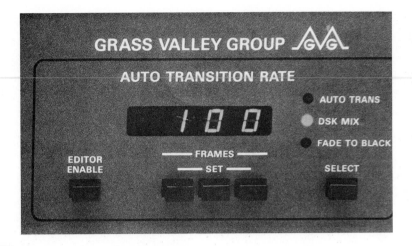

Figure 8.8

The "automatic transition control" section of the GVG 100. This panel allows the technical director to set precise timings for wipes and dissolves without the manual use of the faders. *Photo courtesy of Grass Valley Group, Inc.*

ing a camera 1 signal on the program line. The camera 2 button on the preset bank glows with a softer intensity called a *low tally;* this indicates that camera 2 is selected to be the next camera on the air.

Fader Movement

As we begin to move the fader downward, we will see a *green arrow* begin to glow at the place where the fader arm will be when we have completed the dissolve to camera 2. (This reinforcement of the direction of our lever move is important in more complex operations.) As we continue the fader movement downward, both the camera 1 and the camera 2 buttons will glow brightly as both cameras are seen briefly on the program monitor (a momentary superimposition) during the dissolve.

As the dissolve is completed and the fader lever makes contact at the lower position, we have put camera 2 on the air, and we see camera 2 on the program line monitor. But the surprising thing is what has happened to the two banks. The upper *program* bank now shows its *camera 2* button glowing brightly (high tally); on the lower *preset bank,* the *camera 1* button (the camera from which we have just dissolved) is now glowing dimly (low tally).

Flip-flop

As we completed our dissolve, the two cameras switched positions on the buses, executing what is

called a **flip-flop,** because their positions as *line feed* and *off-line feed* cameras have just been reversed. Looking again at the switcher, we see that even though the fader is in the *lower position,* the line feed camera (camera 2) is shown on the *upper* bank, indicating it is on the *program* bus. It is the brightly glowing tally that reminds us which camera is our line feed and *not* of the position of the fader, as with older switchers.

Automatic Transitions

If we had wanted a dissolve lasting exactly two seconds, we could have used the **automatic transition** feature of the GVG 100 and not used the fader levers at all (since the position of the fader arms no longer indicates which bus is on the air). We would start out by having the program and preset buses set up exactly as in the beginning of the previous example, with the fader arms in the upper position. (Remember: we could just as well have started with them in the lower position.) We would then have used the **auto transition rate** controls at the upper right-hand corner of the unit. (See figure 8.8.) Keeping in mind the thirty-frames-per-second rate explained in chapter 6, we would use the *set* controls to put the transition rate at sixty frames.

In this same group of controls, we would use the *select* button to move the red indicator light to the *auto trans* position. The *mix* button for the "transition

Figure 8.9

Corner insert. This effect may either be used as a transition from one camera to another or to hold two pictures on the screen for a period of time.

type" and the *bkgd* button for the "next transition" are still pressed (see figure 8.7). By pressing the *auto trans* button, we will achieve a perfect 2-second dissolve from camera 1 to camera 2. The "flip-flop" will occur as before. The faders are not moved, although they can be used to *override* the automatic dissolve at any time.

For an instantaneous cut between cameras 1 and 2, we would only have had to press the *cut* button (right next to the *auto trans* button) instead of the *auto trans* button itself.

Wipe Transitions between Cameras

In making a transition between two consecutive pictures, there are times when neither the take nor the dissolve is suitable. An example might be if you want to draw special attention to a picture or series of pictures. The *wipe transition* often accomplishes this perfectly—by letting the viewer see portions of both pictures as the separation line moves through the screen. Used excessively, the wipe calls attention to itself as a gimmick, but when used with discretion, it is an important part of a director's visual vocabulary.

Many production switcher/SEG units in use today have dozens of *patterned wipe* designs—ranging from the traditional vertical line moving horizontally across the screen (or the horizontal line moving vertically down the screen) to diagonals, diamonds, circles, and all manner of boxes, to the jagged shark tooth effect, which is the cliché of the late-night horror movie show.

Split Screens and Corner Inserts

Just as the superimposition may be thought of as a dissolve suspended in midtransition, so might the **split screen** and **corner insert** (or any one of a number of special use inserts) be thought of as a wipe effect that has been halted in midpoint. As a common application of a "suspended" wipe transition, the *split screen* is a means of combining two pictures with either a horizontal or vertical (and occasionally diagonal) line separating the screen into two distinct areas—with a different picture (from separate cameras or other video sources) in each part of the screen. By means of the special effects faders, relative sizes of the two pictures can be adjusted.

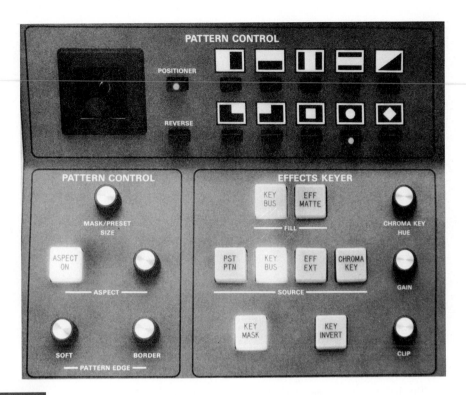

Figure 8.10

The "pattern control" section of the GVG 100. The pattern control buttons allow the technical director to select specific patterns for wipes and inserts. It also has controls that can further position and shape the patterns.   *Photo courtesy of Grass Valley Group, Inc.*

By manipulating the horizontal and vertical special effects faders separately, it is also possible to achieve a *corner insert.* (See figure 8.9.) This places the inserted camera picture in any quadrant of the screen. In a televised baseball game, for example, when you see the runner at first base within a small insert in the top right-hand corner of the primary "behind-the-plate" wide shot, you are actually seeing a corner wipe that has only been taken part of the way—in what could have been a full-screen wipe from one camera to another. Again, the exact size and proportion of the corner insert can easily be adjusted by the control levers.

A further technical advance is the *multiple-source split screen.* With this device, it is possible to split the screen into a number of individual sections, each with a separate picture. Again, these separate divisions can be positioned and shaped to meet a variety of artistic needs. When four picture sources are shown it is known as a **quad split.**

Another useful special effect is the **spotlight** which enables the operator to dim the entire screen except for one circle of light that can be shaped, changed in size, and positioned anywhere on the screen with a joystick. This effect can also be considered as a special application of the suspended wipe transition.

Execution of the Wipe Transition

The method of handling the patterned wipe transition is not too difficult once one understands the basics of the dissolve transition. Returning to the specific example with the GVG 100, we first need to push the *wipe* button for "transition type" next to the fader arms (see figure 8.7), canceling the *mix* transition button. On the "pattern control" section of the switcher (see figure 8.10), the *select button* (under the pattern with a confirming red light) determines the basic shape of the wipe. Keep in mind that the new video from the preset camera will appear in the *white* area of

Two monitors illustrate the difference between a super and a key. The left-hand monitor shows white lettering from a character generator supered over the woman's face. The right-hand monitor shows the same lettering keyed over the woman's face.

the pattern shown on the button. With the *center circle wipe,* the new picture will emerge on the screen as a circle in the middle of the picture; its image will be widened by the movement of the fader.

There is also a *reverse* option in which the *black* area of the pattern represents the new camera. Other controls allow for changes in *position* and *shape* of the circle or other selected design. You can also adjust how *hard* or *soft* you want the edge of the wipe to be and how wide you want to make the *border* between the two video source pictures. The *auto transition* feature discussed previously can be used for the execution of wipes as well as for dissolves.

Keyed Special Effects with Two and Three Sources

For the majority of multiple-picture combinations, the superimposition has been totally replaced by the *key* effect that "cuts out" and combines solid images from two or more video sources.[3] The basic principle of the key is a process by which differences in brightness and/or color are used to insert one picture into another. Often the analogy of a "cookie cutter" is used

to explain how one image electronically *dominates* all or part of a second background picture to produce a *key effect,* such as white letters over a studio camera shot. Unlike a superimposition where the two images bleed through onto each other, the key cuts a clean electronic hole into which it inserts its signal. Figure 8.11 illustrates the difference between a super and a key.

In many such effects, a *wipe pattern* is used to create the *outline shape,* and a *third source* is used as an input to fill the hole with another picture. Another version of this three-source effect, known as an **auto key** (formerly labeled the "external" key), uses one video source to establish the external shape of a letter or figure—in effect, stamping out an image much like a stencil might cut out a shape. The key effect then uses a third source to fill in the picture and color of the "stenciled out" part of the design.

As an example, we will use the least complex of these special effects—white titles keyed over a camera shot. This is termed a **self key** (also known as a **luminance** or **internal key**), because the dominant brightness level of the lettering cuts its own electronic pattern in the background picture. However, even this simple special effect should always be previewed and adjusted before it is used.

Let us say that we are going to use the key at the beginning of a program. The director's command would be to "Prepare to fade up from black to a key of titles on the CG over camera 1." The technical director would press *black* on the *program (background)* bank, *camera 1* on the *preset (background)* bank, and *button 5* (for titles from the character generator) on the *key bus* (refer back to figure 8.7). In this case, camera 1 is the *preset background,* and the character generator will be the *key* source. The fader arms can be in either the upper or lower position to start the exercise. (Remember, their position does *not* relate to the bank that is feeding the program line.)

The two *next transition* buttons in the *effects transition* area allow us to select the source bus or busses used in the next transition or effect. In this case, we press *both* the *bkgd (background)* and *key* buttons, because when we come up from black, we are going to fade to a key consisting of *two* images—the preset background from camera 1, and keyed over it, the lettering originating from the character generator on the *key bus 5* position.

In the *effects keyer* section (see figure 8.10), we must press both *key bus* buttons, because the *key bus* will be both the *source and* the *fill* of the effect. (If we were preparing a three-source key, we would punch up different sources for the source and for the fill.)

Once the selections have been punched up on the *preset background* bank (camera 1) and on the *key bus* bank (the character generator), the **preview monitor** will display the key effect of those two sources (see the following discussion). Because the difference in brightness between the lettering and the background is always a matter of delicate balance, a look at this preview monitor will now tell us just what adjustments must be made. The **clip knob** sets the *brightness* threshold for the key source video that allows the letters to "cut" the electronic hole, and the **gain knob** sets the *sharpness* of the key effect itself. After viewing the result of these adjustments, the director gives the command, "Fade up on the key effect," and the technical director executes the fade-in to the effect by moving the fader arms from wherever they are to the opposite position. The key effect is brought up on the

line, and we see the results on the **program (line) monitor.**

On the GVG Model 110, there is a feature called **key memory** that is built into the unit. It will remember and note the *clip* and *gain* settings for a source image that has been used previously. When that source is used a second time, the clip and gain settings will automatically be returned to their previously established levels. Other state-of-the-art SEG/switchers have even more amazing electronic memory innovations (see section 8.4).

Picture Monitors

At this point, it should be obvious that the video monitors in the video control room are essential to the proper use of the switcher as well as for camera operations.[4] For that reason, it is important to discuss some of the specific monitors that are essential to the explanation of the above switcher operations.

Even in a moderate-sized studio, there may be up to a dozen different monitors, each performing an important individual function (see figure 8.11). Each video source will have its own monitor. Each studio camera, character generator, and video recorder will have a small individual monitor. In addition to these 7- to 10-inch units, there will be several larger monitors. The most crucial of these is the *program (line) monitor* which shows the actual picture that the switcher is sending to master control for live transmission or recording. This is the one that the director must watch constantly as a final check on the program picture content.

The other large monitor, often to the left of the program monitor, is the *preview monitor* which is used heavily by the technical director to adjust keys and other special effects in advance of their use—and to show the director just how these effects or any upcoming shot will look. For some types of production, directors may ask for the upcoming camera shot to be displayed so that any need for minor adjustment can be more clearly seen.

In complicated network sports programs, this preview function may be done on separate **preset monitors** used only for effects. In some production systems, the preset monitors may be used routinely to preview the upcoming shot so that the director

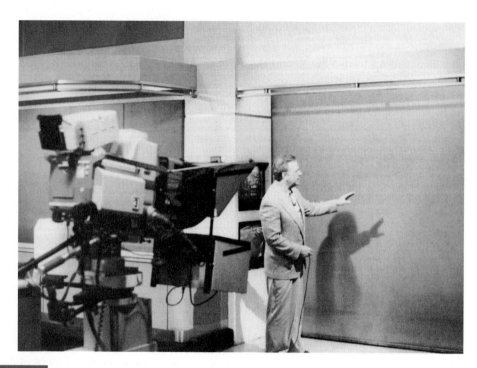

Figure 8.12

Like all weathercasters, KABC-TV's Johnny Mountain actually works against a blank blue or green screen. The orientation of hand movements and visuals is done through the use of monitors to his left and right.   *Photo courtesy of KABC-TV*

will always be able to see precisely what is going on the air next. There may also be a number of preview monitors for remote location feeds in addition to the basic preview monitor. In a live broadcasting situation, an **air monitor** always shows the actual broadcast picture.

8.4

Additional Special Effects and Digital Applications

An additional component called the **downstream keyer** is increasingly being used as television production becomes more complex. It adds an additional effect to a video signal *after* it has passed through the primary selection and combination functions of a switcher. When viewed on a monitor, the output of the downstream keyer looks much the same as the output of the internal key component. It is designed to insert captions or other key effects into the final output of the switcher and, as such, may also utilize

sources such as a character generator or a graphics camera.

The *key memory* feature of the GVG Model 110 was previously described. Other state-of-the-art SEGs have even more amazing electronic memory and execution innovations. For example, the Grass Valley Group Model 300 (see figure 8.1) offers a much more sophisticated memory feature called the *E-MEM*[5] which can combine digitally-produced animated graphics along with color, brightness, and other design information in its memory unit. By pressing a single button, the animated effect/transition can be recalled and executed with no other preparation or commands.

Other features of today's switchers include all sorts of ways to manipulate colors and shapes of backgrounds and borders. The actual *color* itself is adjusted by the **hue** control. The **chroma knob** varies the *intensity* (**saturation**) of a color (the "bluishness" of blue). The **luminance** control regulates the amount of brightness in the image. All these controls interact to a degree that can only be appreciated with hands-on experience.

Figure 8.13

The computer-generated map and other animated effects are chroma keyed through the switcher to produce the visual effect seen on the televised picture. *Photo courtesy of KABC-TV*

Chroma Key

Considered a near miracle when it was first introduced, the **chroma key** is a matting process that is now a staple of much video production. This is a technique in which a specific color—rather than a graphic design or pattern—is used as the electronic key to cut out part of the picture. (Any color can be designated to be used as the key; however, light blue or green is most often used, because it is farthest from any skin tones.) Wherever the foreground or key camera detects the designated hue (and chroma) in its picture, that video information is discarded and background picture signals are supplied from a second source such as a still-store device, graphics unit, camera, or VCR.

Probably the best-known example of this process is seen nightly on the local weathercast during the news. The studio camera has a shot of the weathercaster standing in front of a light blue background (but not wearing any blue item of clothing). (See figure 8.12.) Through the switcher, this picture is combined with the computer-generated local or national weather map that includes cloud movement and other animated

effects. As seen on the home set in figure 8.13, the result is impressive. It is technically impressive, but much of the effect depends upon the weathercaster's skill in pointing out specific areas on the blank wall through the use of monitors not seen by the audience.

Although the use of chroma key is widespread, it is not without numerous potential difficulties. The electronic equipment has to be adjusted delicately. Lighting of the color background of the key camera has to be perfectly even. Considerable attention must be given to selection of costumes and scenery. Slight problems in any of these areas lead to conspicuous troubles such as tearing of the foreground image, an obvious border around the foreground figure, discoloration, or indistinct contours.

Many of these drawbacks have been overcome by newer systems, such as *Ultimatte*,[6] which has supplanted or replaced chroma key in most major professional studios. In addition to conventional color matting features, Ultimatte can render not only highlights and reflections off of glass, but the actual glass object itself will be visibly matted over the background image. The process is sensitive enough that it can capture every strand of a person's hair and even wisps of smoke.

Figure 8.14

The new Grass Valley 2200 component digital SEG/switcher has such features as one-button automatic chroma key setup and four-layer imaging effects. It is much more compact than earlier models designed for a similar workload. Note the use of an LED informational readout.   *Photo courtesy of Grass Valley Group, Inc.*

Digital Effects

One of the digital switcher effects most often seen is the *continuous image compression* that enables the switcher operator to compress the full-frame picture down to the size of a tiny circle (at any speed, to any size) and—with a joystick—to place the shrunken image anywhere on the screen. This is what makes the squeeze zoom possible as a transition. *Image expansion* allows the director to take any segment of the video frame and enlarge it up to four times its original size (beyond which point it becomes unintelligible). A combined phenomenon is *image stretching*. Any portion of the picture can be expanded or compressed in any direction; ratios can be altered; graphics can be shaped to fit the picture.

Other transitional devices—in addition to effects such as the fold-over and squeeze zoom—include: (1) the *video split* that literally takes a picture and pulls it apart in the middle to make room for a new frame, and (2) the *push-off* that simply shoves a whole frame off the tube sideways while replacing it with another image (as opposed to the wipe that does not move the two stationary frames involved in the transition). (See figure 8.14.)

The strongest impact of many of these advances has been in the areas of graphics as they relate to postproduction editing. Once the basic video images have been recorded, the director can sit down with an editor and decide how to time each transition, when to compress this image and bring in another, whether to electronically zoom in on a particular frame, how to shape graphics as they are added later, and so forth. The video editor now has available more sophisticated and less expensive creative opportunities than film editors have ever enjoyed.

Other components developed through the application of digital technology include the *time-base corrector* whose importance to the videotape machine will be discussed in chapter 9, and the *framestore synchronizer* that helps to synchronize the process of inserting live video feeds from distant locations.

8.5
Video Production Commands

In discussing audio production techniques (see chapter 4, section 4.3), we stressed the difference between commands of *preparation* and commands of *execution.* Nowhere is this distinction more important than in giving commands to the technical director. The preparation and execution of the various transitions and effects involve different amounts of switcher operation time. A straight take is ready instantly, but a dissolve to a chroma key effect requires a number of operations, done in a precise order. The commands of preparation must allow for sufficient lead time. Such commands, given over the intercom system, allow camera, VCR, and graphics operators time for their own preparations.

One helpful rule is that the command of preparation for any straight take is "ready." The preparation for any dissolve, super, fade, or special transition or effect that involves getting something set or prepared on another bus, uses the command "prepare." (A few directors prefer to use the command "set up.") Although some directors use the term "standby" as a preparation for both takes and dissolves, this can be confusing to the crew. The use of correct terminology immediately lets the technical director know whether to simply get ready to push a button on the same bus or to prepare or set up another camera or effect on another bus. The command sequence for a direct take from camera 1 to camera 2 is stated by the director as follows:

(Preparation): "Ready camera 2" (or simply) "Ready 2"
(Execution): "Take 2"

The word *ready* lets the technical director know only to place a finger on the camera 2 button on the activated bus.

No matter how rushed the director may be or how fast-paced the program, the director should never skimp on the commands of preparation. If occasionally the director does not have time to give full commands, some abbreviation could be used:

(Preparation): "Ready 2"
(Execution): "Take it" (or simply): "Take"

If time is so short that even this much preparation is impossible (for example, shooting a game show, fast-paced panel discussion, or football game), the command of preparation still must be given priority:

(Preparation): "Two"
(Execution): "Take"

When such abbreviated commands are used successfully, it is usually in a situation where the director and the crew have worked together for an extended period of time. Even so, most directors will return to the safer, more complete commands when time allows.

A dissolve requires a different sounding command of preparation to allow the technical director time to prepare for a more complex series of actions. Assuming you already have camera 1 on line, the correct commands for a dissolve would be:

(Preparation): "Prepare a dissolve to 2" (or) "Prepare 2" (or) "Set up 2"
(Execution): "Dissolve to 2"

For a super, the actions are the same so the commands are much the same:

(Preparation): "Prepare to super 2 over 1" (or) "Set up 2" (implying that camera 1 stays on the air)
(Execution): "Super camera 2 over 1" (or just) "Super 2"

We depart slightly from the basic pattern whenever two cameras are to be *taken* together in a super or key. While these effects involve a movement of the control levers to set them up, the movement is not one of program execution. As previously outlined, the command of execution is "take"—calling only for the technical director to press the *line mix* output button or *take bar*. For this reason, the voice procedure in this case should be as follows:

(Preparation): "Ready to take 2 and 3 in super"
(Execution): "Take super" (or) "Take 2 and 3"

The repetition of camera numbers in the command is optional, but does reinforce the intent of the command.

Much of the discipline necessary for keeping a program under control comes from this pattern of preparation followed by execution. The technical director must be able to depend on this sequence. The pattern is broken when a complicated effect that must be set up in advance is called for. A complicated key, for example, might need to be preset several shots before its use. In this situation, after the command of preparation that acknowledges the time delay in execution, there may be several intervening commands. Then a new command of preparation is issued before the execution command for the key. The command of preparation must be given far enough in advance so that the technical director has a chance to do the preset at a time most convenient during the ongoing program. The director keeps an eye on the preview monitor to see when the key is ready. The commands might be as follows:

(Advance preparation): "We're about to wrap, so preview your key of camera 2 and credits on the CG"
(Ongoing shots in the program continue): "Ready 1, take 1 . . . etc."
(Immediate preparation): "Now set up a dissolve to the key of credits over camera 2"
(Execution of the key): "Dissolve to the credits"

Similarly, any command to preview and adjust—say, a corner wipe or an insert—in the coverage of a live event may be given well in advance of its eventual use on the air. There may be several intervening ad-libbed shots. This can be thought of as a nontime-specific command. For example:

(Advance preparation): "Preview a top-left corner insert, camera 3, of runner off first base, within camera 2"
(Intervening shots ad-libbed): "Ready 4, take 4, . . . etc."

(Adjustment of preparation): "Tighten the framing on camera 3 insert"
(Intervening shots ad-libbed): "Ready 1, take 1, . . . etc."
(Immediate preparation): "O.K. Now, ready to take corner insert"
(Execution of the effect): "Take effect"

One final note—fades to and from black are handled in a manner very similar to the dissolve (the fade to or from black is in essence a dissolve to or from black). Because a sync black picture has such a definite connotation of separation and/or conclusion, many directors reserve the term "fade" for use as a command only to dissolve to or from black. This serves as a safeguard to protect against any inadvertent dissolve to full-screen black.

As special effects generating switchers have become more complex, the numerous visual options available to the director have placed many demands upon the technical director. The director is obligated to use the clearest of command language, which in turn must be based upon an operational understanding of what is involved in achieving execution of those commands. Beyond common courtesy, there is a very practical aspect to this. Ill-timed and poorly-stated commands simply cannot be executed within the time framework that the director may have in mind. Such a disparity can have serious side effects, especially with live programming. Used well, today's state of the art switcher is an impressive instrument. For those learning its operation, the advice is much the same as with all television components. One first gains a clear understanding of basic techniques and then extrapolates those fundamentals to more complex equipment. This is especially true with the switcher.

Summary

The switcher is the key *channeling* and *mixing* device in the video signal flow system. In conjunction with the *special effects generator (SEG)* and *digital video effects (DVE)*, it is also involved in *shaping* the video signal.

The switcher can be thought of as a simple connection panel, with additional *banks* and *fader arms* added to increase the flexibility of the unit. The basic camera transitions and effects used on the switcher include the *take, dissolve, fade,* and *super.*

There are several variations of more complex switchers that, in conjunction with the various video *monitors,* enable the technical director to *preview* and *preset* certain effects. On many switchers, *auto transition* is available so that transitions can be programmed to be of a specific length. Special electronic effects include *wipes, split screens, corner insert,* and *spotlight.* Also available are numerous *key and insert* effects and the *chroma key* and *downstream keyer.*

Effects that are possible because of *digital* technology encompass *image compression and expansion* and *image stretching*—as well as transitions such as the fold-over, squeeze zoom, video split, push-off, and numerous others.

The very complexity of today's switcher serves as an excellent reason for directors to work very hard at developing a style of giving verbal commands that permits the technical director to work at optimum efficiency.

Footnotes

1. Technically speaking, the line and its connectors that runs under each row of buttons is termed the *bus,* and the row of buttons is called the *bank;* however, in common usage, the two terms are used interchangeably.

2. Throughout this chapter, the term technical director (TD) will be used to denote the person who operates the switching unit. The term is derived from professional situations where the person given that title has a much larger engineering responsibility to supervise the entire technical staff and to operate the switcher/SEG only at the latter part of the production effort. There are circumstances when a person may function only as the SEG operator and is usually then known as the switcher.

3. Occasionally the word matte is associated with the key process. The term was derived from the traditional film technique that printed or "matted" inserts within the larger film frame.

4. The video monitor is distinguished from the regular television receiver in that the monitor is usually a high quality unit with ability to reproduce fine detail. It receives a direct unmodulated video signal, as opposed to a modulated radio frequency signal. Thus, there is no audio and no channel selection capability.

5. E-MEM is a trademark of the Grass Valley Group.

6. Ultimatte is a trademark of the Ultimatte Corporation.

chapter 9

The Function and Operation of the Video Recorder

I n 1956, CBS first used videotape for the delayed rebroadcast of its newscast to the western states. The industry immediately saw the possibilities that tape could provide for the *distribution* and *storage* of program material. The *editing* possibilities were equally obvious, but the technology has taken time to develop to its full potential. By 1970 it was being used in televised news, where the crucial aspect of production was "getting it on tape." News footage could then be later edited and in other ways prepared for broadcast. If no tape was available, the story might not appear on the broadcast.

Increasingly, *raw* footage is being transferred by microwave or satellite directly from cameras in the field to recording machines waiting at a central studio location. After preproduction-production editing, the program segments are again stored on individual videotape cassettes for flexible access during the live broadcast. Similarly, soap operas, situation comedies, and countless other types of production have placed large amounts of material on *original master* tape recordings for later editing during the **postproduction** process.

9.1 Developmental Background

One of the reasons for this increasing use of videotape has been a series of new options relating to the structure and quality of the signal. Over a decade ago, the original **composite** format was improved by providing the option of having the color and brightness signals separated into what is called a **component** signal. There is often a further division, as with the *Betacam* component signal, that requires two separate lines for just the color signal.

The most important change has been the move from the original **analog** waveform (reflecting the structure of light or sound waves) to a **digital** form that is almost entirely immune from distortion or

Figure 9.1

The rear connection deck of a Panasonic AJ D580 (D-5) VCR shows the connections necessary to receive, record, convert, and output an impressive range of digital and analog signal combinations, including those using the newer multiple-pin connectors that match disc units and the newer digital formats. *Photo courtesy of Panasonic*

Figure 9.2

The front view of the Panasonic AJ D580 (D-5) shows one of several LED operational displays designed for convenience and speed in editing. Its compatibility with D-3 units put it in demand during the 1996 Olympics. *Photo courtesy of Panasonic*

Figure 9.3

The Avid Media Recorder is a disc-based VCR replacement, specifically designed for recording incoming satellite feeds and videotape to hard-drives in preparation for nonlinear production. The VCR unit digitizes material already on tape.

interference. Of even more importance, however, is the fact that this signal can be controlled and stored through the use of digital computer technology. One negative effect was a resulting profusion of new analog and digital tape formats that used composite or component signals in various combinations and tape sizes (D-1, D-2, D-3, etc.). This, in turn, forced the manufacturers to design videotape machines that had both input and output capacity for a number of these signal options. For example, an incoming digital component picture could be recorded and then fed out as an analog composite signal. Figure 9.1 shows the rear panel of a Panasonic AJ D580 (D-5) video recorder that has compatibility of this sort as one of its main features. As one of the workhorses of the 1996 Olympics broadcasts from Atlanta, its compatibility with the D-3 format made it invaluable for editing. Note the many inputs for digital and analog signal combinations and especially the horizontal *multiple pin* connectors that are important when transferring to digital disc and for related editing applications. In the front view (see figure 9.2), notice the LED opera-

tional display that includes four vertical VU meters used in editing the four audio tracks.

Even with the numerous tape formats, for the past decade, there has always been a degree of signal compatibility made possible by multiple conversion options, like those on the AJ D580. However, announcements made by Panasonic and Sony at the 1996 convention of the National Assn. of Broadcasters may have changed all that. While both manufacturers said that they had agreed on a consumer-level digital camera and related tape format, their new professional-level digital tape formats would not be compatible. Upcoming section 9.4 will examine this situation more fully.

The possibility of an increase in the already large number of competing videotape formats has caused many in the industry to consider carefully the implications of the latest example of technological convergence, the multichannel video file server. Known more often as simply a **server,** models like the Avid Media Recorder (figure 9.3) have been in use for a number of years at large stations and networks. With computer control, its multiple digital disc drives and

Figure 9.4

The Spotbank hard disc-based server from Odetics can be programmed to control up to twenty-four devices such as digital discs, VCRs, and switchers in order to feed programs and spots for broadcast. Its built-in redundancy protects against program loss.   *Photo courtesy of Odetics Broadcast*

other components are designed to receive and store compressed digital video. It can feed scheduled programs and commercials for broadcast and, simultaneously, send stored footage to a news editing suite. There are a number of configurations on the market. Some are entirely disc-based and others, like the Odetics *Spotbank* shown in figure 9.4, can use existing videotape units for archival storage of news footage or valuable program material. One key feature of newer units is a bank of discs that provides instant redundancy in case of disc drive failure. Theoretically, the number of channels that could be built into one unit is only limited by the cost factor. An overabundance of new videotape formats means a potentially large expense for the purchase of new VCR machines for much of the industry. If the use of servers can keep the use of tape to a minimum, the relative cost could turn out to be low.

One cost-effective step has existed for several years in the Avid CamCutter™ shown in chapter 1,

figure 1.16. Replacing tape, it has a Fieldpak™ hard disc drive that fits into a larger dockable recording unit for field transmission or recording and editing at a base location. The system is not only designed to minimize the use of tape, but also to speed video through editing to broadcast.

The CamCutter system combined with the server technology fits right in with the already well-established **nonlinear** digital editing process that is also based on digital disc and computer control.[1] With its ability to insert audio and video into existing segments (in much the same way that one adds an additional sentence to an already completed paragraph with a word processor), the nonlinear method of editing has brought about great changes in the way today's video product is assembled. Some of the procedures relating to this new editing approach will be compared to traditional videotape editing in the next chapter.

While there is no doubt that all of this new technology will be put to use by the industry, the final

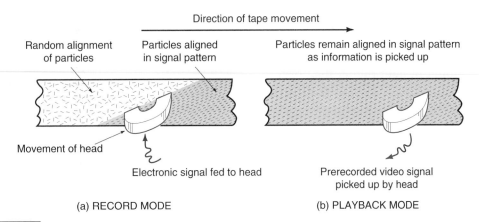

Direction of tape movement

Random alignment of particles

Particles aligned in signal pattern

Particles remain aligned in signal pattern as information is picked up

Movement of head

Electronic signal fed to head

(a) RECORD MODE

Prerecorded video signal picked up by head

(b) PLAYBACK MODE

Figure 9.5

Video recording and playback heads. (a) **Record Mode.** The electronic video signals sent to the record head activate the magnetized head to align the iron oxide particles on the tape to retain a permanent (until erased) pattern of the recorded electronic video signal. (b) **Playback Mode.** The prerecorded video signals on the videotape generate a small amount of electrical current in the playback head that is an exact duplicate of the original video signal.

changeover to a component/digital signal also has some relationship to the introduction of the **High Definition Television (HDTV)** format to the American public. This much heralded, but somewhat delayed, new video standard is also referred to as the **Advanced Television (ATV)** format. It features an upgraded digital/component signal that uses roughly twice the number of scanning lines as the existing system. Current plans are for a screen ratio of 9 by 16 as opposed to the traditional 3 by 4 ratio of screen width to height. Final approval was delayed until 1997 by an ongoing series of disagreements about such things as the color system, compression technology, and screen size among various factions representing video, film, and computer interests.

9.2

Principles of Video Recording

The concepts behind the development of video recording were based upon a technology that had already been used for sound. Organized sound energy from an amplified source can be made to align particles of iron oxide on a tape through the action of a magnetic **recording head** passing in contact along the tape. As shown in figure 9.5, these alignment patterns are actually an electromagnetic memory of the original analog waveform. When the tape is moved past the magnetic head in the **playback** mode, this action reproduces the original frequencies and amplitudes exactly as they

were recorded, and the resulting signal can be amplified and transduced into pictures and sound.

The development of reliable color tape machines and a related editing capacity was, however, slow in coming. Much of the problem was due to the fact that it takes roughly 600 times as much signal information to record a color picture as it does to record sound. New methods of moving tape and recording on tape had to be developed. Because the recording process relates to the nature of the video signal itself, a quick look at the material in chapter 6 on the structure of the video signal will make this easier to understand.

A Brief Review of the Video Signal

The **CCD** (charged coupled device) chip, functioning as an **image sensor,** and the home picture tube **raster** are both organized into 525 horizontal scanning lines. Of that number, varying numbers of these lines (over 90 percent) are used purely for picture purpose. (The remaining lines are used for other functions, such as titling for the hearing impaired.) In chapter 6, figure 6.5, a number of 480 has been assigned as being typical of many sets. Each of these horizontal lines is composed of varying numbers of separate illumination points called **pixels**. To maintain a 3 by 4 frame ratio, the number of pixels per line would have to be 640. Simple multiplication gives us a grand total of 307,200 picture elements on the face of the Charged Coupled Device (CCD) making up the electronic mosaic in the camera.

As the lens focuses the incoming light from the subject onto the CCD image sensor, each one of the pixels is individually energized in direct relationship to the specific amount of light hitting the pixel. This process produces the signals that are the electronic version of the optical image focused on the face of the lens. In tube-type cameras, a stream of electrons (the **scanning beam**) is shot at the **target** at the front of the tube—essentially a similar plate of pixels—by means of electromagnets located just forward of the **electron gun,** which is the source of the electron beam. In the CCD camera, this "scanning" function is accomplished by vertical and horizontal **shift registers,** which in effect, collect the sequential output of the pixels.

This scanning process actually occurs in two phases. Starting at the top left of the picture, the odd-numbered lines are first scanned to produce a top-to-bottom picture **field.** Only one-half of the illumination points have been used to produce this picture. Once this half-picture has been scanned, the scanning beam starts at the top left of the picture again, and this time all the even-numbered lines are scanned to produce another picture field. There are sixty of these half-picture fields occurring every second. This odd-even field alternation, called **interlacing,** is designed to cut down on the unwanted "flicker" effect of the picture (sixty half pictures a second cause less flicker than thirty full pictures per second). This interlacing of fields adds up to a theoretical figure of thirty **frames** per second, although no complete frame ever really exists as a static entity.

Horizontal and Vertical Synchronization Pulses

An examination of this process in greater detail reveals that additional factors are needed to ensure the stability of the picture. It is imperative that the scanning sequence in the camera, whether tube or chip type, be precisely synchronized at every stage of its journey through the switcher to all other recording and editing equipment in the studio during broadcast, as well as to at the home receiving set. A series of specialized pulses—generated independently of the color and luminance portion of the video signal—are used for this purpose. First, there is a **horizontal sync pulse** that activates the video system at the beginning of each scanning line and turns

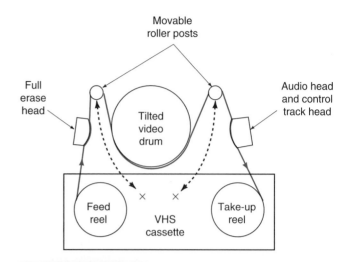

Figure 9.6

The VHS "M" wrap system of transporting tape past the circular record-playback head after it has been retracted from the cassette.

it off for a brief retrace period **(blanking)** as the beam returns to the beginning of a new line on the left side of the picture tube.

At the completion of each field, there is a similar retrace period as the scanning beam returns to the top left of the picture. At this point, a **vertical sync pulse** is used to coordinate the start of each new field. While there are only two vertical sync pulses for every 525 horizontal sync pulses, they must nevertheless be considered as an extremely important part of the video sequence. Because it denotes the beginning of a new picture field, the vertical sync pulse has an important application in videotape editing.

The previous rather technical explanation has been presented because it is vital to an understanding of the conditions for successful recording and playback of video on tape.

Helical-Scan Videotape Recording

The first professional videotape **quadruplex** machines used a 2-inch wide tape. At one point of its movement, the tape curved around slightly less than one-half of a rotating disc containing four video heads—hence its name. Each head scanned only one-sixth of the picture, making slow motion and freeze-frame pictures impossible.

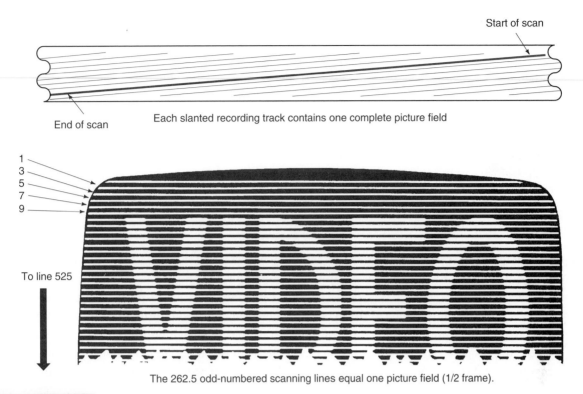

Start of scan

Each slanted recording track contains one complete picture field

End of scan

1
3
5
7
9

To line 525

The 262.5 odd-numbered scanning lines equal one picture field (1/2 frame).

Figure 9.7

Helical-scan slanted track. The continuous video signal from one slanted video track contains enough information to record 262.5 odd-numbered scanning lines (one complete field) and to play back the field on the picture tube.

The answer to this and several other problems was to be found in the **helical-scan (slant-track)** videotape recorders developed in the late 1960s. Introduced originally as low-cost alternatives to the quadruplex machines, these recorders were at first only used for nonbroadcast applications such as college production courses and industrial training, as well as for an early form of off-line editing. In the intervening years, the basic helical-scan concept has become the worldwide standard, giving rise to numerous camera/VCR fomats that are differentiated according to tape size and signal type.

Transport Mechanisms

The various mechanisms that move the tape from the feed reel to the take-up reel are called the *transport system.* Many hours of tape may pass through this very complicated assembly each day, and the slightest deviation of speed or path can have serious negative effects upon picture quality. It is not surprising, therefore, that the transport system found on professional equipment is designed, manufactured, and assembled like an expensive watch.

The heart of the tape drive is the **servo capstan** mechanism that pulls the tape through the tape machine. It takes signals from the **sync pulses** on the **control track** (below) of the tape itself to reproduce the exact speeds of the tape at the moment that it was originally recorded.

Figure 9.6 does not show the location of this transport unit, but it does show how the tape is pulled out of the relatively simple VHS cassette so that it can be partially wound around the tilted video drum.[2] The figure does show the *erase* head located "upstream" of the video head, and the location of the *audio heads* and *control track heads* that govern the speed of the tape as mentioned above.

Head Assembly

Many improvements in machine capacity were made possible by the innovative design of the helical-scan video head assembly. Each of the angled parallel lines shown in figure 9.7 represents one continuous scanning of the tape by one of several video heads mounted on the tilted circular drum shown in the

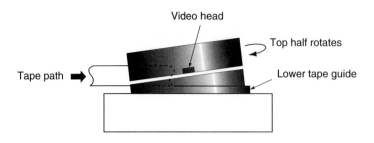

Video head

Top half rotates

Tape path ➡

Lower tape guide

Figure 9.8

Helical-scan videocassette drum assembly. The playback/record heads are attached to the rotating top half of the tilted head assembly.

same figure. Each single scan contains exactly the video information needed to record one complete 262.5-line picture *field.*

As the tape is pulled around the head drum, successive parallel angled (helical) tracks are scanned. In the *record* mode, the heads leave a magnetized memory of the picture signal from the camera. In the *playback* mode, a still picture is produced when the tape movement is stopped, because the video heads maintain a constant scanning speed on the diagonal of the tape. The heads scan the same area of the tape to reproduce the same picture field over and over again.

If the tape is moved at a slower-than-normal speed, a slow motion effect is achieved. As long as the revolving head speed remains constant, the video sync of the picture is maintained—no matter how fast or slowly the tape is pulled around the head drum. Remember that this 262.5-line picture *field* used to produce the *freeze-frame* or *slow-motion* effect contains only one-half of the video information necessary to reproduce a full 525-line picture *frame.* On consumer-level machines, this results in a somewhat washed-out picture. On professional units, information is "borrowed" from an earlier frame and is used to fill out the rest of the 525-line "slo-mo" picture.

Helical Scan Formats

In the early 1970s, the Sony ¾-inch **U-matic** format became the first broadcast quality helical-scan videotape unit. With its convenient cassette, it fit the needs of news and sports field production work and quickly became the standard. Its original analog/composite signal has been upgraded lately to an analog/compo-

nent format known as U-Matic SP. The head assembly (see figure 9.8) for the U-Matic is typical of all helical-scan machines. The first ½-inch professional Sony **Betacam** composite format has undergone many generational improvements over the years. It became Betacam SP, then Digital Betacam (which could play back the nondigital SP format), and finally the digital Betacam SX model. All of these formats used versions of the original *Betacam* transport system.

The Panasonic AJD 580, shown in figures 9.1 and 9.2, is a continuation of that company's line of products leading up to the digital D-5 level of cameras and recorders. A certain design compatibility that exists among such companies as Panasonic, JVC, Canon, and others is the result of a business relationship with the Matsushita corporation of Japan. Until the mid-1990s, these companies all used the "M" wrap and its related transport system in the majority of their VHS and professional VCR units (see figure 9.6).

9.4

Videotape Track Functions

At the time that this edition was being prepared for publication, the consumer/industrial level DV format had just come on the market. Similarly, the several new professional tape formats derived from DV, but incompatible with one another, were also just on the market. Because of this uncertainty and coupled with the fact that budgets at most educational institutions will possibly preclude much involvement in those formats in the near future, the first and largest part of

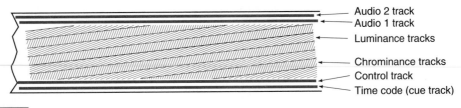

Audio 2 track
Audio 1 track
Luminance tracks
Chrominance tracks
Control track
Time code (cue track)

Figure 9.9

Configuration of ½-inch Betacam format (not to scale). Note that alternate video tracks carry the luminance information, while every other video track carries the chrominance signal.

this section will be devoted to the formats that will continue to be used at most institutions.

Obviously, a videotape has to contain more information than just picture signals. In the interests of simplicity, figure 9.9 shows the configuration of tracks used on an earlier Betacam format. Later VCR formats have added even more audio tracks that are used for sound mixing during editing as well as for second language and descriptive applications.

The Video Track

The portion of the videotape that carries the series of slanted video scanning lines is known as the **video track;** this occupies roughly 80 percent of the tape area in helical-scan formats. It is here that the information dealing with the picture signal, color, and brightness is carried. Every second, sixty of the slanted tracks are scanned to produce sixty fields—resulting in the rate of thirty completely scanned picture frames per second.

As shown in figure 9.9, this older Betacam system used a two-track system similar to those used today. One video track carries the *luminance* (brightness) information, and the next track carries the *chrominance* (color) information. Note that on professional machines there are also two "flying" erase heads—one for each track—revolving around the drum head to accomplish the function of the stationary erase heads shown in figure 9.6. Their ability to start and stop erasing at a specific frame is essential to editing. In addition to the video tracks, an increasing number of other tracks are simultaneously contributing to the picture and sound. Along with the two or more *audio* tracks, there is a *control* track and a separate "address" or *cue* track at the bottom of the tape.

The Control Track

Earlier sections have described how the continuous picture display on a monitor is synchronized with the original camera picture by means of *vertical* and *horizontal synchronization* pulses. For every 262.5 horizontal pulses, there is one vertical pulse that initiates scanning of a new odd or even-lined picture field.

When the television picture information is recorded, these *sync pulses*—and some related information—are separated from the color and brightness signals and recorded on an individual band or *control track* of the tape. During the playback of recorded videotape programs, the sync pulse serves an additional important purpose. The playback machine reads the signals and uses them to regulate the speed at which the *capstan* pulls the tape through the transport system—as well as the speed at which the video head wheel turns. This *servo control system,* in effect, tells the playback VCR exactly how fast the tape was moving when it was originally recorded. When a broadcast picture is received at home, it is these sync pulses that "lock together" the camera or studio tape machine signal with the home TV set.

The Cue Track

The title **cue track** is derived from a time when it was used for verbal editing cues. Now, it is used to lay down the signal for an editing location system called the **SMPTE time code.** This location system produces a digital clock-like numerical readout or *address* for each hour, minute, second, and frame recorded on the videotape. It can reflect the "real time" at which the tape was recorded, or it can be

Display of time-code information. The SMPTE time code address system, stated in hours, minutes, seconds, and frames, can be used by a computer-based disc controller to locate any frame in less than one-half second.

added later, showing time elapsed from the beginning of a production or from some other reference point on the tape. The readout, as illustrated in figure 9.10, can be displayed on the picture monitor by a process similar to the way titles are matted over any picture source.

For some editing applications, the **window** display becomes a part of a **workprint** tape dub and is seen as a permanent part of the picture. Also, during the editing process, the time code can be viewed by means of LED (light-emitting diode) readouts located at the control panel and on the machines themselves. In most current editing systems, a computer can "read" the unseen time code to locate predetermined edit points for the execution of cuts, dissolves, and special effects. Time-code referencing is especially important for programs such as *Wide World of Sports*—or the Olympics—where tapes from a number of recorders in many different locations must later be edited together in precise chronological synchronization.

The Audio Track

The **audio track** hardly needs further explanation. The technology involved is exactly that of conventional sound recording. It must be noted, though, that the quality is somewhat less than that of professional audio equipment used in recording studios. The television industry is just beginning to take advantage of its capacity for stereo and high-fidelity sound—up to the 15,000-Hz level now heard on FM radio. As more home receivers are sold with this *MTS* (multichannel television sound) capacity, more stations and cable systems are making the necessary modifications for increased audio fidelity.

The audio track configuration of some consumer and "prosumer" formats allows for audio dubbing (editing). Early VHS format group models had only a single linear mono track. When a Hi-fi track was later added, it was *layered* under the video track and, thus, could not be edited without disturbing the video track. The mono track can be edited, but its quality is somewhat less. 8mm cameras and recorders using only AFM (audio frequency modulation) cannot be edited, because the audio is blended with the video. PCM (pulse colde modulation) units have a separate track that can be edited. The new DV format offers a choice of either two or four tracks in a PCM audio system. The four-track option allows for editing, but the CD-quality is slightly less than when only two tracks are used.

Track Configuration of the New Digital Formats

The Panasonic DVCPRO camcorder/VCR format, designed for field acquisition of news footage, keeps the control and cue tracks bottom and top as shown in figure 9.11. Just above the control track at the beginning of the scan there is the small Insert Track Information (ITI) sector that provides signals for automatic tracking, insert editing, and audio dubbing. Moving upwards there is a small signal separation gap and then the area for audio recording. After another separation gap, there is the relatively large video area. Ten such scanning lines produce a NTSC video frame. After another protective gap, there is the sub code area that combines time code and other location identification signals. To protect against format isolation, the AJ-D750 VCR is impressive in the area of compatibility with almost complete digital, analog, and server interface. (See figure 9.12.)

Interestingly, the format (designed for the industrial-level videomaker) that served as the inspiration for the more advanced DVCPRO format uses much the same tape configuration, but does not have either

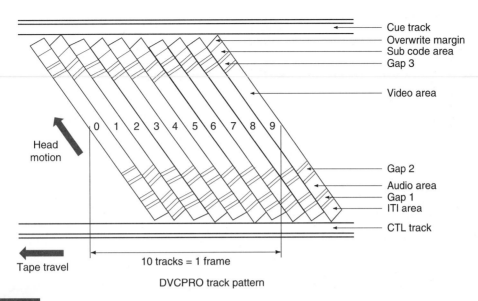

— Cue track
— Overwrite margin
— Sub code area
— Gap 3

— Video area

— Gap 2
— Audio area
— Gap 1
— ITI area

— CTL track

Head motion

0 1 2 3 4 5 6 7 8 9

Tape travel

10 tracks = 1 frame

DVCPRO track pattern

Figure 9.11

The configuration of tracks on the DVCPRO format tape shows considerable change from the original slant track for the Betacam shown in figure 9.7. The transport speed is much faster, and ten scans are needed to complete one NTSC frame.

Figure 9.12

As a new digital format, the Panasonic AJ-D750 DVCPRO editing recorder is designed to be compatible with a wide range of other digital, analog, and hard drive formats. Its ¼-inch tape comes in three cassette sizes, the largest of which holds 1 hour and 23 minutes of video.   *Photo courtesy of Panasonic*

a control or a cue track. Presumably this information is included in the ITI or sub code areas.

The Sony DVCAM format that also grew out of the industrial DV format has omitted any capacity for such things as closed captioning, but its intended use in the high end industrial area really doesn't call for any such capacity. In what may prove to be a prudent move, JVC has opted to create a new component digital format for professional and industrial use that is based on the successful S-VHS signal. Its new Digital

S VCRs will be "backward compatible" so that existing ½-inch S-VHS tapes can be played and edited in the new format. It uses the same size S-VHS size metal particle tape. In most ways, the JVC track configuration is similar to that of DVCPRO and Sony DVCAM formats. All of the new digital formats make use of the metal particle video tape instead of the original metal oxide coating still used on older formats.

9.5
Video Recorder Operations and Controls

The setup and operation of any VCR machine involves the use of components that generally fall under three headings: *connectors, control mechanisms,* and *visual indicators.* The arrangement, appearance, and even terminology may vary with the manufacturer—but once one knows what to look for, these basic components can be identified on any video recorder.

First, since videotape machines work in conjunction with other electronic units (cameras, microphones, other recorders, speakers, monitors, editing equipment, etc.), as a primary step, you must be able to make these hookups accurately and quickly. Second, you must learn how to manipulate the collection of knobs, switches, levers, and push buttons that are used to start, stop, or change the basic audio and video functions of record, playback, and editing. Third, you must be able to monitor and understand those things that tell whether or not the machine is operating the way you want it to—informational feedback provided by items such as monitors, lights, and meters.

Connections

In a studio situation where equipment and its related cables are permanently in place, the connection process takes place primarily at the patch bays, where labeled receptacles indicate the sources and termination points of feeds. Often the camera, VCR, and other pieces of equipment are semi-permanently connected, so you, as an operator, do not need to deal with the connections unless you do not obtain proper picture and sound.

However, much of the small format video for educational and industrial purposes—and much of the semi-EFP production for training purposes—involves a temporary "lash-up" of video recorders, cameras, mics, monitors, and associated gear in out-of-studio *field* locations. Whether in the studio or in the field, the operational linking of components will be most efficiently accomplished when three interacting factors are kept in mind:

1. The nature and purpose of all signal feeds
2. The direction and pathway of all signal flow
3. The structure of the connective hardware

If you know *what* your signal is supposed to do, it is easier to know *where* it should be going and *how* you are going to connect it to get it there.

Signal Flow

The first thing to keep in mind when making any connection is simply whether you are dealing with an *input* or an *output.* You should first look at a wiring diagram. If one is not available, the very act of making a sketch of the probable *sequence of signal flow* will bring some order to the process. Does the receptacle into which you are putting one end of a cable represent the signal output of a component? If so, with that connection made, the other end of the cable obviously becomes the new output of the signal—and as a result goes into an input receptacle to continue the movement of the signal. It must be emphasized that incorrect connections not only cause operational delay, they also can cause serious damage to equipment by overloading circuits.

Signal Levels

One of the main principles involved in the connection process is understanding the different compositions and strengths of signals that one deals with in making those hookups. In addition to differentiating audio from video feeds, one must realize that some lines, such as **radio frequency (RF)** signals, carry both audio and video.

The basic concept of amplification differences was introduced when discussing audio patching in chapter 3, section 3.2. The same principle applies to the way in which the video recorder handles audio and video. The recorder has a provision for the input of an external microphone ("mic in"). This low-level signal

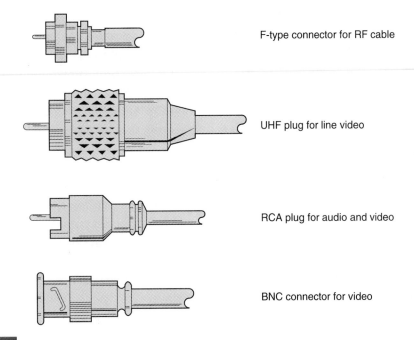

F-type connector for RF cable

UHF plug for line video

RCA plug for audio and video

BNC connector for video

Figure 9.13

Basic video plugs and connectors. Much of the multiple-pin hardware for the new digital formats is undergoing a process of standardization.

is then amplified to *line level* within the machine before being recorded on tape. However, previously amplified signals (an audio recorder, for example) are only to be plugged into "line" audio inputs. If these are plugged into a "mic" input, you will get a distortion from the double amplification.

Connecting Hardware

Connective hardware for audio and video equipment involves a wide variety of receptacles and matching plugs. For example, *line video* may utilize a BNC, UHF, or RCA plug. *Audio* is usually handled by a phone plug, Sony mini-plug, or RCA plug. With low-impedance mic lines,[3] a three-pin Canon connector is quite common. See figure 9.13 for the most commonly used video connecting hardware. Refer also to chapter 3, figure 3.7, for audio connectors, adapters, splitters, and terminators, some of which are used for video work as well.

Because of all the differences in plugs and receptacles, the connecting process is greatly aided with a good supply of adapter plugs on hand for all setup situations. It should also be noted that a variety of

cables are available with different connectors at the two ends. Such cables often make the most convenient types of adapters. With a variety of these on hand, one can quickly connect a number of components from different manufacturers with some degree of confidence. Caution and common sense should always be exercised when making such connections. As stated in chapter 3, it is not possible to make a high-impedance mic function with a low-impedance cable by simply using an adapter.

Controls

Regardless of the age or simplicity of design, the transport (tape movement) functions on all video recorders will have eight to ten basic controls. Normal speed playback is accomplished by activating the control labeled *play*. On many machines the recording mode is initiated by pressing *play* simultaneously with the *record* button; on other machines, just pressing *record* starts that function. On older and consumer-level cassette machines, the *stop* control not only stops the tape movement, but it also causes the tape to unwind from the video drum and be retracted into the cassette. This allows the *eject* control to be used to remove the cassette from the machine. On these units, "stop" should not be confused with the *pause* control that halts forward tape movement, but produces a "freeze-frame" picture. The tape is still in contact with the heads that are in motion scanning the same slant track again and again. With these older machines, the unit should not be left in this mode for more than a minute or so at one time, as the heads are continually wearing away the oxide on one specific track; tape damage and/or head clog can occur.

On all current professional models designed for editing, the *stop* command will put the machine into a mode that leaves a still picture on the monitor. Even though the tape is in contact with the rotating heads, there has been a lessening of the tape tension to avoid causing excess wear. These late model recorders also have another feature that automatically shuts off this stop/pause mode after it has been left alone for several minutes. The same feature is present in most camcorders also.

To get the tape quickly from one point to another, *fast-forward* and *rewind* controls are used. This is usually referred to as being in the **search mode.** On some units, these two modes will produce a somewhat recognizable picture for "search" purposes. Many VCRs—especially those designed for editing—also will have *variable speed* controls that facilitate slow or sped-up motion, either forward or backward.

The *audio dub* (audio edit) control puts the audio record head into the record mode without activating the video record heads, making possible short audio-only edits or the addition of a whole new audio track.

Tracking and Skew

One other control is important for accurate tape transport. The path of the tape around the video drum is crucial to the playback of a proper picture. Bands of picture distortion sometimes result when a tape recorded on one machine is played back on another with a slightly different horizontal alignment. This problem can usually be corrected by an adjustment of the **tracking** control. The normal operating setting as determined by the factory is located at the top point (12 o'clock position) on the dial. The slight click one feels when passing this point is known as a "detent"

position. After any tracking adjustment is made, the knob should be returned to this position for each new recording or playback.

On most professional units, there is an additional control for the tape transport called **skew.** When the top third of the picture appears to bend to the left or the right, it is usually caused by an incorrect amount of tension on the tape as it passes around the video drum. This is adjusted by means of the skew control knob. Keep in mind that this is a problem on the playback machine, not on the machine to which you are editing or dubbing. As with the tracking control, the knob should always be returned to the detent position before that same machine can be used for a subsequent recording or playback.

Selector Switches

As discussed previously, most video recorders are designed to function with a variety of different types of inputs such as a *camera*, the tuner in a *receiver/ monitor*, or a studio *line* feed. There must, therefore, be an *input selector switch* that differentiates between the various levels and/or sync sources of these inputs. The advice of a studio technician may be needed to determine proper switch positions. Whereas a camera signal from the studio switcher would feed through the line input, a single camera might use some other selector position.

On some machines, there is another switch that separately controls the use of internal or external *sync sources* (on several VCR makes, the alternative to the external position is labeled "defeat.") This *internal sync* position allows the recorder to "strip off" any incoming sync signal and utilize the synchronization pulse from the machine itself during the recording process.

Visual Indicators and Meters

The final area of concern is with visual monitoring and feedback indicators. Although these will vary from machine to machine, there are a number of controls that group together in operational units and directly relate to a visual readout—starting with the *pilot light* that indicates when the *power on/off* switch is activated. The most important of these are the VU meter (chapters 3 and 4) and the similar metered readouts that indicate video signal strength and the

Figure 9.14

The JVC Component Digital S BR-D85U is an outstanding example of a well-designed panel providing quick readability and ease of control. The deck is also compatible with the standard S-video signal.   *Photo courtesy of JVC*

accuracy of video head tracking. An excellent example of an easily-read front panel full of important information is found in the JVC BR-D85U Digital S editing recorder seen in figure 9.14. Unfortunately, the black and white picture shown here does not do justice to its beauty and clarity.

Automatic Gain Control

Most portable recorders have an **automatic gain control (AGC)** option for audio. When this is switched on, the AGC serves as a limiter that keeps incoming audio feeds within a range that does not exceed the capabilities of the recorder. However, the AGC often will automatically boost the "noise" of the line signal when there is momentarily no other incoming signal (a pause in the voice or music source), thereby recording an amplified hiss. The AGC selector switch allows you to defeat this feature.

Most machines will reflect their recording and editing functions with additional video control switches and indicators. There is a *video control* knob that adjusts the level of incoming video—as well as a related *AGC off-on* switch that allows for automatic gain control of the video signal. These are usually grouped with the *video VU meter*.

Warning Indicators

An increasing number of portable recorders are including a number of warning lights and status indicators that provide several types of important feedback to the operator. Sometimes these are on the body of the camcorder, and sometimes indications appear in the camera viewfinder. On some machines, a *pause mode* light serves as a reminder that the heads are continuing to scan the tape. There are also lights that indicate the condition of the *battery*, the presence of moisture that is dangerous to the circuitry (*auto off*), a *tape supply* warning light that lets you know you are coming to the end of your videotape, and a *servo* lamp that warns of improper tape transport.

Counters and Location Indicators

Virtually all recorders have some sort of *counter* or other component that allows an operator to locate predetermined points on a recorded tape. On consumer models and lower-end industrial units, there is usually only a three- or four-digit readout that counts the revolutions of the take-up reel. Since the circumference of the tape on each reel will change as the reels unwind and wind, the operator must keep in mind that a given number of revolutions will indicate different amounts of tape footage—depending upon how far one is into the program.

On most consumer-level VCRs, there is a zero-point *reset* button that, on rewind, brings the tape back to the zero point and comes to an automatic stop. A somewhat more complex *memory control* permits the quick location of a series of selected points with the tape in the fast-forward mode.

These controls are definitely useful, but as we shall see in the next chapter, it was the development of the SMPTE time code that put the use of videotape on a very efficient basis. With its display of the precise hour, minute, second, and frame (figure 9.10) of any particular point on a tape, program segments can be quickly set up for broadcast. Of even more importance are the obvious applications to videotape editing. What had previously been a slow, inexact, and expensive procedure has quickly become one of television's most important tools.

There is a second location method that has a display looking very much like time code, but it operates quite differently. Its numbering system is based on a count of the continuing sync pulses coming from the control track.

Both of these electronic digital readouts help the operator to "feel" the speed and direction of tape movement while operating the *variable speed* control dials. At the straight-up detent position, the tape is in "pause." The more you twist the dial to the right (clockwise), the faster the tape moves forward. As you turn the dial to the left (counterclockwise), the tape moves in reverse (rewind)—again with the speed determined by the extent you turn the dial. On most machines, speeds range from a very slow motion, one frame at a time, to five or more times normal speed.

Successful Performance and Maintenance

The key to successful operation of the videotape recorder—whether for a student instructional project or the operation of the latest digital/component unit—is *familiarity* and *practice.* Instructions and specific controls will, of course, vary significantly from machine to machine. Become familiar with the ones you have access to. Make certain you have taken full advantage of the instructions and directions for the particular models with which you will be working. Especially, follow the recommended care and maintenance instructions. This is particularly important for routine cleaning of the video heads. And then practice. Become familiar with the recorder. Under the guidance of a trained technician or instructor, work with the machine; experiment with it; find out what it will and will not do. Only then can you have the confidence and discipline to handle any video recording and playback assignment given to you.

A major part of your professional discipline will be care and respect for all production equipment—and the video recorder is one of the most expensive and delicate machines you will handle. Everyone will benefit if you follow a few common rules of preventative maintenance.

1. Videotape recorders require a constantly renewed supply of clean, cool, dry air. Heat, moisture, and cigarette smoke are damaging to all electronic equipment—especially VCR machines. Never place books, cassette cases, or papers on top of the recorder; it seriously inhibits the flow of air. Liquid containers and ashtrays—anywhere adjacent to video recorders—are simply disasters in the making.

2. Place a dust cover on the machine when it is not in use—but only after the unit has had time to cool off.

3. When a video recorder is moved, be extremely careful not to bump or jar the unit. Delicate components are easily damaged by slight shocks. Do not attempt to operate a recorder immediately

after it has been moved from a cold to a warm environment.

4. Videotape should not be left in the recorder when the unit is not in use. Tapes should be rewound and properly stored in a cool, dry place.

5. Keep the recorder and tapes at a distance from other equipment that may be generating strong magnetic fields, as these can erase the information on the tapes.

6. Do not tinker with various controls and functions without a clear purpose and idea of what you are doing. Do not fool around, for example, with the color lock control and other critical mechanisms. Maintenance personnel who are unaware of the misadjustments may spend hours trying to find and correct the resulting problems.

7. As the videotape operator, always allow yourself time to think through carefully all connecting and patching procedures—as well as the basic disciplines of machine operation. The time spent always pays off later in time saved.

Summary

The video recording process involves an understanding of the entire electromagnetic concept. For our purposes, we have looked at two aspects of the electromagnetic phenomenon—*electronic principles* (such as the horizontal and vertical sync pulses) and *magnetic principles* (the electromagnetic properties of an electrical current rearranging iron oxide or metal particles) to record a video signal on videotape.

Just as the bulky and expensive *quad*-head machines have been supplanted by the *helical-scan video recorder*, the industry is now looking to *digital nonlinear* storage, editing, and production distribution. It is important that operators understand how the various *audio and video tracks* function as a part of the recording, editing, and playback process. Each tape has a carefully located space for picture information, *control track, cue signals,* and audio track(s).

Operational functions for VCR machines include three main considerations: *connections* (with cameras, switcher, line feeds, microphones, other recorders, speakers, monitors, editing facilities, etc.); *controls* (for all operating modes such as play, record, fast forward, rewind, stop, pause, variable speed, dubbing and editing, input and sync selection, tracking and skewing adjustments); and *indicators* (lights, VU meters, counters, etc.).

This information will be invaluable in chapter 10, as we continue looking at the video recording process as it applies specifically to electronic editing.

Footnotes

1. The book, *Digital Nonlinear Editing,* by Thomas A. Hanian, Focal Press, 1993, provides a good background on a range of technical matters relating to nonlinear editing. It discusses the number of bytes of information necessary for the storage of various levels of video information. Each byte is made up of eight bits of information in the 0 or 1 digital code. In one video frame, a single byte could represent the gray scale value for one pixel of the total picture. The terms kilobyte (KB), megabyte (MB), and gigabyte (GB) denote the quantities of a thousand, a million, and a billion bytes of digital information. For its Media Recorder unit, Avid Technologies cites a capacity figure of 20 minutes of audio and video for a 3 GB drive. Groups of these 3 GB drives can be connected for added capacity. Capacity can vary greatly according to the type of compression technology used in the storage process.

2. As with self-contained audio sources, the term cassette refers to a two-reeled unit in a semiclosed case; the videotape is not exposed to human handling. Once the cassette is inserted into its loading deck, the player mechanism automatically engages the tape around the recording head assembly. A cartridge, now used only for audio, refers to a single-reel container. When the cartridge is inserted into the player, it is automatically threaded; again, human hands do not become involved in the loading and threading operation.

3. Recall the discussion regarding impedance levels (chapter 3, section 3.1). In the studio, where the distance from the mic to the audio console may be up to 50 feet, a low impedance (low-line resistance) cable and microphone are used; however, home VCRs and many industrial-level recorders work with less expensive high-impedance (greater resistance) lines and matching mics that are designed to carry not more than 6 to 8 feet. A mismatch of lines and mics can cause hum or other distortion.

chapter 10

Video Editing: Equipment and Techniques

T hose movie pioneers who made the first silent films soon discovered how powerful a *close-up shot* could be in the telling of a story. Since its beginnings, the dramatic stage had always been limited to the aspect of the entire proscenium as its visual perspective. Considering audience-to-performer distance, most emotions had to be expressed by large arm and body movements. Film, however, could use what humankind has always used to communicate, the expressions of the eyes and facial muscles. The subjective as well as the objective aspects of the visual narrative could be combined through editing. By the 1930s, as a result, motion pictures had become a truly creative art.

10.1

Editing as a Factor in Television Production

When television first began, much of what the audience saw was occurring at that very moment *live* in a studio somewhere. The director did the editing from the control booth, calling for the use of various camera shots as the program progressed. Then, as now, on the director's command the technical director used the switcher to connect the visual flow of the program by means of takes, dissolves, superimpositions, and fades to black. For network level musical

Figure 10.1

This telecine suite is used to transfer increasing amounts of film into digitized video for postproduction editing, graphics, and other special effects work. The original quality of film is often improved by the operation of the *Ursa/Sintel Converter* in the background. *Photo courtesy of Hollywood Digital*

and dramatic productions this approach necessitated a lot of prior planning. With limited amounts of rehearsal time, the problems that could arise during a live 90 minute play would often negatively effect even the best-planned productions.

While the programs of the so-called "Golden Age of Television[1]" were often very impressive, the networks eventually turned to the film industry for much of its dramatic and situation comedy programming. Many in the industry felt more comfortable with the idea that with the traditional single-camera film system of shooting, management could exercise more control over production, especially editing. The distribution of syndicated reruns was made possible by the shift of much of prime time TV to film.

With the introduction of videotape and especially the development of an efficient editing technology, the nature of broadcasting (and eventually cablecasting) began to change again. A new multiple-camera technique known as "live-to-tape" emerged for game and talk shows. Videotape replaced film on newscasts.

In a somewhat ironic move, those dramas, situation comedies, commercials, and rock videos that con-

tinue being shot on film have long since changed over to a process that puts the footage on videotape for all editing and effects work. Figure 10.1 shows a **telecine** suite where the film is not only transferred, but also where color corrections are made and other imperfections are eliminated. Operator skill and some rather expensive equipment are required, but the results are impressive.

Three Categories of Editing for Video Production

Through the years, editing has been used in various ways for a variety of purposes and different types of programs. Sometimes the editing is completed after the main program is shot; sometimes it is accomplished prior to taping the major portion of the show; and sometimes the entire program is edited.

Postproduction Editing of Studio-based Production

The daytime "soaps" and some of the prime time situation comedies are shot using a multiple video camera technique. Two- to three-minute scenes are shot

Figure 10.2

Using disc-based nonlinear technology, the Avid NewsCutter™ expedites the movement of microwaved video from a news scene directly to the editing unit for assembly, effects, and audio voice/over work. Finished pieces are then immediately ready to be fed for broadcast from the same editing unit.   *Photo courtesy of Avid Technology, Inc.*

without interruption with the director calling the shots as in a live production. Later the segments are put into program sequence and slight errors, such as a poorly lit close-up or a late entrance, are corrected by editing in **pickup shots** that are reshot at the end of the scene.

Daytime game and talk shows undergo a slightly less complicated process called **sweetening.** These programs are usually taped start to finish, and it is not unusual to do five shows in one long production day. As stated above, *pickup shots* are recorded for insertion during a later editing session, where a number of other small sound and picture corrections are made.

Some programs, such as rock concerts, that are edited through the switcher and taped straight through from beginning to end will have an additional camera separately **slaved** to an additional videotape recorder. This camera usually is assigned to hold wide-angle **cover shots** or get spontaneous **close-ups.** The director can later edit these shots into the program to smooth out or further enhance what is still basically a switcher-edited production.

Preproduction Editing

In successful news programs the essential ingredient has always been fast-paced, well-edited tape footage. Avid Technology's NewsCutter™ (see figure 10.2) has been designed to take news video as microwaved from a news scene, record it on the disc-based nonlinear system for editing, and then fed it directly on the air from the same unit. Discs from Avid's CamCutter™ can be used immediately as source footage see chapter 1, figure 1.16). If only tape footage is available, it can be quickly digitized to disc. A/B editing,

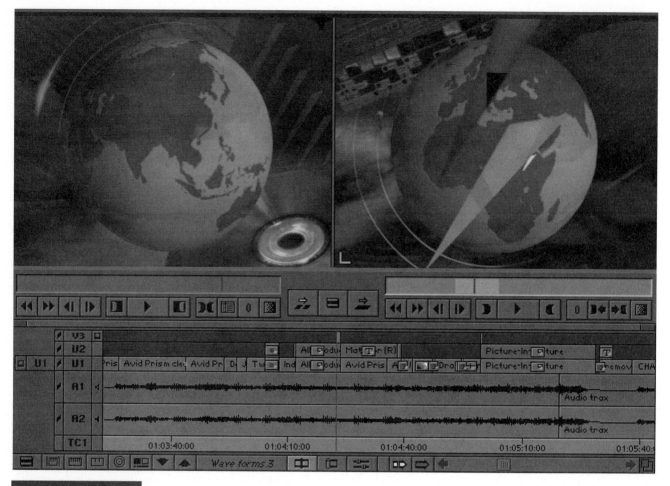

The disc-based nonlinear Avid Composer 8000 handles the demands of fully-edited high-budget productions that call for a wide range of editing capabilities based upon a reliable technical foundation. Note the cleanly designed user interface workscreen shown here. This unit has many features that aid in the location and quality control of video clips as well as the provision for such things as real-time 2D and 3D effects and twenty-four video tracks for layering and compositing.
Photo courtesy of Avid Technology, Inc.

as well as motion and 2D video effects, can be part of the editing process. As with all Avid edit systems, it operates on a Macintosh platform.

Similarly, magazine format shows such as *Entertainment Tonight* depend upon interesting, well-produced tape segments being fed into a *live-to-tape* program format. Much like a newscast, the *ET* show spends more than four hours each day prior to its studio assembly period preparing animated graphics that appear behind the host and hostess as well as on the full screen. Both of the above program types, as well as a number of public affairs and corporate video

formats, share the technique of maintaining a sense of spontaneity by balancing the edited segments with on-camera anchor/host *"wrap-arounds."* The video work done for the preparation of the *interactive multimedia* product is considered also to be in this category.

Completely Edited Production

A single-camera technique is essential for some types of production, whether the **acquisition mode** involves the use of film or video cameras. This approach, which grew along with the movie industry,

Figure 10.4

The disc-based nonlinear PostSuite from D-Vision offers editors the ability to open and edit an almost unlimited number of time lines. Basic 2D and 3D effects are included. The advanced model, PostSuite-EXD, can work simultaneously with composite, Y | C and component analog video at the level of broadcast quality resolution.   *Photo courtesy of D-Vision*

is used for such diverse production work as serious drama, commercials, rock videos, and the currently popular reality-based "police-in-action" shows. It also encompasses the documentary techniques that are applied to corporate and educational video. Camera work involves multiple takes of individual segments shot out of sequence and often at different locations. It gives the director a much higher level of control over all aspects of the production but is expensive and time-consuming.

As stated in the beginning of this chapter, many productions that are shot on film are transferred to video-disc for editing, titles, and special effect work. Much of this *long-form* production work requires considerable storage capacity as a part of the total editing

system plus a number of features to aid the editor, who may be putting in ten- and twelve-hour days. Avid's Media Composer Family (see figure 10.3) is often used for this sort of work. It has some 9,000 installations worldwide. The PostSuite models from D-Vision are said to be popular with those whose early editing experience has been largely with film. It operates on a PC platform using Windows NT. (See figure 10.4.)

When, in the middle 1990s, leaders from the film industry began to get very involved in the final decisions about the technical aspects of the High Definition Television signal, many observers saw this as an indication that an increasing amount of film-based production would eventually turn to digital video. As

Figure 10.5

Using portable D/Vision Pro equipment and software, editor Dan Moore quickly assembles a rough-cut for the director while a feature film is being shot on location. To get the footage, video cameras are bolted to the side of the film cameras.
Photo courtesy of D/Vision

stated in the beginning of this chapter, for the past decade, large amounts of what is shot on film has been transferred to tape or disc for editing, titles, and effects. This system is used for the production of almost all commercials as well as promotional and public service spots. Another indication of the tendency toward the convergence of technologies is seen in figure 10.5. Editor Dan Moore prepares a rough-cut of a feature being shot on location. As the film cameras roll, video cameras bolted to their sides make a simultaneous copy of the footage. This becomes the basis for an edit decision list that can be conformed to the film editing process. Moore worked on location with this system during the filming of *Jurassic Park II.*

10.2
Preliminary Editing Concepts

The primary technical objective of an edit is to place the beginning of a selected segment of picture and sound at the conclusion of a previously selected segment. This basic concept is the same regardless of whether the editing method is linear or nonlinear. The edit is accomplished by means of an electronic transfer of the selected segment from an **original master** (on videotape or digital disc) to the **edited master** which can be to either medium depending upon distribution or storage requirements.

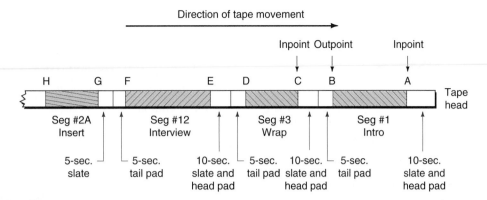

Figure 10.6

Camera segments as recorded on the original master tape. In this example, there are three segments of program material plus one insert segment to be edited in later. These are to be edited together in the order of the indicated segment numbers, but not as recorded.

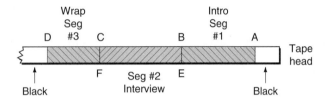

Figure 10.7

Eventual assembly plan for the transfer of the three main segments. As the program segments (from figure 10.6) are assembled, the inpoint of segment 2 (E) is electronically transferred to the outpoint of segment 1 (B). Segment 3 is handled in a similar manner.

The nature of single-camera shooting is such that segments are not only shot out of order, but are often shot several times before a satisfactory **"take"** is achieved. There is also other material on the tape that must be eliminated. In figure 10.6, we see a short version of footage on an original master. The fist 10 seconds of footage (moving right to left) contains an identification of the segment called a **slate.** Often just a chalkboard, it is usually held directly in front of a performer's face. With the tape still rolling, it is removed as the performer waits for a start cue. This last piece of footage, the **head pad,** is important in that it allows for adjustments in editing to any previous segment or title. **Inpoint** "A" is where the person on camera starts speaking and an **outpoint** "B" is where the voice stops and segment #1 ends. This must be followed by roughly 5 seconds more of continuing picture called **tail pad.** When the first segment (scene)

is transferred from the **playback machine** to the **record machine,** at least several seconds of this extra footage must also be temporarily recorded. As above there will be some flexibility in the timing of exactly how closely the next segment will follow when it is joined to the end of segment #1.

Looking again at the original master tape example, we see additional slate and tail pad footage. We also see other segments that are not in sequence with the eventual plan for the segments, as shown in figure 10.7. This plan is the result of an earlier **pre-edit session,** involving the producer, director, and probably the editor, during which scenes are listed **(logged)** in their original shooting sequence. A numerical system described below is used to identify possible inpoints and outpoints as well as some identifying notes on content. Once this process is completed, it can be decided that points "E" to "F" will be segment #2 as a part of a larger **edit decision list (EDL)** that becomes the plan for the final edited sequence.

10.3

Editing Control Systems and Related Equipment

Some basic, but often effective, editing is being done by amateurs at home using their camera or a VCR as a source tape playback unit along with a second VCR as the record machine. Using the above example, the new inpoint is selected on the playback unit, which is then placed in the **pause mode** just ahead of that inpoint. To function properly, the recording VCR must have the capacity to go into pause at a selected outpoint and then be put into a **pause/record mode** at that same point with no disruption of the previously recorded picture. For an edit, the playback is then rolled and the record machine taken out of pause as the selected inpoint is reached on the playback VCR. The all-important technical factor for the method is the existence of a "flying erase head" located on the drum just next to the edit record head. This configuration makes it possible for the VCR to erase previous material on tape and to lay down a new video signal without breakup. After one has later worked with equipment designed for real editing control, such efforts may seem rather primitive; however, the benefits of working through such an assembly process a number of times and getting some sort of product out of one's raw footage (that otherwise rarely gets viewed) makes it well worth the effort.

The Videotape Controller

At the next higher level of assembly, this process of positioning playback and record tapes prior to moving them through the edit sequence is done by an **edit controller.** Some units handle only one edit at a time, but newer models can be programmed to do a single edit or automatically go through the contents of an entire *edit decision list.* Although some controllers may be designed to go into *record* mode directly from the *pause mode* as described above, a **pre-edit roll period**

is usually standard for at least the record machine. The purpose of this feature is to assure proper tape speed when the edit takes place. On most units, the operator programs the edit location and then, on command, the controller automatically rolls to a position for each that is 5 seconds (or more) ahead of the upcoming edit. Both machines then come to a stop and wait for the command to proceed with the edit or for a **preview** that could call for further adjustment. These operations are explained in greater detail in section 10.4.

The Sony AV XL 100 controller, shown in figure 10.8, has a built-in audio mixer and a method of adding titles along with some other computer-like attributes, such as the storage of edit information for later use. Other units have actual character generators with keyboards for adding titles and credits. Most of these professional-level models can be connected to external switchers to allow for dissolves among two or more playback reels.

The Use of Time Code

The essential element in any edit control mechanism is an accurate **address system** that allows the editor to identify numerically any single picture frame on tape or disc, and then return to it quickly and accurately. The original system, devised by the Society of Television and Motion Picture Engineers (SMPTE) is, with variations, still the most-often used. Known as **time code,** its electronic signal is the basis of a system that identifies every single frame of picture from an established point, such as the beginning of the tape or actual time at the shooting location. In chapter 9, figure 9.10, using a 24-hour clock, the numbers would stand for 16:00 hours (4 o'clock), 42 minutes, 43 seconds, and 22 frames.

The numbers are not usually seen on a monitor, except as part of some editing procedures, but the signal that generates those numbers is used by the controller (and computer as explained below) to locate and precisely position videotape for the edit sequence. With a digital disc, these numbers work with somewhat different equipment to accomplish the same purpose. Originally, this information was recorded on one of the tape audio tracks. In newer

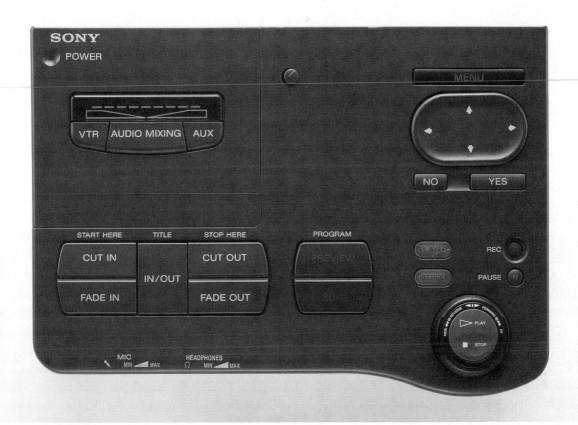

Figure 10.8

The Sony XV AL 100 performs the primary function of positioning two or more tape machines for all phases of the edit process for both audio and video. In addition, it has many computer-like attributes such as being able to store the timecode information needed to perform edits programmed into it.   *Photo courtesy of Sony Electronics Inc.*

systems, it is recorded on its own track or in another section of the tape known as the **vertical interval.** This is the **retrace** area, where the scanning process stops at the bottom of the frame and returns to the top of the frame. Because it uses the vertical interval, this type of time code is known as **VITC (vertical interval time code).**

A much simpler type of location system still functions with some older controllers and tape machines. The sync pulse of the control track serves as the basis of a similar indication of hours, minutes, seconds, and frames. In many ways it can be used very much like SMPTE time code. This sort of control-track editing is very acceptable in training situations but has drawbacks, because the frame location numbers are not permanently recorded on tape. They exist only in the edit controller and in relation to a movable "∅" point,

which can be changed by the operator at any time (possibly by accident). The numbering system is erased each time the tape is removed from the machine, but it can be restored accurately if a definite "∅" point is selected and reused at each editing session.

Computer-based Control Systems

With its incredible ability to count, sort, and remember, it was only natural that computers would be combined with videotape control systems for editing purposes. The software that comes with the edit controller (or separately purchased) is programmed into the computer. This provides for a number of screens and dialogue boxes that are used to do such things as calibrate tape beginnings, adjust for tape machine

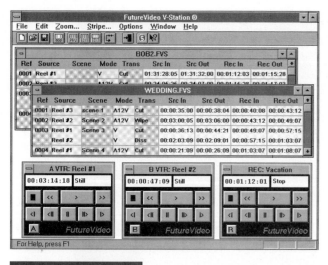

Figure 10.9

This primary EDL screen display, generated by the FutureVideo® V-Station 3300 edit controller, shows inpoints and outpoints in SMPTE time code and other edit-related information to the left. The dialogue boxes below control all modes of VCR tape movement. Other drop-down boxes are used for preview and any adjustment of the EDL.
Photo courtesy of Future Video

start and stop characteristics, and set preroll period times. When all of such things are done properly, **frame-accurate** edits can be achieved that are precise to within several frames.

After carefully examining the available material, the editor and others responsible for the final production work through the preliminary list of footage to create the *edit decision list.* Figure 10.9 shows part of an EDL as entered into the computer through the use of Future Video's V-Station 3300 Edit Controller. Note in the illustration that the operator has entered (from left) a number of items such as source reel numbers, scene numbers, and types of transition, as well as the time code for source and record inpoints and outpoints. The lower area of the screen shows where the computer **mouse** would be used to control the movement of two source machines and the record machine. Some computer-based controllers have attractive optional features that include a screen display of freeze-frame **picons** from the beginning of segments and horizontal depictions of the footage and sound as it relates to the point of edit.

With the completed decision list entered into the computer, the next step would be a **review** of all edits in program sequence. Unlike nonlinear editing (see below), this review function cannot be accomplished in **real time** due to the delay as source machines are rolled to succeeding inpoints on the source tape(s). This operation does, however, give the operator an approximation of nonlinear editing techniques in that changes can be made before any final assembly is done. In professional situations, this process of working with each individual edit to make sure that each segment ending leads comfortably in to the next, getting the timing of a conversation just right, and numerous other subtle and creative elements is known as **off-line** editing. The immediate goal is a start to finish **rough cut** that lets the production be considered as a whole. Changes continue as long as necessary. Only when the producer is satisfied is the final **on-line** assembly process started. At this point, all of the time code numbers and other notes are used to build the control information that is needed to create one final **edited master.** In professional situations, it is not uncommon to have different editors for each type of work.

The equipment for computer/controller linear editing is within the financial reach of almost all educational institutions, those in the "prosumer" level of activity, and a growing number of amateurs. There are several magazines that can be of help in getting to know the sort of equipment that is being used to create an editing suite. The computer that stores such things as the software and the EDL should be in the 486 range with 4 MB of RAM and 5 MB of storage. Cameras used as a tape source and other player/ recorder VCRs must be equipped with control protocols such as the RS 422A, Control-M (5 pin), and control-L (2.5 mm). Machines, such as the Sony SLVR 1000 and the Panasonic AG 1960 (see figure 10.10), are designed with this level of activity in mind. For A/B rolls and over 150 patterned transitions, plus mattes and other special effects, Panasonic's WJ-AVE 55 mixer, shown in figure 10.11, actually works more like an audio/video switcher. The Future Video V-Station 3300 controller, mentioned above, is one of several units designed with this mixer in mind. The manufacturers of all controller units will provide a long list of videotape machines and their protocols that are compatible with their controllers.

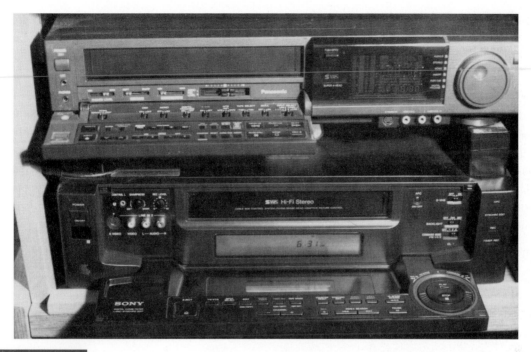

Figure 10.10

The Panasonic AG 1960 shown at the top of the picture has since been updated by the AG 1980. Along with the newer Sony SLVR 1000 shown below, they embody a number of professional features such as multiple inputs and outputs for both sound and picture, and control panels that provide a large amount of information relating to the editing process. They handle both the S-VHS and regular VHS signals.

Figure 10.11

The Panasonic WJ-AVE55 mixer connects to a PC and, interfacing with the controller, performs very much like an audio/video mixer. It is capable of over 150 patterned wipe transitions plus chroma key and luminance key functions ability along with other special effects.   *Photo courtesy of Panasonic*

Remember that there was a long period of time when all professional editing was done using the linear technique. With care and effort, the same impressive results are possible. There is a note of caution that must be added. Some of the programs designed for the *prosumer* level do not provide instruction books that are written clearly enough for the people for whom they are intended. This problem can sometimes be overcome if the telephone technical support advertised by the manufacturer is available and adequate to the needs of the caller. It is wise to have checked out these factors with independent sources before making any large investment in editing equipment.

Nonlinear DPR Computer Control

Although the signals were not digital, the first *nonlinear* editing units to be used commercially were available in the early 1970s. The *CMX 600,* developed by CBS and the Ampex Corporation, provided true **random access** to analog picture information stored on magnetic discs. Other companies used multiple videotape machines (all tapes containing identical material), and still others used laser discs to achieve the benefits of an instant video retrieval. It is the attribute of random access to digital video signals stored on disc that has produced the improvements found in nonlinear editing.

The differences between linear and nonlinear editing can be explained by using the oft-quoted analogy that describes a paragraph typed by an electric typewriter as being in linear form, while a computer with a word processing program can operate in a nonlinear style. We can use the typewriter erase ribbon to delete a specific sentence, but another sentence of exactly the same length must be typed if we wish to make a correction. This is what an *insert edit* can accomplish on an edited videotape; however, with a word processor, we can delete an entire sentence or any other group of words to make a shorter paragraph. We can also add several sentences and make a longer paragraph. Previously existing material following our word insert is automatically moved forward to make room for the new material. This is possible because the digitized information is not permanently recorded on the disc and can be located electronically and moved around at millisecond speeds.

This is exactly what the computer platform can do with digitized video and audio. Once the video has been logged and identified by time code plus a few words of description, it can be located quickly, viewed, and placed in position for a potential edit. An editor can even program *several* alternative cutting sequences and view each of them in *real-time* before making the final edit decision. Nonlinear systems have created a whole new *computer workstation* approach for editing.

Starting with the computer itself, the level of power usually recommended is in the range of a 486 DX66 system with 16 MB of RAM memory. Some of the software manufacturers prefer Windows 95 or NT for their PC-based applications. A number of manufacturers are focusing on the **digital boards** and **sound cards** that make up the **DPR (digital player/recorder)** unit. A Motion-JPEG board with an audio card to the right, as seen in figure 10.12, is a part of FAST Electronic's Video Machine system. These units convert analog signals to **digitized** signals (and back again). Many can be set to determine what ratio of compression will be used to store the digitized signal. The extent of the storage capacity as measured in **gigabytes.** Some kinds of off-line editing can be done with a low quality, highly compressed picture that needs little space. Other work must be done with no more than a 6 to 1 ratio in order to be able to export broadcast quality pictures. It follows then that the capacity of the hard drive could be anywhere from eight GB for editing commercials to twenty or more GB for longer forms. In the long run, GB capacity is determined by the consistent needs of a production organization. According to most working editors, there is never enough. Like the linear systems described above, the nonlinear system also needs a small but important **hard drive controller** that is usually in the form of an internal card.

With all of this equipment, plus assorted monitors, there is still one more important element needed in the mix—the **editing software.** Whichever product is selected, care must be exercised to be sure that the software is able to function at its optimum level with

Figure 10.12

This view of the internal structure of a digital player/recorder (DPR) Motion-JPEG board, along with the audio card, is a part of Fast Electronic's Video Machine system. It enables an editing system to function with tape, disc, or both.   *Photo courtesy of Fast Electronic U.S.*

all of the components of the system. Even if this factor is known, there are considerable differences in the performance of packages on the market. In a purely linear system, dissolves, wipes and other effects must be done through a process called **rendering.** This term means that the same 2-second dissolve that can be done in 2 seconds of *real time* on a linear unit could take several minutes with one nonlinear software package or only one-half minute on another.

On the subject of little-known negatives that are a part of the general wonder of nonlinear editing, there is also the small matter of **batch capture.** This term refers to the process through which one digitizes selected segments of footage from the *original master* onto the hard drive. The word "selected" is used here because, if the gigabyte capacity is small in relation to

that footage, then there must be either some sort of a selection process or the project must be edited in segments. Sometimes this ends up being time consuming and negates some of the benefits that are achieved through the instant access to footage on the hard drive.

Fundamental Concepts of Linear Editing Assembly

In a survey published in the October 1995 issue of TV Broadcast Magazine, 56 percent of those asked said that they would be "going digital" by the end of the century. Another 30 percent said "maybe" to the same

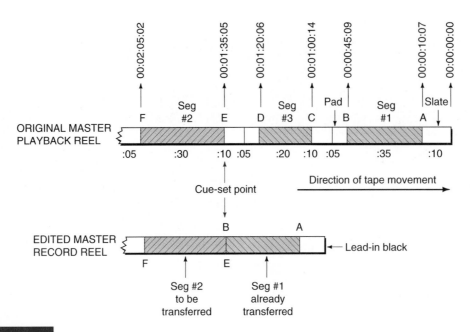

00:02:05:02
00:01:35:05
00:01:20:06
00:01:00:14
00:00:45:09
00:00:10:07
00:00:00:00

| | Seg #2 | | | Seg #3 | | Pad | | Seg #1 | | Slate |
| F | | E | D | | C | | B | | A | |

ORIGINAL MASTER
PLAYBACK REEL

:05   :30   :10 :05   :20   :10 :05   :35   :10

Cue-set point

Direction of tape movement

B   A

EDITED MASTER
RECORD REEL

←— Lead-in black

F   E

Seg #2   Seg #1
to be   already
transferred   transferred

Figure 10.13

Playback and record tapes as they would be positioned relative to the cue-set points entered into the controller. With segment #1 (*A–B*) already transferred from the original master (playback reel) to the record reel, the cue-set point is selected to determine the precise point to begin segment #2 using time code as those displayed here with segment times.

question. In a later survey published by the same magazine in January of 1996, 72 percent of the professional broadcasters who planned to purchase a VCR-machine during that year were going to buy a model with an *analog* signal base. This figure could have been influenced by the fact that 28 percent were planning to buy a disc-based digital server.

Whatever those figures have come to mean, the demise of videotape remains a question in the minds of many. One thing that can be said with some degree of certainty is that educational institutions will probably be among those at the latter part of the transition away from tape. At the present time, a number of schools do have nonlinear equipment. The brief coverage of linear and nonlinear components at the beginning of this chapter is designed to provide a quick background to the more specialized written material generated by each department for its own facilities. Many such departments, however, still teach an introductory editing course with their older linear machines. In many instructor's minds, this is not just a matter of budget. It is also the honestly-held belief that there are certain benefits to be

derived from introducing basic editing concepts with linear equipment. With this possibility in mind, the material presented in the following pages will be presented using the method of only one edit at a time in a semi-automatic mode of operation.

Organization of Segment Sequence

In section 10.1 we established the concept of *segments* and related material such as *head and tail pad* that make up an *original master reel.* Material is *logged* and selected for use at a *pre-edit session* where *edit decisions* relating to the final sequence of segments are made. For purposes of an editing example, let us establish the fact that segment #1 in figure 10.13 consists of the host/interviewer talking directly to the camera. Out-point *B* is the end of a sentence introducing a second person who will appear with the interviewer at the beginning of segment #2. Consider that segment #1 has already been electronically transferred from the playback reel to the record reel. This first edit transfer is really just a simple dub of segment #1 plus the essential 5 seconds of pad at the end.

Playback   Record

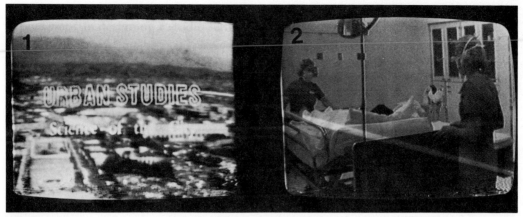

Figure 10.14

Simultaneous display of picture information from both the playback (original source) and record (edited master) machines. The operator watches the picture on the playback machine (*left*) while searching for the starting point of the next segment to be recorded. When located, the machine is put into the pause mode as seen here. During this search, the last frame of the previously recorded segment can be viewed on the monitor (*right*). The operator can easily compare these two pictures while making the edit decision.

Entering Edit Points

The ability of the editor to position these tapes in relation to the video recording and playback heads in each machine is dependent upon the use of the time code numbers as displayed in relation to the segment times in figure 10.13. The operator begins to set up what is actually the first real edit point by locating the numbers for the approximate outpoint of segment #1 on the LED readout for the record machine. The same procedure is followed for the inpoint of segment #2 on the playback machine.

The actual mechanics of using the controller to set up the edit are not complicated. There are a number of ways that tapes can be moved at various speeds to position tape. With the record deck in a slow mode that permits words to be understood, the operator would now lay the end of the cut that has just been recorded, listening for the final word. Depending upon equipment, the technique is to use the control to move the tape back and forth to find that word and then add at least fifteen frames (one-half second) of tape before putting the machine into the pause (freeze-frame) mode. Both the time code readouts and the video monitors provide important visual feedback for the operator during this process. It is important at

this point to keep in mind that a primary consideration in any edit decision involves making sure the short pause between edits always reflects a feeling of the natural pace of speech and conversation.

Now the same procedure is used with the source tape controls to find the precise inpoint that is roughly 1 second ahead of the first word of inpoint *E* of segment #2. When the cut is to a different individual from the one previously speaking, it is usual to provide at least 1 second on the new picture so as to establish or re-establish that person before they begin to speak. This being done, the two VCR machines are set up as is shown in the lower part of figure 10.13. Consider that the two arrows in the illustration indicate the two video recording heads in relation to the position of the segments on tape. The two video monitors could be showing something similar to figure 10.14.

To enter this edit point into the controller's memory, older manual units will have something like a central *set button* (enter) located adjacent to an *in* and an *out* button on both the source and record sides of the controllers. By simultaneously pressing the *set* and the *in* buttons on the source side of the controller and then the same two buttons on the record side, we have entered the edit point into the

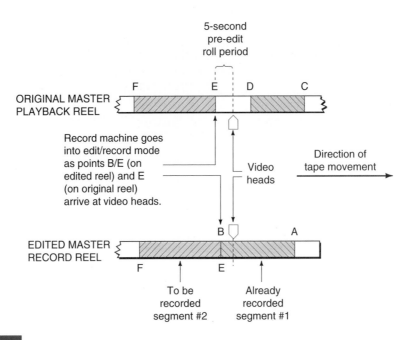

5-second
pre-edit
roll period

F   E   D   C

ORIGINAL MASTER
PLAYBACK REEL

Record machine goes
into edit/record mode
as points B/E (on
edited reel) and E
(on original reel)
arrive at video heads.

Video
heads

Direction of
tape movement

B   A

EDITED MASTER
RECORD REEL

F   E

To be
recorded
segment #2

Already
recorded
segment #1

Figure 10.15

Tapes on the playback and record machines in position for the pre-edit roll period. In this example, segment #1 (A–B) has already been transferred to the edited master record reel on the record machine. The next steps are to preview the upcoming edit, perform the edit, and then review it as performed. In all cases, the preroll period is necessary for the accuracy of the edit transfer.

controller's memory. Tape on the source machine is then rolled to find the approximate end point of the new segment. Again the operator makes sure that there is an extra several seconds of picture beyond the last word. By then pressing the *set* and *out* buttons on the source side of the machine, a completion point for the segment has been set that allows some flexibility with the next edit. The newer computer-driven controllers are built to work with an entire EDL at one time, but they are capable of executing single edits by the entering of in and out time on both the playback and record units.

Preview, Trim and Execution of the Edit

The machines are now set up to perform an edit, but only in rare circumstances would an editor proceed without a *preview* of the exact picture and sound at the transition between the two cuts before going ahead. This function can be accomplished without any actual transfer of the signal to the record tape. On command, the unit sets up as if it were going into an edit. Both tapes go to a *preroll point*, shown in figure 10.15, pause there briefly, and then roll both tapes forward. As the tapes are getting up to playing speed, the record monitor shows the end of its segment and the source monitor shows material in front of the inpoint of the new segment. There must always be 5 seconds of continuous sync picture (or whatever is set up for the preroll time) at the head of the source tape or the preview function cannot take place. At the point of edit, both monitors shift to the beginning of the new segment and proceed for another 5 seconds before coming to a stop.

If at the edit point something did not go as planned, it is possible to make an adjustment in the position of either of the two tapes to change the timing of the edit. Using our example, let's say that the one-half second of picture at the head of segment #2 (inpoint E) seems too short. One solution would be to use just a little more of the silent pad footage at the head of the segment. The **trim** control is designed to do just this by letting the editor program the edit to take place just a little earlier on the source tape. The trim control would be used to enter *minus* frames (lower numbers on the time code display) on the

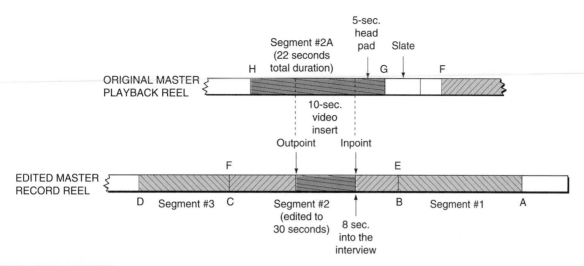

Playback and record machines set up for an insert edit. Ten seconds of video taken from segment #2A (shown in figure 10.6) is to be edited within segment #2 starting eight seconds after point B/E, the beginning of the segment. The two VTR machines are rolled simultaneously from points at least five seconds ahead of the anticipated edit. The edit in and edit out commands can be executed either manually or by the edit controller.

source side of the controller (the end pad of the recorded segment could have been extended as another option). If the editor is satisfied after a second preview, and the edit itself seemed to go as planned, then the *review* control can be used to confirm the edit. Adjustments such as these can make a considerable difference in how the edit looks may only involve as little as plus or minus ten frames.

Insert Editing

With segment #2 transferred, the best option is to continue with segment #3 and then return to the task of making an insert edit *2A*, which consists of a video shot (no sound) of the item that is being discussed in the interview. Such an insertion of "video only" is not difficult, but again there are some aesthetic and technical aspects to be considered. Most controllers still have a specific *insert mode* control option that retains the original control track and uses it for synchronization as the new picture (and sound) are added within a segment. Some editors use this mode for all editing even though they are, in effect, doing a segment by segment *assembly editing*. By first recording a black synchronous signal on the complete tape and then doing all edits within this black, there is an added stability to those edits.

On the aesthetic side, the conversation in segment #2 may provide an obvious cue such as a reference to the item in the close-up shot to be inserted. Prior planning by the director would probably include having the interviewer say something like, "Now on this particular unit . . ." to serve as an inpoint. The outpoint could be a little more subtle. The important thing is to have enough footage after the insert to re-establish the interview shot before the segment is concluded.

Figure 10.16 shows how, with these considerations in mind, the tapes would be set up in relationship to each other for "cut" transitions to and from the insert material. Note the allowance for at least 5 seconds of picture head pad on the playback machine. This is necessary in order to assure proper picture sync at the time of the inpoint edit. As stated previously, the insert will begin 8 seconds past the previously transferred edit point *B/E* and run for 10 seconds. Insert editing is by no means limited to just video. The insert can be combined video and audio using the same technique.

A and B Roll Transitions

Machine-to-machine edits as described up to this point can be used when the desired effect is that of an instantaneous *take*. **Cuts-only editing** can be accomplished

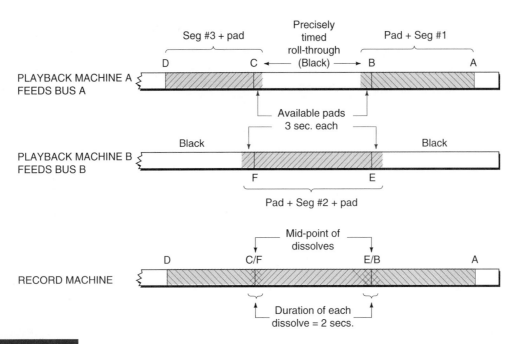

Three VCR machines set up for a dissolve edit. In preparing the *A* and *B* playback videotapes, care must be taken to ensure that every segment and each "roll-through" (black space between segments) is precisely timed—including the exact pads that are wanted. As the two playback tapes are fed into the switcher, the actual dissolve edits (on computer controlled editing units) are accomplished simply by using the fader arms.

with nothing more than two VCRs and a controller; however, when dissolves or special effects are desired, the levers, buttons, and mix banks buttons of a **switcher (video mixer),** as in figure 10.11, must be used. As in any dissolve or effect, this means there must be two simultaneous sources of video signal. Also, when mixing various video sources, the time-base corrector must be used to guarantee that all video signals will lock up with no picture breakup.

To dissolve between two segments, it is necessary to have two separate tape feeds on *A* and *B* source machines. The technique is somewhat the same as in traditional **A/B roll editing** for film, where the final composite film is automatically printed from two specially edited film rolls containing a series of timed intervals of picture and then black leader. For video this system can either be set up for automatic control or be done manually at the switcher during the edit session. The basic principles involved in setting up the tapes are roughly the same in either situation.

When a dissolve (or wipe or other effect) between segments is planned, it is imperative to allow consid-

erably more video pad (compared to editing a straight cut) following the outpoint of the first segment and preceding the inpoint of the second. For example, in the diagram shown in figure 10.17, the edit point *E/B* is the midpoint of a 2-second dissolve between segment #1 and segment #2; however, both playback machines must feed a video signal to the record machine throughout the duration of the dissolve. Although only 2 seconds of pad from each segment are actually needed for the 2-second dissolve overlap, it is always advisable to have extra-protection source video available. Most professional editors would not feel comfortable without a working margin of at least an additional 3 seconds added to each segment. While it may be good practice for a beginning crew to try for A/B roll results in order to get an understanding of the process, the truth is that most such work is usually saved for the sort of video mixers that were described above, where the computer and controller can be programmed for the real control that is necessary for the execution of an edit decision list of any length.

Figure 10.18

A possible future use of videotape may be anticipated in Panasonic's new Postbox, designed to operate with both digital tape and disc. It is envisioned as a complete postproduction unit with several optional levels of M-JPEG in addition to a wide range of sophisticated special effects. *Photo courtesy of Panasonic*

The Workstation Concept That Mixes Digital Tape and Nonlinear Disc

Looking to the needs of a future with a number of possible editing directions, Panasonic has recently put on the market its **Postbox** (see figure 10.18) nonlinear editing system that is designed to combine the benefits of one or more hard disc boxes with one or more VCRs like the DVCPRO AJ-750. As its title would indicate, it is envisioned as an all-around postproduction system offering a character generator with 42 fonts, a paint system, and other special effects including 2D and optional 3D (three dimensional) effects. It offers four levels of J-JPEG image quality.

The magazine survey cited earlier and the sort of equipment described above might well indicate that videotape, analog as well as digital, may be with us at least into the new century. Whatever the case and whatever its flaws, it must be said that tape, from its very beginnings, has served the video industry well.

Summary

Most editing techniques and the equipment that made them a functional part of television grew out of some obvious needs that became apparent as the industry developed. The original "edit-as-you-go" style of earlier live television gave way to a number of impressive videotape-based techniques that suited the needs of the growing audiences for sports, news, and situation comedies.

Videotape editing came to be seen as serving three distinct types of productions in somewhat different ways. The *postproduction* editing on situation comedies and soap operas takes individual short scenes and makes some minor corrections in both sound (applause) and picture (replacement for an out-of-focus close-up) and then assembles all the parts into a whole. The *preproduction* work that puts taped news footage into short concise stories is the backbone of the news program. Newer program types such as the reality-based "police-in-action" shows are shot with a *single-camera* technique that depends upon a *complete editing* job for final assembly.

For most of its history, editing for television has been *linear* in structure. All footage existed on tape, and to view it, one had to roll through it in the sequence of its location on that tape. Editing of any complexity was divided into an *off-line* planning and trial assembly stage. This was followed by a final assembly stage, termed *on-line editing.* The original *edit controllers* were eventually improved so that they could manipulate the tape with some facility. When *computer control* was added, an off-line editor still had to roll back and forth through tape but did so only for the purpose of creating a series of *edit decisions* that became the basis of the on-line assembly phase.

Nonlinear digital video editing makes possible the concept of *random access* to any frame of video that has been *digitalized* and placed on a *magnetic disc.* This means that an editor can instantly call up any segment (cut) of video and place it and other segments in a trial order for viewing in the off-line stage of editing. When this process has established a final edit decision list on a digital disc, the on-line computer-controlled unit can perform the final assembly with both speed and technical perfection.

The equipment is truly impressive, but the lesson for students continues to be that technology is worthless without the creative knowledge that can make it live up to a worthwhile potential. Linear, tape-based equipment will very possibly serve as the introductory medium for students for a number of years to come.

Footnotes

1. The "Golden Age of Television" is a term used about programming of the 1950s, and particularly refers to the anthology dramas such as "Marty" and "Requiem for a Heavyweight" that were produced and aired live.

chapter 11

Pictorial Elements: Sets and Graphics

 n this chapter, we will examine the two major pictorial elements that make up the visual aspects of television production—graphics and sets. Although these two topics will be discussed separately throughout most of the chapter, they both encompass several concepts that will be considered first, namely pictorial design functions and pictorial design factors.

Figure II.I

An abstract news set previously used for a local news program.   *Photo courtesy of KABC-TV, Los Angeles*

Pictorial Design Functions

Pictorial elements (like many other facets of television) are multifunctional. They can be used to convey information, and they serve to enhance or create emotional reactions within the audience members.

Informational Aspects

First, the *informational aspects of pictorial design* must be considered. They are concerned with conveying appropriate information cues to the audience as accurately and efficiently as possible. In the case of a dramatic setting, you ordinarily want to tell the audience as much as possible about the time and locale of the action. Where is the scene taking place? What is the historical period? What time of day is it? You may also want to give other pictorial cues. What is the sta-

tus of the main character? Where does he or she live? (Of course, there are many dramatic programs where this type of information is deliberately concealed from the audience to create suspense or dramatic surprise.)

Nondramatic programs also need to convey this kind of information data. Are we in a newsroom? A classroom? A corporate office? Are we on a stage in front of a live audience? Are we in a pulpit? How much do we need to tell the viewers about where they are and what they should know about their surroundings? All television staging considerations should start out with these types of questions.

With graphics, the informational considerations are even more important. The overwhelming use of graphics—especially for simpler productions and basic formats—is to convey information. What is the name of the program? What is the name of the person talking? How much of our tax dollar goes to education? What does the race course look like? How does the piston engine work? How bad was the accident?

Figure 11.2

A view of a working newsroom used as actual on-the-air background for a news set.   *Photo courtesy of KCBS-TV, Los Angeles*

In designing graphics, the need for clarity is paramount. The director and graphics person must always be asking, "How can I get this information across as clearly and efficiently as possible?"

Emotional Aspects

Second, the *emotional* or *psychological functions of pictorial design* must be considered. Many subtle messages can be conveyed by the total production design. All the scenic elements—sets, props, furniture—combine to give a "feel" or "image" to the program. In a news program, do you want the image of an advanced technological communications center, of an abstract setting (see figure 11.1), or of a working newsroom (see figure 11.2)? In an instructional TV program, do you want the image of a typical academic setting or of a research lab? In a religious program, do you want the image of a traditional church service or of an avant-garde contemporary movement? In a variety program, do you want the image of a conventional stage presentation or the electronic collage of a music video? Again, it is important that the director and designer begin with these types of questions before any decisions are made regarding the design or assemblage of set pieces or graphics.

In dramatic programs, of course, the overall *atmosphere* or *mood* is very important. Staging elements—combined with lighting—will tell us much about things such as the mystery of an event, the state of mind of the hero, the lurking tragedy, the atmosphere of a family gathering, the majesty of an accomplishment, the power behind a particular move, the potential danger behind a closed door, or the emptiness of a certain thought. The designer should always be concerned with maintaining or building the mood or feeling of every particular scene.

The emotional function of design also includes creating a *style* or **continuity** for the program. This style should carry through to all the pictorial elements used in the production; each pictorial element should look like it *belongs* with every other element. For instance, many news programs have more than one set. In some cases, a station has a news bureau in another city and, thus, part of the newscast originates from the set located there. These "satellite" sets should match the main set, exhibiting similar style cues such as color and decoration.

Maintaining this type of consistency is especially important in designing graphic elements. Most news programs, for example, use a particular lettering style,

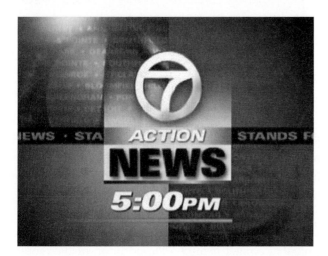

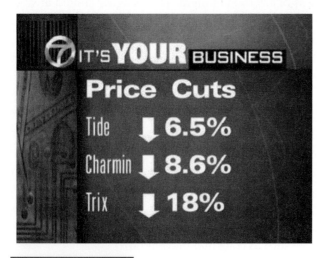

Figure II.3

This selection of graphics from a Detroit television station demonstrates the concepts of style and continuity. Note how elements such as lettering style and the channel 7 logo are used in each. This helps maintain a consistent look. *Photos courtesy of WXYZ-TV, Detroit* logo, or color scheme throughout all their graphics. Figure 11.3 shows an example of how various graphic elements in a program can be designed to enhance continuity.

Thus, every pictorial design should serve both an *informational* function and an *emotional* function. The set should not only tell us what time of day it is, but also give us a hint as to what is going to happen this day. The graphic should not only give us information, but also emphasize how important the information is.

11.2
Pictorial Design Factors

Artists and critics discourse long and eloquently about the many different factors that constitute aesthetic criteria—unity, harmony, texture, color, rhythm, proportion, and so forth. It is beyond the scope of this book to get into any detailed treatise on aesthetics of the still and moving picture. The beginning production student should be aware, however, of at least three pictorial design factors: (1) balance and mass; (2) lines and angles; and (3) tone and color.

Balance and Mass

The concept of balance was introduced in chapter 6, section 6.3 in connection with camera work. Asymmetrical balance is generally preferred over formal symmetrical balance. The larger a mass, the nearer it must be to the center of the scene in order to preserve a sense of balance with a smaller mass (see figure 11.4). In addition, the placement of mass within a scenic element will tend to affect the stability of the picture. A heavy mass in the bottom part of the picture implies

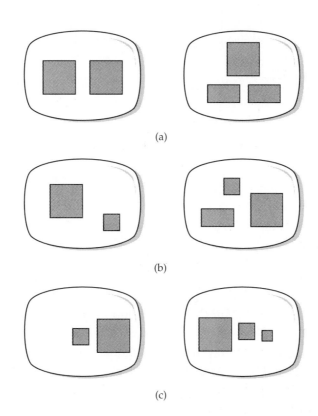

(a)

(b)

(c)

Figure 11.4

Symmetrical and asymmetrical balance. (a) Symmetrical balance usually results in a rigidity and precision that is usually not desired—except for certain formal settings. (b) Asymmetrical balance usually is more interesting and dynamic, resulting in a more fluid and creative mood—and just as well balanced aesthetically. (c) An unbalanced picture can result, however, if care is not taken to position the asymmetrical elements with respect to their weight and mass. Temporarily, this may be desired.

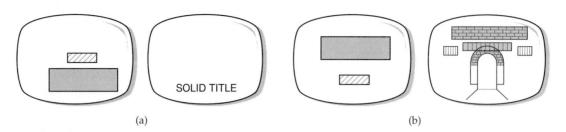

(a)   (b)

Figure 11.5

Location of mass in the picture. (a) Heavy weight in the bottom of the frame tends to give an impression of stability and security. (b) If the top of the picture contains more mass than the bottom, the result is a feeling of uneasiness and suspense.

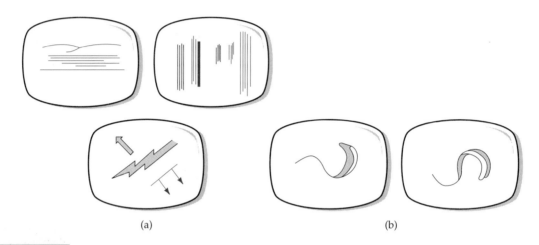

(a)   (b)

Figure 11.6

The effect of straight and curved lines. (a) Horizontal lines are restful, inactive, stable. Vertical lines suggest solemnity, dignity, dominance. Diagonal lines represent action, movement, impermanence. (b) Curved lines generally imply change, beauty, grace, flowing movement. With an upward open curve there is a feeling of freedom and openness. A downward open curve has more of a feeling of pressure and restriction.

firmness, solidarity, support, and importance. A heavier mass in the top part of the picture projects more instability, suspense, and impermanence (see figure 11.5). These considerations of balance and placement have strong implications for the design of sets and graphics as well as for camera composition. A graphic title with lettering in the bottom of the frame projects a solid, strong opening. A scenic unit with heavy ornamentation near the top implies a feeling of uneasiness and suspense.

Lines and Angles

The use of dominant lines is one of the strongest elements available to the scenic designer. Straight lines suggest firmness, rigidity, directness, and strength.

Curved or rounded lines imply softness, elegance, and movement. The direction of the dominant lines in a picture will carry strong connotations. Horizontal lines represent serenity, inactivity, and openness; vertical lines are dignified, important, and strong; diagonals imply action, imbalance, instability, and insecurity. (See figure 11.6.)

Lines and angles can also be used to reinforce or exaggerate perspective, giving more of an illusion of depth. Painted on the studio floor, *false perspective* lines can reinforce a great feeling of depth. Lines can also be worked into other scenic elements. This kind of false perspective is limiting, however, in that the illusion works from only one specific camera location. (See figure 11.7.)

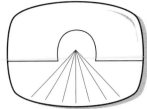

Figure II.7

Lines and perspective. A false perspective can be created by careful use of scenic elements and even by painting perspective lines on the studio floor.

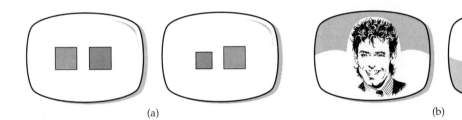

(a)   (b)

Figure II.8

Tone and balance. (a) A darker tone tends to imply more mass; thus the darker tone will overbalance the lighter mass **(left)**. A smaller dark mass can be used to balance a lighter mass that is larger **(right)**. (b) A darker tone or darker color at the top of the picture or scenic element will tend to imply a top-heavy feeling of depression **(left)**. The lighter tone or brighter color at the top gives a feeling of more solidarity and normalcy **(right)**.

Tone and Color

The predominant tones determine, to a great extent, the overall emotional image of a production. Light tones result in a delicate, cheerful, happy, or trivial feeling, whereas dark tones result in a heavy, somber, serious, or forceful feeling. Tone also affects balance. A dark tone carries more mass, weighs more, and can be used to balance a larger mass that is light in color or tone.

The position of various tones or blocks of dark and light mass in a picture also affects its stability and emotional quality. A dark mass at the top of a picture tends to induce a heavy, unnatural feeling of entrapment and depression; heavier tones in the bottom of a picture give it more of a stable base. (See figure 11.8.)

As shown in colorplate B, color is usually discussed in terms of three characteristics: **Hue** is the actual color base itself (red, green, purple, orange, and so forth); **saturation** refers to the strength or intensity of a color (how far removed it is from a neutral or gray shade); and **brightness** (or *lightness*) indicates where the color would fall on a scale from light (white) to dark (black). The considerations mentioned for tone apply to color; for example, highly saturated colors (a vivid red) appear heavier—for purposes of balance—than unsaturated colors (a grayish red).

Various hues are also subjectively classified as *warm* (yellows and reds) or *cool* (blues and greens). Warm colors appear to be "heavier" than cool colors. Much of the secret of achieving good color balance is the art of mixing various hues that are compatible, balancing highly saturated colors with grayer shades, and selecting the right brightness of a particular hue (for example, baby blue rather than navy blue).

All these elements of design—balance, line, tone—must be kept in mind as you look specifically at the elements of graphic composition and set design.

II.3

Computer-Generated Graphics

Many years ago, most TV station graphics consisted of title cards made by applying rub-on or stick-on letters to sheets of cardboard that were then placed in

front of the camera. Occasionally, stations had "high tech" equipment—metal type (circa 1889)—which, when pressed onto a sheet of acetate with pigment on one side, melted an impression of the type onto a card, usually burning the operator's hand in the process. If a chart or graph was needed, an artist drew it by hand, sometimes aided by a compass and protractor. Those days are long gone. Now, most graphics are constructed with the aid of a computer.

Computer equipment for creating and manipulating graphics falls into three main categories: **character generators, graphics generators**, and **electronic still store** (ESS) units. As with many pieces of television equipment—especially computer-based equipment—the lines that separate these categories often are blurry. Some pieces of equipment, for instance, can perform all three functions. However,

in order to understand how computerized graphic equipment works, it is useful to examine these functions separately.

Character Generators

If you have used a word processing or desktop publishing program on a computer, you are familiar with the basic concept of a character generator (CG). CG units, which often look like an electronic typewriter (see figure 11.9), allow the user to type words which can be output as a television signal. The first CG units, which appeared in the 1970s, were decidedly limited by today's standards. Many produced crude, jaggy lettering and provided few automated functions.

Today's character generators provide many more features and produce very high quality output.

A graphics tablet and digitizing pen are basic tools for any electronic artist.

CG operators can perform functions such as copying and pasting, and can choose from a wide variety of sizes and lettering styles, or **fonts.** Modern character generators also can produce many special effects such as boldface, italics, drop shadow, outline, and multicolor lettering. Many can even add graphic elements like lines, boxes, or even a station's logo to the screen. Character generators normally operate with a "screen" or "page" metaphor—information is typed in and saved as various screens or pages for later recall. With the push of a button, the operator can move to the next page, go back to the last page or even skip to a completely new page. In a television newscast, for instance, the anchor's name might be on one page and the name of a reporter on another page. During the show, the CG operator can easily move from page to page.

Character generators also can perform special effects with text material. *Rolling* moves the text up or down the screen, an effect often used for closing credits. *Crawling* moves the text horizontally across the screen in a single line; you may have seen this effect used for special news bulletins or for stock information on financial news networks. Other effects include flips, spins, and *page turns,* where one screen of information "peels away" like a page in a book to reveal another screen. All of these effects can be preprogrammed into the character generator, so at show time the operator can execute the desired effect with the touch of a button. All the information entered into a character generator can be stored on computer disk for later recall.

Graphics Generators

Graphics generators, which also are called **paintboxes,** produce sophisticated graphic elements such as pictures, maps, or diagrams. Most paintboxes also have lettering capabilities, although many do not provide easy access to editing functions like CG units. Paintboxes allow the operator to "paint" and "draw" on an electronic "canvas," and the result can be output as a television signal. Using tools such as a **mouse, graphics tablet,** and **digitizing pen,** the operator can produce specialized artwork (see figure 11.10).

Paintbox operators may produce artwork from "scratch" or they may start with an existing frame of video. Figure 11.11 shows how video can be used to create paintbox graphics. The paintbox can perform many functions, including resizing, rotating, and changing colors. Paintboxes also can create **animations,** or graphics, that appear to move. In reality, the illusion of movement is created by using several frames, each one slightly different from the last. You have probably seen an example of this type of animation on your local television station's weathercast, where clouds appear to move across the country.

(a) A still photo of Madonna is retrieved from the video library. The first step is to use the graphics pad and pen to outline her head and block out all of the distracting background so that only the desired portrait remains.

(b) After a similar library shot of Roseanne is retrieved and treated to remove the background, the two portraits are positioned for one of the planned on-air shots.

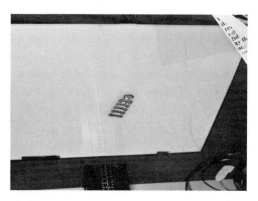

(c) In order to convey the atmosphere of Italy (the locale for the Madonna/Roseanne story), a small picture of the Leaning Tower of Pisa is pulled from the "flat art" file and placed on the copy stand.

(d) This picture of the tower is shot with the video "capture camera," and the image can then be integrated into the other electronic graphics.

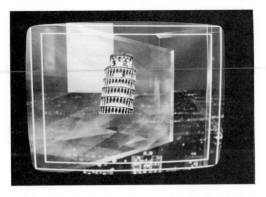

(e) The tower is positioned and layered into an existing *Entertainment Tonight* mosaic.

(f) For one segment of the story, Roseanne's image is layered (matted) over the tower. The degree of blending and transparency of the images is controlled with the light pen and "paint" program options.

(g) For another segment of the story, a "Madonna" logo is retrieved from still art and shot with the "capture camera."

(h) The black-and-white "Madonna" logo is reversed, a drop shadow is added, and it is positioned over the tower.

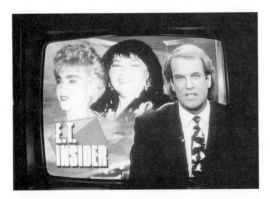 

(i) Two of the on-the-air results with the electronic graphics keyed in behind the host.

Figure 11.11

Many steps are involved in creating a series of graphics for a highly visual production such as *Entertainment Tonight*.
Photos courtesy of Paramount Studios, Los Angeles

This gasoline commercial uses morphing technology to turn a car into a tiger.   *Photos courtesy of Exxon Company, U.S.A. © Exxon Corporation 1991*

Over-the-shoulder graphics, such as this one indicating *"Your World Tonight,"* can be stored, indexed, and recalled using an Electronic Still Store (ESS) unit.   *Photo courtesy of WXYZ-TV, Detroit*

Sophisticated effects such as **morphing,** where one object transforms into another, also can be performed using animation (see figure 11.12).

Like character generators, graphic generators can save their information to computer disk for later retrieval. Special effects such as animations can be preprogrammed so that they will play at the touch of a button.

Electronic Still Store Units

The graphic example illustrated in figure 11.11 gives you a hint of what electronic still store (ESS) units can do. ESS units can "capture" individual frames of video, store them, and index them for easy retrieval. For example, you might capture a video frame of each member of a basketball team using an ESS unit. You can assign a specific number to each frame, and then, by typing a number into the ESS unit's keypad, you can instantly call up the desired frame. You also can add graphic elements to frames using a character generator or paintbox and save the combined product. Many television stations use ESS units to store over-the-shoulder graphics for their newscasts (see figure 11.13). These graphics are indexed by number ("1000" for the automobile accident graphic, "1001" for the city council graphic, for instance) and can be easily

(a)

(b)

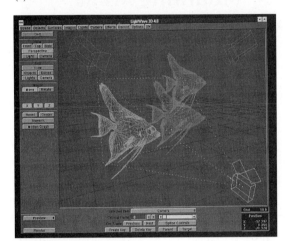

(c)

(d)

Figure 11.14

NewTek's Video Toaster® system provides what the company calls a Television-Studio-in-a-Box™. (a) a Video Toaster® workstation (b) a control screen for the Flyer nonlinear editing add-on card (c) the LightWave 3D™ control screen (d) a 3D special effect produced with LightWave 3D™   *Photos courtesy of NewTek, Inc.*

called up and reused as appropriate. ESS units store frames in digital form on computer disk.

Proprietary versus PC-based Systems

There are a variety of systems available for performing graphic functions. Some are *proprietary* systems, meaning that they have been designed "from the ground up" to perform a specific function. Other systems are PC-based, using a normal personal computer as a starting point. By adding specialized software and hardware, PCs can be made to function as character generators, graphics generators, still store units, or

combinations of the three. PC-based systems are often more cost-effective for operations with low budgets and have the additional advantage that they can be used for other functions such as word processing or bookkeeping.

NewTek's Video Toaster® was a pioneering effort in the PC-based graphics system. The Video Toaster, based on Commodore's Amiga PC, combines character and graphic generation, electronic still store, and a switcher with digital effects. Introduced in the late 1980s, the Toaster's "Studio-in-a-Box™" features make it popular with schools and other groups that want to do affordable production. NewTek also produces accessories for the Video Toaster, including LightWave 3D™, a graphics modeling program, and the Flyer, an add-on card that allows Video Toaster users to perform nonlinear digital video editing (see figure 11.14). The Amiga's specialized video chips

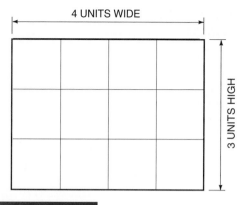

4 UNITS WIDE

3 UNITS HIGH

Figure 11.15

Regardless of the size of the television graphic—whether it is 4 centimeters wide or 8 feet wide—it must always be in the 3 to 4 aspect ratio if it is designed to be used full frame.

and NTSC output made it the platform of choice for the Toaster's designers; Macintoshes and IBM PCs, by contrast, need add-on boards to produce NTSC output. However, Commodore went bankrupt in 1994 and no longer produces the Amiga. NewTek has responded by adapting the Video Toaster technology to other platforms, including the Macintosh and IBM PC. Several other companies are producing similar PC-based production systems.

11.4

Other Graphics

Sometimes it is necessary to use graphics other than those created by a computer—an award-winning photograph, a map of the world that you want to show in its entirety and then zoom in on Egypt, or a page from an old manuscript. When this is the case, you must prepare the graphic so that it will look good on TV.

Aspect Ratio

To the extent possible, you should prepare the material with a *3-to-4* **aspect ratio**—the television screen is three units high and four units wide. Nothing can be done to change that ratio. Regardless of the size of the graphic, it still has to fit into that 3-to-4 ratio. (See figure 11.15.) Computer graphics automatically give you that aspect ratio, but graphics that come from other places can be any size. If you are starting from

scratch, you can make sure you create the proper aspect ratio, but if you are using something like an old manuscript page, it is not going to be the proper aspect ratio.

However, you do have options. You can show only part of it; you can have the camera tilt from the top to bottom of it; or you can mount it on a larger board that is the proper aspect ratio and show borders around it. **High definition television (HDTV)** has a 16-to-9 aspect ratio. Thus, graphic elements produced for HDTV use should conform to this ratio.

Mounting Areas

In general, you should mount all graphics that are going to be used in a studio. This makes the graphics more stable and keeps the camera operator from shooting off the sides of them. The mounting board (usually a stiff cardboard) should be significantly larger than the actual graphic in order to allow for proper framing. Noncomputer-generated graphics are usually thought of in terms of total size, scanning area, and essential area. (See figure 11.16.)

All material that is prepared on a physical graphic card will not necessarily be seen on the home receiver. There has to be some room around the border of the card for numbering and identification of the graphic, handling, smudge prints, and so forth. Let us call this the *border area* and assume that it will not be used for any information at all. The camera will never intend to shoot this area. To give ourselves plenty of room, let us assume that this margin should be about one-sixth of the total card: that is, if the card is 24 inches wide, we will take off one-sixth, or 4 inches, from each edge. This leaves us with a total usable width of 16 inches.

The remaining area that we have left is called the **scanning area.** This is the area actually to be scanned by the television camera. If we started out with a card that measured 18" by 24" and reduced that border one-sixth the dimension of the card on all sides, we should now have a scanning area of 12" by 16"—still in the 3-to-4 ratio.

Still, not everything in the scanning area will be transmitted through the entire system to reach the home TV set. The scanning system of the camera monitor may be slightly misaligned, so the camera

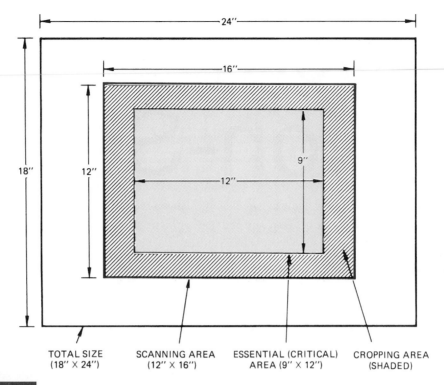

TOTAL SIZE
(18" × 24")

SCANNING AREA
(12" × 16")

ESSENTIAL (CRITICAL)
AREA (9" × 12")

CROPPING AREA
(SHADED)

Figure 11.16

Relationship of scanning area to essential area. In this particular example, suppose you are working with a card that is actually 18" × 24". The scanning area is two-thirds of the total card size, or 12" × 16" (which includes the shaded area). The essential area is three-fourths of the scanning area (or half of the total card size); that is, 9" × 12" (indicated by the area in color). The cropping area (shaded) is the portion of the scanning area that may be seen by the television camera, but that may or may not be seen on the home television receiver.

operator will inadvertently cut off part of the graphic. The home TV set may clip off, or **crop,** some of the picture. To be safe, you should decrease the total width of the usable scanning area by taking off about one-eighth on all sides. Starting with our original card 24 inches wide, we would now have a remaining width of about 12 inches.

The remaining area is known as the **essential area.** All the crucial information that we want to transmit through the system must be placed in this zone. This amounts to about one-half of the original card size. It is still a 3-to-4 ratio. The information that is outside of the essential area but still within the scanning area (the shaded area in figure 11.16) may or may not be seen on the home receiver. Depending upon the various components in the total transmission system, some of this information may reach the home set; some of it will be cropped. This informa-

tion, therefore, must be part of the total graphic design, but it cannot be essential.

Graphic Aesthetics

Regardless whether graphics are computer-generated or physical, they should be pleasing to the eye and easy to read. Several factors are important for attaining this objective. They include the symbol size, simplicity and style, and color contrast.

Symbol Size

As a general rule of thumb, lettering on television should be *no smaller than one-fifteenth of the screen height.* If the critical area of a physical graphic card is 15 inches high, that would mean that lettering could be no smaller than 1 inch high. If no line is less than

(a) # Serif

(b) # Non-Serif

Figure 11.17

These two text examples show the difference between serif and non-serif type. Serifs are the small protrusions on the ends of letters, as indicated by the circled portion of the letter "f". (a) Serif type (b) Non-Serif type

one-fifteenth of the height of the critical area (and assuming some space is left between each line of letters), this would mean that normally *no more than seven lines of information* should be included on a computer page or a TV graphic card. Of course, artistic considerations—balance and arrangement of mass—might dictate that much less material be used.

Given the ease of creating bountiful clean, crisp lettering with a computer-graphics generator, the temptation is to flood the screen with information. But seven lines should generally be considered the maximum number of lines for a normal TV graphic. Think not of the high quality monitor directly in front of you in the control room; think rather of the myopic viewer at home sitting across the room from the slightly fuzzy old TV receiver.

Simplicity and Style

If there is one primary rule about the preparation of TV graphics, electronic or physical, it is simply this: *Keep it simple*—all lettering, all design elements, and all artwork. The screen is too small and the scanning lines are too blurry to permit any fine detail work.

This is particularly true with lettering styles. Letters should be bold, thick, and well-defined, with a sharp, firm contour. As illustrated in figure 11.17, some styles of lettering have **serifs,** or small extensions on the tips of the letters. In printed text, these extensions help "guide" the eye from one letter to the next and one word to the next, helping ease eye

strain. But because of television's scanning process and lower resolution, serifs often flicker or disappear on screen. Consequently, lettering styles with serifs should be avoided for television work. However, some serif type styles have been specially designed for television use and can work rather well. You should still use caution, however, to make sure that the serifs show up properly on the screen. You will notice that the overwhelming majority of type styles used in television do not have serifs.

Any other artwork on a graphic card with lettering should also be kept simple. If it is too detailed, the audience will not get a chance to comprehend it; if it is too confusing and domineering, the audience will be distracted from the lettering.

All nonverbal graphics—pictures, cartoons, drawings, and slides—also must be kept as simple as possible. Drawings or photographs showing a certain component or step in a process must show only what is absolutely necessary. One of the main problems in trying to use visuals prepared for other media (for example, charts from a book or photos from a magazine) is that they invariably contain too much detail. They are designed for a medium without the pressing temporal limitations of television. Usually, they are visuals designed to convey as much information as possible in a single picture; they are designed for detailed study and comparison. Television, by contrast, may need to use three or four graphics sequentially to impart the same information. Do not try to crowd everything into one picture.

This admonition is particularly true with *maps*. It is safe to say that no prepared maps (designed for nontelevision application) can be used safely on television. Any television graphic that tries to squeeze in more than twenty-five words is really too cramped, and the information is too small. Most maps have to be redone for TV. Use only outlines of countries or natural geographical bodies and a few key labels or key locations. Keeping simplicity is often particularly difficult with computer graphics. There are so many temptations. But just because you have 16 million colors, 40 fonts, and 125 wipe patterns, don't feel you have to use them all. If you are just trying to capture the viewer's attention, you can flaunt a few special effects, but if you are trying to convey information, remember that often less is better.

Color Contrast

A third factor that can help determine the readability of either a physical or computer-generated graphic is color contrast. Working with color graphics, it is important to use hues that contrast and complement each other without actually clashing. (See color plate B.) Artistic judgment and experience will help determine which hues go well together. It is often very effective to combine different saturation levels of the same or closely related hues. Contrast in brightness levels also is effective in making certain segments of a graphic stand out.

With most basic computer graphics generators, thousands or even millions of colors are possible. Take time to experiment with your system, and see what combinations of hues, saturation, and brightness work best for your purpose.

Video engineers like to have just a little white and a little black in a picture for reference points. Thus, a good graphic would be one that has two or three shades of brightness plus a little white and black for sparkle and interest. Avoid graphics that are all black and white or that consist entirely of high-contrast colors.

One problem to avoid is the use of colors of the same brightness or saturation in preparing graphics. Two different hues (say, red and blue) will contrast best if you also consider differing levels of saturation and brightness. A dark brownish red will contrast better against a brilliant royal blue than against a dark navy blue.

In fact, contrasting saturations of the same hue (for example, a vivid chartreuse and a grayish olive green) provide considerable contrast. And even contrasting brightness or lightness of the same hue and saturation (for example, a light pink and a dark rose) provide essential contrast and legibility.

Working with graphics can be very rewarding. Computers have made the process fairly simple and fast, but the main responsibility, the creation of something that is aesthetically pleasing, rests in the hands and minds of human beings.

II.6
Set Design

Set design, like graphics, has been invaded by the computer. **Production designers** and **art directors** frequently plan the overall look of a production and the specific set pieces by using computer programs. Graphics software helps them create a visualization of what will later become massive set pieces and furniture. Some programs allow them to "enter" a set and look at it from a number of different angles. Programs also help them keep track of what supplies will be needed to construct the sets, what the cost will be, and what is finished and yet to be completed.

For purposes of ordering different items, constructing needed units, and considering storage and construction, people involved with set design and execution will find it convenient to think in terms of three broad categories of scenery and staging elements: settings, set dressings and furniture, and hand props.

Settings

The term *setting* usually refers to all the major scenic pieces that make up the background and surrounding environment of the scene. This category would, in turn, include about three different kinds of scenic elements: *standard set units,* such as **flats, twofolds,** and other standing background pieces; *hanging units,* including various cloth drops, hanging drapes, and the **cyclorama** (or **cyc**) that might cover two or three walls with a flat, neutral surface; and *set pieces* that include pillars, steps and stairways, arches, platforms, wagons (platforms on casters), fences, lampposts, and so forth.

Set Dressings and Furniture

The terms *set dressings* and *furniture,* along with the label *stage props,* are used by different practitioners to mean slightly different things. Basically this category includes all those major items that are involved in *dressing* the set, filling out the naked setting represented by the flats and major set pieces. This includes all the major furniture items (desks, lecterns, chairs, tables, appliances, and so forth) and large exterior stage props (bicycles, cannons, trees, and other natural or man-made objects). The term *set dressing* is often used to refer even more specifically to those smaller items that are used to make the set look lived in—lamps, pictures, books and magazines, household plants, vases, and other furnishings. *Set dressings* and *stage props* come from different sources, depending upon one's ingenuity and budget: a studio's prop storage, a secondhand store, or one's own living room.

Hand Props

A specialized, but extremely important, category is that of *hand properties*—those items that are actually handled and manipulated as part of the television production. They include all those props needed for a dramatic production (telephones, bottles, kitchen tools, food, books, glasses, or weapons), or for a commercial (a box of cereal or a can of dog food), or for an instructional program (globes, models, or chemistry apparatus). Obviously some of these items overlap with other set dressings, the distinction being that hand props are actually *used* in the program, rather than being planted as *decoration.*

11·7

Staging Requirements and Considerations

Settings, set dressings, and hand props do not exist in a vacuum. They must be integrated with the equipment and actors that are part of any production.

Camera Movement

No matter what the set looks like, there must be provision for adequate camera movement. Several cameras will have to be free to have access from different angles in the setting. This usually poses no problems with settings that have few set units and very little furniture. A talk show set with a desk and several chairs set against a cyc is easy for cameras to move around in. What creates problems are elaborate realistic settings with windows and doors and a great deal of furniture. For this reason, sets are usually constructed as just two-walled or three-walled sets. The open wall (the missing side of the set) is used for camera access. In three-walled sets, the walls do not have to be set at exactly 90 degrees; they can be left open at oblique angles so that the camera can have even more access. In some sets (occasionally a four-walled set may have to be used), it is possible to position cameras behind the flats or other scenic elements and shoot through a window, doorway, hole in the bookcase or fireplace, or other camouflaged opening.

Microphone Placement

The setting also must provide for adequate microphone placement and, if on a boom, movement. Although the wireless microphone is increasingly used in studio dramas—soap operas and situation comedies—the beginning audio operator must learn how to cope with staging concerns involved with wired microphones. For most dramatic productions (since lavalieres usually are not worn, hanging mics result in bad audio, and hidden microphones are not encouraged), some sort of boom or giraffe or fishpole is used. This can lead to two kinds of problems.

First, if the set is small and the boom is large, there will be movement and coordination troubles; cameras will also have to maneuver around the boom and microphone cables; adequate room has to be left open. Second, the mic boom can cause shadows. If the lighting has not been carefully worked out with the precise boom placement in mind, there will be a strong possibility of unwanted shadows from the horizontal boom or fishpole. This could be more of a problem in a setting with a plain background than in a busy set that may make a shadow less noticeable. In most cases, however, either the mic boom or the light-

Back-lighting problems with scenic flat. In this kind of situation, either the back light will have to be mounted higher, the light will have to be repositioned closer to the flat, the flat will have to be moved back (closer to the back light), or the talent will have to move forward, farther away from the flat.

ing instrument will have to be repositioned somewhat, or the light will have to be barndoored off the boom.

Lighting Instruments

Other lighting problems can be caused by certain kinds of setting arrangements. Occasionally, pillars or other foreground set pieces may block crucial front lighting from a certain angle. Sometimes a strong key light may throw a very distracting shadow on a close-up shot of some small object; or if the talent's lighting is too close to the set (flat or cyc), the key light may throw too much illumination on the set. One of the most common problems, however, is the blocking of the back light by a flat. If the flat is too high for the studio (a 10-foot flat might be high if the studio has a low ceiling), if the flat is out too far into the studio from the back light, or if the talent is standing too close to the flat, it will be difficult to hit the talent with the back light. (See figure 11.18.) In this case,

something—the back light, the flat, or the talent—will have to be moved.

To minimize the problems between sets and lighting and make for ease of operation for both the staging and lighting crews, large set pieces such as flats should be put up before lighting begins. However, furniture and set decorations should not be put into place. This allows the lighting people to light according to the general placement of the sets without having to maneuver their ladders around pieces of furniture. Once the lighting ladders are put away, the set can be dressed. Some minor lighting changes may then be made, but these usually can be adjusted from the floor or with the aid of one small step ladder.

Talent Movement

Finally, the setting has to take into consideration all anticipated movement by the talent. How much action is required? Will several people be moving in the same direction simultaneously? How much space is needed for certain movement (a dance step or tumbling demonstration)? Is there plenty of room for all entrances and exits? Will the talent be forced to maneuver so close to the set walls that part of their lighting will be cut off? Or, if the performers work too close to the set, will they cast unwanted shadows on the flat or cyc? Once the director is satisfied that there is enough room for talent movement, lighting instruments, microphone placement, and camera movement, he or she is ready to look at the functional aspect of using scenery.

11.8
Using Sets and Scenic Elements

The physical manipulation and handling of all scenery units—construction, assemblage, and storage—is a major study by itself. Television scenery is closely related to stage and film scenery; anyone who has ever worked in technical theater or visited the back lot of a major motion picture studio has a feel for the scope of the scenery and props department. All we can do in this text is touch upon some of the basic elements involved in making scenery units, assembling them for studio use, and storing them for repeated use.

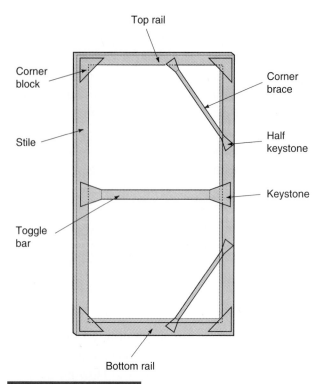

Corner
block

Top rail

Corner
brace

Stile

Half
keystone

Keystone

Toggle
bar

Bottom rail

Figure 11.19

Construction of an ordinary flat. Standard construction of a simple wooden flat consists of a frame made of 1″ × 3″ pine with ¼″ plywood for the corner blocks and keystones. The front of the frame is typically covered with canvas or with plywood (or pressed hardboard). If a solid wooden front covering is used, then the corner braces will not be needed.

Construction

The basic scenic unit for television, like that for the stage, is the *flat*—a cross-braced wooden frame faced with either canvas (which is lightweight, but too flimsy for repeated heavy use) or thin pressed board or plywood (which will take more abuse, although it is heavier to work with).

The layout for a standard flat is shown in figure 11.19. Flats can be made in any size, but common heights are 10 feet for larger studios and 8 feet for studios with lower ceilings. Widths also will vary, although they are seldom broader than 5 feet (the width that one person can comfortably handle with arms outstretched).

Whenever wider widths are needed, flats can be hinged together semi-permanently. Two flats hinged together are known as a *two-fold.* Three flats similarly

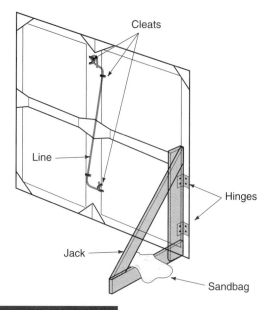

Cleats

Line

Hinges

Jack

Sandbag

Figure 11.20

Connecting and bracing flats. Cleats on both flats allow the units to be lashed together by a line that is permanently tied onto one of the flats. The jack is a hinged stage brace that, when weighted, forms a good self-supporting unit.

connected (seldom will you see more than three) are known as a *three-fold.* When a wider span needs to be covered, the flat units are temporarily lashed or connected together. (See figure 11.20.)

In addition to standard wooden construction, studios use other rigid but lightweight materials, such as foam board and corrugated feather board, for making flats and other scenic elements.

Construction of other set pieces (stairways, platforms, and so forth) is more complicated, requiring heavy bracing and sturdy framing for the amount of abuse and wear they will be subjected to. (See figure 11.21.)

Cycs can be either a permanent solid cyc (faced with plywood or some other hard surface, which may tend to give audio problems) or a cyc cloth (canvas, duck, or gauze, depending upon the desired texture and reflectance quality desired). Cycs as a rule are designed to be used while stretched taut, giving a smooth limbo background, although they may be hung loosely in pleats to give the appearance of opened drapes. Canvas cycs also can be painted and used as the backdrop for a set, as illustrated in figure 11.22.

Figure 11.21

A section of an airplane fuselage shows construction that is typical of specialized set pieces.   *Photo courtesy of Universal Studios, Universal City, CA.*

Figure 11.22

Canvas backdrop painted to serve as a street-front scene.   *Photo courtesy of Universal Studios, Universal City, CA.*

Figure 11.23

Fiberglass "dirt skins" are made from burlap impregnated with fiberglass mixed with dirt or any other desired soil texture.
Photo courtesy of Universal Studios, Universal City, CA.

Drapes, which are usually of a heavier material and often darker, can be either pulled taut or pleated, depending upon the desired effect. Darker, low-reflectance drapes are effective backing for **cameo lighting.** Drapes are usually used in smaller widths than a cyc and can ordinarily be easily rigged or hung for specific applications. A cyc, on the other hand, often is permanently mounted, covering two or even three walls of a studio.

If any amount of action or camera work is going to focus on the ground, the floor covering must be considered. Most studio floors are generic tile that blends in well with most productions. But a story line that calls for a realistic plot with dirt or a sandy beach can cause problems. Figure 11.23 shows one answer— the use of a **dirt skin** to simulate a patch of natural earth. Similarly, natural vertical surfaces—cliff faces, rocks, mine walls—must be carefully constructed to simulate the real thing. These upright pieces, how-ever, must be constructed from fairly rigid material such as fiberglass (see figure 11.24). A more common solution is to take the production out of the studio into the real world and use an actual beach, cliff, or mine for the shooting.

Assembling

Most flats are built with special hardware that facili-tates easy temporary joining of two or more units. The stiles of the flats can be fitted with **cleats,** so that a line can be used to lash two flats together quickly. (See figure 11.20.)

Other methods of joining flats include the use of various metal fasteners (such as *L-plates,* which have drop-in fasteners and loose pin-hinges) and the use of large *quick-fix* clamps that can be used to clamp the stiles of two adjoining flats together. Most flats also have some sort of bracing or supporting unit, so they can be completely freestanding as a self-supporting unit. Several different types of stage braces are used. One of the most common is the **jack** or hinged wooded brace. (See figure 11.20.) When the flat is in place, the jack is swung out behind the flat at right angles to the front of the flat and held in place with stage weights or **sandbags.**

Rigid fiberglass pieces can be used to simulate the texture of mine walls or other rough surfaces.   *Photo courtesy of Universal Studios, Universal City, CA.*

A metal brace used for semipermanent support of a flat.
Photo courtesy of Universal Studios, Universal City, CA.

When flats are assembled for a set that is likely to remain in place for a prolonged period, they often are permanently secured with a stage screw. Figure 11.25 illustrates the use of a metal brace screwed into the floor for a set that is part of a long-running situation comedy.

Most set pieces are solid and freestanding units that need no special bracing when assembled for use in the studio. However, many of them—such as stairway units—do need to be fastened to other units or flats to make them as secure as possible. Door flats also need to be securely fastened to other set units to guarantee that the doorway will function properly without sticking or falling down when used. Some set pieces, such as *parallels* (collapsible platforms), can be partially disassembled and folded for storage. They must be carefully put together and securely set up before being used.

Storage

In many small stations and educational institutions, scenery storage can be a serious problem. There is never enough room to house everything that is needed, and scenery storage always seems to be the area that suffers the most. This can be a particularly critical problem, because so many of the flats and special set pieces can be reused over and over in a variety of ways—with different set dressings—in a number of configurations. Yet, they have to be stored somewhere and catalogued for easy retrieval.

Flats and other narrow units are usually stored in racks, which are simple frames designed to hold a number of flats in an upright position. Each rack can be designed and labeled to hold similarly matched scenic units (for example, living room flats, office flats, green-speckled flats, log cabin flats, and so forth).

Props and other small items can be stored on deep shelves in the storage area. Again, it is important that each shelf and/or cubicle be clearly labeled:

"telephones," "dishes," "bottles," and so on. Even furniture and other large stage props can be stored in multitiered shelves. Large overstuffed chairs, sofas, and heavy tables can be stored on the floor level; medium-sized chairs and tables can be stored on another level (4 to 5 feet off the floor); and lightweight chairs and stools and small appliances can be stored on a third level (perhaps 7 to 8 feet above the floor).

II.9
Studio Techniques

In moving into actual studio usage, the director and staging director need to be aware of several other factors, including the floor plan, lighting effects, and special staging effects.

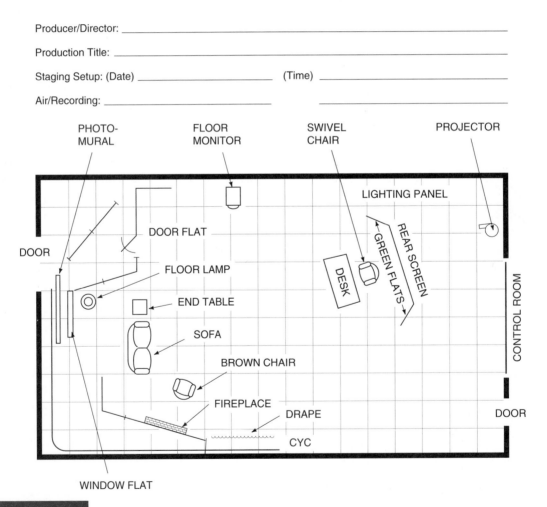

Producer/Director: _____

Production Title: _____

Staging Setup: (Date) _____ (Time) _____

Air/Recording: _____ / _____

Figure II.26

Sample staging floor plan. In this particular floor plan, the squares on the floor correspond to three-foot tiles actually laid on the studio floor. In other floor plans, a lighting grid or pipe battens might be superimposed over the studio layout.

Floor Plan

First, as we have stressed throughout this text, the success of any television production is dependent to a great extent upon the discipline exercised in preproduction planning. As with the considerations of the lighting director, much valuable studio time and frustration can be saved by careful planning and plotting of the basic set.

A good floor plan allows the director to make the most economical use of all studio and staging space. Sets can be planned efficiently; equipment can be placed with precision. The director can plan how best to take advantage, for example, of the *cornerset*—a two-walled setting positioned in a corner of the studio—that provides good set backing for many types of productions (better than a flat backdrop), while allowing great depth and freedom of camera movement (more so than with a three-walled set).

A typical studio staging floor plan will include the placement of all flats and other set pieces and the exact location of all stage props and furniture. It is important that all flats and furniture be drawn to exact scale; otherwise the director's shooting angles, the talent's movement, and the lighting design will all

be off. Computer programs designed to help develop floor plans are very helpful, because they keep the scale consistent and can be used to "move" items around as often as necessary. Figure 11.26 shows a typical plot plan, drawn to the scale of 1/8 inch to 1 foot. Once the accurate floor plan is drawn, it will be used by the director, floor manager, audio person, talent, and even the lighting director (to confirm and complement the lighting plot). It is therefore essential that the plan be prepared with as much detail and precision as possible.

Lighting Effects

In addition to the regular lighting required for illumination of the production area, other special lighting effects should be considered as part of the overall staging design. We have already mentioned the use of the **cucalorus,** or **cookie,** pattern (see chapter 5, section 5.4) to cast various shadow patterns (venetian blinds, prison bars, Moorish latticework, and so forth) on the set wall. (See figure 11.27.)

Colored gels can be used to throw colored lights on a plain cyc or other surface. Subtle lighting changes (with the dimmer) can be employed to change color or shadowing as dramatic action unfolds. Other creative lighting effects (determining shape and texture, modifying reality, and establishing mood) were discussed in chapter 5, section 5.3. Staging and lighting must be considered as one integral production element; they cannot be looked at as isolated, independent components.

Special Staging Effects

Several different types of mechanical and optical *staging effects* can be used. Although some of the effects depend on expensive equipment and elaborate arrangements, others can be adapted to most studio situations.

Large electric fans can create *wind* effects. Dry ice plunged into a tub of hot water creates *fog.* (Both of these effects cause studio noise that can be compensated for in a number of ways, including sound effects CDs.) *Lightning* and *explosions* are best suggested by lighting effects (off set) coupled with sound effects.

To produce a *fire* effect, shake silk strips on a stick in front of a spotlight to create flickering shadows or superimpose video footage of a flame over the set (since flame is translucent, the super effect works

Figure 11.27

Use of a cucalorus pattern to project a shadow on the back wall of a set.

well). Again, use sound effects to present a total contextual effect. *Smoke* can be added by carefully pouring mineral oil in a container on a hot plate.

Rain can be simulated by preparing a **rain drum** graphic—a continuous loop of black paper with white streaks splashed on it rotated on a round surface (you can use an old bass drum); super a slightly defocused shot of the drum over the scene (with the actors in wet clothing). Again, add sound for a total effect. *Mirrors* can be used in a variety of ways. For example, a large mirror suspended from a lighting grid can be used to get a shot looking straight down onto a demonstration table or into a cooking pot. Mirrors also can be used in musical productions. High and low shots—for example, dancers' feet on a bandstand program—can be obtained by using a double-mirrored periscope.

Gobos are another handy staging device that enable a camera to frame a shot through some special foreground design. The gobo is a cutout (for instance, a simulated gunsight or keyhole) that is positioned several feet in front of a camera; it is an obvious stylistic effect that can be used judiciously to good advantage. Other optical devices using special filters and prisms also can be utilized in more sophisticated situations.

Production Problems

Finally, mention should be made of several common troubles that periodically plague even the best staging plan. One is the difficulty of obtaining a consistent background from all angles. Whether a person is using a lighted cyc or a realistic set of flats, care must be taken to make certain that the set is evenly lit so that each camera, shooting from its particular angle, will be getting the same background shot. Also, care must be taken to ensure that the sets are wide enough—that there is enough cover at each end of the set—so that a camera shooting from outside angles will not be shooting off the set.

Troubles frequently occur with functional furniture. Chairs, stools, and sofas must be appropriately matched with talent. Some common furniture problems include: the *swinging swivel chair*, in which guests vent their nervous energy by rotating back and forth; the *precarious perch*, which involves sitting uncomfortably on top of a high, hard stool; and the talent *swallower*, overstuffed chairs and sofas that are so plush and soft that the person sinks down so far the director is left with nothing but a shot of knees. Make sure you use solid furniture that is comfortable but firm.

One last production problem that has ruined many a final take is the *forgotten prop*. In any kind of production that relies on hand props (dramas, demonstration shows, training programs), there is always the danger of failing to return a given prop to its starting point after a rehearsal. The gun must be returned to the bedside table; the magician's paraphernalia must be repacked and checked; a new set of vegetables must be prepared for the cooking demonstration; the toys must be put back in the clown's sack; and so forth. Both the talent and the stage manager should double-check after the dress rehearsal to be sure that everything is in place for the final production.

Summary

Good pictorial design for graphics and sets starts with consideration of both *informational* functions and *emotional* functions of the picture. Basic elements of design that should be considered in every production include *balance and mass, dominant lines,* and *tone and color.* Color components include *hue, saturation,* and *brightness.*

Computer graphics have progressed very rapidly, both in *proprietary* systems and in systems tied to personal computer platforms. These systems come in three broad categories: *character generators, graphics generators* and *electronic still store (ESS)* units. Some systems can perform more than one of these functions and, in some cases, all three.

Sometimes physical graphics, such as photos or maps, must be used. They should be in the 3-to-4 *aspect ratio* and should be mounted to take into account *scanning* and *essential* areas. Easy to read graphics should contain no more than seven lines of text, should emphasize simplicity, and should use hues that complement and contrast with each other.

Set design also has been affected by the computer, which can help designers visualize design parameters. Scenery elements include *settings* (standard set units, hanging units, and set pieces), *set dressings and furniture,* and *hand props.* In designing a studio setting, consider also *camera movement, microphone placement, lighting instruments,* and *talent movement.* In handling pieces in the studio, you should know the basic *con-struction* of a flat, how flats can be *assembled,* and the best way of *storing* flats, set pieces, and properties. Some other studio techniques involve the preparation of a staging *floor plan,* use of *lighting* effects, other special *staging* effects, and dealing with basic problems of backgrounds, furniture, and props.

chapter 12

Interactive Media

omputers have become a fact of life in television production. In previous chapters, you have seen how computers have had an impact on the way television professionals work in areas such as graphics, video editing, and audio production.

But while computerized videotape editors and character generators merely change the techniques of conventional production work, the marriage of computer technology and traditional media also is creating new ways to communicate. The convergence of computers, digital technology, video, and audio is at the heart of the so-called *new media*.

Like many of the buzzwords of the computer age, establishing a precise definition of what the new media are is difficult. In general, new media are characterized by **user interaction** and **dynamic content,** meaning that the consumer of the media is not passive, but rather actively controls the media and selects the content he or she wishes to experience. New media are also referred to as *multimedia, hypermedia,* or *interactive media,* and while there may be subtle differences in the precise definitions of these terms, for clarity this chapter will use the term "interactive media."

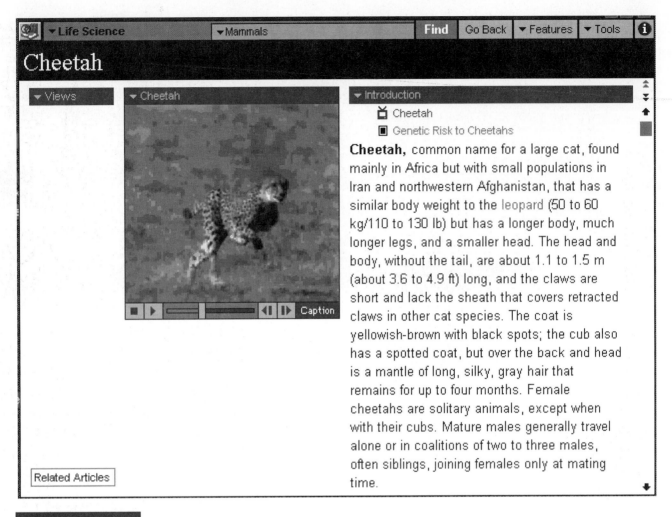

Figure 12.1

Interactive Encyclopedias, such as Microsoft *Encarta*™, allow users to experience a variety of media interactively. Here, users can read about cheetahs and see a video clip of a cheetah running.   *Encarta*™ *is a trademark of Microsoft Corporation. Screen shot reprinted with permission from Microsoft Corporation.*

You have probably seen examples of interactive media. Many museums and other public attractions now have interactive kiosks that enable visitors to find information by selecting options on a video screen. Home computer users can purchase interactive encyclopedias on CD-ROM disks that allow them not only to read words and view photos as they would in a printed encyclopedia, but also to see moving video and hear sounds. (See figure 12.1) Using a computer connected to the **Internet,** a user can access a variety of information sources around the world, complete with video and sound. There are many other examples, as you will see in this chapter.

The important thing to remember as you read this chapter is that interactive media production represents not only a convergence of media, but also a convergence of skills. Many of the same principles, for instance, that guide the production of graphics for an evening television newscast still apply to producing graphics for interactive media presentations; the same fundamentals of audio, lighting, camera work, and editing that make for an effective documentary or sitcom also will make for an effective interactive media production. The advent of computers doesn't mean you can forget traditional audio and video production principles; in fact, they become even more important.

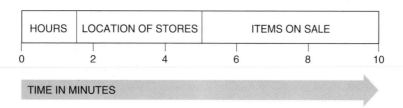

Figure 12.2

A time-line representation of a linear informational kiosk.

12.1

Interactivity and Dynamic Content

Most traditional media are **linear,** meaning that their content has a specific beginning, middle, and end. Such media are also static; their content cannot be changed by the consumer of the media. For instance, when you watch an episode of your favorite sitcom, you normally begin watching at the start of the program and watch until the end, and you cannot affect the content of the program. Certainly, you *could* record the program on videotape and then "skip around" to various parts, but this would be a tedious process, and the result probably wouldn't make much sense. And even then, you would not be able to actually change the show's content.

Interactive media, on the other hand, are characterized by their **nonlinear** design and dynamic content. Nonlinear means that the presentation does not have to proceed in a predetermined order. You have already seen this term used in the chapter on videotape editing, and its meaning in this context is similar. But while nonlinear videotape editing affects the production *process,* nonlinear media refers to the finished product. This is where the concept of interactivity comes in; interactive media presentations are normally designed to allow the consumer to "navigate" through them. The consumer does not merely passively take in the media content, but rather actively controls how it is presented. The same presentation, in fact, may be experienced by different people in different ways; it can change according to each consumer's wishes. For that reason, consumers of interactive media are usually referred to as *users,* because that term implies actively employing something—putting it to use—rather than the passivity connoted by terms such as "viewer" or "listener."

To see how these concepts work, let's examine in detail a hypothetical interactive presentation. The owner of a shopping center wants to provide an automated way for shoppers to find out three kinds of information: 1) the location of particular stores; 2) the shopping center's hours of operation; and 3) what items stores have on sale each week. Imagine that the owner has hired you to create a kiosk to dispense this information.

Your first instinct might be to produce a linear, tape-based presentation. You could shoot videotape footage of products that are on sale, use a graphic to show a map of the shopping center, and compose text on a character generator to indicate its hours. You could then edit this information, along with a narrator's voice, onto videotape, producing a presentation that might run 10 minutes. Illustrated as a time line, the program might look like figure 12.2. Your informational kiosk, then, would consist of a television monitor and a continuously-looping videotape that would play the 10-minute program over and over.

But it is unlikely that such a presentation would meet the needs of shoppers. Most of them are probably looking for just one of the three categories of information given on the tape, and if they happen to arrive at the kiosk just after that information has been given, they will have to wait 10 minutes to see it again. In a busy shopping environment, it would be inconvenient for shoppers to stand around that long waiting for the information.

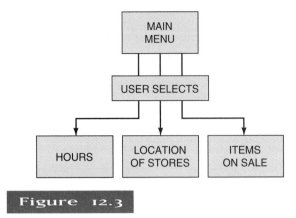

Figure 12.3

The structure of a nonlinear informational kiosk.

A more effective approach would be to design an interactive presentation. You could still use many of the same elements—graphics to show locations of stores and hours, video footage of sale items, and a narrator's voice—but you would make them part of an interactive presentation. Using a **multimedia authoring program** you could assemble the graphics, sound, and video so that they could be accessed in a nonlinear fashion, allowing the shopper to instantaneously "jump" to the desired information. Figure 12.3 shows a graphical representation of how the program would work. Rather than having to wait through unwanted material to get to the desired information, the user can choose which part of the presentation to access and immediately access it. As shown in the illustration, the user selects the part of the presentation to view.

Later in the chapter, you will see how to facilitate this type of user control, but for now it is helpful to understand the concepts of **screens** and **menus.** In an interactive presentation, different portions are often referred to as screens. The above example, for instance, has four screens as shown in the illustration. Each screen may contain various information and types of media. For example, the "Sale Items" screen would contain text and pictures. Menus are screens that allow the user to make choices.

The **main menu** is usually the first screen that the user sees and, from this menu, makes a selection. In the example, while the kiosk is not in use, the main menu will be displayed on the monitor. When a user

selects an item from the menu, the presentation then displays the selected screen. The user can then return to the main menu in order to access other information if desired. The presentation would be programmed to return to the main screen after a certain length of time if no further selections are made. Thus, shoppers might approach the kiosk to find out how much shopping time they have left. They would select "Hours" from the main menu, and then read the information. Since they need no further information, they would probably simply leave the kiosk and continue with their shopping. After a certain amount of time—say 30 seconds—the presentation will automatically return to the main menu so that it will be ready for the next user.

Varying levels of interactivity can be built into presentations. The example just cited has a fairly low level of interactivity; the user simply chooses from among three sets of "canned" information. To increase interactivity, we could ask for more input from the user and make the presentation more dynamic. For example, the user could use a keyboard to type a question such as, "What stores have jeans on sale?" The presentation would respond by immediately moving to the part that shows what stores are having sales on jeans. Media presentations that respond to specific user requests in this manner are called **adaptive presentations.** Such higher levels of interactivity lead to more dynamic content, as users can tailor the presentation to their personal interests. Incorporating such increased interactivity, as you might imagine, also takes more work.

I2.2

Elements of Interactive Media

Computers are central to interactive presentations. In some cases, the computer may be well disguised; the user of the interactive presentation may not even realize he or she is operating one. But a computer is necessary in order to bring together the various media that make up the presentation and to allow the user to navigate through it.

In order for a computer to bring together different types of media, those media must be in **digital** form, meaning that they are represented electronically by a series of "on" and "off" signals, as discussed in chapter 1. Since video and audio normally exist in **analog** form, they must first be digitized. Once digitized, audio and video signals become merely "data" as far as the computer is concerned. A properly equipped computer can thus bring together digital video, audio, words, pictures, and any other elements that are in digital form.

Computers perform three main functions in interactive presentations: *storage, delivery,* and *manipulation.* They can store digital information on a variety of storage media, from the traditional 3.5-inch floppy disk to CD-ROMs, hard drives, and optical drives. They also deliver that data from the storage area to the place where it is needed. In the case of a stand-alone computer kiosk, this involves simply moving the data through the computer to the monitor, but in cases where more than one computer is hooked together, or **networked,** the data must move a greater distance. Network connections are said to have a certain **bandwidth** that measures how much data they can carry. Finally, the computer is nearly constantly manipulating, or changing, the digital data.

This manipulation is performed chiefly by the computer's **central processing unit (CPU),** an electronic chip that is, in effect, the computer's "brain." Any time digital data is changed in any way, displayed on the screen, or moved from one location to another, the computer's CPU is put to work. Because some of the elements of interactive media—especially digital video—are highly complex in digital form, powerful computers are required to produce and run interactive presentations. To be suitable for interactive media work, a computer must have sufficient capabilities to store, move, and manipulate digital media information. More information on specific requirements will be presented later in this chapter.

Text

Text is normally displayed on the computer's monitor, although the computer may have the ability to print text on paper as well. Text may consist of labels ("Main menu"), instructions ("Click here to continue"), or substantive content. Long text passages may be displayed in a *scroll box* that allows the user to move "up" and "down" through it. The user can normally control how long text is displayed on the screen, thus allowing the presentation to be adjusted for different reading speeds.

Graphics

Graphics are usually displayed on the computer's monitor, although they, too, can be printed. Graphics may consist of original artwork composed with a computer program such as Adobe *Illustrator,* or they may be digital copies of existing artwork. Using a **scanner** and appropriate software, photographs and other printed material may be digitized. Individual video frames also can be digitized into graphics using **video capture** hardware and software. Users may be given control over how graphics are displayed. For example, they may be able to "zoom in" on static graphics in order to see more detail.

Animations are created by assembling individual graphics to create the illusion of movement. Much like video creates the illusion of movement by displaying a series of static "frames" in rapid succession, a computer can rapidly display a series of static graphics to create a similar effect. Animations can be used to demonstrate movement. For example, an animation showing how electrons move around the nucleus of an atom might be used in an educational science presentation. Presentations may be designed so that users can control when animations play and how quickly and may allow them to "pause" animations.

Audio

Audio is normally played through the computer's sound system. It can be made a part of interactive presentations either in conjunction with video clips or as a separate element. Digitized audio might consist of voice, music, or sound effects. Using an appropriate audio card (a circuit board and components that plug into the computer) and software, an audio signal can be digitized.

Users may have the ability to control when an audio clip plays and may be able to "pause" the clip if they wish. They also may be given control over how loudly audio plays over the computer's speakers.

Through the use of **MIDI** (Musical Instrument Digital Interface), a computer can control certain musical instruments—especially electronic keyboards—making them play particular notes. Some sound cards have built in MIDI synthesizers that can mimic various musical instruments.

Video

Video is normally displayed on the computer's monitor, although in some applications—especially those using videodiscs—it may be displayed on a separate monitor. Using a video capture card and software, video is digitized and compressed. Compression is necessary because uncompressed video has extremely high storage, bandwidth, and processing requirements. Various compression methods, including *MPEG, Motion-JPEG, QuickTime,* and *Video for Windows,* are available.

The size and bandwidth of digitized video also can be cut down by using lower resolutions, fewer colors, or slower frame rates. Resolution, which is a measure of the video frame's size, is normally indicated in **pixels.** Common resolutions include 320 pixels wide by 240 pixels high and 640 pixels wide by 480 pixels high. You also may digitize the signal using fewer colors, although digitized video with fewer than 256 colors tends to look cartoon-like. Finally, you might digitize the video with fewer than the standard 30 frames per second. Each of these techniques lowers the quality of the image, however, and should only be used in situations where the highest-quality video is not required.

Users may control when video clips play and may be able to "pause" or "rewind" the clip just like an animation. Users also may be able to choose whether the video fills the entire screen or only a portion of it.

Links

As you have seen throughout this chapter, a recurring characteristic of interactive media is user control. This control is facilitated through the use of **links,** which connect one part of the presentation to another. Virtually any part of an interactive presentation can be a link. When the link is activated, it "triggers" a designated action.

This action may be as simple as emitting a short "beep" sound or as elaborate as playing a full-motion video clip with sound. For instance, a presentation may include a line of text, "Click here to see the video clip," that is designated as a link to a video clip. Thus, when the user clicks the mouse on that line of text, the video clip plays. Links may be used to move the user to a new location in the presentation, allowing a quick "jump" to a new screen. Text designated as a link is often called **hypertext.**

Pictures also may be defined as links. When the user clicks on the picture with the mouse, something happens. Different parts of a picture may be defined as different links. For instance, an interactive presentation may display a picture of the solar system on the screen. When the user clicks different parts, different things happen. When the user clicks on Mars, additional information about Mars and a more detailed picture of the planet may be displayed. Clicking the Sun may cause the picture to animate, showing how the planets revolve around the Sun. Graphics used in this manner are called **image maps.**

The most common type of link is the **button,** which is a small graphic made to look like a button on an appliance. Buttons may be labeled with text ("Continue" or "Stop," for example) or they may have small pictures that define their function (a red hexagon to represent "Stop," for example). Video clips are often accompanied by a series of buttons that mimic the functions on a VCR, as shown in figure 12.4. Thus, users can "pause," "play," "rewind," or "stop" a clip by pressing the appropriate button.

There are several ways to activate links. Most commonly, they are activated by clicking a mouse, typing on a keyboard, or touching the screen. In some presentations, the user may be able to talk into a microphone; the computer will then interpret what is said and make an appropriate response. The user may, for example, say "Go back" to make the presentation return to a previous location.

12.3
Types of Interactive Media

Interactive media are continuously expanding into new areas as computer technologies evolve and as new ways of combining interactive control and multiple media develop. The interactive media frontier is

Figure 12.4

Buttons that allow users to control video clips in interactive presentations can be designed to look like the familiar controls found on a VCR.

an exciting one for users, producers, and companies that develop interactive programs. Goldman Sachs, a Wall Street investment firm, has coined the term "Communacopia" for the seemingly endless variety of new ways to combine and use media.

Some forms of interactive media, such as **video on demand** which allows subscribers of cable or satellite services to order movies and other programming at the exact time they want it, involve very little actual "authoring" of content. Instead, the challenges of providing video on demand are technical considerations of delivering an existing product. At the other end of the spectrum, **virtual reality** which simulates activities such as flying a jet plane, hang gliding, or walking through dungeons and mazes requires specialized equipment and a massive amount of programming.

This chapter focuses on interactive media presentations that lie "in between" those two. The emphasis here is on presentations that involve original content and that can be produced using relatively modest computer equipment. Those types of presentations fall into two broad categories—stand-alone systems and World Wide Web-based systems.

Stand-alone Computer Systems

Personal computer technology has developed to such a point that even modest home systems can be used to create and view interactive material. PCs—whether IBM or Macintosh—lie at the heart of the majority of interactive kiosks and presentations used in business, education, and medicine. With a few required add-ons that will be discussed later in this chapter, most modern PCs are able to handle fairly elaborate interactive programming.

Nearly all interactive presentations designed for home use are distributed on CD-ROM disks. These disks normally contain data files for video clips and other content, as well as a program that facilitates interactive control. This program allows the user to navigate through the material contained on the disk. CD-ROMs come in many varieties with literally thousands of titles. Among the most popular are interactive encyclopedias, as mentioned at the beginning of the chapter. Other CD-ROMs concentrate on home maintenance, auto repair, military history, golf, and many other topics. Some allow users to play elaborate interactive games, with digitized video images taking the place of the cartoon-like graphics of early computer games. Educational CD-ROMs are available for students of all ages. CD-ROMs also have become a popular marketing tool, and many companies now distribute advertising and other information on them.

Interactive kiosks, which are becoming a mainstay at shopping centers, museums, and theme parks, normally run on PCs. Such kiosks are programmed to provide very specific information to users. Some videotape rental chains, for example, have installed interactive units to help customers find information about movies they want to rent. These units allow movie enthusiasts to search for information on

Figure 12.5

Interactive Media exhibits at the Rock and Roll Hall of Fame and Museum, designed by The Burdick Group of San Francisco, allow guests to interact with music and video clips. This exhibit is titled "The 500 Songs that shaped Rock and Roll."
Photograph by Timothy Hursley

particular movies, actors, or directors, and even view short video clips of selected films. At the Rock and Roll Hall of Fame and Museum in Cleveland, music enthusiasts can hear music clips and find information about their favorite artists at interactive media stations (see figure 12.5).

Kiosks are sometimes connected via networks, allowing users at different locations to access the same information. A growing number of banks and financial institutions are installing *Video ATMs* that allow cus-

tomers to access their accounts and other information from various branches. Such networks may be set up on a **video server** model in which a powerful central computer stores digital video and other data and then distributes it to other machines when it is requested.

World Wide Web-Based Systems

Networks can span entire communities, states, and even countries. The Internet, which is a massive net-

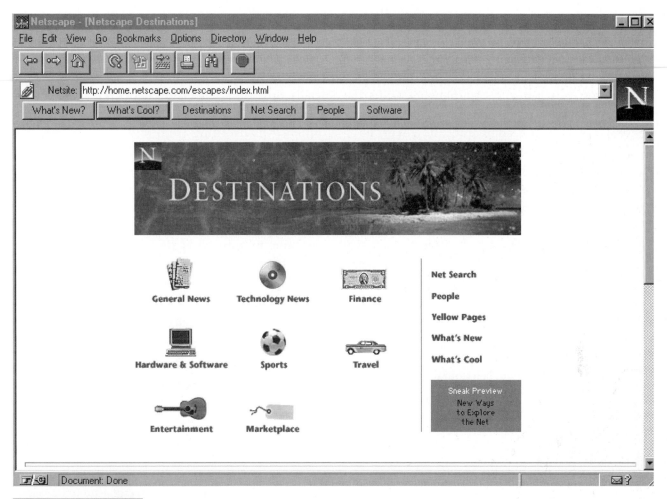

Figure 12.6

Web browsers, such as Netscape *Navigator*™, allow users to access information on the World Wide Web (WWW). The small pictures shown on the screen, such as the ones labeled "General News" and "Sports," are links to other information.
Courtesy of Netscape Communications Corporation

work of computers around the world, allows users to access information on a seemingly endless variety of topics. You have no doubt heard the Internet referred to as "The Information Superhighway" for its vast informational resources. However, the Internet has been criticized for its lack of organization, and it often is hard for even experienced users to find what they're looking for.

The advent of the **World Wide Web (WWW)** has helped to make the Internet's information more accessible and appealing. Through the use of **Hypertext Markup Language (HTML),** a computer language

that allows the creation of interactive presentations using text, pictures, sound, and video, the World Wide Web provides a standard format for Internet users. By using a **browser** program such as Netscape *Navigator*, a user can access information from computers located around the world. (See figure 12.6 and color plate E.) Browsers also allow users to interact with this information; by clicking on a particular picture or piece of text, for instance, the user can move to a new location or access different information. A browser is programmed to read HTML *scripts*, which look a lot like a normal text file. The scripts contain instructions to display text, pictures, and other media as well as links, as shown in figure 12.7.

HTML itself is a relatively limited language for providing high levels of interaction, and the fact that information must travel over a network limits the amount of data that can reasonably be contained in a presentation. Several companies, however, have developed add-ons to HTML that allow for more significant interaction. Sun's *Java* and Macromedia's *ShockWave* are two examples. An advanced version of HTML, **Virtual Reality Modeling Language (VRML)** allows web users to "steer" through 3D landscapes. Still, it must be understood that Internet-based systems where content is stored on an off-site computer and accessed via HTML are normally not able to match stand-alone systems in terms of speed and interactivity.

World Wide Web technology also can be used on smaller networks. Many organizations run **intranets** that are essentially smaller, self-contained versions of the Internet. Intranet users can utilize HTML and browsers to access information from other computers on the network.

Who's Producing Interactive Media?

You have seen that the term interactive media encompasses a variety of applications and techniques. Not surprisingly, interactive presentations are produced by a wide range of groups. Software companies—both giants such as Microsoft and smaller companies—produce interactive media, and many schools, businesses, and institutions produce in-house presentations. Hundreds of small companies, often called "boutiques," that specialize in producing Interactive Media are springing up around the country. Also, companies that in the past have concentrated on "traditional" media—like video production houses and television studios are now getting into interactive media. There are opportunities to start small interactive media businesses with relatively modest investments, much like the desktop publishing businesses of the late 1980s and early 1990s. Interactive media producers may work as part of a large team of videographers, editors, graphic designers, and others, or they may work alone, solely responsible for producing all aspects of a project from start to finish.

The number of corporations interested in interactive media continues to grow, boding well for future opportunities in interactive production. We are seeing joint ventures between telephone companies and cable providers, television networks and software makers, and many others. A key goal of all of these alliances is profiting from interactive media. It is likely that at least some of these much-hyped alliances will fail, and that some of the highly-touted promises of the new media will never materialize. But interactive media has already staked out a significant place in the industry, and it is likely that the stake will continue to grow. And people who can combine a solid foundation of production technique with an understanding of computers, interactivity, and non-linear design will be in increasing demand.

12.4
Tools of Interactive Media

Interactive media are very closely tied to computers. Therefore, they require both hardware, the actual pieces of equipment, and software, the programs that allow for the creation and use of the interactivity.

Hardware

Computer hardware is constantly changing. Components that were "state-of-the-art" a short time ago now may be obsolete. Constant innovation is increasing the capabilities of every component, from the CPU to the mouse. The following is a general guide to components used in interactive work. For a particular application, you may not need all of these components, but you should be familiar with what they do.

Computer

Both the IBM PC and the Macintosh computer are suitable for interactive media work. More expensive workstations, such as those made by Silicon Graphics and others, are also well-suited to authoring. Ideally, an IBM PC should have a Pentium-class processor and a Macintosh should have a PowerPC-class processor. A processor's power is determined by its speed, usually measured in megahertz (MHz). Thus, a 166 MHz Pentium is faster than a 100 MHz Pentium. While there are many variables in processor model

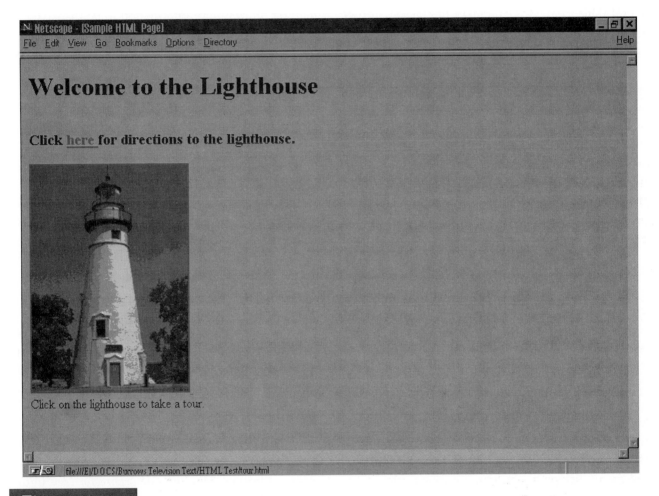

```
1   <HTML>
2   <TITLE> Sample HTML Page </TITLE>
3   <H1> Welcome to the Lighthouse </H1>
4   <BR>
5   <H3> Click <a href="directions.html"> here </a> for directions
    to the lighthouse.
6   <a HREF="tour.html"><IMG SRC="lighthouse.gif"> </A>
7   <BR>
8   Click on the lighthouse to take a tour.
9   </HTML>
```

Figure 12.7

Here is an example of a simple HTML script (top) and how it looks when viewed with a browser program (bottom). The numbers in the box to the left of the script are not actually part of the script; they are shown to explain what each line in the program does. Line (1) Identifies the file as an HTML script. Line (2) Is the title of the page; it appears in the title bar of the browser. Line (3) Uses Heading level 1 for the line of text indicated. HTML allows different levels of headings, differing in size and type style. Line (4) Inserts a line break command that makes subsequent text start on a new line. Line (5) Uses Heading level 3 for the line of text indicated. The portion <a HREF="directions.html"> designates what follows as a link. In this case, when the user activates the link, it will move to a new page called "directions.html". The </a> command designates the end of the link. Thus, the word "here" is designated as a link to the file "directions.html". Line (6) Places the picture of the lighthouse on the screen with the section <IMG SRC="lighthouse.gif">. The portion, <a HREF="tour.html"> designates the lighthouse picture as a link to the file "tour.html." Thus, if the user clicks on the lighthouse picture, he or she will be taken to the tour section. Line (7) Inserts a line break. Line (8) Places the indicated text. Line (9) Indicates the end of the HTML script. In this case, the scripts "directions.html" and "tour.html" would need to be written separately.

and speed, Pentium processors are normally at least twice as fast as 486 and lesser model IBM PCs, and PowerPC Macintoshes enjoy similar advantages over Macintoshes with 680x0-series processors. No matter what processor is used, 16 megabytes of system memory is the minimum for work involving digital video, and 32 megabytes or more may be required.

Storage

There is an ever-growing range of options for storing digital data. Hard drives remain the fastest storage media, and they are available in increasing capacities. Removable drives are becoming more popular, although most are slower than hard drives. The storage medium of choice for distributing interactive media remains the CD-ROM, although the new *Digital Video Disk* (DVD), which can hold seven times as much data, may become the next standard. All of these storage media are **random access,** meaning that any portion of the stored data can be accessed nearly instantaneously.

Tape, on the other hand, is not random access. As you know, if you need to access a particular piece of information stored on a tape, you may have to go through the time-consuming process of rewinding or fast-forwarding. For this reason, the increasing number of affordable digital videotape formats discussed in the first chapter has had little impact on interactive media production.

Audio and Video Digitizing Cards

Audio cards that can digitize stereo audio are generally standard equipment on most PCs sold today. There are also a wide variety of video cards available, and many differences in terms of frame rates, compression formats, and resolution. Both audio and video cards come with software packages that allow you to perform digitization, although for advanced applications it may be necessary to purchase more specialized software, such as Adobe's *Premiere.*

Input Devices

The mouse and the keyboard are the two most common input devices for home PCs. For kiosks, a touch screen that fits over the computer's monitor and responds when a user touches it is widely used. (See figure 12.8.) Touch screens are preferred on presentations designed for public places, because they are easy to use and cannot be tampered with as easily as a mouse or keyboard.

Monitor and Video Card

Monitors are available in various sizes ranging from 14 inches to 20 inches and more. Naturally, a larger monitor allows more information to be displayed on the screen. Video display cards, which allow data to be displayed on the monitor, vary in terms of speed, memory, number of colors, and resolution.

Other Peripherals

Scanners are used to digitize printed material and are available in hand-held and flatbed styles. Photographic slides can be scanned with a slide scanner. Lower-cost scanners may only digitize in black and white and in lower resolutions. For some interactive applications, you may want to use a printer to give the user hard copies of information. There are many varieties available with different features, including the ability to print in color.

Software

Because the general types of interactive media are stand-alone and World Wide Web-based, it stands to reason that software programs fall into these categories, too.

Stand-alone Authoring Programs

There are a variety of programs available for stand-alone authoring. Macromedia's *Director* (see figure 12.9) and *Authorware Professional* and AimTech's *Icon-Author* allow you to combine various media into interactive presentations. Presentations produced with these programs are made into *runtime modules,* allowing them to be used on other computers. Thus, while you need to have the authoring program installed on your computer to produce the presentation, the finished product will run on machines that do not have the authoring program installed on them.

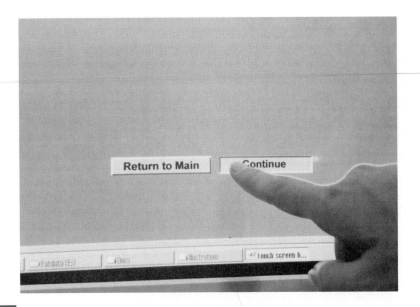

Figure 12.8

Touch screens allow users to activate links by simply touching a particular area of the computer screen.

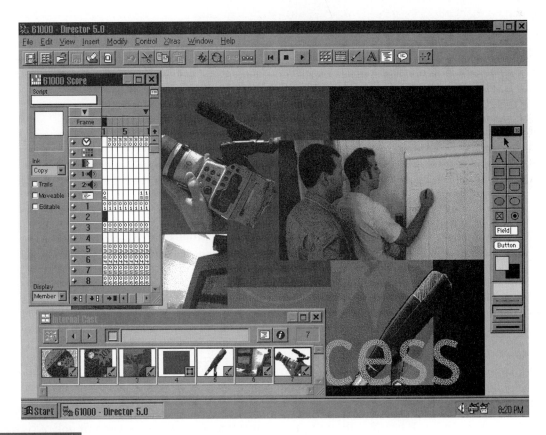

Figure 12.9

Multimedia authoring programs, such as Macromedia's *Director*, allow producers to combine various media into interactive presentations.   © 1996 Macromedia, Inc. All rights reserved. Used with permission. Developed by Bluewaters Productions

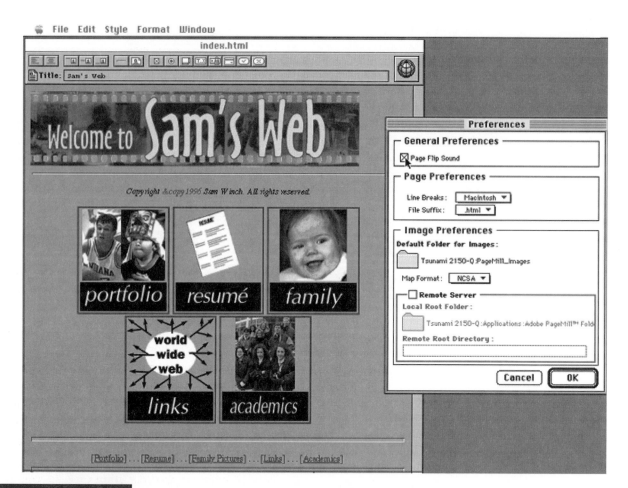

Figure 12.10

Although HTML code can be written using a word processor, programs such as Adobe's *PageMill*™ are designed specifically for authoring HTML presentations. These programs allow the producer to lay out material and specify links on the screen; the program will automatically create the HTML script to make the presentation run.   *Adobe® and PageMill™ are trademarks of Adobe Systems Inc. Artwork courtesy of Samuel P. Winch*

Web-based Authoring

Since HTML is a text-based computer language, you can write HTML programs using a word processor. However, there are a growing number of programs available that make it much easier to assemble HTML presentations without manually writing code. (See figure 12.10.) For viewing HTML presentations, you will need a browser such as Netscape *Navigator*™.

Other Programs

Since both stand-alone and web-based authoring programs are designed chiefly to assemble various media, you may need other programs to prepare your media. For instance, programs like Adobe's *PhotoShop* can be used to manipulate digitized pictures and pro-

duce original artwork. You might also use a word processing program, such as Microsoft *Word* or Corel *WordPerfect*, to key in long text passages and then bring the information into your presentation.

Interactive Media Production

Throughout this chapter, we have emphasized how interactive media represent not only a convergence of media, but also a convergence of skills. The concepts that apply to writing, editing video and audio, shot composition, and graphic design for "traditional" media still apply to interactive media. A poorly lighted interview, for instance, will look just as bad as part of an interactive presentation as it would as part of a documentary or news broadcast. Interactive production does introduce many new and exciting technologies, but it is important to remember that these "bells and whistles" do not change sound production techniques and disciplines.

Since a number of programs are available for putting together interactive media presentations that differ significantly in operation, it would not be practical to give you a step-by-step guide to producing an interactive presentation. Instead, the remainder of this chapter will discuss the overall processes of interactive production, using a hypothetical example at the end to illustrate key points.[1] The best ways to learn to use a particular system are to carefully read the manuals that come with the software, to practice the tutorials that are provided, or to work with someone who has experience with the program. Unfortunately, the learning curve on many authoring programs is very steep, and you may find yourself quite frustrated at times. Like most pursuits, however, once you survive the initial difficulty you will soon find yourself moving rapidly toward mastery of the program and the process.

Interactive Media Planning

As with any type of production, you will need to do thorough preparatory work before you even begin the physical production process. Your interactive production should be well-planned, meaning that you have a clear sense of what it is designed to do (sales, training, entertainment, etc.) and who the target audience is. Your presentation should have a defined set of objectives, outlining the specific information you want it to convey. You will then have to determine what types of media are best suited to these objectives and audience. Would moving video work best in a particular situation or would animations be better? How much text information is needed to make a particular point clear?

It is important to remember that you do not have to use every media in every interactive presentation. It is possible, for example, that you can meet your objectives without using video or animations. Don't include extraneous media just for the sake of doing it; this will only make unnecessary work, confuse the user, and bog down equipment. Having said that,

keep in mind that few presentations can be effective without at least some text and graphics.

In both the preproduction and production processes, you also will need to keep in mind considerations related to *environment* and *resources*. Environmental considerations have to do with where the presentation will be used. Will it end up as a kiosk in the middle of a busy shopping center or will it be a CD-ROM that individuals will use on their home PCs? Your final product should be appropriate for the environment in which it will be used. Resource considerations involve the equipment the presentation will be used on. You know, for example, that full-motion video requires tremendous processing, storage, and transmission resources and will, thus, tax less-powerful computer systems. A highly interactive, beautifully designed presentation loaded with moving video and animations that runs great on a Pentium-based computer may hopelessly bog down a lesser machine. Remember, too, that if you are working on an HTML-based presentation the data will have to travel over a network connection. That fact, combined with HTML's more limited interactive capability, means that web-based presentations tend to be less elaborate.

Very early in the preproduction process, you also need to consider the level of interactivity of your presentation. The level of interactivity, as mentioned earlier, determines how much input you will require from the user and how much power the user has to control the presentation. The presentation may require very little user interaction, or it may depend on nearly constant user input. There are no hard and fast rules for determining an appropriate level of interactivity; it depends on the situation. In general, however, interactivity should be designed to give the users a feeling of control without burdening them with a lot of unnecessary work. In some situations, such as training presentations, it is better to design in a higher level of interactivity in order to make the user feel involved in the learning process. Remember the objectives of your presentation, and design in a level of interactivity appropriate to achieving those objectives.

The level of interactivity has a direct influence on the flow of the presentation. As you know, the power of interactive media is its ability to be used in a non-linear fashion. The simplest type of interactive

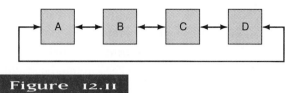

Figure 12.11

Structure of a linear interactive presentation. The arrows between the screens represent user control.

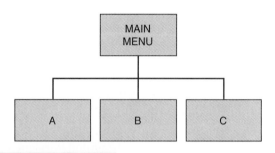

Figure 12.12

A menu-based interactive presentation.

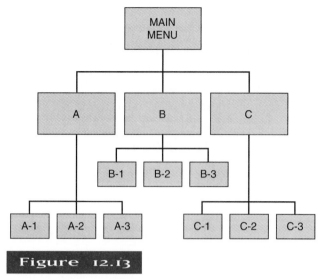

Figure 12.13

A more complex version of a menu-based interactive presentation using submenus.

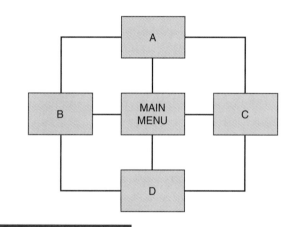

Figure 12.14

Some presentations are not based on a menu design.

presentation, however, as illustrated in figure 12.11, is essentially a linear presentation that requires user input to move from item to item. The presentation is designed only to flow from element A to B to C to D. While the user may be able to move "backward" to previous parts of the presentation, there is no provision for branching to different locations. This type of design, while interactive, is still linear.

A more effective presentation can be created by using a model that is both interactive and nonlinear. The model illustrated in figure 12.12 is quite similar to the shopping center kiosk example cited earlier. In this example, the user is presented with a series of choices that allow him or her to select particular parts of the presentation. The user may decide to ignore the information in one branch, for example, and proceed directly to another. This model allows the user to more efficiently move to a particular piece of information. Menu-based designs also may utilize submenus, as illustrated in figure 12.13, to facilitate increased user control. Other presentations may have a less structured design that does not rely on a menu paradigm, as shown in figure 12.14.

It is important to make your presentation's structure as simple as possible while still meeting its objectives. This relates directly to designing in an appropriate level of interactivity, as you don't want to send the user through fifteen menu levels when three will do. You also want to avoid allowing the user to get "lost" in a presentation that is too complicated or confusing. Links that will allow the user to "go back" to the previous screen or return to a main menu should always be available. You should not send users down "dead ends."

You will probably find it helpful to make a "map" of your presentation similar to the ones in figures 12.11 through 12.14. Doing so will help you visualize both the user input and flow of the presentation. Once you have established these parameters, you will need

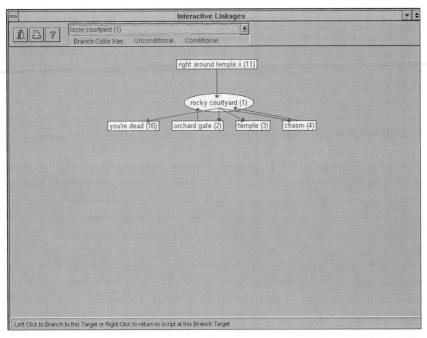

(a)

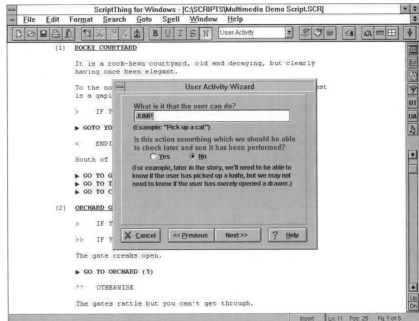

(b)

Figure 12.15

ScriptPerfection Enterprises' ScriptThing™ allows multimedia authors to write scripts for various screens of their presentation and view how those screens are linked (a). Authors can also keep track of user actions (b). *Screens courtesy of ScriptPerfection Enterprises*

to address issues such as treatments, storyboarding, and budgeting (see chapter 13 for more information). Storyboards should be made for each screen in your presentation, showing a hand-drawn representation of how it is to be designed and indicating links, if any.

When you are finished, you should have an individual storyboard for each block on your map. Some specially designed scriptwriting programs can help you plan out links and an overall structure to your presentation (see figure 12.15).

Interactive Media Production

Once you have your presentation thoroughly planned out, you will then begin gathering the information and various media that will be a part of it. Text will need to be written, video shot and digitized, animations produced, graphics and audio digitized, and so on. Once these are secured, you are ready to put them together using an appropriate authoring program.

If you have thoroughly planned your presentation, putting it together should be relatively easy. Work from your presentation map, scripts, and storyboards to produce what you have planned out. Your presentation should have an overall "look" that remains consistent throughout. This means that your selection of fonts, colors, and backgrounds should convey a sense of unity. Graphic elements, such as buttons or logos, should be consistently designed as well.

Your presentation's opening screen, or main menu, is in many ways its most important element. The main menu should be attractive, and should clearly indicate what the presentation is designed to do. In this sense, the main screen should provide orientation for the user, preparing him or her for the presentation. The main menu should provide links to the main parts of the presentation.

Throughout the presentation, links should be clearly labeled, letting the users know what will happen before they activate them. Vague links, such as "Click Here," should be avoided. Links should provide feedback when the user activates them, either through an audible "beep" or some other sound, or by briefly changing color on the screen. Throughout the presentation, links should help guide users by giving them a clear sense of where they are in the presentation and what their choices are.

These principles should give you a good idea of the basic concepts of interactive media production. You will need to tailor these concepts to your particular hardware, software, and objectives. There is an ever-growing number of reference sources available that discuss topics such as the operation of particular programs and design issues in greater detail. Remember, too, that you must apply what you have learned in other areas of television production as well.

12.6

An Interactive Media Production Example

Assume that you have been asked by the chairperson of the Communications Department at your school, Collegiate University, to produce an interactive pre-

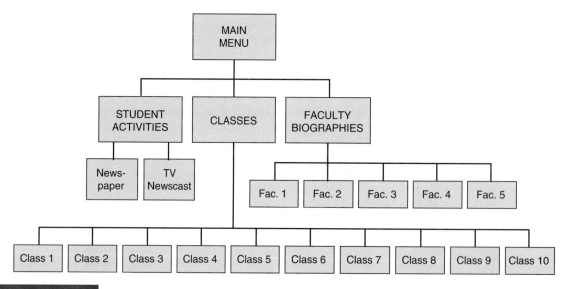

Figure 12.16

A graphical representation of the structure of the interactive presentation designed for Collegiate University.

sentation for the department. The chairperson wants to use this presentation as a way to interest high school students in the department. Prospective students will access this presentation over the Internet using World Wide Web browsers. The chairperson wants to provide information about student activities and classes, and biographies of the department's faculty. After a series of planning meetings with the chairperson, you agree that you will use the following media:

1. Text: brief description of the department, student newspaper, student TV newscast, classes, and faculty biographies;
2. Graphics: picture of department's building, picture of students working on newspaper, picture of each faculty member, Collegiate University logo;
3. Video/Sound: brief (approximately 15 second) clip of student TV newscast.

This mix of media seems appropriate to accomplishing the assigned task. Since the presentation will be accessed by a wide range of students (likely with a wide range of computer equipment) over a network, the presentation will not include a lot of video.

You then decide on a relatively simple design: a main menu and three submenus, as shown in figure 12.16. The three submenus correspond to the three main objectives cited by the chairperson: student activities, classes, and faculty biographies. From the main menu, users can choose one of these three areas to explore. The submenus then branch further. The Student Activities submenu has two branches, the student newspaper and the student TV newscast. The Classes submenu has ten branches, one for each class offered by the department. The Faculty Biographies submenu has five branches, one for each faculty member. On each page of the presentation, a link to return to the main menu will be provided. A sample storyboard for the main menu of the department's interactive presentation is shown in figure 12.17.

The completed main menu page, shown in figure 12.18, illustrates the principles of consistency and clarity discussed in the previous section. The design

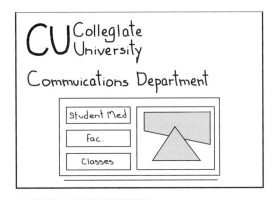

Figure 12.17

A hand-drawn storyboard for the main menu screen of the Collegiate University presentation.

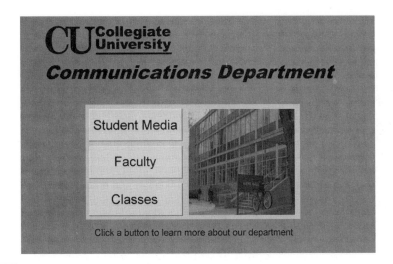

Figure 12.18

The main menu screen from the Collegiate University presentation.

elements shown on this page, such as the font styles, button styles, and layout, would be carried over to the rest of the presentation. The main screen describes what the presentation is designed to do, is attractively designed, and has links that are clearly marked.

Summary

Interactive media represent a convergence of media. Using computers, various media such as *text, graphics, audio* and *video* can be combined into presentations. These presentations are characterized by *interactivity,* meaning that the user can control how information is presented, and by *dynamic content,* meaning that the same presentation can provide different information to different users. Using *links,* interactive presentations allow the user to tailor the presentation to his or her specific needs. Computers lie at the heart of interactive presentations, providing the means of combining the various media and facilitating user control. *Stand-alone* computer systems allow the user to access information contained on a single machine, while *World Wide Web*-based systems allow the user of one computer to access information from many different computers. Although producing interactive media presentations can require specialized equipment such as *video digitizing cards* and *touch screens,* most personal computers sold today are capable of running interactive presentations.

Producing interactive presentations, a process that is also called *authoring,* requires many of the same skills as traditional media work as well as specialized skills. You should plan carefully, taking into consideration such factors as which media to use, what the *environment* will be, what *resources* the users will have, the level of interactivity, and the flow of the presentation. There are a wide variety of applications for interactive presentations, and many tools—both hardware and software—for producing them.

Footnotes

1. A good source for more information about interactive authoring is Fred T. Hofstetter, *Multimedia Literacy* (Second Edition) (New York: McGraw-Hill, Inc., 1997). There are also numerous books on HTML authoring available, as well as tutorials for programs such as Macromedia *Director.*

chapter 13

Producing

s mentioned in chapter 2, section 2.1, producing involves bringing everything together for a successful production. This encompasses coming up with an idea, committing that idea to paper, making sure it can be accomplished given available resources, overseeing the whole project so it reaches fruition, and then evaluating it to see if it reached its goal.

The *discipline* of thorough preproduction planning in this process can not be emphasized strongly enough. The success of every production is determined, to a very great extent, by the way that problems are solved—before they occur.

13.1

Types of Producers

The nature and scope of a project may determine how many people are involved in producing. A public access cable talk show may have one "guiding light" who produces, writes, and hosts the show and handles the expenses out of his or her own pocket. A network situation comedy series may have one or more executive producers, one or more producers, a line producer, and a number of assistant and associate producers.

Executive Producers

Executive producers are people who oversee a number of different productions. For example, a production company (such as Carsey-Werner, owned by Marcy Carsey and Tom Werner) may have several network series in production, in syndication, and in development. Each series has a hands-on **producer,** who does the day-to-day work, but the owners of the company, who made the deals with the networks and who are in the process of making other deals, make decisions regarding the overall scope and direction of the series—hence the term executive producer. Your instructor probably serves as executive producer for your class projects.

Line Producers

Some productions, primarily movies, have a **line producer.** This is a person representing the producer who is on the set each day, mainly making sure that all is progressing properly so that the movie will be finished on-budget and in time for its scheduled airing.

Associate Producers

Many productions have **associate** or **assistant producers**—people who help producers who would otherwise have too much to do. For example, a game show may have one assistant producer whose job it is to acquire free prizes for contestants, while another assistant producer is in charge of screening potential contestants. Whether someone is an assistant or associate producer is not related as much to what job they are in charge of as to their level of experience and skill; an associate producer is paid more than an assistant producer.

Hyphenates

Sometimes people will be **hyphenates.** They take on multiple roles such as producer-director or producer-writer or even producer-writer-director.

There are advantages and disadvantages to handling a number of different roles. Most people evolve into becoming hyphenates because they want *creative control.* A writer who has been displeased with how a director has interpreted his or her script will decide to become the director for the next script. Directors who feel they are unnecessarily curtailed by cost conscious producers may want to make their own decisions about how to prioritize spending. Producers who work hard to develop a project and raise the funding may want to ensure that their vision is carried out during the production phase.

Although being a hyphenate can lead to greater creative control, it is also more work. Given the time pressures of most TV productions, one person can become exhausted trying to polish a script, find Civil War-era guns, and plan camera angles all at one time. Also few people have all the aptitudes necessary to undertake multiple jobs. Someone who is highly skilled in getting the best performance possible from actors may not be equally skilled in handling financial statements. Multiple inputs, undertaken *harmoniously,* can also enrich a production. One person, given too much responsibility, can flounder—or become an ego maniac. Often the reasoned judgment that comes from bouncing ideas off others can lead to a richer end product.

Regardless of how the producing chores are divided, however, somewhere along the way they will involve scripts, budgets, personnel, production paper work, and schedules.

Scripts

To be successful, even the simplest productions need something committed to paper to serve as a guideline. That something is referred to as a **script.**[1] The producer uses the script to organize the elements needed for the program and often to sell the idea of a series or program to someone who will pay the production costs. As with most other elements of TV production, scripts vary both in form and complexity.

Treatments

Most commercial network series start with a **treatment.** (See figure 13.1.) This is several pages, written in regular prose form, that tell the overall premise of the series, describe the main characters, outline the basic plots for several of the episodes, and highlight the strong points of the idea. A producer (or executive producer) from an outside production company (with a track record of success) can make an appointment to see the appropriate network executives for a **pitch** meeting—a session that lasts about half an hour during which the producer tries to convince the network executives that they should buy the series idea. The producer presents the information in the treatment orally and usually leaves the written treatment behind for the executives to study.

If the network executives like the idea, they will commission (pay for) one or more complete program scripts. If they like the scripts, they will order a **pilot,** a produced program that is to be one of the series. If they like the pilot and decide to schedule the series on a regular basis, they will give the go-ahead for more scripts and productions. Throughout this whole process, the production company producer negotiates with the network regarding both creative and financial elements.

Many other types of programs also use treatments. Magazine, talk, and game shows that are planned for **syndication,** cable TV, or local broadcast often evolve from treatments presented to programming executives. In these cases, the treatment will indicate the target audience, define the series goals and objectives, describe the overall idea for the series, and outline some of the planned segments. In addi-

"The Campus" is a high energy series aimed at teens and young adults. It takes place on a college campus and features the adventures, problems, and experiences of four roommates.

Mark, a sophomore, is good looking and athletic. He is on the basketball team and seems destined to become one of its stars. He attracts coeds easily, but deep down he is uneasy with them. He comes from a wealthy family and seems to "have it all." However, he has trouble knuckling down and studying and is constantly on the verge of academic problems that will disqualify him from basketball. He's such a nice guy, however, that his friends try to come to his rescue and figure out ways for him to get through his classes.

Frank, on the other hand, has an easy time in classes, but always seems to have hard luck in social situations. He says the wrong things, wears the wrong clothes, spills his soft drink on a girl he is trying to win over, and generally falls prey to social indiscretions. He and Mark do not get along very well.

Juan tries to smooth the waters between Mark and Frank. He's not as bright as Frank or as athletic as Mark, but he's well rounded and a good mediator. He is on a scholarship and does not have much spending money. Mark sometimes tries to buy his allegiance by giving him material things, but Juan does not respond well to that. He works most evenings so does not have much time for social life.

George is the jokster of the group. In trying to make light of situations, he often utters what turns out to be prophetic philosophy. He likes to play practical jokes on people, especially Mark's girl friends, but he does not mean any harm. He is not particularly good looking, but he is a likable person.

In the first episode of the series, all four arrive back on campus for their sophomore year. Frank, Juan, and George had planned to room with each other and had thought their fourth roommate would be someone they had all befriended in their freshman year. However, that person has dropped out of school and Mark has been assigned to their room. He is unhappy about the situation. He thought he would be in special housing for athletes, but there had not been room for him.

Frank and Mark clash immediately and Frank goes to the housing authority to try to get Mark removed from the room. However, he is unsuccessful. Juan, realizing they will probably all have to live together, talks separately to both Mark and

1

Figure 13.1

The first page of a treatment that might be prepared by an independent production company to give to a network executive.

tion, individual programs such as made-for-TV movies or documentaries often have a treatment as a starting point.

A newscast script proceeds very differently. If a network or station has decided to present the news, no one needs to spell out specific ideas with a treatment—the ideas come from the news of the day. The newscast script is written during the course of a day (or several hours) as the producer and news director decide what is the most important news. Reporters and writers put together individual stories and transitions between stories that are eventually read by newscasters. Usually the producer for a newscast is a *staff producer.* In other words, that person works full-time for the network or station overseeing one or more newscasts each day. This is unlike many network series, where the producer is a member of an *outside production company.*

Varying Script Forms

Because programs and circumstances differ, script forms also differ.[2] The type of script needed for a drama would be overkill for a talk show. A music video that is highly postproduced can use a script with less structure than a news script that must give accurate mistake-proof guidance for a live broadcast. A multimedia game that is interactive needs a different type of script than a TV game show that is not interactive. Although many different script forms have evolved over the years, the main ones that you, as a television student, are likely to encounter are film-style scripts, two-column scripts, rundowns, outlines, and storyboards.

```
INT. - ELEGANT RESTAURANT - NIGHT

     Joan and Philip, both dressed in stylish clothes, sit at a table.
     Philip has leaned forward and is talking softly to Joan.  She is
     leaning back and appears to be somewhat distant.

                         PHILIP
          I really want to come back, Joan. I miss the
          children and I'm tired of living out of a suit-
          case.

                         JOAN
                    (sarcastically)
          That's tender.

                         PHILIP
                    (exasperated)
          Now what did I do wrong?

                         JOAN
          You're just acting like your same old selfish
          self.  Everything revolves around you.  No
          consideration for me.  Not even any sign of
          love.

                         PHILIP
          But, of course, I care about you.  I don't need
          to tell you that.

                         JOAN
          That's a matter of opinion.

                         PHILIP
          Now you're being like your old sensitive self.
          I just don't get it.

                         JOAN
          That's right, Philip.  You just don't get it.

     Joan gets up from the table angrily and walks away.  She realizes
     she has forgotten her purse, returns for it, glares at Philip and
     walks toward the door.  Philip looks hurt and confused.

INT. - CITY STREET - NIGHT

     Christopher is seen driving his car, weaving in and out of
     traffic.  He pulls over to the curb and blinks his lights off and
     on.  A large dark figure carring a briefcase emerges from the
     shadows, opens the car door, throws the briefcase in the car, and
     receeds back into the shadows.  Christopher drives off.

INT. - PHILIP'S OFFICE - DAY

     Philip is going through a stack of papers, but he seems to be
     having trouble concentrating.  Mildred comes in the door with a
     stack of phone messages.
```

Figure 13.2

An example of a page of a film-style script. Note the separation of the scenes and the indentation of the dialogue.

Film-style Scripts

As might be evident from their name, **film-style scripts** (see figure 13.2) are the type that have been used for years to produce theatrical movies. The main characteristic of this script is that each scene is *separated* from the next so that each can be considered individually. Materials produced from film-style scripts are usually shot in a number of different locations with all the scenes from one location being shot on the same day or succeeding days. A script that highlights times of day, locations, and whether these locations are inside (interior-INT.) or outside (exterior-EXT.) can help a producer with preproduction planning. The producer uses the descriptive paragraphs to determine what will be needed in the way of props and set pieces.

Also, the director shoots each scene a number of times using only one camera. For example, the first time the camera might film a two-shot of a man and woman arguing. The second time the scene is shot, the camera would record a close-up of the woman delivering her lines and reacting to the man's lines. The third time through, the close-up would be of the man. Then, during editing, the various shots are cut together. The script form, by showing each distinct scene, helps the director figure out what to shoot. The

```
                          NIGHTLY NEWS

            VIDEO                              AUDIO
    TAPE: OPENING CREDITS          SOUND ON TAPE.  Runs :30.

                                   Ends with drum beat.


    TWO-SHOT - STEVE AND SHARON    STEVE: I'm Steve Anderson.

                                   SHARON: And I'm Sharon

                                   Hendricks here with the latest

                                   news.


    STEVE                          STEVE: Fire fighters are still

                                   at the scene of a three-alarm

                                   fire on Market Street that

                                   destroyed two buildings

                                   earlier today.  Fred White has

                                   this report.


    TAPE: FIRE REPORT              SOT: Runs 2:56. Ends with

                                   "could have been a lot worse."


    SHARON                         SHARON: The Japanese are still

                                   trying to assess if any damage

                                   was caused by this morning's

                                   earthquake. The quake was

    GRAPHICS: MAP OVER SHOULDER    centered two hundred miles

                                   from Tokyo and registered

                                   7 point 1.  Two strong

                                   after shocks have been felt.
```

Figure 13.3

A sample page from a two-column news script. Note how the video and audio items line up with each other.

dialogue is indented, keeping it separate from the writer's descriptive material about the scene. This gives the director room for notes and helps the actors pinpoint their lines.

Film-style scripts are very complete. They include all the words that will be spoken by the actors, describe all the primary action that will take place, and indicate basic moods and emotions. Of course, sometimes the words are altered by the actors or director, and the interpretation and execution of actions and emotion is the province of the director (hence, the occasional conflict about *creative control*).

Just about anything that is shot single-camera can use a film-style script, but it is most often associated with dramatic productions.

Two-column Scripts

The film-style script is not appropriate for multicamera productions that are shot live or live-on-tape. The descriptions would get in the way and location does not change. More appropriate is the **two-column script** (see figure 13.3) that pairs the video elements on the left-hand side with audio elements on the right-hand side. The producer can find all the materials that will need to be gathered together, especially since elements such as music and insert tapes are capitalized.

The director, who must act quickly, can easily see what visual images should be on the screen as the talk progresses and can set up cameras for what will be coming next. Usually the left-hand margin of a two-column script is fairly wide so that the director can make notes.

```
                    RUNDOWN SHEET

                 "PROFILES" - NO. 37

                                        SEGMENT    TOTAL
      SEGMENT   SOURCE         ITEM            TIME     TIME

        1       VCR            Opening Credits.         :25      :25

        2       Cam 2          Host welcomes Jane
                Host mic       Collins from Personnel.  :20      :45

        3       Cam 1,2,3      Host and Jane discuss purpose
                Studio mics    of the department, how it
                Graphics for   interfaces with each employee,
                  guest ID     and its organzation.
                               ENDS: We can see this on a
                               chart.                  3:00     3:45

        4       Graphics of    Jane discusses the chart of
                  chart        the department's organiza-
                Studio mics    tion.                   1:00     4:45

        5       Cam 1,2,3      Host and Jane discuss com-
                Studio mics    pany benefits.
                               ENDS: Let's look at the tape
                               your department produced
                               about this.             1:30     6:15

        6       VCR            Tape about benefits.
                               ENDS: Music and copyright
                               credit.                 5:35    11:50

        7       Cam 1,2,3      Host and Jane discuss how
                Studio mics    employees get additional
                               information.             2:10    14:00

        8       Cam 2          Host thanks Jane and closes
                Studio mics    program.                 :30    14:30

        9       VCR            Closing credits          :30    15:00
```

Figure 13.4

This is a rundown for one of a series of 15 minute programs that might be produced as a corporate video to highlight the job functions of people within the company. Note that exact wording cues are written in some places so that the director can move smoothly from one element to another.

There are many variations on two-column scripts, depending on the type of program for which they are used. Some include every word of dialogue. Editorials and commercials, for example, need to be precise—no ad-libbing allowed. Dramas, such as soap operas, that are shot in-studio with multiple cameras can also use fully-scripted, two-column scripts. Other programs, such as magazine shows and newscasts, include all the words to be spoken by the anchors, but just include basic information about edited field reports that are to be rolled in so that the director can bring them in and take them out without any flubs. Still others, such as talk shows and game shows, indicate the general topics to be discussed or questions to be asked, because the answers, of course, can not be scripted ahead of time.

Rundowns

Rather than using a two-column script, some talk and game shows (and other programs for which little can be scripted ahead of time) use **rundowns.** (See figure 13.4.) These list the various segments that will be included in the program and are most often used for routine programs that are produced on a daily or weekly basis, such as *Today* and *Meet the Press.*

Specific information is given for each segment. This information may vary from one form of program to another, but generally it includes the source for that segment (videotape roll-in, studio cameras, graphics, remote feed), what the segment contains, and how long the segment should run. If a program has a set length, such as 1 hour, the total running time may be indicated so that the director can tell if the overall program is running short or long. Cues in and out of segments help the director prepare for transitions.

Producers use the rundowns to make sure all the guests are confirmed and ready to appear in the proper order. Usually these programs are directed by the same person day after day, so the director has a routine and is mainly concerned with knowing about

```
                    MUSIC VIDEO FOR
                "I LOOK SO GOOD IN YELLOW'
                         BRIAN

    The video will consist of four different set-ups:
         1. Brian, dressed in a variety of yellow clothes, lip
    syncing in a nightclub setting.
         2. A chorus of children dressed in yellow singing the "Oo la
    la la la" refrain.
         3. Brian, dressed in a yellow shirt and lip syncing, walking
    a dog dressed in a yellow dog jacket.
         4. The three back-up singers in a department store trying on
    ugly colored shirts and finally finding yellow ones they like.

    We will build two sets in the studio, one for the nightclub scene
    and the other for the children's chorus.  The nightclub scene
    will have a 1940s look to it and will consist of a sequined
    curtain and a floor stand microphone.  The audience will not be
    shown.  An intense spotlight will highlight Brian's yellow
    clothing.

    The children's chorus (about twenty 8 to 10 year olds) will be on
    risers against background flats that are painted with geometric
    shapes in primary colors.

    The dog walking scene will be shot on a street that has many
    trees and colorful flowers that will show in the background.

    The scene with the back-up singers will be shot in the men's
    clothing store late at night when the store is closed.

    As the track begins, we see Brian in the nightclub scene dressed
    in yellow pants and a black shirt.  As the first verse
    progresses, he adds (in jump cut fashion) additional yellow
    clothing--a shirt, shoes, a jacket, and finally a large floppy
    hat.

    At the first "Oo la la" chorus, we cut to a long shot of the
    children singing.

    Next, Brian is seen walking the dog.  At first the dog is not
    seen, but it is obvious from the leash and the way Brian is being
    pulled that a dog is present.  When the next "Oo la la" section
    comes, the dog and its yellow jacket will be revealed.  Both the
    children and Brian will be heard for this "Oo la la," but the
    children will not be seen.

    The video returns to the nightclub lip syncing until the words "I
    hardly know anyone who wears yellow shirts" at which point the
    back-up singers are seen rummaging through shirts on a "sale"
    counter in the men's clothing store.
```

Figure 13.5

An outline for a music video. Both general and specific ideas are given and the various set and remote locations are enumerated.

anything unusual that is incorporated within a particular segment.

Sometimes rundowns include fully-scripted material that can be written ahead of time. When they do, they look somewhat akin to a two-column script in that they include a column for video and another for audio. The line can blur between a *detailed rundown* and a *nonspecific two-column list,* but how to categorize the script is not nearly as important as whether or not it is useful for the talent, producer, and director.

Outlines

The line also sometimes blurs between rundowns and outlines. **Outlines** list the various elements of a pro-

gram but usually in less specific terms than rundowns. They are often used for pieces such as music videos (see figure 13.5) that are shot and then edited. Because of this, they can include some of the type of detail found in film-style scripts. The producer and director both have time to digest the information, and the shooting itself is usually undertaken with one camera from a variety of angles.

Documentaries often lend themselves to outlines. They can indicate general items, issues, or circumstances to be investigated, but the real conclusions and findings cannot be planned until the material has been shot.

Outlines do need to indicate to the producer the props, sets, locations, and other production elements that will be needed to ensure a successful shoot. They must give the director a general idea of what to shoot, but they allow plenty of room for improvisation.

Storyboards

Storyboards (see figure 13.6) show pictures of each visual element and describe the actions and/or indicate the dialogue below each picture. They are usually used for short productions such as commercials or music videos, and they are a basic element of an interactive media script (see chapter 12). A drama could certainly be storyboarded, but it would involve a great deal of tedious artwork and pages and pages of paper. Sometimes directors will storyboard complicated scenes of a drama to better visualize them, but the storyboard, as a script form, is usually associated with short productions.

In general, directors like to work from storyboards because they are so *visual.* Although a director may superimpose his or her own ideas over the storyboard script, it gives a good starting point. Producers have to examine storyboards very closely to make sure all the props and other elements needed for production will be ready.

The type of script you choose to use—film-style, two-column, rundown, outline, storyboard—will depend on the type of program you are undertaking and the type of material you feel most comfortable with. Scripts are primarily a blueprint for production. People who try to produce without a script are asking for trouble in the same way that builders would be asking for disaster if they tried to construct a house without following a basic blueprint.

13.3

Budgets

Students often do not give much thought to budgets, because their monetary needs are small. The college provides the equipment; cast and crew members come from the class and do not need to be paid; props can be borrowed from dorm rooms or willing relatives. But in the "real world" of TV production, budgets are *very important.* A producer who goes over budget is not likely to stay employed. Moreover, budgets are usually part of the presentation package when a producer is trying to convince a network or syndicator that it should support a particular program idea.

Graduating students who understand the procedures of budgeting are likely to be looked upon as more *valuable* than graduates who have mastered only creative or technical talents. For that reason, it behooves you to practice budgeting by figuring out what it would cost you to produce your class projects if you were doing them in the outside world.

Costs of Productions

TV production expenses are usually divided into **above-the-line** and **below-the-line.** The above-the-line costs are creative in nature and include the pay given to talent, producers, directors, and writers. Below-the-line costs are more technical in form and include the salaries of the crew, the cost of the staging area and equipment, and the money needed for supplies such as scenery and make-up.

Costs vary greatly depending on many factors: whether the crew is union or nonunion; the recognition value and reputation of the talent; the length of the production; the number of complicated effects needed; the part of the country or world in which the production is taking place; and whether the equipment and facilities used belong to the production company or are rented from other companies.

Pay Rates

Most major production companies, networks, and some local stations are unionized and agree to pay at least the minimum cast and crew wages stipulated by the various **unions** that represent the technical people—International Brotherhood of Electrical Workers (IBEW), International Alliance of Theatrical Stage Employees and Moving Picture Machine Operators (IATSE), etc.—and the **guilds** that represent the creative people—Screen Actors Guild (SAG), Directors Guild of America (DGA), American Federation of Radio and Television Actors (AFRTA), Writers Guild of America (WGA), etc. Every several years the unions and the producing organizations negotiate these rates. Over time, the contracts have become

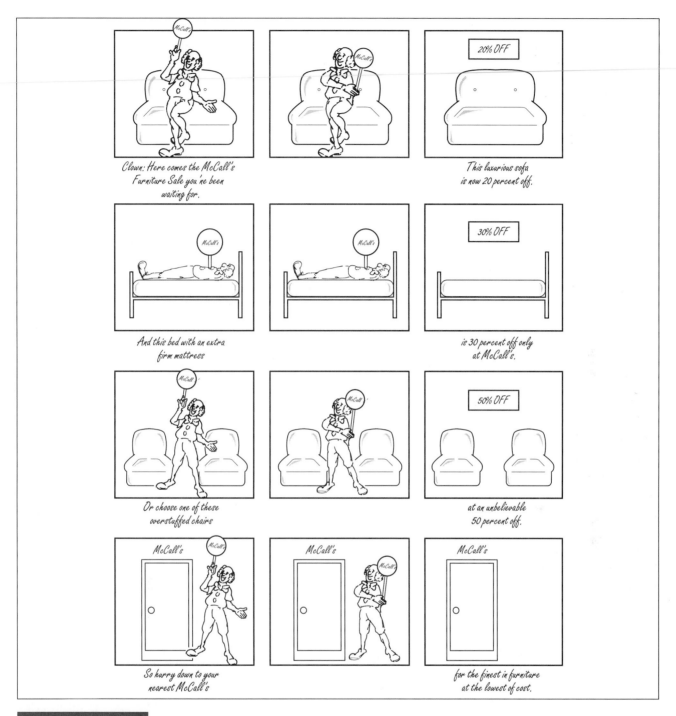

Figure 13.6

A storyboard for a commercial. This enables the director to visualize all the action and how it juxtaposes with the words. The accuracy of this visualization is much more important than any artistic considerations.

SELECTED TELEVISION INDUSTRY PAY RATES

Directors
    If the program length is   the director is paid a minimum
                                         of appproximately
    0 to 15 minutes $3037
    16 to 30 minutes   5235
    31 to 60 minutes   9299

Producers
    Producers are usually paid about the same as directors

Writers
    If the program length is   the writer's minimum is a
                                      total of approximately
    0 to 15 minutes $3489
    16 to 30 minutes   5664
    31 to 60 minutes   10,976

Performers
    These types of performers   receive approximately this
                                          amount of pay
    Principal performers $559 per day
    Stunt performers   559 per day
    Singers   603 per day
    General ability extra   72 per day
    Special ability extra   82 per day

Technical and Crafts People
    Technical director . . . . $35 per hour
    Lighting director . . . .   30 per hour
    Camera operator . . . .   30 per hour
    Audio operator . . . .   34 per hour
    Audio assistant/Boom operator . . . . . .   26 per hour
    Tape editor . . . .   34 per hour
    Other technical personnel (graphics, . .   30 per hour
       VCR, teleprompter operators, etc.)
    Assistant director/Script supervisor . .   35 per hour
    Floor director . . . .   30 per hour
    Stage hands . . . .   23 per hour
    Electricians . . . .   24 per hour
    Scenic artist . . . .   31 per hour
    Set decorator . . . .   29 per hour
    Set painter . . . .   23 per hour
    Propmaster . . . .   27 per hour
    Costume designer . . . .   29 per hour
    Costumer . . . .   22 per hour
    Make-up artist . . . .   27 per hour
    Hair stylist . . . .   23 per hour

Figure 13.7

Selected TV industry pay rates. These are approximate rounded-off figures of pay for various union positions. Note that some of these people are hired by the day, project, or hour. In reality, union provisions are much more complicated, taking into account such factors as how long a person has been in the union, how many hours or days they work total, overtime pay, meal breaks, and working conditions. These figures are intended simply to help students approximate their production costs if they hired union people.

quite complicated, but figure 13.7 shows some of the major pay provisions for performers, directors, producers, writers, and technical and crafts people that should help students practice budgeting their own productions.[3]

Shoots that are nonunion can pay whatever people are willing to work for, but the unions and guilds fine their own members if they work for anyone for less than union rates. Most of the truly skilled people are in the unions, so a nonunion crew is likely to be less capable than a union crew. Of course, people who are highly prized within the industry can demand much higher pay than that stipulated by the union and guild minimums.

The trend within the television industry is to hire **freelance** cast and crew by the hour, day, or project as indicated in figure 13.7. However, sometimes people are hired on a more permanent basis, usually

FACILITIES RATE CARD

Studio and Control Room Rental $500 per hour

(Includes a 35' by 35' studio with cyc, lighting grid and lights,
3 industrial grade CCD cameras with teleprompters, and up to 5
microphones; and a 12' by 20' control room with an 8-in 4-out
audio mixer, switcher with 2 effects buses, graphics generator,
and 1 play and 1 record VCR.)

Additional Equipment

```
    Extra microphones . . . . . . . . . . . $  3 each per hour
    Extra cameras . . . . . . . . . . . . .   50 each per hour
    Digital video effects . . . . . . . . .   50 per hour
    1/2" S-VHS VCR . . . . . . . . . . . . .   20 per hour
    8mm Hi-8 VCR . . . . . . . . . . . . . .   20 per hour
    3/4" U-matic VCR . . . . . . . . . . . .   20 per hour
    1/2" Betacam VCR . . . . . . . . . . . .   80 per hour
    1" VTR . . . . . . . . . . . . . . . . .  100 per hour
    Digital VTR . . . . . . . . . . . . . .  150 per hour
    Cuts-only 3/4" editing . . . . . . . . .   80 per hour
```

Set Pieces

```
    Easels . . . . . . . . . . . . . . . . .   10 each per hour
    Plain flats . . . . . . . . . . . . . .   15 each per hour
    Chairs . . . . . . . . . . . . . . . . .    5 each per hour
    Tables . . . . . . . . . . . . . . . . .    5 each per hour
    Risers . . . . . . . . . . . . . . . . .   10 each per hour
    Piano . . . . . . . . . . . . . . . . .    20 per hour
```

Figure 13.8

A facilities and equipment rate card. Studio rental fees and the cost for renting individual pieces of equipment vary greatly depending on the size of the studio, the quantity and sophistication of the equipment, and the part of the country where the rental is taking place. These figures are based on a facility and equipment similar to that found on many college campuses.

referred to as **staff** positions. A news producer, for example, would be hired by a local station to work with the local news day after day, year after year. That same station might have a staff director who directs a public service show one day and a children's program the next. Similarly five or six staff camera people might handle most local production—news, public affairs, children's programs—supplemented occasionally by freelance camera operators. Staff people usually receive less per hour than freelance people, but they are assured of steady employment, while their freelance counterparts must be constantly seeking new jobs.

Facilities and Equipment

Facilities and equipment are also major costs associated with production. If something is produced **in-house**—that is, within a production facility that has its own studio and equipment—the cost could be considered to be next to nothing, because everything that is needed is already in place. However, the facil-

ity must be maintained and the equipment must eventually be replaced, so even a local public affairs show produced at a local station is usually "billed" (on paper only) for use of the facilities.

When a producer rents an outside facility, costs are real and can be easily budgeted. Most organizations that rent studios and/or equipment have a **rate card** listing the cost for a fully equipped studio or for the various pieces of equipment that the client might wish to use. The rate card shown in figure 13.8 lists the costs for a studio with three cameras and other commonly used production equipment as well as the rates for additional equipment. Once again, students can use these numbers to practice budget construction.

Supplies are figured at what they actually cost. If the production calls for a wig, the producer (or assistant producer) must actually locate an appropriate wig and find out how much it will cost. One supply that is necessary for all taped programs is videotape stock. The actual cost of the stock will depend on which tape format is being used.

BUDGET WORKSHEET

Production Name_____

Producer_____

Director_____

Date(s) of Production_____

DESCRIPTION	ESTIMATE	ACTUAL	NOTES

ABOVE-THE-LINE
Producer
_____

Director
_____

Writer
_____

Principle Performers
_____

Bit Performers
_____

Off-Camera Announcers
_____

Extras
_____

Musicians
_____

Other
_____

_____

TOTAL ABOVE-THE-LINE   _____   _____

BELOW-THE-LINE
Crew
Technical Director
_____

Lighting Director
_____

Camera Operators
_____

Audio Operator
_____

Audio Assistant
_____

Tape Editor
_____

Graphics Operator
_____

VCR Operator
_____

Teleprompter Operator
_____

Assistant Director
_____

Floor Director
_____

Stage Hands
_____

Electricians
_____

Figure 13.9

A budget worksheet (continued on page 273). This worksheet should help you determine what the costs will be for your production. Use the space under each person or item to indicate how you arrived at your estimate. For example, 3 camera operators for 4 hours at $30 each = $360.

```
Art Director                    _____

Set Decorator                   _____

Set Painter                     _____

Propmaster                      _____

Costume Designer                _____

Costumer                        _____

Make-up Artist                  _____

Hair Stylist                    _____

Other                           _____

                                _____


Facilities
Studio Rental                   _____

Extra Equipment                 _____

                                _____

                                _____

Set Pieces                      _____

                                _____

                                _____

                                _____

Props                           _____

                                _____

                                _____

Costumes and Make-up            _____

                                _____

                                _____

Tape Stock                      _____

                                _____

TOTAL BELOW-THE-LINE    _____      _____

GRAND TOTAL             _____      _____
```

Figure 13.9—Continued

Constructing and Adhering to the Budget

Once all the information regarding costs has been gathered, the producer must actually construct the budget. It is laid out with the above-the-line costs separated from the below-the-line costs. Figure 13.9 shows a worksheet that can be used for a typical TV production budget. Computer spreadsheets are particularly helpful for budgeting.[4] Using them, produc-

ers can determine what costs would be under various circumstances—with three cameras versus four cameras; hiring two different audio operators versus paying one audio operator overtime; with and without the scene that requires renting a helicopter.

The Role of the Unit Manager

The people working with or for the producer who deal the most with budgets are the **unit manager** and/or **production manager.** Sometimes these titles are used interchangeably, but most commonly a person who works for a *production facility* is called a unit manager and a person who works for an *independent production company* is called a *production manager*. For example, a unit manager might work for a network that produces some of its own shows and rents out its facilities and crew members to others (corporations, advertisers or production companies). The unit manager would be in charge of drawing up and adhering to the rate card and scheduling the facilities for use by both in-house producers and outside clients. This person has the responsibility for seeing that the production costs do not exceed the contracted amount paid (on paper or for real).

Production managers are usually associated with a *particular project* rather than a particular facility. They determine what costs will be incurred by the project in terms of people, facilities, supplies, and other requirements. Working closely with producers, they draw up the budgets. Then, during production and postproduction, they keep track of all expenses to make sure the budget is not being exceeded.

Budget Overruns

If a budget is being overrun, the producer is the one who must solve the problem. At times the producer can raise additional money to cover the shortfall; sometimes the producer can convince the director to work faster; other times some element of a program must be cut so that costs can be saved.

Budgeting is a difficult process. Costs must not be exaggerated or people will not be willing to undertake the production. But sufficient money must be provided so that the program is successful. As money becomes tighter, *more care* must be given to drawing up and adhering to the budget.

13·4

Personnel

In addition to seeing that the script and budget are generated, another major duty of the producer is hiring the various people who will be needed for the production. The most important person whom the producer hires is the director. Sometimes once the producer hires the director, he or she steps out

of the hiring process, and the director hires the rest of the cast and crew. Of course, if the producer, director, and crew members are all on staff at a production facility, no actual hiring takes place, but the producer may lobby to have the most appropriate (and skilled) of the directors and crew members assigned to the project.

Casting

If the project is a drama or sitcom, **casting** is very crucial and producers often want to be involved. The usual procedure is that the producer and/or director draw up a list of the characters needed, along with their physical and psychological traits. (Often this is taken from the treatment or script). This list is given to various **agents** who then select actresses and actors they represent and send them to an audition where they read lines of the script. Then the director, producer, and others who have a vital interest in the production select the cast members. Sometimes specialized **casting agencies** are hired for productions with large casts, such as made-for-TV movies. The director may be involved with hiring the principal actors, but the casting agency alone fills the minor parts.

Although dramas present the greatest challenges for finding talent, other forms of shows also involve hiring or selecting talent. For example, great care goes into selecting contestants for game shows. The number of people wishing to try their luck on these shows far exceeds the number needed, so producers (or associate producers) look for people who are lively or unusual and who will perform well when the TV cameras are on. Talk show producers try to line up people who are well-known (or eccentric) and who will interact well with the host or hostess. Public affairs producers look for people with something to say who can present their points in a dynamic (or at least not boring) manner.

Actors who appear on dramas or sitcoms sign *contracts* that stipulate how much they will be paid and what their general obligations and working conditions are. Nonprofessionals should also be asked to sign **performance releases** (see figure 13.10) so that they cannot come back at a later time and ask for money or other privileges. One student producer learned this lesson the hard way. He had a sword swallower

PERFORMANCE RELEASE

In consideration of my appearing on the TV program

_____
(title)
and for no subsequent remuneration, I do hereby on behalf of
myself, my heirs, executors, and administrators authorize

_____
(producer)
to use live or recorded on tape, film, or otherwise my name,
voice, likeness, and performance for television distribution
throughout the world and for audiovisual and general education
purposes in perpetuity.

        I further agree on behalf of myself and others as above
stated that my name, likeness, and biography may be used for
promotion purposes and other uses. Further, I agree to
indemnify, defend, and hold the producer harmless for any and all
claims, suits, or liabilities arising from my appearance and the
use of any of my materials, name, likeness, or biography.

Conditions:

Signature_____

Printed Name_____

Street Address_____

City and Zip Code_____

Phone Number_____

Date_____

Figure 13.10

A sample performance release. All people who appear on a television program who have not signed official contracts should be asked to sign a form such as this.

appear on his student production and neglected to get the proper release form signed. Later he showed the production on a cable TV public access channel, and someone called the sword swallower to say she had seen him. The sword swallower, thinking the student was making huge amounts of money distributing the tape, sued for $100,000 in retroactive pay and residuals. Although the student managed to avoid paying the sword swallower, he had to hire and pay a lawyer to fight the suit. That student producer will never again forget to get each person to sign a release.

Crew Selection

The producer for any show will definitely hire the production manager and assistant producers, if needed. She or he may also be involved with selecting camera operators, scenic designers, makeup people, and the like. One of the most important considerations is gathering together a group of people who work together harmoniously. Frequently, producers and directors have people with whom they have worked in the past that they want to work with again, because they have a common understanding of the TV production process. This makes it hard for new people to break into the business, but it usually ensures a successful production.

If talent must be brought in from a great distance, if the production lasts for many hours or if any of the shooting is done at a remote location, then the producer must make arrangements for _transportation,_

GROUP 2

PROPS

ITEM	WHO IS BRINGING IT	NOTES
umbrella	Jorge M.	
world globe	Susan T.	will get from library
purse	Kim S.	
waddling duck	Chris B.	bring it a week early to test it on camera
lamp	Maria G.	get permission form signed by dorm counselor

Figure 13.11

A list of props as a student producer might prepare it for a class production.

lodging, and *meals.* Creature comforts are definitely the domain of the producer.

13.5
Production Paperwork

Because one of the duties of the producer is to make sure all elements of the program are in the right place at the right time, a producer usually makes and double-checks *lists.* The type of lists needed vary from production to production. A drama will need lists that detail costumes, sets, props and who is responsible for each. (See figure 13.11.) An ongoing talk show will need a list of potential guests and dates when they are to appear. A game show will need a list of prizes that have been or may be acquired for free. Often the production manager draws up these lists, because they relate closely to budget determinations.

Copyright Clearance

Producers must also keep track of **copyright.** Nothing that has been copyrighted (e.g. poem, short story, photograph, music, videotape footage) can be used on a show unless the owner has *granted permission.* Obtaining permission involves writing letters to copyright holders and then keeping careful track of what has and has not been cleared. (See figure 13.12.) Sometimes copyright holders specify particular stipu-lations, such as a special wording in a credit at the end of the program. Producers must make sure these requirements are executed.

The most commonly used copyrighted material in programs is music. Some TV stations pay **music licensing companies** (ASCAP, BMI, and SESAC) then have the right to use music represented by those companies, which is most of the popular music. However, most independent productions (including student productions) must clear copyright to use material that is not copyrighted.

Clearing copyright can be a difficult chore for the producer. Often just finding who owns the copyright can require extensive research. With music, the copyright holder could be the composer, the arranger, the publisher of the sheet music, the record company, or some combination of them. Usually when they are found, they want money, so copyright clearance can be *expensive.*

Music that is old enough to be in the **public domain** can be used without copyright clearance. Usually that means the composer has been dead at least fifty years, but sometimes a particular arrangement of a song can be copyrighted and the rights to that are held by someone who is still alive.

A way to get around copyright clearance is to have music composed specially for the production. This, too, can be expensive if the composer is to be paid. Student productions have an advantage in this

```
Date

Name
Licensing Department
Music Publishing Company
Street Address
City, State, and Zip Code

Dear Person's Name:

I am producing a student television production entitled ("Name of
Program") for which I would like to use part of your musical
composition ("Name of Music"), composed by (Name of Composer.)  I
would like to acquire a non-exclusive synchronization license for
this musical composition.

I would like permission to use this material for broadcast,
cablecast, or other means of exhibition throughout the world as
often as deemed appropriate for this stuent production and for
any future revisions of this production.  Your permission
granting me the right to use this material in no way restricts
your use for any other purposes.

For your convenience, a release form is provided below and a copy
of this letter is attached for your files.

Sincerely yours,


Your Name


I (We) grant permission for the use requested in this letter.

Signature_____

Printed Name_____

Title_____

Phone Number_____

Date_____
```

Figure 13.12

A sample of a letter you might write to obtain clearance for music.

regard, because universities usually have music students eager for the experience of composing in return for a credit. There are also services that provide copyright cleared music very inexpensively.[5] The problem with much of this music is that it is not very distinctive—it all tends to sound alike.

The producer's problems are similar when it comes to videotape or film footage. If the opening credits require a shot of an airplane taking off, you cannot simply tape a takeoff from some movie you have seen on TV and use it without permission. You could have someone take portable equipment to the nearest airport and shoot the shot, or you could acquire it from a company that supplies stock footage.

Permission to use *written material* (poems, stories, charts) can usually be obtained from the publisher of the book in which it appears, while permission to use a painting that is in an art book may require permission of the artist, the photographer who took the picture of the painting, the publisher of the book, the museum where the painting is hanging, or some combination thereof.

Record Keeping

The producer must keep careful records of legal documents (including actor contracts and performer releases), receipts for purchased supplies, damage done to sets or locations, and other paperwork that is

CALL SHEET

Date_____

Program Title_____

Episode Number_____

Producer_____

Director_____

Studio Location_____

_____

PERFORMERS

NAME   POSITION   REPORT TIME

_____

CREW

NAME   POSITION   REPORT TIME

Figure 13.13

An example of a call sheet.

generated during preproduction, production, and postproduction. This paperwork is necessary for a variety of reasons. First, if the producer leaves and a new producer is hired, he or she will have the necessary information to continue production. It also supplies the cast and crew with specifics so that they can do their jobs correctly. Some of the paperwork is used for tax purposes, while some is needed in case of (or hopefully, to prevent) lawsuits or investigations.

13.6

Schedules

Scheduling is another part of the producer's duty. Sometimes this is relatively easy. An ongoing series produced in a studio is likely to tape at the same time each day or each week. The set will be the same each time, and for the most part, the cast and crew will remain unchanged. For such productions, the producer usually posts a **call sheet** (see figure 13.13) on the studio door or somewhere that is easily accessed

by cast and crew. This lists the time that everyone is to appear and gives a general idea of what will be shot. The time may generally be the same from week to week, but the call sheet takes into account aberrations. For example, if a complicated makeup job is called for in a particular episode of a series, the person being made up and the makeup person will need to report earlier than usual.

Scheduling is more complicated for a studio show that is produced only once. The producer must find a time or times when all the performers are available, often a difficult task, because people appearing on a one-time only basis are likely to have other obligations. The producer must also work with the unit manager to assure that a studio will be available at a time when all the performers are free. If a producer wants a particular crew member, such as a certain audio operator, that further complicates the scheduling process.

Shoots that cover real events, such as news and sports, have their schedule set for them. The equipment and crews must be available and in place when the event takes place. The scheduling is easiest if the time of the event is known well ahead of time. However, news, by definition, does not occur that way. For this reason, most stations and networks have equipment that is dedicated to the coverage of news events.

Most complicated of all are programs that involve field production. Multiple locations are added to the problems associated with having cast and crew available. Also everyone is usually a long distance from the studio and cannot return for something that was forgotten. For these reasons, producers draw up thorough **shooting schedules** that list all the elements needed at each location. The process of producing and shooting away from the studio is discussed more thoroughly in chapter 15 dealing with field production.

13.7

Evaluation

Once a program is finished, the producer has another function—evaluation. The program should meet its goals. For network TV, the main evaluation process is ratings. A series with high ratings stays on the air and one with low ratings is cancelled. But many other forms of programs need much more sophisticated evaluation. The producer of a cooking show designed to show people how to bake a cake should test participants after they have viewed the program to see if people really can bake the cake. Demographic studies should be undertaken to make sure a program designed to appeal to 8- to 11-year-olds is actually watched by that age group. Interactive multimedia, in part because it is so new, requires a great deal of evaluation, some of it to make sure the goals are being met and some just to make sure the program works in its entirety.

Only by honestly evaluating past productions can producers create even better programming.

Summary

Producing is a crucial process that can make or break the overall organization and execution of a production. A producer is responsible for making sure that none of the details involved with a show are forgotten.

Sometimes producers are *hyphenates* and take on directing and/or writing chores as well as producing duties. Often they have a number of people working for them such as *associate producers, assistant producers, production managers,* and *line producers. Executive producers* oversee a number of projects.

Producers are in charge of making sure an appropriate *script* is generated. Often they must first sell the idea for a series or program to network executives by *pitching* the idea contained in a *treatment* and then making a *pilot.*

Different forms of scripts are appropriate for different types of programs. Dramas usually use a *film-style script,* while news and information programs are more likely to use the *two-column script. Rundowns* are useful for programs, such as talk shows and game shows, that are similar from week to week and contain interviews and other unscripted material. *Outlines* are appropriate for music videos and other program forms that are rather nonspecific. *Storyboards* are most often used for commercials and other highly visual or interactive materials.

The producer is also charged with drawing up and adhering to the *budget.* A typical budget is divided into *above-the-line* and *below-the-line* costs and includes salaries, facilities, and supplies. People are hired on a *freelance* or *staff* basis and facilities usually have a *rate card.* Union and guild rates for various technical and creative positions come into play. *Unit managers* and *production managers* play an important role in budget creation and adherence.

The director is hired by the producer, and both are often involved in hiring the rest of the cast and crew. *Casting* is a particularly important part of hiring that often involves agents and casting agencies. Nonprofessional talent should always be asked to sign *performance releases.*

Producers generate lists of things needed for the production to help people organize their jobs. They also clear *copyrights* and obtain music and stock footage.

Scheduling is another domain of the producer. This can be a fairly simple process for regularly scheduled, in-studio productions, but it becomes increasingly complicated for field production.

Once a program is produced, it should be *evaluated* so that future programs can be even better.

Footnotes

1. This book does not pretend to be a text in scriptwriting. What is given here is merely an overview of script forms. For more information on scriptwriting, see such books as Syd Field, *Screenplay: The Foundations of Screenwriting* (New York: Dell, 1982); Ronald D. Dyas, *Screenwriting for Television and Film* (Dubuque, IA: Brown and Benchmark, 1993); Jurgen Wolff and Kerry Cox, *Top Secrets: Screenwriting* (Los Angeles: Lone Eagle Publishing Company, 1992); Richard A. Blum, *Television and Screen Writing* (Stoneham, MA: Focal Press, 1995); Peter Mayeux, *Writing for the Broadcast Media* (Newton, MA: Allyn and Bacon, 1985); and Ray DiZazzo, *Corporate Scriptwriting* (Stoneham, MA: Focal Press, 1992).

2. A large number of computer programs are available to help television writers compose their scripts. Some of the most commonly used are *Scriptor* from Screenplay Systems, 150 East Olive Avenue, Suite 305, Burbank, CA 91502; *AVScriptor*, 4705 Bay View Avenue, Tampa, FL 33611; *ScriptWright* from Indelible Ink, 156 Fifth Avenue, #228, New York, NY 10010; and *Movie Master* from Comprehensive Video Supply, 148 Veterans Drive, Northvale, NJ 07647.

3. For more information on wages and salaries, see *Paymaster,* a publication put out by Entertainment Partners, 3601 West Olive Avenue, 8th Floor, Burbank, CA 91505, that lists all the generally accepted minimums and working conditions.

4. Computer budgeting programs made for the television and film industries include *Movie Magic, Turbo AD,* and *Cost Tracking.* All these can be purchased from Quantum Films Software Division, 8230 Beverly Boulevard, Suite 17, Los Angeles, CA 90048.

5. Some libraries that supply copyright cleared music are Blue Ribbon SoundWorks Ltd. (404-377-1514); Canary Productions (800-368-0033); DeWolfe Music Library (800-221-6713); FirstCom/Music House/Chappell (800-858-8880); Killer Tracks (800-877-0078); Metro Music (212-799-7600); The Music Bank (408-867-4756); and Sound Ideas (800-387-3030). For more details, see "Production Music Libraries on Audio CDs," *Mix,* September 1995, pp. 127–129.

chapter 14

Directing

A director is part manager, part artist, and part psychiatrist. Directors are the ones who give instructions to cast and crew, who make sure the production is aesthetically pleasing, and who handle the reasonable (and unreasonable) demands or quirks of those involved with the production.[1]

Directors must adapt their directing styles to fit their own personalities, the capabilities of the on-air talent, and the needs of the particular show they are directing. Some directors are, by nature, more authoritative than others, and give concrete, distinct direction. Others rely more on psychology and attempt to obtain superior performances by letting the talent and technicians feel they are the ones in charge of their own actions. Professional actors, such as those participating in a drama, require different handling than nonprofessionals who might be making a first-time appearance on a public affairs program. A children's program with many youngsters on it requires a more patient approach than a late-night talk show.

The "Manager" Role

As the overall "boss," the director must oversee what everyone else involved with the production does. In addition, the director has many specific tasks that are primarily his or her domain that are part of managing the program. These include blocking the production, marking the script, preparing shot sheets, conducting rehearsals, and actually calling the show. In addition, the associate director, working with the director, must plan the exact timing procedures for the show.

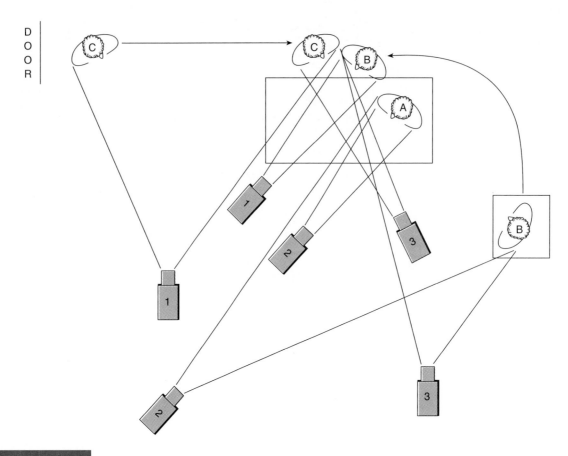

Figure 14.1

A blocking diagram as a director might draw it. In this scene, characters A and B are talking when character C comes in the door angrily and goes behind the sofa. Character B rises from the chair and goes behind the sofa where characters C and B argue. Character A reacts to the argument. Camera 1 pans with C as he moves from the door to behind the sofa and later has a close-up of B. Camera 2 shows A and B talking and then gets a reaction shot of A. Camera 3 follows B from the chair to behind the sofa and later gets a close-up of C.

Blocking

Once you, as the director, have determined the purpose of the script and are sure it is the approximate length you want (see chapter 2, section 2.2), you should start thinking about *blocking*—the placing of actors and cameras in particular spots. This is more complex for dramas and comedies than it is for public affairs programs, but all programs need some form of blocking. Think through how the actors or performers will best relate to each other?

Should the talk show host sit in the middle of two guests or to the right of both of them? Should the husband lean against the back of the wife's chair or sit down in the chair next to her? Don't forget to think about actor comfort. An actress who has to turn her head unnaturally in order to see the leading man is going to be too uncomfortable to deliver her lines well.

Also think through the relationship of the actors to the cameras. Where should the daughter be positioned so that camera 2 can capture a good close-up of her reaction to her father's chastisement? On which burner of the stove should the chef stir the pudding so that camera 3 can obtain an effective shot?

Directors often draw **blocking diagrams** to help them visualize the shots ahead of time. (See figure 14.1.) Using these diagrams, they can plan moves and think through how the people and the equipment will interact with each other. One useful blocking technique for directors is to *start blocking in the center of the program.* Pick the most crucial or difficult part of the

③	Camera number three
< or F.I.	Fade in
KEY or K	Key
T	Take
⩵ or D	Dissolve
SD	Slow dissolve
> or F.O.	Fade out
Q	Cue
⌐	At this point, cut, dissolve, or cue
D. I.	Dolly in
D.B. or D.O.	Dolly back or dolly out
PREP ②	Prepare camera 2
③ TO___	Camera 3, get ready for . . .
2-sh	Shot of two persons
3-sh	Shot of three persons
O/S	Over-the-shoulder shot
CU	Close-up shot
MS	Medium shot
LS	Long shot
ECU or XCU	Extreme close-up
MLS	Medium long shot
MCU	Medium close-up

Figure 14.2

Standard script-marking symbols.

production and figure out your camera pattern for that segment first. Once you know how that segment has to be blocked, you can figure backward to see how you will want to work your way up to that position. Continuing to work backward, you will be able to determine how you want to set up your cameras for the beginning of the program.

In planning multicamera blocking, you must keep in mind that the action is continuous, and you will not be able to stop to readjust the prop in someone's hand. You must also keep in mind the position of all the cameras so that they are not visible in any of the shots. And you must consider the position of actors and cameras so that shots can flow appropriately from one camera to another. With single-camera shooting, you can stop, but actors must perform in exactly the same fashion over and over again so that all takes are consistent (see chapter 15, section 15.2).

Marking the Script

Once you have thought through the blocking, you can *mark* your copy of the script so that you can call commands effectively during the program. Indicate which cameras you are going to use for which shots, what instructions the technical director and camera operators will need, where the audio cues will have to be, what cues the talent will need, and so forth. Most directors develop their own shorthand for marking their scripts, but some commonly used symbols are shown in figure 14.2.

Depending on the program and the director's experience, scripts are marked in varying degrees. A major studio comedy special might involve hundreds of abbreviated cues, instructions, and notes. With a fairly routine ongoing program, script preparation may take no more than a few pencilled reminders of

Roll opening tape	VIDEO	AUDIO
	TAPE: OPENING CREDITS	SOUND ON TAPE. Runs :30.
		Ends with drum beat.
Open mic		
② *2-sh*	TWO-SHOT - STEVE AND SHARON	STEVE: I'm Steve Anderson.
		SHARON: And I'm Sharon
		Hendricks here with the latest
		news.
① *MS*	STEVE	STEVE: Fire fighters are still
		at the scene of a three-alarm
		fire on Market Street that
		destroyed two buildings
		earlier today. Fred White has
		this report.
[PREP TAPE]		
Roll tape	TAPE: FIRE REPORT	SOT: Runs 2:56. Ends with
		"could have been a lot worse."
30 sec.		
③ *MLS*	SHARON	SHARON: The Japanese are still
		trying to assess if any damage
		was caused by this morning's
		earthquake. The quake was
[PREP GRAPHICS]		centered two hundred miles
K graphics	GRAPHICS: MAP OVER SHOULDER	from Tokyo and registered
		7 point 1. Two strong
		after shocks have been felt.

Figure 14.3

This is an example of how a novice director might mark a news script.

unusual cues. (See figure 14.3.) As a beginning director, you will probably feel more comfortable with a
heavily marked script. Just the process of noting all
the commands you will need to make will help you
when you are in the director's chair.

Preparing Shot Sheets

Once you have thought through your camera shots
and marked your script, you can prepare **shot sheets**
for your camera operators. These are abbreviated
descriptions of every shot that a particular camera has
to get. A shot sheet is compact enough to be attached
to the rear of the camera, where the operator can
quickly refer to it. They are not particularly useful for
interview shows, where the director is calling shots
on-the-fly depending on who happens to be talking.
But they are very valuable for complex, fully-scripted
programs, where every shot has been carefully

CAMERA 1	CAMERA 2	CAMERA 3
3. LS, Mary in doorway	1. Wide Sh., Kitchen, hi-angle boom down.	2. CU coffee cup, pan to ash tray
5. LS, David in doorway	4. MS Mary. Follow her	6. MS Mary (she rises)
7. MS David (he walks into O/S)	12. 2–sh., Pan L as David crosses behind Mary	8. O/S Mary
9. O/S David	15. MS David. D.B. as he comes to her. Open to 2–sh.	10. CU Mary
11. CU David	17. CU Mary	13. MS David
14. MS Mary (she sits)	19. 2–sh. (tight)	16. MCU David (bust-–shot)
20. Loose 2–sh. (Mary rises)	21. (Crane up) Hi angle 2–sh. D.I. & crane down to single of David	18. CU David
22. O/S Mary (in doorway). She walks toward David. David turns to camera.	25. Single David (wide). D.B., follow as he walks to Mary. Open to 2–sh.	23. 2–sh. as Mary turns
24. CU David	27. CU Mary's hands	26. (Hook wheels) 2–sh. D.I. to ECU Mary
28. 2–sh. Mary walks past camera. Hold on David	31. MS Alice	29. MS Mary
30. MS David. Pan to door as Alice enters	34. MS David (he sits)	32. Loose 2–sh. (Mary, David)
33. 3–sh., favoring Alice	37. ECU David	35. Loose CU, Mary
36. CU Alice	40. (Crane down) Loose MS Alice. Follow her to table. Follow action w/cup. Crane up & D.I.	38. ECU Mary
39. CU Alice		41. ECU Mary
42. Wide 3–sh., follow action		43. CU of knife

Figure 14.4

Representative shot sheets.

worked out by the director—and where the cameras will have to be moving quite a bit to get various shots as requested.

Figure 14.4 shows the three shot sheets for a three-camera drama. All the shots have been numbered in the order in which they will occur. The camera operators tape or clip these shot sheets near their viewfinders. Sometimes all the camera operators have all the shot sheets, so they know not only what they will be shooting, but also what the other cameras will frame. In other instances, each camera operator would use only his or her own shot sheet.

Conducting Rehearsals

Program types differ greatly in the number and types of rehearsals they have, ranging from virtually none for a football game to several days for a sitcom. You want everything to be well enough rehearsed that the program runs smoothly, but, at the same time, you do not want to over-rehearse to the extent that the material becomes stale to both talent and crew. Sometimes outside factors, such as the amount of money that is budgeted to pay the actors or the amount of time the studio is available, affects your rehearsal schedule.

But in considering rehearsals, you may wish to think in terms of several different kinds: **pre-studio rehearsals, floor rehearsals,** and **control room rehearsals.**

Pre-studio Rehearsals

For many extensive productions, especially dramas and comedies, you will want to have some rehearsals prior to coming into the studio. Studio time is too precious to start from scratch with basic blocking. Using a rehearsal hall, an empty studio, or a living room, you can begin working with actors. Specific areas can be measured off and marked with masking tape or furniture to represent major staging areas, and much of your blocking of action can take place—as well as quite a bit of the dramatic interpretation and working on lines.

For nondramatic productions, there are also many good reasons for pre-studio rehearsals. Demonstration shows, educational programs, political broadcasts, and the like, can benefit from having an early **dry-run** session, where the director and talent can work together on the basic staging of the program.

Studio Floor Rehearsals

When the director and the production crew start to work in the studio, the director usually will spend some amount of time on the studio floor before assuming the director's chair in the control room. Depending on the type of production, either the talent or the technical crew might benefit most from your presence in the studio. If the talent is particularly insecure or if the technical coordination of a production is really complicated, you might spend quite a bit of your time on the studio floor. On the other hand, if the talent is in control of the situation and the technical elements are no special problem, you probably would benefit from getting into the control room as early as you can.

The first rehearsal techniques you will be most likely to conduct from the studio floor will be a **walk-through rehearsal.** This might be either a *talent* walk-through (if they are not really sure of their positions and movements) or a *technical* walk-through (to explain major camera moves, audio placement, and scene changes). In many instances, the walk-through is a combination, taking both the talent and crew through an abbreviated version of the production.

Control Room Rehearsals

The full rehearsals are usually conducted with the director calling shots from the control room. The initial type of full-facilities rehearsal is called a **camera rehearsal.** For the first time, the camera operators are operating the cameras and all other technical personnel are at their positions.

This first camera rehearsal may be a **start-and-stop rehearsal.** In this approach, you interrupt the rehearsal every time there is a major problem. You correct the trouble and then continue the rehearsal. It is quite a time-consuming process—although it can be effective if you have the luxury of enough studio time.

Another approach to the first camera rehearsal is the **uninterrupted run-through.** In this approach, the director attempts to get through the entire production with a minimum of interruptions. If time is short—and if problems are minor—you keep on plowing through the rehearsal regardless of what happens.

Finally, there is the **dress rehearsal.** Theoretically, this is the final rehearsal—a complete, uninterrupted, full-scale rehearsal after all the problems have been straightened out. In practice, this stage is rarely reached. Realities of the medium are such that there simply is never enough studio time to do as polished a job as you would want. In many instances, the director will wind up with a combination start-and-stop and dress rehearsal.

When time is short, you must economize and try to make the most efficient use of the time available. Do not stand around waiting for others to finish their jobs before starting your rehearsal; you can rehearse even while the lighting crew is still trimming the lights and while the audio engineer is establishing music levels. In an abbreviated walk-through rehearsal, at least make certain you get through all the rough spots in the production; *rehearse the open and the close* and *the crucial transitions* that call for coordination of several kinds of movement. Pick your priorities; do not get hung up on small details (such as worrying about the possibility of a boom shadow) when you have only a few minutes to work out major problems (the talent doesn't know where he or she should move next).

Timing

As a director, you want to make sure that your associate director (AD) is effectively handling timing of the program. One way for the AD to do this is the use of a **segment timing sheet.**

Segment Timing Sheet

It may take several forms and be used in different ways. One sample format is shown in figure 14.5. In this particular example, there are five columns for the AD to use. The first column is for a brief description of each segment in the program. The next four columns are for timing notations of one kind or another.

"Unit" means the actual length of the *individual segment.* "Cume" is for the *cumulative time* of the program up to that point. The "Ideal" column is the estimated time that each segment *should* run; both the ideal unit-segment times and the ideal cumulative time should be figured out prior to setting foot in the studio.

The "Rehearsal" column is for jotting down the unit times as various segments are worked through in

SEGMENT (Description)	IDEAL (Unit)	Cume.	REHEARSAL (Unit)	Cume.	DRESS (Unit)	Cume.	AIR (Unit)	Cume.
1. TEASER	(:20)	0:20	:25			:25		:25
2. OPENING TITLES	(:30)	0:50	:40			1:05		1:10
3. INTRO	(1:05)	1:55	1:30			2:15		2:20
4. CHART	(2:00)	3:55	1:50			4:00		4:10
5. DEMO.	(4:00)	7:55	4:45		(4:15)	8:15	(4:20)	8:30
6. INTERVIEW	(5:30)	13:25	6:00			13:45	(5:00)	13:30
7. WRAP-UP	(:30)	13:55	:20			14:05		13:55
8. CLOSE	(:35)	14:30	:45			14:50		14:30
			16:15					
			(+1:45 over)					

Figure 14.5

Sample segment timing sheet.

a start-and-stop rehearsal. It is difficult to get an accurate picture of the actual cumulative times at this point, but the total of the unit times should give the AD a rough picture of how long or how short the program is likely to be. This column also allows the AD to figure backtiming so that certain segments start on time.

The "Dress" rehearsal column should give the AD a clear picture of how the actual cumulative times compare to the ideal times. The "Air" column is filled in as the program progresses. It lets the AD know how much to tell the talent to *stretch* or, in figure 14.5, how much to *cut* in order to come out on time. In this program, for example, we can see that several segments ran long, so the interview segment had to be cut short (from an ideal of 5½ minutes to an actual 5 minutes).

There are many variations of timing sheets. Some will include *time in* and *time out* cumulative columns. Some will work with only one or two columns. This sample, however, should give the beginning AD an idea of what is needed to get the program timed accurately.

Talent Timing Cues

In many programs, such as the one illustrated in figure 14.5, the talent would need time-remaining cues in specific segments. Thus, working from the *ideal* times, the host would get, for example, a "30 seconds remaining" cue at 3:25 into the program (as a reminder that there are 30 seconds left in the chart talk) and at 7:25 (30 seconds left in the demonstration). The talent might want time cues to get out of the interview segment on time (that is, a 30-second cue at 12:55) or simply time cues to get through with the wrap-up summary on time (that is, a 30-second cue at 13:25).

Care must be taken that the talent clearly understands what these intermediate segment cues are so that they will not be confused with time remaining in the body of the program.

Program Time and Body Time

This brings up one other point of potential confusion. The AD must be concerned both with *getting the talent wrapped up on time* and with *getting the program off the air on time.* In figure 14.5, the talent needs a 30-second cue at 13:25, because he or she has to be completely wrapped up and finished at 13:55 (leaving the director 35 seconds for the closing credits). Also, the director has to have a 30-second cue at 14:00 in order to get the program off the air and into black at precisely 14:30.

Thus, the AD has to work with both **body time,** the actual *length of the program content* including the host's closing summary but not the show's closing credits, and with **program time,** the *total length of the show* from fade-in to fade-out.

Calling Commands

Once rehearsals are finished and you, the director, and your AD have solved any potential timing problems, you are ready to actually tape the show (or send it out live). You are the one who makes sure all the audio and video material will be ready when you need it, and you make the decisions as to what will happen when. In actuality, you may delegate some things to your AD, such as making sure the proper camera shots are set up, but you have the overriding authority and responsibility.

If the program is being taped, the first thing you need to do is start the VCR that is going to record the show. You do this by saying, "Roll record tape." When the tape has stabilized, the VCR operator will say "Speed," and you can then begin. Sometimes there are preliminary things you need to put on the tape, such as color bars, tone, and a slate. In other situations, those will already be on the tape, and you start right in with the program.

Crew Commands

Each production varies in terms of the exact commands you need to give, but a director might give different crew members the following kinds of commands:

Technical director—Various transitions, such as cuts and dissolves. The technical director will also set up special effects, but those are usually planned ahead of time, because the director does not have time during production to give elaborate instructions as to what type of effect he or she desires. When the effect is needed the director will call for "effect 1" or "effect 5."

Associate director—Quick comments regarding things, such as pickup shots, that need editing. Actually, the associate director is more likely to be giving instructions to the director (such as time remaining in the program) than the other way around.

Audio operator—Fade music or other audio elements in and out; open and close mics.

Graphics operator—Change graphics and bring them in and out (unless they are brought in through the switcher by the technical director).

Video operator—Start and stop the record tape and any roll-in tapes.

Lighting director—Bring up or fade out lights if lighting changes are part of the show.

Teleprompter operator—Usually this person rolls the script without instruction from the director, keeping pace with the talent. Commands would come only if there are problems.

Stage manager—Cues and timing information to relay to the talent.

Camera operators—Shot designations such as close-ups or wide shots and zooms or pans.

Boom operator—This person usually works independently following the talent, but the director might need to instruct the boom operator to raise the boom, if it or its shadow looks as though it is going to appear in the picture.

Production assistants—These people may take their instructions through hand cues from the floor director, or the director may need to tell them to flip charts or remove some prop.

Command Principles

There is really no right or wrong way to give commands, but there are certain principles that will enable you to give directions as clearly as possible. For example, refer to talent (when talking to the stage manager) by name—"Cue Dr. Morgan," not "Cue him"—to avoid misunderstandings. Refer to camera operators, on the other hand, by numbers; you are less likely to slip up and get confused. Make sure you use correct and precise commands of preparation to the technical director (see section 8.5) and to all other production positions; the commands of preparation are as important as the commands of execution.

Figure 14.6

Director (center) calling shots during a production, flanked by the TD and AD.

Keeping the lag time of various equipment and personnel in mind, give your cues in a sequence designed to get things happening when you want them to. In opening your program, say "Fade in music" and then "Fade in camera 2." It always takes a second or so before the music will be heard (if it is properly cued up), but the camera is there with the push of a lever. Similarly, always cue talent before putting his or her camera on the air. "Open-mic-cue-talent-dissolve-to-two" is often given as one command of execution. By the time the floor manager reacts and throws the cue and the talent takes a breath and starts to talk, the camera will be on the air.

Watch and *listen* to your monitors. Always be aware of exactly what is going on over the air. If a pic-

ture is not what you want (what the viewer needs), then change it. The viewer watching his or her home receiver could care less about your sinus headache or your fight with the talent or the camera cable with the bad connection; all he or she knows is what comes out over the receiver, and if it is bad, it is bad.

Also, always check your camera and preview monitors before calling a shot to be put on the air. Make sure the camera you want to dissolve to or the special effects you want next are prepared and ready to be put on the air. You cannot afford to get buried in your marked script while ignoring the realities of the picture and sound you are sending out. (See figure 14.6.)

Figure 14.7

Comparison of wide shot and close-up. Whether in a variety show, drama, or panel discussion, the same need exists to balance wide shots (*left*) with close-ups (*right*).

14.2

The "Artist" Role

Many things related to managing also affect aesthetics. For example, the director must think of the aesthetics of the picture frame while planning blocking or marking the script or preparing the shot sheets. But beyond that, the director must think of artistic principles that will make a program pleasant to watch. Many of these principles involve **continuity**—a broad term that refers to keeping things the same throughout an entire program.

These principles have developed over the years as part of a language of film and television. People viewing a movie or TV program expect certain conventions, and violating them confuses the audience. However, these principles are not laws of the land. In fact, they are made to be violated, because sometimes you want to disorient (or frighten or shock) your audience. Music videos have certainly breached every camera and cutting continuity principle—and have done so effectively. But if a program is straightforward information or entertainment, a director should abide by the conventional language. In addition, understanding a principle better enables you to know how and when to violate it.

We will discuss a number of production conventions that directors should keep in mind. Although the focus of the discussion will be on multicamera production, some of these conventions also hold true for single-camera shooting. Many of them are easier

to obey in multicamera shooting, because all the shots are seen on monitors, and errors will be more obvious than they will be when shots are taken individually.

Shot Juxtaposition

Early filmmakers quickly came to the conclusion that when one picture is immediately replaced by another, an interaction occurs in the mind of the viewer that communicates something more than if each picture were viewed separately. This intriguing concept obviously can have direct bearing on the process of shot selection for any television program. Each shot must be thought of as being part of a flow of images, each with a relationship to the one that precedes it and the one that follows it.

For this reason, the succession of pictures should be motivated by the basic tenet, "Give the viewers what they need to see when they need to see it." To a great extent, this is determined by a juxtaposition of *collective* shots showing the whole picture—the relationship of all elements in the scene—and intimate *particularized* shots giving the viewers the closer details they want. (See figure 14.7.)

The generalities of a scene or program situation are established by the **wide shot** (also referred to as a **long shot** or **cover shot**). Then the director cuts to a **medium shot** or a series of medium shots to give the audience particularized details. When something small or intimate needs to be seen, the director uses the **close-up.**

Of course, the terms *wide shot, medium shot,* and *close-up* are relative and vary from one type of pro-

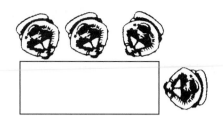

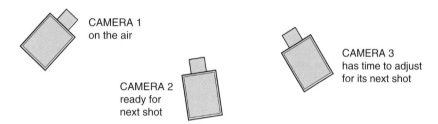

CAMERA 1
on the air

CAMERA 2
ready for
next shot

CAMERA 3
has time to adjust
for its next shot

Figure 14.8

Sequence of camera shots. In this illustration, the director has just used camera 3 (before taking camera 1); therefore, camera 2 will probably have more time to get the next shot lined up.

gram to another. The left-hand picture shown in figure 14.7 is probably a wide shot for a discussion program. However, if this were a children's program with toys to be demonstrated flanking the four people, this shot would be considered a medium shot. Likewise, the right-hand shot in figure 14.7 would be considered a close-up for a talk show, but for a drama in which the girl's earring played a major role, this might be the medium shot and the earring would be the close-up.

Nevertheless, the pattern of wide shot to medium shot to close-up should be observed so that the audience comprehends the total environment and can then relate to particular areas of that environment. Of course, as mentioned above, this "rule" is often violated for perfectly good reasons. Starting with a close-up of a dagger builds suspense and draws the audience into the scene. Where is this dagger and why is it sitting there? Only after the audience's curiosity has been aroused does the director use a wide shot to reveal the location.

Camera Selection

Even with the opportunity to preplan or block out the camera work in multicamera television programs such

as dramas, the ongoing production technique forces the director to make some rather quick, on-the-air editing decisions, because the exact moment of the take is crucial. With talk and game shows, of course, there is truly an ongoing series of changes in camera use every time someone new breaks in to talk. A basic challenge is to always have the proper camera ready for a shot at the exact moment the situation calls for it. On the part of the director, this requires an ability to be able to think *simultaneously* on at least two levels—what is on the air right now and what is going to be on the air next.

Thought Process

With a three-camera structure, the thinking process might work something like this: Camera 1 is on the air. You, as director, have the choice of using camera 2 or 3 for the next shot. Camera 3, however, has just been used on the previous shot. Camera 2, therefore, has more time to make a framing adjustment or even change position. (See figure 14.8.)

By using the commands of preparation and execution properly (see chapter 8, section 8.5), the director can select the next camera to be used, allowing sufficient lead time to set the next shot. It is accepted studio procedure in a three-camera setup to place camera 1 on the left, camera 2 in the middle, and camera 3 on the right. This setup allows the director to keep track easily of the relative positions of cameras on the floor and the angle of shots available to them.

Obviously, cameras usually are not employed in a repeated 1-2-3-1-2-3 rotation. In order to observe the wide shot, medium shot, and close-up requirements of any program, at least one of the three cameras at any given time will usually be designated as a wide-angle cover shot camera. This is especially important in shooting unrehearsed programs, such as panel discussions, where there are sudden changes of the individuals speaking. The technique on such a program is to cut to a wide shot on the change of voice if a close-up of the new person is not immediately available. The director then has a chance to ascertain who is talking and call for the close-up. The most glaring error on any kind of program is for an unprepared director to be caught with a speaker or performer still on camera when that person is no longer speaking or performing.

In a rehearsed program, when the camera blocking has been worked out in advance, the director can temporarily commit all cameras to close-up shots, having planned to return to a cover shot at a later specific time. Generally, however, the wide-angle and close-up shot balance requirements are such that at least one camera is always kept on a cover shot.

Crossing Camera Angles

Another principle involving camera selection deals with *crossing camera angles.* In many staging setups, the natural pattern will have two people facing each other. In order to frame the best headshots, cameras should shoot across each other's angles; that is, each camera should be shooting the person or object farthest away from the camera. (See figure 14.9.) The camera on the right (camera 2) should be getting the shot of the person on the camera left, and vice versa. In this way, each camera gets a view of most of the talent's face. If camera 1 shoots the talent on the left, it will get no more than a profile of the talent. The same holds true for camera 2 if it shoots the person on the right.

Shot Relationships

When changing from one shot to another, the two pictures should relate to each other in both an informational and aesthetic setting. The subject in two succes-

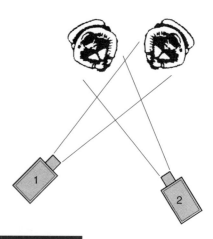

Figure 14.9

In order to get the best head-on shots, cameras should be set up so they shoot across each other.

sive shots should maintain continuity in that it should be *readily recognizable.* You would not want to cut to such a different angle that the viewer would not immediately recognize the subject from the previous shot.

Cutting Ratio

One of the most common errors of shot relationship involves wide shots and close-ups. If you were to cut from the left-hand shot in figure 14.7 to a close-up of the girl's earring, most of your viewers would be totally lost, because they would not have noticed the earring in the wide shot. One good rule to follow is that you should always keep your camera cuts within a **three-to-one cutting ratio;** that is, do not take to a shot that is *three times larger* or *three times smaller* than the preceding shot.

Jump Cutting

For aesthetic reasons, you should avoid taking or dissolving between cameras that have almost exactly the same (matching) shots. The result would be that the scene remains essentially the same, but the picture *jumps* slightly within the frame. On unrehearsed shows, the camera operators may inadvertently come up with almost identical shots; therefore, it is up to the director to watch carefully for this **jump cutting**[2] on the control room monitors.

Position Jumps

Another problem to avoid is the **position jump**—having a primary subject jump from one spot on the

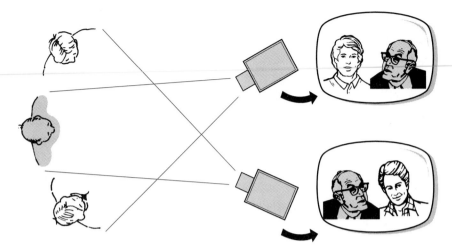

Figure 14.10

Subject jumping positions. With both cameras shooting a standard two-shot, the central talent appears to jump from one side of the screen to the other as we take between shots.

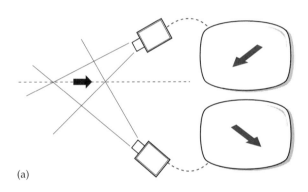

(a)

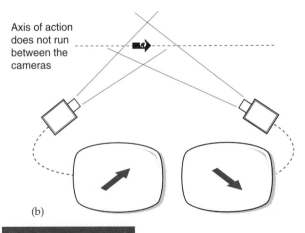

Axis of action does not run between the cameras

(b)

Figure 14.11

Axis of action. (a) WRONG. If cameras are placed on both sides of the imaginary axis of action, the screen direction will be reversed when cutting between cameras.
(b) CORRECT. When both cameras are on the same side of the axis of action, they will both perceive the action moving in the same direction.

screen to another position in the next shot—an apparent loss of continuity. This can occur, for example, if three people are lined up facing two cameras and each camera is getting a two-shot of two adjacent persons. The center person will be on the left of one picture and on the right side of the other camera's picture. (See figure 14.10.) This position jump can be avoided by having one camera go to a three-shot before cutting or, conversely, by cutting to a close-up single shot.

Axis of Action/Conversation

Another basic principle involves *screen direction*. In successive shots, we want to make certain that all action is flowing in the same direction and that each screen character is facing in one consistent direction. If an imaginary line is drawn extending the path in which a character is moving, we can call this the **axis of action.** As long as all cameras are placed on the same side of this axis, the action will continue to flow in the same direction. If cameras are placed on different sides of this axis of action, however, the apparent screen direction will be reversed when cutting between the cameras. (See figure 14.11.) Directors, therefore, always try to avoid having cameras **crossing the line.**

Closely related to the axis of action is the **axis of conversation.** If the imaginary axis is drawn through two persons facing each other, all cameras should be kept on the same side of this line. Otherwise the

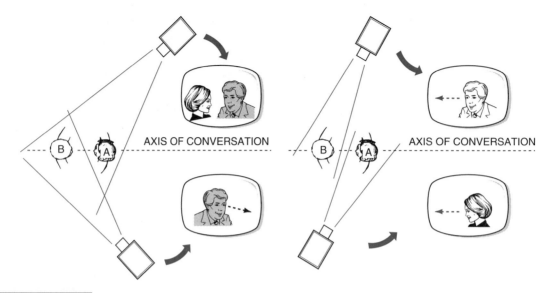

Figure 14.12

Axis of conversation. In the *left* illustration, Actor B changes screen direction as we cut from one camera to the other. In the *right* illustration, both actors appear to be looking in the same direction, making it difficult for the viewer to establish the relationship between the two.

screen direction (the direction in which a person is looking) will be reversed when you cut to the other side of the line. This imaginary line—the axis of conversation—will shift, of course, as performers move. Figure 14.12 shows two common errors in crossing the axis of conversation.

Jump cuts, position jumps, and crossing the line problems are all examples of mistakes that are easier to spot in multicamera production, where the shots can be seen in relation to each other as they are being selected, than they are in the field, where shots cannot be compared. It is much easier for a director to accidentally cross the line when a long shot is recorded in the morning and its accompanying close-up is shot in the afternoon, than it is for a studio director who is watching all the monitors.

Transitions

Many of the mechanics of continuity are carried out by the actual camera **transitions**—the manner in which the director changes from one picture to another. Over the years, these transitions have adopted meaning that audience members readily understand. The director must be aware of the psychological and visually conditioned impact of each—

when to use one and when to use another. These transitions can be accomplished in postproduction editing as well as with the switcher during a multicamera studio production.

Cuts

The instantaneous **cut** or straight take replaces one picture immediately with another. It implies that there is *no change in time or locale.* It happens right now. The audience is not moved anywhere, except to a different perspective of the same scene. It is the basic transition. It is the device that the audience has accepted since the beginning of the motion picture film for changing a point of view without making any major dramatic change. In terms of grammar, it is the end of a sentence—a period—and the beginning of a new sentence.

Dissolves

The **dissolve,** simultaneously fading out one picture and fading into another picture, creates a temporary overlapping of images. Dramatically, this implies a *change of place* or a *change in time* (usually a lapse of time). It shows a relationship with the previous shot, but there has been a change; the audience has been moved somewhere else or somewhere later in time. Grammatically, the dissolve corresponds to the end of a paragraph or possibly even to the end of a major section of a chapter.

In musical programs, the dissolve is often used purely for aesthetic reasons—a slow dissolve of a singer from a medium to a tight close-up profile, or a close-up of the dancer's feet dissolving to a long shot of the dancer. No change in time or locale is implied in this case—just a pleasant visual effect. In musical productions, the dissolve can be used as an artistic connecting or relating transition, whereas it has the opposite effect in dramas.

Dissolves are slow, and therefore, have an affect on the *pace* of a program. For example, an effective series of fast camera cuts can lose its intensity if a dissolve is suddenly used. If a director does not want to lose intensity, the dissolve should not be used. If the dissolve stops for awhile in the middle, creating a **superimposition,** this serves to intensify whatever is being expressed by the individual images.

Fades

A **fade** from a camera to black or a fade up from black implies a very *strong separation.* It is used in going from one segment of a program to another—from the talk show interview to the used-car commercial. Dramatically, the fade is the curtain falling—the end of a scene or an act. Grammatically, it would be the visual counterpart of the end of a chapter or story.

Defocus

One specialized transition that can be used with no fancy electronic effects is the **defocus;** the camera on the air defocuses and dissolves to a similarly defocused shot on another camera, which then comes back into focus. This usually implies either a *deranged state of mind* or a transition *backward in time.* As with other specialized transitions, it tends to call attention to itself and must be used very sparingly.

Wipes

The **wipe**—taking one picture off the face of the screen and replacing it with another—also calls attention to itself. Most of the time, it has no special grammatical significance except to say, "Isn't this a *fancy*

transition!" Some wipes, however, have developed grammatical significance. For example, in sports productions, a wipe from the center to the sides indicates an instant replay.

Digital Effects

Digital technology has brought new dimensions to transitions. Graphics programs and digital manipulators used in conjunction with the switcher allow for an array of bursts, flips, tumbles, and spins. These are used mainly as attention-getters and are often employed during opening credits to *grab the audience.* They should be used sparingly during the body of the program, because they draw attention to themselves and away from the content of the show.

Timing of the Transition

Understanding the different types of transitions helps to explain the *how* and *why* of changing cameras, but a word needs to be said about the *when.* Generally, camera changes must be adequately motivated; there has to be some reason for cutting at a particular point. The audience should want to see something else. ("Give the viewers what they need to see when they need to see it.") Without proper motivation, you should avoid the temptation to change the picture just for the sake of change. The following discussion on the timing of camera transitions applies equally to the timing of editing shots together in the postproduction process for single-camera production.

One of the strongest motivations for cutting is to capture action. When the action starts, you need a wider view. When the talent walks to a new area, you need an establishing shot. When cutting on action, you should always try to cut *just prior to the action*— not too long before it nor immediately after it. Ideally, as soon as the action starts, the audience needs to see the wider shot. Cutting to a movement that is in progress creates a jarring effect similar to a jump cut.

In a similar vein, you usually should not cut to a camera that is in the *middle of movement*—panning, tilting, or zooming. Occasionally, it is alright to cut (or preferably dissolve) from one moving camera to another that is moving in the same way. For example, if a camera is panning right, a cut can be made to another camera that is also panning right at the same pace.

Cutting to a camera panning left or zooming in or to a stationary camera would be very jarring. But, of course, there are situations where this abrupt effect is desired.

During an interview or panel program, the strongest motivation for cutting is when a speaker *starts to talk*. The audience wants to see who is talking. The ideal timing of the take is precisely between the two speakers—not 3 seconds after the second speaker has started. As a practical matter, cutting during an ad-lib discussion program will usually involve a delay of 1 second or so. To counteract this, the director has to be sensitive to the body language and facial expressions of all participants (watching the off-the-air camera monitors). Who has his mouth open? Who just leaned forward? Who just took a deep breath? Anticipate who the next speaker is going to be.

Include appropriate, judiciously spaced **reaction shots** also. How are the listeners reacting? Which listener is especially animated? In timing reaction shots, *do not* cut at the end of an obvious statement or during a break in the speaking; it will look too much like a cut to the wrong participant. Reaction shots are most effective in the middle of a speech.

During musical numbers, time your cuts to fit the music. (In slower tempos, purely for an aesthetic "feel," dissolves may be a better transition.) The cuts should be crisp and clean, following a regular rhythmical pattern—cutting on the beat every 4 bars or 8 bars—as the music dictates.

14.3

The "Psychiatrist" Role

Any video production involves the work of a team of people. You, as the director, are the team captain and must motivate people to do their best work. Sometimes this involves at least listening to problems that have nothing to do with the production at hand—the illness of the camera operator's father, a child-care problem that the associate director is having.

Other personal problems that you must deal with are very much related to the production, in that they involve interactions among members of the cast and crew.

Familiarity

Cast and crew members (and college classmates) who work with each other over and over for a continuing series often become like *family*. This has the same advantages and disadvantages as other family situations. They come to know each other well and can anticipate each other's moves. However, like brothers and sisters, they get on each others' nerves and develop rivalries and incompatibilities. You, like a good mother or father, should realize that this will happen occasionally and try to make sure it has positive rather than negative outcomes. A disagreement on microphone placement between the audio person and the lighting director can be healthy, because it can lead to better lighting and better sound. However, if the antipathy between the two grows to the point where the audio person purposefully places a boom microphone where he or she knows it will give the lighting director problems, the feud has gone too far.

You must be sensitive to minor problems developing between crew or cast members and nip them before they become major. Usually the best way is to sit the people involved down and have a frank, open discussion between them. Doing nothing and hoping the problem will go away rarely works.

New Relationships

When the people involved with the shoot have not worked with each other before, the director's job can be even more complicated. You must mold these people into a workable whole, taking advantage of the skills and personality traits each brings to the production. Initial rehearsals usually take longer when crew members are strangers, because all of them are trying to find their specific roles. Which of the camera operators should be given the complicated zooming shot? Should the audio operator use his or her own initiative in deciding how slowly to fade in the music or wait for specific instructions from the director? How much background information should the stage manager give the talent?

The best way for you to handle a *new* cast and crew situation is to start the rehearsal session by holding a meeting and talking through the entire program,

Figure 14.13

Before production, the director spends a little time talking with two performers who have never been on camera before.

specifying each person's role at various points. As the rehearsal proceeds, changes and discrepancies will alter these roles, but at least everyone will have had the same starting point; all people will have not only ideas about their specific roles, but also general understandings about the roles of all others.

A variation on a new situation is one in which the crew and some of the performers (e.g. the game show host, the talk show hostess, the soap opera regulars) are the same for each production, but others of the talent are new (e.g. the game show contestants, three local politicians, an "uncle" visiting a soap opera regular). These people must be made to feel at home so that they can perform at their best. As the director, you should welcome them and spend a little time orienting them. (See figure 14.13.)

Directorial Style

Your style as a director can also affect the psychological makeup of interpersonal relationships. Some directors are authoritative and give precise instructions, such as specifying exactly how much **headroom** a camera operator should allow or telling an actress precisely when she should wrinkle her nose. Others let cast and crew members make more decisions—the actress works out her own facial expressions and the camera operator frames the shot; the director only intervenes if something is incorrect. Either method can work: the former assures quality control, but it can antagonize creative people who like to exercise their own judgment; the latter can lead to extra creative input that enhances what the director wants to do, but it can also lead to chaos if various cast and crew members run counter to each other.

Your best bet is to be yourself—but be consistent. If you feel most comfortable letting cast and crew members make many of their own decisions, do so, but don't expect initiative one moment and then clamp down on it the next.

Expectations

A director should be able to assume that the people working on a production have both the *discipline and technique* to do the job. If any crew members are not

Figure 14.14

Typical setup for an *L*-shaped staging arrangement for a discussion program.

exhibiting one or both of these characteristics, you should have a talk with them, outlining expectations. If this does not work, you should try to remove the person from the crew. However, in union situations (and student situations), this may not be possible. The director must then use psychological persuasion to motivate the person as much as possible.

Most production situations work very well, however. Cast, crew, and director develop a sense of unity and exhilaration wherein the sum of the whole is greater than any of its parts.

14·4

Production Project: The Discussion Program

Now that we've discussed many of the elements that are needed for successful directing, let's take a look at how you, as a beginning director, might handle your first production—a fairly simple discussion show. An actual suggested discussion project is given in Appendix D, along with several other production project ideas.

The discussion show, that sometimes maligned but nevertheless ubiquitous stalwart of television program-

ming, provides an excellent format for understanding the fundamental principles involved in directing.

Staging

The majority of discussion shows utilize some variation of either one of two basic staging configurations: an *L-shaped grouping* that places the host on the end facing down a row of other participants (see figure 14.14); or a *semicircle,* in which the host is generally placed in the center (see figure 14.15). This conformity of staging is not as much a lack of originality on the part of the directors as it is their recognition that these seating plans provide an arrangement whereby the guests can best relate to each other and the host, and at the same time, provide the director with the best camera angles of the participants.

On these programs, it is best to use four cameras. One of the cameras holds a wide shot of the entire group at all times, and another camera holds a shot of the host for use at any time in the program. The primary assignment of the other two cameras (cameras 1 and 4 in figure 14.15) is that of providing close-up shots of those persons facing their direction—by crossing their angles. If there are only three cameras available, the shoot becomes more difficult. You should always keep a cover shot of the entire group in

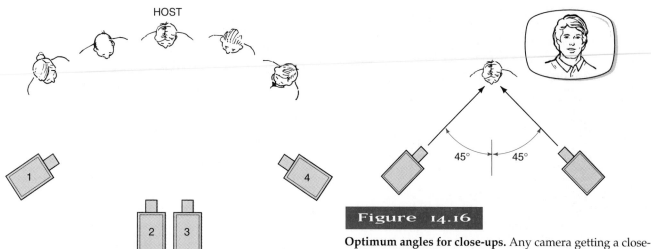

HOST

Figure 14.15

Camera pattern for semicircular staging. In this typical "talk show" camera pattern, one center camera (either 2 or 3) remains on a cover shot of the entire group while the other center camera (3 or 2) holds a close-up of the host.

Figure 14.16

Optimum angles for close-ups. Any camera getting a close-up shot should be as perpendicular to the talent as possible. The camera should not be more than 45 degrees from a head-on shot for a good close-up.

case someone who is not on one of the other cameras starts to talk. In all probability, the cover shot will have to be alternated from one camera to another as the program progresses.

In a discussion program, the participants relate not only to the audience, but also to each other and, as a result, face not to the front but in the direction of the persons to their right and left. Depending upon the role of the host/moderator, the other participants will tend to face in his or her direction during much of the program.

Lighting

Two suggested lighting plans for an L-shaped seating configuration have been presented as sample lighting plots in chapter 5, figures 5.22 and 5.23 (see section 5.5). A review of that section of material will be of value in the preparation of lighting plots for any of the several main seating configurations.

On a discussion program, care must be taken to ensure that the face, especially the eyes, is properly lit from all potential camera angles. The locations of the cameras provide a good guide to the location of the main lights in relation to the subjects. The amount of light reflected back from each subject to the camera must be individually balanced to produce an equal

intensity. Differences in hair, clothing, and complexion can produce unsuitably dark or light close-up shots. When taken in succession, such shots are noticeably objectionable.

Shot Continuity

Earlier in this chapter, reference was made to *wide-angle, medium,* and *close-up* shots in terms of their respective abilities to communicate collective or particularized program information. Wide-angle *cover* shots are used within a program sequence to re-establish the relationship of program participants to each other and to the elements of the set. It is the *collectivizing* view of all those production values that contributes to the program as a whole.

By contrast, the medium and close-up shots are a *particularized* view of a person or object at a precisely appropriate point in the program sequence. As such, the information conveyed is selective and personal, even to the point of being intimate. The eyes and facial muscles add an important dimension to the total meaning of what a person is expressing in words. This is especially true of actors or other personalities who often speak in public or on television. For this reason, the most effective close-up shots are those in which the camera angle is not more than 45 degrees from a head-on position. (See figure 14.16.)

Transitions

The most important production value on a discussion program is the precision with which the camera shots follow the spontaneous flow of the conversation. Each time a new person begins to speak, the camera on the air—whether a cover shot or a close-up—should include that person. To linger for more than a split second on someone who has just stopped talking or to cut to the wrong person is very distracting to the audience.

Ideally, each change of voice should be accompanied by a change of cameras to a close-up shot or one that predominately features the person talking. On a three-camera show that features four guests and a moderator, this is not always possible. By carefully watching the panel for clues as to who may be speaking next, the director may somewhat improve the chances of having the shot ready.

Most directors solve the problem by having a cover shot of the entire group available for use at all times. When a close-up shot of a new speaker is not readily available, a take to the cover shot performs several important functions. Primarily, it includes the person who just started talking, and it gives the director a chance to be certain who is speaking before assigning a camera to the shot. In a fast-paced discussion, this alternative is the only way the director can stay with the quickly changing flow of conversation. Once the cover shot has been taken, the close-up need not be used immediately. The director can let the wide shot re-establish the collective aspect of the group while waiting for the end of a sentence as a convenient point to cut to the close-up.

During a discussion program, the situation often calls for shots other than a close-up of one participant in the total group. Shots including two or three persons not only add pictorial variety, but also are quite useful when several people begin a rapid interchange of short statements or questions and answers. Smaller group shots have an added dimension—showing the silent, but often revealing, expression on the faces of persons other than the speaker. A brief close-up shot of someone moving his or her head in agreement or disagreement—a reaction shot—is especially useful when one person has been speaking for an extended period of time.

On the other hand, the director must be alert to group shots in which those persons who are not talking are looking away from the speaker. Whether or not intended, the visual effect is one of boredom and, as such, has a negative impact on the program as a whole.

Camera Blocking

The range of shots available to each camera in a program situation is dependent upon the two interrelated variables of camera and subject position. On a discussion program, where the staging options are somewhat limited, the director generally uses the seating arrangement as a starting point in the camera blocking process. Primary camera positions can then be selected on the basis of the best angles for the close-up shots and the important requirement of wide-angle cover shots.

All the shot possibilities for each camera should be plotted so that each camera operator can work within the parameters of established shot assignments. The use of a definite shooting plan aids in having critical shots available when they are needed, and at the same time, helps in holding down the talk on the PL intercommunication system.

The direction of conversational flow may vary at different times during a program. For this reason, directors usually develop several shooting plans to cover all contingencies. Figure 14.17 shows two such plans that could be used in the coverage of an L-shaped arrangement. Plan A is designed to provide maximum close-up coverage of the three panel members, with the moderator being seen only on the wide shot on camera 1. Plan B is set up for situations in which the moderator takes a very active role in the program, and as a result, needs a close-up shot ready at all times.

Plan A has obvious limitations, but it has a basic utility in predictable situations, such as a period in the program during which the host is bringing out individual responses from each participant. The beginning and ending of discussion programs usually assume this structure.

A director would probably quickly shift over to Plan B during the more active phases of the conversation. By holding camera 3 on a cover shot, camera 1 is

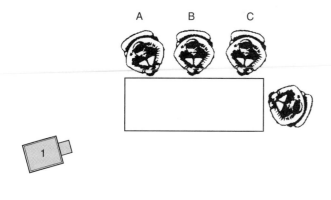

Figure 14.17

Camera patterns for L-shaped staging. Plan A: *Camera 1* remains on a wide-angle cover shot. *Camera 2* gets close-ups of panelists as they face camera right and two-shots or three-shots of panelists. *Camera 3* gets singles of panelists as they face camera right and over-the-shoulder shots (with host in foreground). **Plan B:** *Camera 1* gets close-ups of moderator/host, two-shots of host and panelist C, and singles and two-shots as panelists turn to camera left. *Camera 2* gets close-ups of panelists as they face camera right and two-shots or three-shots of panelists. *Camera 3* remains on a wide-angle cover shot.

able to get a close-up shot of the moderator. Camera 1 also has the option of getting close-up shots of those who turn camera left for a two-person conversation. In this situation, camera 2 then has the option of a close-up of the other person or a two-shot of both speakers. The reverse structure is also possible with camera 1 on the two-shot and camera 2 on the single of the person facing camera right.

Even taken together, these two shooting plans by no means exhaust the possibilities available within an L-shaped seating configuration. The use of camera 2 as a cover camera from either a left-side or right-side studio position opens up another series of coverage patterns. The suggestion of cameras 1 or 3 for cover shots stems from the fact that their angle to the set allows for a more interesting grouping of all participants in the frame. Each person's face occupies a larger proportion of the frame than in a wide shot

from the center—which also results in empty space at the top and bottom of the frame.

In the press of a fast-moving program, the director often is tempted to give up the cover shot and use that camera temporarily for smaller group shots and close-ups. It is an option that even the most experienced directors use with considerable care. Invariably, when all cameras are committed to the three people who are dominating the conversation, the fourth (off-camera) voice suddenly starts speaking.

Calling Shots

In a discussion program, it is essential that preparatory commands always be used in conjunction with the commands of execution. An inexperienced director might be tempted to think that a needed shot could be put on the air instantaneously if only the command of execution were given. To do so, however, would be to increase appreciably the possibilities for error. The spontaneous nature of talk programs makes the command of preparation doubly important. The technical director needs this lead time to be certain that the right shot is readied. Of equal importance is the possibility that the camera operators need this time for final adjustment of the framing or as a warning to hold a shot they might otherwise be in the process of changing.

A good procedure for the director on a fast-moving talk show is to give a "ready" for a probable next shot as soon as possible after the previous shot is on the line. This does not remove any option for a subsequent change in the upcoming shot; it simply aids the director in staying ahead of the action. An example of how the director can inform the crew of several probable courses of action would be as follows.

"Ready camera 3 . . . take 3" (cover shot). "Ready camera 2 on a close-up of guest C . . . camera 1, hold the moderator close-up, but be ready to move over to guest B."

In this situation, guest C has just interrupted the moderator. The director can afford to wait on the cover shot to see whether guest C will continue talking or whether the moderator will start talking again. At the same time, the director has noticed that guest B also is trying to break into the conversation.

Now that you have begun to appreciate some of the basics of directing a discussion show, you and your classmates should be able to undertake the program production project in Appendix D. This discussion format can be used for a repeated number of production exercises within the class. A minimum running time of 5 minutes for each exercise is suggested so that each director has an opportunity to become familiar with the pattern of the conversational flow and the related continuity of camera shots. A realistic element can be added by having the AD and the stage manager feed the moderator countdown cues for time remaining in the exercise. Directors should be prepared for the fact that the transition from the body of a program to the closing segment can be difficult unless cues and other instructions are given well in advance.

Summary

The director's job, regardless of the style of the individual director, is a combination of manager, artist, and psychiatrist. The director decides both camera and actor *blocking*, often with the aid of a *blocking diagram*. For this, he or she must keep in mind creature comforts and shot framing that is often continuous. The director *marks* the script in a manner that will help during production and also prepares *shot sheets* for the camera operators.

Rehearsals that the director may want to hold include *pre-studio* (perhaps including a *dry run*), *floor* (such as a *walk-through*), and *control room* (*camera rehearsal*, *start-and-stop* rehearsal, *uninterrupted run-through*, and *dress*).

The AD often uses a *segment timing sheet* to keep track of timing. He or she also decides on *talent timing* cues, usually given on a time-remaining basis. *Program timing* and *body timing* are both concerns of the AD.

During the production, the director *calls* commands to all others on the crew, remembering to call performers by their names and cameras by number. The commands should be designed so that everything happens when it should, and the director should watch the monitors closely.

Many directing principles revolve around *continuity*. The director should think of *shot juxtaposition*, especially as it relates to *wide shots, medium shots,* and *close-ups*. In addition, the director should think through which camera to use when, in part, so that cameras can *cross angles*. Shots should maintain the proper relationship, taking into consideration the *cutting ratio* and the need to avoid *jump cuts* and *position jumps*. Cameras should not *cross the line*, but should be on the same side of the *axis of action* or *axis of conversation*.

A director needs to think through transitions to decide whether to use a *cut, dissolve, fade, defocus, wipe,* or *digital effect*. The timing of the transition is also important, including such principles as cutting right before the action.

A director must pull together the disparate personalities of cast and crew, be they people who work together often or people who do not know each other. By using different techniques, he or she must mold the groups into a well-oiled, functioning *team*.

Footnotes

1. Several books that contain good advice for directors are: Alan A. Armer, *Directing Television and Film*, 2nd ed. (Belmont, CA: Wadsworth, 1990); Steven D. Katz, *Film Directing Cinematic Motion* (Los Angeles: Lone Eagle Publishing Company, 1992); and Ron Richards, *Director's Method for Film and Television* (Stoneham, MA: Focal Press, 1992).

2. When the term jump cutting is used in field production, it means something slightly different. The picture still jumps on the screen, but it is because something has been cut out. For example, if the mayor is talking at a press conference and the reporter edits out part of the speech, the mayor's head may appear to jump at the point of the edit.

chapter 15

Field Production

ost of what we have discussed in previ-
ous chapters has dealt with *live* or *live-
on-tape multi-camera* productions shot in
a studio environment. However, many
productions are shot totally or partially in out-of-
studio locations with one camera. This technique is
often called **"film-style shooting"**, because most
motion pictures are shot with one camera that takes
shots one by one from all the various angles
employed in multiple-camera shoots. It is also
referred to as **field production,** because it takes place
in the field rather than in a studio.

There are numerous similarities between studio
production and field production, mainly because
much of the same equipment is used. A microphone
is a microphone whether it is on a game show set or at
the scene of a fire. Pictures should be focused and
well-composed, and talent should maintain eye contact, whether in the studio or in the field. And yet,
there are many differences caused, to some degree, by
the lack of control that exists outside of the studio.

Many extraneous noises cannot be stopped; the sun
and clouds cannot be controlled; crowds often cannot
be maneuvered to remain outside of the camera's
shot. In addition, postproduction editing takes on a
much greater role, because the single-camera technique obviously does not utilize the switcher during
the production.

This chapter will concentrate on single-camera
field production, looking at the similarities and differences between it and studio production. It is organized in a manner that is similar to the rest of the
book,[1] beginning with a general introduction and
then covering cast and crew, audio, lights, cameras,
video recording, editing, pictorial elements, producing, and directing. In that way, this chapter will serve
as a review of the rest of the book while, at the same
time, introducing concepts that are crucial to this
increasingly popular form of production for news and
public affairs, dramatic programs, music videos, documentaries, corporate videos, interactive productions,
instructional programs, and so forth.

15.1

Introduction

Single-camera field equipment is younger than multi-camera studio production, mainly because the original TV equipment was so bulky it could not be handled in the single-camera configuration. However, with the introduction of the ¾-inch U-matic format in the early 1970s, cameras and recorders ventured out of the studio, first to cover news and then to produce other forms of programming.

Field equipment, like studio equipment, changes rapidly. With each year, cameras, microphones, and lights become smaller, lighter, and "smarter" in that they are capable of allowing their users to increase creativity and flexibility. The introduction of nonlinear editing has brought new stature to film-style shooting and has greatly increased its flexibility.

Field production, like its studio-based sister, requires both *discipline and technique*. It involves the development of a professional attitude and a knowledge of equipment and aesthetics. (See chapter 1, section 1.1.)

Techniques

One of the reasons techniques are so important is that miles away from "home base," you cannot turn to the instructor or technician when you have a problem such as no picture in the viewfinder. This means that all crew members must know how to operate the equipment well. You and other crew members must also be well grounded in aesthetics, because you cannot see the finished product as you are taping the individual shots. You must be able to visualize how the shots will cut together.

Discipline

In some ways, field production requires more discipline than studio work because, once away from the studio, you cannot easily return for a forgotten item. You must plan very thoroughly for all eventualities. Teamwork, combined with a cooperative spirit, is a *must*. People are usually together for longer periods of time in the field than they are in the studio, especially if they commute back and forth together or stay in one location for several days. The tendency to "get on each others' " nerves must be overcome.

15.2

Cast and Crew

One of the reasons that discipline is so important is that crews are usually smaller for field productions, so it is hard to cover for anyone who is undependable.

Crew Size

One reason crews are smaller is that much less gear is involved. Only one camera is used to shoot, eliminating the need for all but one **camera operator.** With a **camcorder** configuration, this person also doubles as the **video operator.** No one is needed to operate a **switcher;** the camera picture goes directly to the VCR, because there is no need to cut between two or more cameras. Teleprompters, because they are so bulky, are rarely taken to shoots, eliminating the need for a **teleprompter** operator. Graphics are generally added during postproduction, not during shooting.

Because there is no control room, the director is on the location set in the midst of all the action, thus eliminating the need for a **stage manager.** Because timing is usually not crucial for scenes that are later going to be edited, an **associate director** can also be superfluous at a field shoot. However, there is often a person called a **script supervisor**[2] who keeps notes and watches for continuity problems so that what is shot can be effectively edited.

Some crews, especially for news, are as small as two people—one to operate the camcorder and another to hold the mic and interview talent, thus serving as producer-director-talent-script supervisor-audio operator. In fact, some "crews" are now only one person—the camcorder has a large viewfinder that pivots so that the operator can see the image while interviewing someone in front of the camera. Other shoots have larger crews that include a producer, a director, an audio operator, a camera-VCR operator, a lighting director, a script supervisor, and a production assistant or two to handle any other miscellaneous duties. (See figure 15.1.)

As with most task-oriented working groups, an efficient operation must have a clearly established

(a)

(b)

Figure 15.1

Crew configurations differ depending on the taping situation. For the first taping (a) only two crew members were needed, because the footage was being shot silent to go with music during the opening credits. The director told the children what to do and the camera operator taped the material. For the second taping (b), which was much more complicated, five people attended—the producer who was coordinating with the people running the children's art workshop; the director; the audio operator; the camera operator; and a combination lighting person and script supervisor.

plan for areas of responsibility and authority. Whatever the size of the crew, each individual member of the shoot should have a *clear idea* of his or her responsibilities—but with the understanding that flexible working arrangements may find each one helping out with other jobs.

Cleanup

One of the absolute essentials that all crew members on a field shoot must handle carefully is *cleanup.* If a crew member carelessly leaves a mic cable on the floor of the studio, someone else will probably find it later and put it away. But if a mic cable is left in the middle of a park, it will quickly disappear. Everything must be conscientiously disassembled, coiled, stowed away, and neatly packed—in part, as a courtesy to the next people who use the equipment and, in part, because such care adds to the life of the equipment. Cleanup requires discipline. It is not glamorous work, but it must be done.

Cast Considerations

Most of what applies to talent in a studio production also is true for a location shoot (see chapter 2, section 2.14). Sincerity and proper projection are important to

any television performer. Constantly scratching your ear will be as distracting in front of the local courthouse as it will be in front of a studio talk show set.

However, in many ways, performing at a field site is more difficult than being on camera in a studio. For starters, there will be no teleprompter, which means you must handle your own notes or script and must know your lines and material well. Because there also are fewer crew members, there are fewer people to help out with talent requests.

Nonsequential Shooting

One of the hardest parts of film-style shooting, though, is that scenes are shot out-of-order. This can create **continuity** problems and difficulties for performers.

Sometimes it is necessary for an actor to *switch emotions* on and off for the convenience of a shooting schedule. Often two scenes will be shot back-to-back, because they are at the same location, but the emotional content of two shots may be diametrically opposed. You might be called upon to portray the emotion felt about the tragic death of a friend two days before the death of the friend has been acted out.

Figure 15.2

Reporters and interviewers often have to tape reaction shots after the interviewed guest has departed. (*Left*) During the interview, the single camera would have been behind the male interviewer, focusing on the female guest answering questions. (*Right*) After the guest has departed, the camera should be repositioned to shoot the interviewer repeating the same questions for later editing.

Even within one scene, lines are sometimes shot out-of-order. When actors' close-ups are shot, they deliver their lines often without benefit of cues and other lines in the rest of the scene. Frequently, the characters they are supposedly talking to are not even on the set. Imagine professing mad passionate love—to a camera.

Because innumerable shots are taken of one scene, you must perform the same in each take so that the material can be edited together. This means you must follow **blocking** very precisely. You cannot walk beside the sofa in the long shot and behind it in the close-up, because doing so would cause a continuity problem. Of course, there are many professional actors who have learned to perform well nonsequentially. But crew members must let them have their "space" so that they can build up to the required emotions.

Taping out-of-order is a problem for talent in nondramatic shoots also. Because the camera is on the guest during an interview, the interviewer's face will not be seen. This means that after the interview has been completed, reverse-angle shots must be taped of the interviewer asking the questions over again. This is often very difficult if you are the interviewer. You

must sit there and earnestly ask questions of a camera lens—because the person being interviewed has already departed. (See figure 15.2.)

This brings up a related *ethical* problem that reporters, in particular, must face. How much can the wording of the questions change between what was asked during the actual interview and what is asked on the reverse-angle shots taped later? The answer should be, "Not much." If the question is changed significantly, the guest's answer may take on an entirely different meaning. Networks and stations have policies regarding the need to keep the questions the same. Because of this, a continuity person should listen to the original interview and jot down the exact wording of the questions that are asked. An audiotape recorder, of course, can serve the same purpose. Then the interviewer can review the questions before the reverse-angle shots are taped.

Sometimes even more difficult than asking questions after the fact is the need to react after the fact. In almost all single-camera interviews, shots of the interviewer listening and reacting need to be recorded—usually after the guest has departed—so that they can be edited into the interview to prevent **jump cuts.** This requires the interviewer/reporter to just sit there

Figure 15.3

The audio operator is positioning the boom so that it will pick up sound as well as possible without getting in the shot.
Photo courtesy of Amy Phillips

looking at an empty chair and smiling or frowning every once in awhile; this is a difficult acting job—especially for novices. People tend to break up into laughter or to exaggerate movements such as nods of the head.

15.3

Audio

As with other technical components, many of the elements of field production audio are the same as those for studio audio; any differences are caused primarily by the uncontrollable elements of the outside world. As a starting point, ask the same questions concerning frequency, pickup pattern, impedance, and usage categories for both studio and field productions (see chapter 3, section 3.1).

Microphones

Sometimes the answers are different, however. Generally, microphones need to be more directional for field locations because of all the extraneous noise. By the same token, mics that are less sensitive (and therefore need to be located closer to the talent) are desired, because they will pick up less of the background noise.

Also, because of the transportation jolts and rough handling that field equipment is subjected to, mics for location shoots usually are of a more rugged design—**dynamic** rather than **condenser.** *Quality* and *frequency response* often have to be sacrificed for *dependability* and *ruggedness.*

Fishpoles and **hand mics** tend to be used most frequently in the field. The fishpoles (see figure 15.3) are common for dramas, where the mic should not be seen in the picture. Hand mics are common in interview situations, where the presence of the mic is accepted. Another type of mic, the **shotgun,** is used in situations where the subject being taped is far from the camera and cannot be miked easily (a lion in the jungle or a man on a horse). Shotgun mics are highly directional and can pick up sound from long distances. However, because of the high directionality, they must be pointed at the subject accurately so that they pick up the desired sound. Wireless mics come in very handy when subjects need to move around a great deal.

At times you may want to attach the microphone to the camera to eliminate the need for someone holding it. This is usually *not* a good idea, since the camera is located at some distance from the person talking and is likely to pick up noises close to the camera much more efficiently than it picks up the talent. As a general rule, in the field, microphones should always be as close as possible to the people talking—closer than in studio production—because of all the background and extraneous noise.

Control Equipment

The sophisticated control room equipment that produces clean, well-balanced sound is not available at a remote site. There are no patch bays, equalizers, or separate audiotape recorders. Usually there is not even a board—just a "ballpark" meter and some cheap headphones. Audio on a location shoot is only *transduced* and *recorded*—and usually *monitored.* Channeling, mixing, amplifying, and shaping (chapter 3, section 3.1) are all accomplished in postproduction, and yet, great care must be taken to keep recording levels within a consistent range so that they can be matched when edited. Any differences in the levels of sounds will become very obvious when different shots are assembled together in the editing process.

One way to assure consistent levels is to utilize the **automatic gain control (AGC)** available on most tape recorders. This automatically raises the volume of sounds that are soft and lowers the volume of loud sounds. AGC is *not* always the solution to keeping audio levels within a consistent range, however. This is because AGC can be the cause of another serious sound problem encountered with outdoor audio. The AGC cannot distinguish between desired and undesired sound; it boosts anything that is low. Therefore, when no one is speaking, the level of the background noise is automatically amplified—producing a hissing or roaring effect.

Because there is a built-in delay factor of 1 second or so, the effect is most noticeable at the beginning of segments or during long pauses. Attempts to erase

this unwanted sound involve the risk of upcutting program audio.

Audio **balance** is particularly difficult if two people are talking and one has a very soft voice while the other has a booming projection. AGC cannot completely compensate. Sometimes the better solution is to record each person through his or her individual mic onto a separate track, and then try to match the volumes in postproduction.

Audio Tracks

Many of the ½-inch, 8mm videotape, and digital formats are capable of recording sound diagonally, in the same manner that the picture is recorded. One method of recording sound this way is referred to as **hi-fi** (or **AFM-audio frequency modulation**), and the other is called **PCM (pulse code modulation).** Both of these methods allow for high quality stereo recording and playback. With hi-fi recording, the sound is recorded with the picture and *cannot* be separated from it during editing. With PCM, the sound is recorded on its own real estate and can be separated for editing purposes.

S-VHS recorders have a **linear** analog track as well as a digital track, and most ¾-inch videotape recorders include two linear audio tracks, usually identified as *channel 1* and *channel 2.* Channel 2 is generally the better one to use for recording because, on most common formats, it is located as an inside track on the videotape. Channel 1 is at the edge of the tape, so it is more subject to any distortion if the tape wrinkles even slightly. Also, channel 1 is often used to record a separate time code, so many facilities routinely use only channel 2 for audio. (See figure 15.4.)

Sometimes, you will be able to choose whether you want to record linear, hi-fi, PCM, or some combination of them. When you have options, you should note how the audio was recorded, because this information will be needed when editing begins.

Portable Mixers

If you have a large number of different audio sources that need to be recorded at the same time, you will need to take a portable audio mixer on location with you. (See figure 15.5.) You can then feed several mics through the board, set their levels individually, and

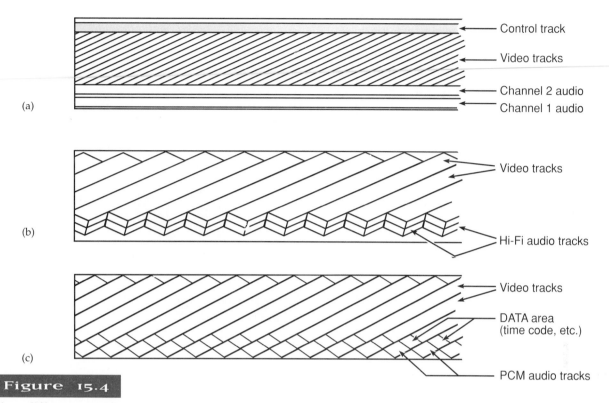

Control track

Video tracks

Channel 2 audio

Channel 1 audio

Video tracks

Hi-Fi audio tracks

Video tracks

DATA area
(time code, etc.)

PCM audio tracks

Figure 15.4

Three different ways that audio is recorded on field systems. (a) The hi-fi audio track rides with the video and cannot be separated from it during editing. (b) PCM audio is recorded on a slant-track following each video field. (c) Two linear (longitudinal) tracks are available on some formats, including U-matic.

Figure 15.5

A portable audio board can help enhance the audio of a field production. *Photo courtesy of Shure.*

record this mix-down on the videotape on one of the linear channels or on the hi-fi or PCM track.

However, setting up such an audio board takes additional space and time, both of which are often unavailable on a field shoot. Also, if the shoot is taking place in a small area, you must be careful to listen for phase problems caused by placing the mics too close together.

Wildtrack

Audio operators on location should always make sure they record some separate **wildtrack** sound—background sound from the location recorded with no specific voices. Sometimes this is for a specific purpose. For example, a narrator may be standing next to a machine that is important to the story line, but the machine has a distinctive sound. In the final edited program, shots that include the machine are to have a voice-over narration, which is to be recorded later in the studio. If the director wants to have the sound of the machine as a part of the background under the narration, then a wildtrack of that sound must be recorded for a later audio mix.

At other times the wildtrack sound is just general background noise that can be used to cover abrupt transitions during postproduction editing. Good sound operators will make a practice of recording numerous pieces of wildtrack sound as protection against unforeseen editing problems.

Extraneous Noise

The audio operator must also listen carefully to the sound that is occurring and being recorded while a take is being shot. The human brain *subconsciously* filters out unwanted sound. The noise of an airplane flying overhead often goes unnoticed by two people engaged in conversation; they effectively hear only each other. But this **selective attention principle** does not work with videotaped presentation. An unnoticed airplane recorded on an audio track will come through loud and clear on playback. For that reason, the audio person must listen intently and stop production if an unwanted noise is too evident.

In many ways, a person operating audio on a field shoot must have a disciplined "feel" for audio. He or she must have enough experience to

Figure 15.6

This Lowel portable lighting kit contains the lights and supporting equipment needed for effective field production. *Photo courtesy of Lowel-Light.*

know how something will sound in the final edited program.

15.4
Lighting

The basic **three-point lighting** approach (see chapter 5, section 5.5) is appropriate for field shoots as well as in the studio. Likewise, **contrast ratio, color temperature,** and other principles of lighting (see chapter 5, section 5.2) apply, at least in theory, to location work. Once again, problems occur when dealing with uncontrolled situations. In this case, the problems associated with lighting indoors are quite different than those found outside.

Indoor Location Lighting

Since lighting grids are far from common in university classrooms, corporate offices, hospitals, and other locations, portable lighting apparatus must be brought to the field shoot by the production crew. *Portable lights* (see figure 15.6) usually are mounted on stands that can then be placed in positions roughly approximating those of the basic **key, fill,** and **back** lights.

Often this is difficult or impossible to accomplish because of lack of space or because the light stands will show in the camera's picture. The back light is particularly tricky, because it is essentially impossible to position it correctly without having the stand visible in a long shot. Occasionally, clip-on **internal reflectors** can be clamped onto a door or tall piece of furniture to serve as a back light. However, many field productions are shot with only key and fill lights.

In fact, many news shoots utilize only one light; it is mounted on the camera and is used only for basic illumination. The result is a very flat, nonaesthetic, washed-out effect which is, nevertheless, better than shooting a silhouette.

The lighting instruments taken on a field shoot are usually limited, too. **Scoops, ellipsoidal spots,** and even **Fresnels** (see chapter 5, section 5.4) are too bulky to lug along. And certainly the vast array of lights available in the studio cannot be taken. The main portable lights used are **broads** (see chapter 5, figure 5.12), but their beams are somewhat difficult to control.

Lighting Control

Lack of a dimmer board adds to the control problems. In order to increase or decrease the intensity of a light, the stand must be moved in accordance with the principles of the **inverse square law** (see chapter 5, section 5.6). However, space limitations may hinder this. Space and time limitations also hinder the use of scrims, barn doors, flags, and other devices that could help diffuse or shape the light.

Power

Another big problem is securing adequate electrical power. A studio is specially wired in anticipation of the power that will be needed to meet extensive lighting demands. People's homes and offices are not. Lighting properly with key, fill, and back lights all plugged into one circuit is almost guaranteed to blow the circuit breaker.

For this reason, it is particularly important to learn ahead of time where the circuit breakers are, how many amps each circuit is rated for, and which outlets are on which circuit. You should also become familiar with the basic formula: *watts = volts × amps.* (This is often referred to as the "West Virginia" for-mula, $W = VA$.) The watts will be written somewhere on the lamp of your lighting instrument—usually 500, 1,000, or 2,000 watts. Amperes should be indicated on the circuit breaker—usually 10, 15, or 20 amps. Voltage is regulated by the power company and in most ordinary circumstances will be 110 volts. (In industrial settings, it may be 220 volts.) Therefore, if the circuit breaker is rated for 10 amps and the voltage is 110, you can plug in lights totaling 1,100 watts on that circuit. To be on the safe side, use a figure of 100 for the voltage (this also makes the arithmetic easier). So a 20-amp circuit could handle 2,000 watts.

However, you cannot assume your lights can use the whole circuit. The total wattage of all appliances and devices on the circuit must be taken into consideration. The office copier or the home refrigerator may be using the same circuit that you want to plug into. One group of students were taping at a factory; they had been recording without problems for an hour or so when suddenly the lights went out. Lunchtime had arrived and the employees began using the company microwave oven that was on the same circuit as the lights.

Usually you must plug in lights on at least two separate circuits and, generally, this means using plugs in two different areas. In many homes and offices, outlets in one room are all on the same circuit, and you may have to go several rooms down the hall to use a different circuit. This means you must take along extension cords.

Safety

The use of extension cords raises another question—the problem of safety. First of all, make sure that the extension cords you plan on using are rated for the electrical load you expect to plug into them. Using cords that are not heavy-duty will result in tripping the circuit breaker—or worse yet, overheating and starting a fire.

Also, electrical cable strung all over the floor is likely to cause people to trip—often unplugging the light and/or bringing down the light stand (as well as causing bodily injury). Where cords must be laid along the floor, cover them with a wide tape to help ensure that they will not be tripped over. Ideally, you should run the cords along the walls and up over

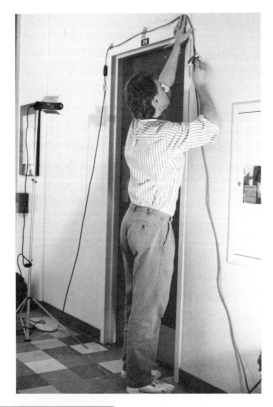

Figure 15.7

Crew member taping a power cord above a doorway to ensure that no one will trip over it during the recording.

Fresnel *Mole Solarspot.* This 2,500-watt HMI (hydrogen medium-arc-length iodine) light is used in field production where it is necessary to match the color temperature of sunlight. The control unit known as a *ballast* protects the lamp from sudden surges of power and provides for longer bulb life. *Photo courtesy of Mole Richardson.*

door jambs. (See figure 15.7.) For these taping purposes, you must bring along heavy-duty tape—preferably something like *duct tape* that is a very strong adhesive. Where cords must be taped to painted surfaces, it is best to use *masking tape* that will not peel off paint when it is removed.

Lights also create a safety problem because of their heat. They should not be placed where someone is likely to bump into them accidentally. Also, they should not be placed where they are touching curtains or paper and could thereby start a smoldering fire. At the end of a shoot, they should be turned off *first* and packed away *last.* This gives them time to cool before crew members must handle them.

Available Light

One other problem associated with shooting indoors comes from available light. If at all possible, you should turn off all regular lights and just use the quartz lights from your portable lighting kit. However, sometimes available lights can be used for general illumina-

tion—if they are of a color temperature close to 3,200 degrees **Kelvin** (see chapter 5, section 5.2). Regular incandescent light bulbs can usually be used, but fluorescents should definitely be turned off. Not only may they result in a recording with a definite blue tint, they may also create a hum or buzz on the sound track.

Outdoor light coming through windows should also be avoided, if at all possible, because it is about 5,500 degrees K—far bluer than the 3,200-degree K quartz lights. The problem is not with the outdoor light itself, but with the fact that you are *mixing* types of light—daylight and quartz. If you set the camera's filter for quartz light and some of your light source is from daylight, your footage will look blue. If you set the filter for daylight, the footage will be orange, because you are using some quartz light. **Gels** are made to place on windows to change the color temperature of the outdoor light, but they are expensive and difficult to install. A simpler solution is to avoid mixing the types of light.

Figure 15.9

As an example of a technique used in portable lighting, these four 12,000-watt HMI instruments were focused through a scrim to produce a soft, flat illumination for an interior scene.

Outdoor Location Lighting

If you are shooting outside, your main source of light is the *sun.* This has both advantages and disadvantages. You do not need to worry about light stands or power requirements. However, you have no control over the sun. It changes position; it can be overly intense; it darts behind passing clouds. Its color temperature changes as the day progresses (ranging from 4,500 to 12,000 degrees K) so that scenes shot at noon will not match scenes shot at 5:00 P.M. Not only will these scenes have a color switch, but they are also likely to show different lengths of shadows, different molding of facial features, and different amounts of glare. This is a particular problem if long shots are taped at noon while close-ups, which are to be intercut, are not shot until 5:00 P.M.

Second Light Sources

Sometimes the sun is so bright that you need *extra* lights. This seeming contradiction is caused by the fact that a bright sun can wash out facial features. It acts, in essence, like a very bright key light. To counteract this, you can add artificial lights to create the effect of a fill. Of course, these lights have to be the same color temperature as daylight.

One way to do this is to cover the quartz lights used indoors with special filter gels that convert the

Figure 15.10

Foil reflector. The two-sided reflector is an invaluable part of outdoor location shooting. The partitioned foil-leaf side (shown) produces a soft diffused light. A smooth silver paper surface on the other side produces a brighter, more intense light.   *Photo courtesy of Mole Richardson.*

3,200-degree K light to 5,500-plus degrees K. However, the filters cut down on the efficiency of the light, so more lights are needed than normal. Another way is to use **HMI** (hydrogen medium-arc-length iodine) lights that are made to produce 5,500-degree K light (see figure 15.8). These lights have a separate **ballast** that protects the lamp from power surges.

To minimize problems from the sun passing behind clouds and changing color temperature as the day wears on, you can actually use large HMI floods to create an artificial source of sunlight (see figure 15.9)—even for interior scenes.

If auxiliary lights are needed, getting power to them can be a problem. Powerful battery-operated lights do exist, but they are not commonly or inexpensively available.

A more feasible alternative for obtaining a second light from a different direction is to use a reflector. A commercially available *foil reflector* (see figure 15.10)

Figure 15.11

In this setup, reflectors are being used to bounce the sunlight onto the two actors sitting on the sand, providing both fill and back light.

can be used to bounce sunlight onto a subject's face from almost any direction. And if the sun is behind the subject (functioning as a back light), you can place the reflector in front of the subject to provide a satisfactory key light. Even if a professional reflector is not available, you can use any large piece of white material (a white poster board, for example) in an emergency to provide some fill light from a complementary direction. Obviously, the more highly polished or reflective the surface of the reflector is, the more efficient it will be. (See figure 15.11.)

Lighting Individual Shots

Overall, lighting can be one of the biggest headaches of field production. However, there is one very distinct advantage that location lighting has over live-on-tape lighting—location lighting allows each shot to be lit individually. When a studio program is shot with three cameras simultaneously, lighting must be general enough that it will provide acceptable illumination for any camera shot

that is to be used. Often in multiple-camera shooting, compromises have to be made in setting the lights, and few shots are really properly lit. With location shooting, however, the camera is stopped after each shot, and the lights can be reset to light the next shot optimally.

Cameras

Most of the aesthetic principles of picture composition (see chapter 7, section 7.4) apply in the field as well as in the studio. So do the general principles dealing with f-stops, depth of field, lens ratio, focusing, and filters. (See chapter 6, sections 6.3 and 6.5.)

Camera Controls

However, in a studio, once cameras are set, the characteristics under which they shoot remain fairly constant. White balance set at the beginning of a studio program, for instance, can be depended upon to give accurate color throughout a taping.

White Balancing

Such is not the case with field production. **White balance** must be reset frequently as lighting conditions change, because the white balance control adjusts the strength of the basic video level to suit the composition of the light that is available for an individual shot. It "reads" a designated item as *white* and then readjusts the electronics associated with the other colors so that they will render true color. (See section 6.5.)

As the sun peeks in and out of clouds, the light source changes, and you need to readjust the white balance. The changes in the sun's color temperature over the course of a day also require changing white balance. Going from outdoors to indoors definitely requires repeating the white balance procedure.

Fortunately, white balancing is easy—just the push of a button on most cameras. In fact, some cameras automatically white balance as changes in color temperature occur. If the camera you are using does not automatically redo white balancing, however, your main white balancing problem may simply be remembering to do it. Also, you must remember to bring something white to the shoot to be used for **reference white**—a piece of paper, a white sweater.

Filters

A related item very easy to forget in the process of field shooting is the changing of the camera **filter** (see chapter 6, section 6.5). Most cameras have four filters—for instance, one for indoor quartz light (which also works for outdoor sunrise and sunset), one for sunny daylight, one for cloudy outdoor shooting, and one that acts as a cap.

When you move from outdoors to indoors, or vice versa, you must change the filter, or your footage will have a decided orange or blue cast. The outdoor filters are orange to compensate for the fact that quartz light is "orangish" and daylight is "bluish." The main difference between the *sunny daylight* and *cloudy outdoor* filters is the amount of **neutral density** in the filter. Neutral density lessens the intensity of the light by

making the filter darker; therefore, the *sunny* filter has more neutral density than the *cloudy* filter.

Gain

Many portable cameras have **dB (decibel)** gain switches to use in instances of low light. This boosts the electronics so that the camera "sees" better in the dark. However, using this switch makes the picture grainier and also shifts the color somewhat. It should be used only when it is absolutely impossible to add light—generally in the covering of a news story.

Power

Another problem in the field is the power source for the camera. Most cameras can be operated either on regular *AC* (household alternating current) or on *batteries*. Whenever possible, AC should be used, because it is more reliable. However, cameras do add wattage to electrical circuits that may already be taxed from your portable lights.

Batteries have a disadvantage in that they do run out of charge—usually when you are in the middle of shooting your most important scene! If you do use batteries, make sure the battery is fully charged before you are scheduled to take the camera on location.

Secondly, while in the field, make sure you are not unintentionally discharging the battery when you are not shooting. By all means, disconnect the battery while you transport equipment from one location to another. Some cameras have a *standby* position that keeps the electronics operational but cuts down on battery use. This should be used while shots are being set up and rehearsed. Cameras differ as to how they conserve on battery power, so be sure to find out when the battery is and is not engaged on your particular camera.

Camera Mounts and Movement

Keeping a picture steady on a portable camera can be a problem. You usually do not have the luxury of the sturdy **pedestals** and **cranes** available in a studio (see chapter 7, section 7.1). What you are more likely to have is a three-legged **tripod** and/or a strong shoulder.

Whenever possible, the tripod should be used; it is steadier than the strongest of shoulders. Many student shots have been ruined because the camera operator or director did not want to take the time to put the camera on the tripod—thus fulfilling the axiom, "There's never time to do it right, but there's always time to do it over."

Pans, tilts, and zooms can all be executed very effectively on a tripod mount. However, assuming you do not have the benefit of a field crane, movements such as trucks and dollies do require the human body to simulate wheeled movement. Improvised dollies and trucks can sometimes be achieved with wheeled conveyances such as a child's wagon or a grocery cart.

Achieving smooth movement can be difficult, especially in a crowd. Shakiness in news footage is accepted by the audience, because the camera is being used *subjectively*. It is the audience eye, showing people what they would see were they there—including the bumping and jostling. But, even so, camera operators should try to keep the picture as steady as possible at all times.

Camera operators and directors must also be willing to reposition the camera frequently for both aesthetic and informational purposes. This requires effort and muscle on the part of the person operating the camera, but it is needed for everything from reaction shots of the reporter reasking questions to low-angle shots to convey a sense of power.

Camera Care and Maintenance

Care of the camera must also be a high-priority item for the camera operator. The high level of activity and unanticipated problems on any location production occasionally mean that some of the usual equipment precautions may be temporarily forgotten. Cameras are very vulnerable to the careless treatment they may be given on a field shoot. The lens should be capped between scenes and whenever the camera is moved, because that is a time when stray objects such as pebbles can accidentally strike a camera.

Many types of professional location productions pose enormous engineering challenges for the optimum functioning and protection of cameras and other equipment. Special housings and mountings have to be used for many adverse situations: dust

protection in arid country; heaters for arctic conditions; gyroscopic mountings for helicopter shots; and underwater housings for perhaps the most adverse environment of all. (See figure 15.12.)

In all probability, you will not be shooting in any of these extreme conditions for class projects but, if you are operating the camera, you should realize that you are in charge of an expensive piece of rather delicate equipment that must remain operational for many future projects.

15.6

Video Recorders

Most modern-day field production is undertaken with camcorders, either Betacam, M-II, VHS, S-VHS, Video 8, Hi8, or one of the digital formats. (See figure 15.13.) Therefore, the camera and recorder are the same piece of equipment, and the camera operator also becomes the videotape recorder operator. A button that is easily accessible when someone is holding the camcorder turns the recorder on and off. Sometimes ¾-inch U-matic equipment is used for field production and, when this is the case, the camera and recorder will be separate. The field recorder usually used for U-matic is smaller than the one used in the studio. It will only hold a cassette with 20 minutes of tape on it, not the 30-minute and 60-minute cassette sizes usually used in the studio.

Setup and Connections

In a studio setting, all the video equipment is more or less permanently connected. Such is not the case in the field. It is up to crew members to know how to attach all equipment. Although a camcorder may have a microphone attached to it, audio should be routed separately from an external mic whenever possible because, as discussed previously, the microphone should be as close as possible to the talent. The VCR input for a microphone may be a *Cannon* connector, a *phone* plug, an *RCA,* or a *mini-plug.* (Review chapter 9, figure 9.13.) Make sure you check before you leave the studio/control room to confirm that the connector on the end of the microphone cable is the same as that required by the VCR. If it is not, get an **adapter plug** that will convert from one type of connector to the other. You will also want to connect

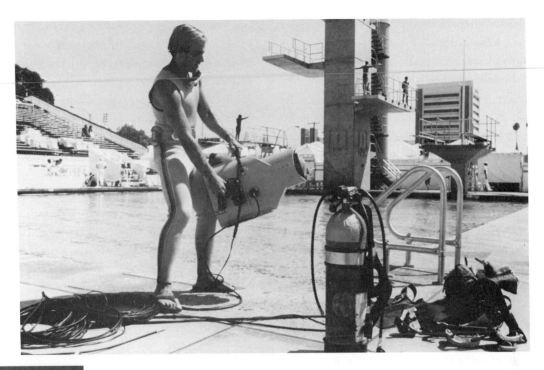

Figure 15.12

Underwater camera housing. Special equipment for underwater television coverage, such as this housing for Olympic diving events, represents an extreme in protection against environmental elements. *Photo courtesy of ABC Sports.*

Figure 15.13

A digital camcorder. *Photo courtesy of Sony Electronics, Inc.*

headsets into the earphone output on the camcorder, usually with a mini-plug.

Monitors are sometimes attached to VCR outputs so that the director can see what the camera operator is framing. The usual connectors for this are *BNC* or *UHF*, and again you should take care to make sure the proper cables and connectors are brought to the location to connect the VCR and monitor. Monitors can be unwieldy because, when they are connected to the camcorder, they must be moved if the camera is moved. This can inhibit the camera operator's flexibility. The viewfinder of most camcorders can serve as a viewing device. After something is shot, the tape can be rewound and played back through the viewfinder so that the director can check it. This takes time, however, so many field shoots take place without monitoring. This requires trust and complete communication between the director and the camera operator.

If the camera and recorder are separate, a **multipin connector** is often used to connect them. Within one cable, this contains wires for various functions—*video* (from the camera to the VCR); *audio* (in case a microphone attached to the camera is used); *power* (so that the VCR can operate from the camera's power source); *remote control* (so that the VCR can be operated by a switch on the camera); and *return* (so that the camera viewfinder can function as a monitor to view tapes after they are shot). Having a multipin connector gives a great deal more versatility to a production situation, but multipin connectors are expensive and not all separate cameras and VCRs can accommodate them.

One good approach to the discipline of field production is to lay out all of the cables and connectors you will need for your particular assignment—and then plug everything together and operate it before you leave—just to make sure you have everything.

Taping Procedures

The camcorder/VCR operator should set the audio level and check all controls before taping begins. You should make sure the machine has been up to speed at least 10 seconds before anything crucial is taped and, likewise, keep the machine running for about 10 seconds after the shot is completed so that a strong control track will be available for editing.

The VCR should not be left in *pause* for long periods of time, because this will wear the oxide off the tape and clog the video heads (see chapter 9, section 9.4).

During taping, the person in charge of recording should be watching all the "vital signs," most of which appear on indicators in the viewfinder monitor—end-of-tape warning, battery condition, low light, and so forth. In most instances, this person will also be framing shots and listening to the headphone to make sure the audio is recording properly. Because the person is doing so many tasks, he or she must be extra careful to make sure the recorder part of the camcorder is operating properly. The best of shots will be useless if they are not recorded properly and ready to be edited.

15.7
Editing

Many of the options and operations of editing are the same for multicamera and field production. The linear systems that use an **edit controller** and **source** and **edit decks** (see figure 15.14) are most likely to be found in educational institutions, but both those facilities and the professional world have largely moved to the newer **nonlinear** digital editing systems (see figure 15.15). The editing procedures involving **time code, assemble** and **insert** modes, determining edit points, previewing, trimming, reviewing, A/B rolling, and the like (see chapter 10, section 10.4) are the same regardless of whether the source material was shot in the field or in the studio.

What is different, however, is the emphasis placed on the editing process and the expanded role of audio editing.

The Editing Process

Because much of the editing done in conjunction with studio-based production is intended to correct mistakes made during production or to put together short roll-ins to be played during production, the editing can usually be accomplished rather quickly.

Such is not the case with material shot single-camera. The program is *literally* put together during

Figure 15.14

This Sony EVO 9700 Hi8 editing system is typical of what facilities use for linear editing.   *Photo courtesy of Sony Electronics, Inc.*

Figure 15.15

This Avid system is typical of what is used for nonlinear editing.   *Photo courtesy of Avid Technology, Inc.*

For students, a two-person editing team can be a very efficient way to work. Many professionals, however, prefer to work alone whenever possible.

postproduction—a process that is often long and drawn out. As all professional producers know, the process of "getting into" this final phase of postproduction is a crucial time. Much of the strength—and discipline—of a good producer is an ability to generate the sense of momentum and enthusiasm that is needed to complete a production. In live television, the relentless clock focuses everyone's attention; in single-camera postproduction, the constant pressure of a knowledgeable guiding hand is needed.

It may be difficult to understand the time frame that is necessary for the editing process; an inexperienced crew may initially waste a considerable amount of energy and effort. Usually, this phase passes as crew members become more efficient at their assigned responsibilities and the leadership and organization become more evident—just as they did during the shooting process.

Although many professional editing sessions involve only the producer or the director working in conjunction with the editor (or even the editor working alone with only a detailed set of notes), student postproduction sessions should, as much as possible, become a *learning process* for the entire team. Without proper organization, however, this process can drift into noisy chaos. The important thing is that there has to be someone who is acknowledged as being definitely "in charge." This may be the producer, the director, or the editor, but it should be the same person who has initiated and established the basic structure of the project.

Editing sessions, which can last for hours, should be set up so that while the person operating the edit control unit is executing each transfer/edit, a second person or team is finalizing the next edit decision—locating the precise reel number, footage/revolution counter number, and exact word cue for the inpoint and outpoint. (See figure 15.16.) Other people can be working on constructing the graphics that will be used for the opening and closing. Still others can be composing and/or mixing music and other audio elements. As with the production phase, the producer and/or director should give each person a clear idea of what his or her role is in the postproduction process.

Audio Editing

For a studio production, audio is usually mixed while the program is being taped. Music is brought in at the beginning and end of the show, and sound effects are incorporated as the production is under-way. Single-camera productions shot without benefit of a sophisticated audio board do not lend them-selves to audio mixing during the production phase. Obtaining good dialogue, interview audio levels, or on-camera narration is all that can really be expected in the field.

As a result, for professional single-camera pro-ductions, audio editing is often undertaken separately from video editing. While one person is editing the picture and the principle dialogue shot in the field, other people are attending to music and sound effects. Dramatic productions are the most complicated from an audio point of view. Someone, often the director, must first determine where audio elements are needed. Where will the music be brought in and taken out? What sound effects are needed? Which sounds taped in the field need to be rerecorded because they are not good enough? Once all this has been decided, a musician is asked to compose the music, someone obtains effects from sound effects CDs, and sometimes some members of the cast are brought back into a studio where they record their lines over again—a process known as **automatic dia-logue replacement (ADR).**

After all the sounds have been gathered, they are placed on a **multitrack** tape or in one of the digitized computer **workstations** that handle audio or audio and video. Here the sounds are positioned so that they are heard where they are needed during the pro-duction. They are also **mixed** together so that they are in a proper volume relationship with each other. For example, the music should not be so loud that the voices cannot be heard, and the sound of a gunshot should be louder than the sound of rain in the back-ground. The average TV drama, commercial, docu-mentary, or top-flight industrial production has a final sound track that is the result of the skilled mix-ing of anywhere from sixteen to thirty-two separate sound tracks together onto the final mix track.[3]

Audio training facilities for most colleges and uni-versities do not approach this level of sophistication—although inexpensive audio software that operates with off-the-shelf computers is enabling some univer-sities to have at least semi-sophisticated audio mixing capability. Additionally, many TV production stu-dents have not had the opportunity for a substantial course in audio production.

Therefore, it is all the more important that the preparation for the sound track must start with the very first planning of the shape of the project. The director and producer should question each other continually as to the exact details of how each sound or combination of sounds (on-camera narrator, voice-over narrator, background noise, music, sound effects, and so forth) is to be achieved. Some of the sound work can be accomplished while pro-duction is still underway. For example, if you know you are going to need the sound effect of a dog barking, you can find it well ahead of the day you need to mix it with other sounds. One often hears the phrase, "We'll fix it in post . . ." This is an in-vitation to audio disaster. If you have not thor-oughly thought out the procedure during pre-production planning, it is often too late to fix it in postproduction.

15.8

Pictorial Elements

Pictorial elements receive less attention in field shoot-ing than in studio shooting. Graphics are usually added after the fact, and sets are determined by the nature of the location. Nevertheless, the basics of pic-torial design exist in the field as well as in the studio.

Graphics

Graphics are essentially nonexistent in actual field shooting. Some consumer cameras have built-in **char-acter generators** so that graphics can be included during taping, but these are generally used only for slating/identification purposes. Occasionally, an on-set wall chart may be shot as a cutaway, but it is not

Figure 15.17

Hallway to be considered for a location shoot. How many problems can you spot if you plan on using this hallway for a location production? How will the mixture of indoor and outdoor light affect color temperature and white balance settings? What can be done about the potential glare? How will the automatic iris function as the talent walks along the corridor—moving in and out of extremely bright spots? What will be the safest angles to use?

likely to be designed for television, so the camera operator must frame it as well as possible under the circumstances.

If actual physical charts or illustrations are to be included in a program, they are better shot in a studio where lighting can be *controlled*. Most graphics, of course, are computer generated (see chapter 11, section 11.3). All of these will be incorporated into the program during the postproduction editing.

Sets

Sets, as such, do not usually exist either. The main reason you go on a location shoot is to obtain realistic scenery and settings that are not possible with constructed sets in a studio. However, when you are scouting to find proper locations, keep in mind the *pictorial design elements* discussed in chapter 11, sections 11.1 and 11.2. For example, yellow and reds are warm colors, and greens and blues are cool colors—whether they are in a studio or out in the country. Whether you are shooting indoors or out, the principles of balance and mass, lines and angles, always apply.

Unless you find some very cooperative people or you are willing to pay a great deal of money, you cannot usually change much in a location setting. You *can* clean up someone's desk so that the clutter will not be visually distracting; but you *cannot* readily change the color of the walls, the location of trees, or the placement of windows.

When shooting interior scenes, windows do present particular problems in that they cause glare and interfere with proper lighting. The best advice is to *avoid* shooting into windows. However, it may not always be possible to avoid a passing shot of a window; perhaps it is absolutely necessary to pan with the talent while he or she walks across a room, passing in front of a window. In such a situation, you should consider disabling the automatic **iris** control; set the **f-stop** manually for the best interior (nonwindow) lighting, and keep it consistent as the talent passes in front of the window. This will result in an overexposed background through the window, but the alternative (if the automatic iris is left on) is to allow the talent to turn to a silhouette when passing in front of the window.

In one sense, the setting is much easier (and less expensive) to deal with in a remote location than in a studio, because very little, if anything, needs to be constructed. However, an improper setting can totally destroy the concept and atmosphere of your program. (See figure 15.17.) You can wind up with the wrong colors, architecture, period furnishings, traffic flow, backgrounds, and so forth. Therefore, you may have to spend many hours scouting and searching for just the right setting.

Real locations are invariably much "busier" than studio sets; they will have a lot of elements that are extraneous to what you will be taping—furniture, props, wall coverings, table objects, appliances, and so forth. As a result, you must pay particular attention to make sure you do not wind up with shots that have light switches or flower pots that look like they are growing out of someone's head.

Producing

As with studio shoots, producers are the people in charge of the *overall organization* of a field shoot. (See chapter 2, section 2.1.) Their busiest time is before the shoot actually begins, but they are responsible for making sure the production finishes *on time* and *on budget*.

Scripting

The same forms of scripts can be used for field shooting as for studio shooting—**film-style scripts, two-column scripts, rundowns, outlines,** and **storyboards**. (See chapter 13, section 13.2.) For most forms of field production, the script is absolutely essential before planning or production can take place. Sometimes there is the tendency on the part of student crews to place a camera on someone's shoulder and assume that the location will provide the necessary material. More than one student production team has found that all of those great ideas they thought of back in the studio just seemed to disappear into thin air once they arrived at the shooting location. The very *act* of putting things down on paper is an important test of the feasibility of the operational plan.

There are times, however, in field production when it is appropriate not to use any script at all. The most obvious example is when covering breaking news stories. But even then, some research can be undertaken ahead of time. Reporters usually keep track of the number of crimes that have been committed in a certain area, the backgrounds of the major political figures, the actions being taken by the local city council, and similar items. This material can be incorporated into what is reported from the scene.

Finding a Location

Producing a location shoot is similar to producing a studio program in that all elements must be in the right place at the right time. However, this is usually much more complex for a field shoot, because everything is out of its usual habitat. Equipment logistics, travel arrangements, power supplies, and coordination of props and talent all involve extraordinary consideration.

One of the crucial initial steps a producer must undertake is to make sure someone selects and surveys the production location. For large dramatic productions requiring many locations, a person given the title of **location scout** will undertake the job of finding, visiting, and winnowing down the possible production sites. The location scout might find ten homes where a 1940s murder mystery could be shot. But some might be a great distance from where other scenes are being shot, some might be in noisy locations, and some may not have an appropriate looking porch. The location person will narrow down the choices and present them to the producer and/or director. At this point, most directors and some producers like to visit the potential sites to make the final selection. Having the camera operator along to give input on these location scouting trips can also prove invaluable.

Surveying a Location

For other types of programs you know approximately where you will be doing the shoot, and you go mainly to see the lay of the land. If, for example, you are interviewing a doctor about a new medical breakthrough, you will want to shoot at the hospital where the instruments used for the procedure will be available. You go there ahead of time to see how large the room you will be shooting in is, to find out where the electrical plugs are, to determine how you can best cut out background noise, etc.

Fast-breaking news stories are another matter. Obviously, it may not be possible to check out the location for these ahead of time. However, some places where news is likely to occur, such as the city council chambers or the police station, can be "cased" ahead of time and notes made so that crews that need to go there have some idea of what they will face.

If you shoot in a studio regularly, you are aware of the location of power outlets, the positions of the cameras, the types of curtains and set pieces available, the location of lighting instruments, and other similar information. With each field shoot, these elements are different. That is why it is *essential* that the area be scouted ahead of time. If the only available plugs are out in the hallway and you have not brought extension cords for your lights, you will be faced with a major production problem.

When you go to a location, it is wise to have a list of things you want to check. A general *checklist* is shown in figure 15.18, but there will also be elements specific to each production that need to be discerned.

One of the first things you should do as part of a location survey is obtain the name of a person who is in charge—someone who gives you the permission to shoot at any particular facility, someone you can contact when you arrive with equipment, and someone to turn to quickly when any unexpected problems crop up. Who has the keys? Whom do you contact when you trip a circuit breaker?

You may wish to draw up a floor plan of the location and take Polaroid shots of the scene to share with other crew members and to remind you of important details as you plan specific shots. Or, better yet, take along a camcorder and tape the location.

If you are shooting outdoors, or if you are shooting indoors with any natural light, you will want to scout the location at the *same time of day* that you will

be doing the shoot so that you can see exactly what you will have to deal with in terms of sunlight, shadows, and windows.

What about possible interruptions and conflicts? Do scheduled events at the location conflict with the shoot? Heavy equipment starting up? Airplanes taking off? If you are shooting on campus, for example, will the end of a class period send large numbers of people walking through the shot? What about those campus chimes? Make note of these items so that you are not in the middle of a take when any of these distractions occur. Listen for continuous extraneous noises, such as an air conditioner or telephones ringing, that will interfere with your audio. Try to obtain permission to turn them off while you are shooting. If you cannot, plan to work with more directional and less sensitive mics closer to the talent.

Stock Footage

Some productions require some shots that will be in difficult or expensive locations—an airplane that has crashed on a remote mountainside, a koala bear asleep in a tree. If the principal talent does not need to be in these shots, they can be obtained from prerecorded material. Most professional producers turn to commercial companies that supply **stock footage.** The price is high (a minimum fee of $300 is not uncommon), but these companies have videotape and film to cover a wide variety of situations. News departments that used to discard their old news stories now carefully index them on computers and file everything they shoot for possible later use.

Students who cannot afford professional stock footage should first examine the resources of their own university. Sometimes some former student will have shot the local area from a helicopter and this footage will be made available for future student shoots. Large companies that turn out numerous public relations films will often allow use of portions of footage if you give them a credit. The copyright laws that govern the use of all stock footage are rather strict and should always be observed.

LOCATION SURVEY CHECKLIST

Type of material being shot_____

Time of shooting_____

Potential location of shooting_____

    Principal contact person_____

    Address_____

    Phone number_____

Camera:

    Where can the camera be placed?
    What, if anything, is needed in the way of camera mounting devices or platforms?
    What, if anything, is needed in the way of special lenses?
    Will any objects interfere with the camera shots? If so, how can this situation be corrected?

Lighting:

    What types of lights will be needed?
    Where can the lights be placed?
    What light stands or particular light holders will be needed?
    What, if any, special lighting accessories will be needed?
    How can any problems regarding mixing indoor and outdoor lighting be solved?
    In what ways will the sun's position at different times of day affect the shooting?
    What kinds of problems are shadows likely to cause?

Power:

    Is enough power available or will a generator be needed?
    Where is the circuit breaker box?
    Who can be contacted if a circuit blows?
    Which circuits can be used and how many watts can be run on them?
    How many, if any, extension cords will be needed?
    What power outlets can be used?

Sound:

    Are there background noises that may interfere with audio? If so, how can they be corrected?
    Where can the microphones and cable be placed?
    Are any particular microphone holders or stands needed?
    What types of microphones should be used?
    How much microphone cable will be needed?

General:

    Where is parking available?
    Where is the nearest telephone?
    If passes are needed to enter the premises, how can they be obtained?

Figure 15.18

A location checklist that is very useful when looking over an area that might be used for taping.

Low-end Camcorders (VHS and Video 8)	$75 per day
Higher Grade Camcorders (S-VHS and Hi-8)	100 per day
U-matic SP Recorder and 3-CCD Camera	400 per day
Professional Digital Betacam or M-II	800 per day
Tripod and Head	60 per day
Monitor	40 per day
Portable Light Kit with Four Lights	55 per day
HMI Light	175 per day
Microphone	15 per day
Portable Audio Mixer	45 per day
Walkie Talkie Communication System	15 per day
Audio Sweetening	70 per hour
Graphics Generation	40 per hour
Cuts-only Linear Editing	80 per hour
On-line Linear Editing	185 per hour
Nonlinear Editing	200 per hour

Figure 15.19

These are approximate costs for renting equipment and facilities.

Budgeting

Budgeting for field production work is very similar to budgeting for studio productions, in that budgets include **above-the-line** and **below-the-line** categories. (See chapter 13, section 13.3.) The main variation is that different equipment will be used and a greater emphasis will be placed on editing. Figure 15.19 gives you some equipment rental figures to help you budget for field shooting:[4]

Conceptualization and Preproduction Planning

Before a program or segment of a program is taped on location, you should conceive it in its entirety. How each individual shot is planned and executed is dependent upon how it will be utilized in the final edited program. In other words, both planning and camera work must be carried out with the eventual editing process constantly in mind.

To aid in this process, video producers have developed a number of different forms. Some of the same paperwork used for studio production is used for field production. For example, you should ask performers to sign **performance releases** (see chapter 13, figure 13.10), and you should clean any music and other **copyrighted** material that is going to be used for the final edited production (see chapter 13, figure 13.12).

However, because field productions usually involve a variety of locations and their inherent uncertainties, producers must examine the scripts very carefully to determine production needs and schedules.

BREAKDOWN SHEET

Program: *PARK MINI-DOC*

Location: *Park with a slide & swing*

Segment Number: *3*

Synopsis: *Mary Ellen talks of the need for greater*
safety standards for playground equipment

Cast	Props	Equipment
Mary Ellen Thomas	*Jump rope*	*1/2 portable VCR &*
Jason	*Tricycle*	*camera*
Tiffany		*Reflector*
		Mike & cable

Crew	Special Needs	Comments
Tom	*Mike cable must be*	*Should be shot at a*
Susan	*able to reach the slide*	*time when children*
Tasha		*are there*

Figure 15.20

The breakdown sheet lists all the talent, crew, facilities, and other elements needed for every scene.

Breakdown Sheets

If you are planning to shoot a complex production that involves a number of individual scenes shot in different locations, **breakdown sheets** are indispensable. They list—for each scene to be shot—a synopsis of the scene, the location, the people who will be needed, the props, and any special considerations. (See figure 15.20.)

As previously mentioned, program material in extensive field productions is almost always shot out of order, so you use your breakdown sheets to juggle your production shooting and determine the order in which scenes will be shot. Usually the primary element for determining shooting order is *location*; all scenes occurring in the park will be shot at one time, even though they will be interspersed at various points throughout the program. However, sometimes the primary element for determining shooting order is the talent; if someone who is crucial to the production can only work one day, all the shots involving that person will have to be shot on that one day, even though this means traveling all over town. On rare occasions, shooting order may be determined by a prop; if you need to rent a vintage automobile, you might want to shoot all scenes with it on one day so that you can cut down on rental fees.

Sometimes it is wise to make lists of props, costumes, cast members, etc. from these breakdown sheets. These lists are similar to what might be made for a studio shoot (see chapter 13, figure 13.11), but usually there are more lists made, because the elements needed for a field shoot are more complex. For example, one list might include all the locales that the location scout needs to find; other lists might include all the animals or all the automobiles needed. Studio productions usually do not include these elements.

Shooting Schedule

Once you have assembled all the breakdown sheets in order, you can develop a **shooting schedule.** This lists everything that is to be shot during each day, giving

Program: _PARK MINI-DOC_

Date	Time	Description	Cast	Location
4/20	1:00	Mary Ellen discusses playground equipment and safety needs (seg 3)	Mary Ellen Thomas Jason Sorkin Tiffany Barr	Alcove Park
4/20	2:30	Mary Ellen discusses need for flowers (seg 7)	Mary Ellen Thomas Mr. Hamilton	Patterson Park
4/22	11:00	Interview with park supervisor (seg 2)	Mary Ellen Thomas Dr. Belling	Dr. Belling's office, Park building
4/22	1:00	Interview with park planners (seg 9)	Mary Ellen Thomas Mr. Loomis Mrs. Robbins	Planning offices, Park building

Figure 15.21

The shooting schedule is indispensable for coordinating location shoots on a major production.

the description, the cast, and the location. It is used throughout the shooting and, of course, must be revised when production gets behind schedule. (See figure 15.21.)

Stripboards

Many producers (or their **production managers**) use **stripboards** to aid them with their shooting plans. Sometimes these are actual boards that can hold long strips of paper indicating the locations and characters needed each day. Computers are now heavily employed for all forms of preproduction paperwork, including stripboards. Figure 15.22 shows a stripboard made with the aid of the computer program *Movie Magic*. When the production needs to be reorganized because some scene didn't get shot, the strips can be moved around by clicking on them with a mouse and dragging them elsewhere. Strips of the old-fashioned paper stripboard can also be easily moved, making stripboards a very flexible production planning device.

In addition, you can devise your own lists, forms, schedules, or pictures to help conceptualize and organize your material. Like the major multiple-camera studio production, every hour spent in preproduction planning and scripting will save countless hours of valuable crew time on the shoot. Careful script preparation and preproduction planning are perhaps the most crucial *disciplines* involved in single-camera field production.

Directing

Directing in the field is quite different from directing in the studio, mainly because the director is on the set rather than in the control room. However, a director's duties during preproduction are similar to those for a studio shoot—becoming familiar with the script, and planning for equipment, cast, and crew (see chapter 2, section 2.2). The main additional chores revolve around those related to finding locations.

During Rehearsals

Rehearsing for a field shoot should involve the same procedures as rehearsing for a studio program (see chapter 14, section 14.1). However, because the

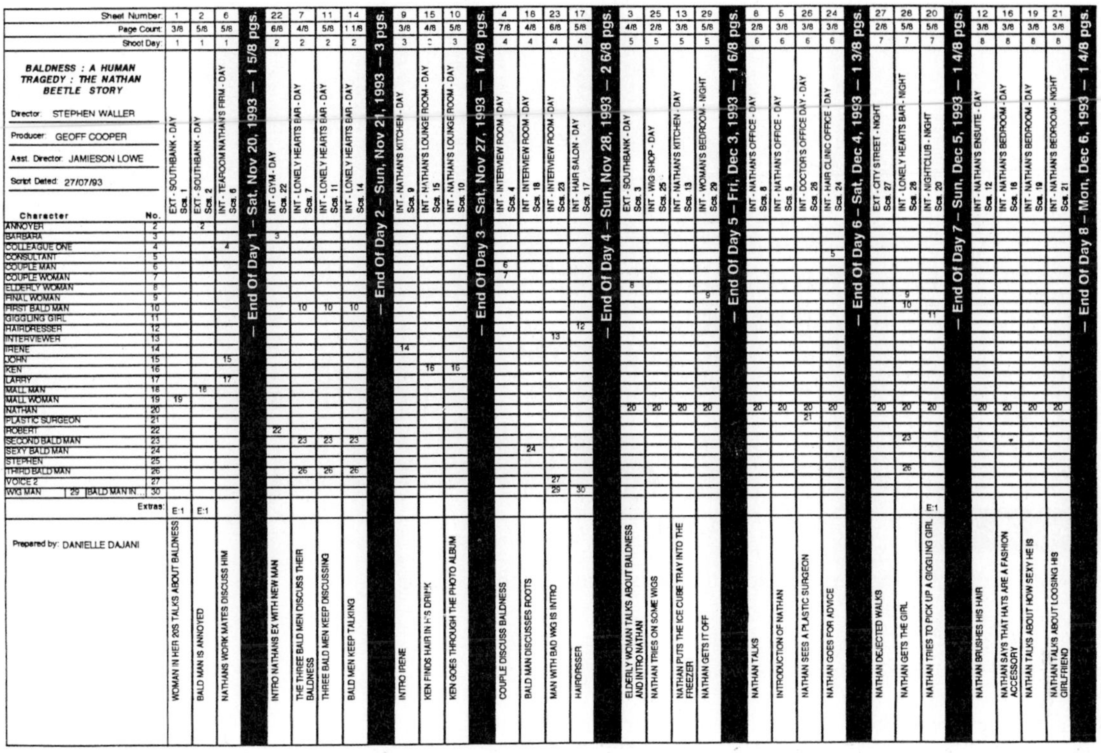

BALDNESS : A HUMAN TRAGEDY : THE NATHAN BEETLE STORY

Director: STEPHEN WALLER
Producer: GEOFF COOPER
Asst. Director: JAMIESON LOWE
Script Dated: 27/07/93

Prepared by: DANIELLE DAJANI

Character	No.
ANNOYER	2
BARBARA	3
COLLEAGUE ONE	4
CONSULTANT	5
COUPLE MAN	6
COUPLE WOMAN	7
ELDERLY WOMAN	8
FINAL WOMAN	9
FIRST BALD MAN	10
GIGGLING GIRL	11
HAIRDRESSER	12
INTERVIEWER	13
IRENE	14
JOHN	15
KEN	16
LARRY	17
MALL MAN	18
MALL WOMAN	19
NATHAN	20
PLASTIC SURGEON	21
ROBERT	22
SECOND BALD MAN	23
SEXY BALD MAN	24
STEPHEN	25
THIRD BALD MAN	26
VOICE 2	27
WIG MAN	30

Figure 15.22

This computer-generated stripboard was produced using the program *Movie Magic*. *Computer work courtesy of Stephen Waller.*

amount of time you can utilize a remote facility is often limited (you can't interrupt the work on a factory floor or monopolize the merry-go-round in a park), you often do not have the luxury of rehearsal in the field—which suggests that you substitute other creative alternatives. Can you at least have a **run-through** with the primary talent to familiarize them with the actual location? How about rehearsing in a substitute location? Rehearsal hall? Your living room?

During Production

On the day of production, many events occur that have nothing in common with studio production. First of all, the equipment must be packed and taken somewhere. You, as the director must make sure that all crew members *double-check* that everything needed is packed and is in working order. If you get to a location site without any videotape, you are in big trouble.

Laying Bars

The taping procedure, itself, is quite different from that in a studio. If a camera has a **color bar generator,** at least 30 seconds of **color bars** should be recorded on the tape before anything else. This is to allow you or the editor time to adjust controls that will enable the tape to be played back with proper color balance during the editing sessions.

Slating

Each shot needs to be slated. As soon as the VCR is up to speed, one of the crew members (often the script supervisor or a production assistant) should hold a cardboard sign, small chalkboard, or professionally prepared **slate** in front of the camera. This should indicate the scene number, take number, director's name, and description of the shot.

The *scene number* should be the same as that on the script and the *take number* is the number of times that same material has been shot—take 1 for the first

Figure 15.23

The slate should contain all the pertinent identifying information that will be needed for later editing.

attempt, take 2 for the second, etc. While this written slate is being taped, the person holding it should read the information into an open mic so that both a video and audio slate are recorded. (See figure 15.23.)

Of course, this formalized slating procedure is not always possible—especially with fast-breaking news. If a production crew has an opportunity to record a criminal being apprehended, you certainly would not want to take a chance on missing the crucial action while you prepare a proper slate.

Taping Procedure

Once the slate is recorded, with the camera still rolling, the director should say "Action" and, after waiting several beats, the talent should begin.

After the segment is taped, all talent on camera should hold their positions for at least 5 seconds while the camera continues to roll. These beginning and ending procedures are crucial for the editing function in that they provide both the necessary sync information and adequate **pads** for maintaining proper pace. (See chapter 10, section 10.2.)

If you, as the director, are satisfied with the take, you should proceed to whatever is being taped next. If the take is not acceptable, shoot it over again.

Logging

Someone, usually the script supervisor, should keep a careful production log of every shot; this should include the scene number (which should be the same as the scene number on the script and the slate), take number, description, length of shot, and any special comments. (See figure 15.24.) The script supervisor should indicate if a take is bad, so that the editor does not have to bother looking at it. Often, particularly if the taping procedure is hectic, this **logging** is done after shooting is complete.

Continuity

In a complicated shoot, such as a drama, the script supervisor's main job has to do with keeping track of **continuity.** He or she makes notes concerning what the actors were wearing, where certain props were set, in which direction the action was flowing, how heads were tilted, and which hand actors used to make certain gestures. If the actor was wearing a tie when he knocked on the door in the scene shot on Monday, he should be wearing that same tie when he enters the living room in the scene shot on Thursday. If the interviewee's hand was clutching the book he was holding during the long shot, his hand should be clutching the book for the close-up that will be edited into the shot.

Slate	Count In	Count Out	Comments
University Security Office Seg 3 Shot 4 Take 3	Lt. Jones. 253 "My Job...	270... this problem."	Best one
Security Office Intro. Meyer Seg 3 Shot 1 Take 1	275 "Lt. Jones...	287... no parking."	
——————— Cassette #2 ———————			
Parking lot student #1 Seg 4 Shot 1 Take 1	025 "Well everyday...	037... no spaces."	Stumbled over words
Parking lot student #1 Seg 4 Shot 1 Take 2	045 "Everyday...	051... really mad."	
Parking lot student #2 Seg 4 Shot 2 Take 1	059 "I don't see	071... parking ticket."	

Figure 15.24

Excerpt from sample production log.

Shot Variety

Probably the most important production technique associated with field shooting is that of making sure enough varied shots are taken—mainly so that they can be used, if necessary, as **cutaways** during editing (to avoid **jump cuts**). If, for example, the taping involves an interview, the single camera will be on the guest throughout the interview. After the interview is over, the interviewer should be taped asking the questions over again. **Reaction shots** of both the interviewer and guest listening should also be taped. And close-ups of anything the guest talked about should be recorded. Take a long shot of the location with the two people appearing to be talking. Tape some over-the-shoulder shots and zoom-in reaction shots. In general, record as many different shots as you think you might conceivably be able to use in editing.

Dramatic scenes almost always include at least a cover shot of everyone involved, close-ups of each person delivering his or her lines, and reaction shots of each person.

Handling Talent

A common problem in many news or documentary shootings is people who do not want to be on television. Usually these are people who are in the news in a negative or controversial way and, as a result, try to avoid being interviewed. The degree to which these people should be pursued depends on the nature of the assignment, the context and reputation of the program, and the personalities of all involved.

Some people do not want to be on TV, because they know they come across poorly. If these people are not crucial to obtaining the message, they should not be used—they may be self-fulfilling prophecies. And certainly, there is little justification for pursuing an interview with the grieving relative of a person who has just been killed.

At the other end of the spectrum is the common problem of unwanted talent. Random people do not wander into a studio very often, but when a shoot is being conducted on a city street, the curious are bound to appear. If a drama is being taped, crew members (or off-duty law officers) are often hired for crowd control purposes—placed at the edges of the scene to keep onlookers out of the shot.

But there is no guaranteed way to keep people out of shots that involve fast-breaking news stories. Egomaniacs and self-proclaimed clowns who strut around in the background and make faces (or obscene gestures) at the camera can be a real nuisance. If the director deals with these people in a firm but pleasant manner, such behavior can sometimes be modified.

Handling Crew

As with a studio shoot, the director must work to build *camaraderie* among the crew members. Poor interpersonal relationships can really damage a field shoot, because usually people cannot even get away from each other. In some instances, they are stuck together for days or weeks.

Because the director is on the set at a location shoot, he or she cannot give commands (zoom in, pan left) during taping—they would be picked up on the mic. Shot composition and other details must be worked out ahead of time by the director and crew.

During Postproduction

The directorial role during postproduction is obviously greater for field shoots than for studio productions, because material shot single-camera film style must be edited. In fact, the actual show is made in the editing room. Because of the generally uncontrolled conditions during shooting, postproduction can be quite a tedious prospect. It can also be quite rewarding, however, if preproduction and production have been carried out effectively—and the potential for a successful program is apparent.

Aesthetics

Most of the aesthetic principles regarding design and studio camera shots (see chapter 14, section 14.2) certainly apply in field shoots. However, some of them take on an even increased importance. For example, the concepts of **axis of action** must be watched even more closely in the field, because so many shots are taped out-of-order. The director must be able to envision shots that will be edited together even though they may not be taped immediately after each other. For example, if a long shot of someone running is recorded before lunch and a close-up of the person running is shot after lunch, the camera must not **cross the line** of the long shot when it is used for the close-up. Otherwise, when the two shots are cut together, the person will appear to change direction.

Similarly, it is easy to shoot material that will violate the **3-to-1 cutting ratio** when you do not shoot **wide shots, medium shots,** and **close-ups** one after the other.

But the compensating factor is that when you shoot single camera, you can take the time to carefully construct each shot so that it enhances your message and appeals to the eye.

Summary

Single-camera field production is both similar to and different from multiple-camera studio production. Both *disciplines* and *techniques* are needed to an even greater degree in the field because of small crews and distance from homebase.

Crews are small, because less equipment is needed and because everyone is on the set. Crew participation in *cleanup* is particularly important. Actors and performers often have difficulties, because there is no teleprompter and scenes are shot *out of sequence.*

Microphones most likely to be used are rugged *dynamic* ones used as *hand mics*, on *fishpoles*, or as *shotguns.* Audio boards are usually not taken on a location shoot. The *AGC* can be used to balance levels, although it will boost noise in addition to the wanted sound. Field sound is recorded utilizing *hi-fi, PCM,* or *linear* tracks. Crews should remember to record *wildtrack* so it can be used for editing.

Often *three-point lighting* is difficult or impossible to accomplish because of tiny shooting areas and lack of places to hang lights. The variety of lights available in a studio cannot be taken in the field; the primary type of light used on a location shoot is the *broad.* Care must be taken when plugging in lights to make sure they do not blow *circuit breakers,* and overall safety precautions must be taken. Color problems can occur if light is *mixed,* with some coming from incandescent lights and some coming from outside daylight. The best procedure is to use either indoor or outdoor light. If shooting occurs outdoors, the sun is the primary light source. However, often it is so bright that it must be supplemented with *HMI lights* or *foil reflectors.*

Cameras must be *white balanced* and the proper *filters* must be selected based on whether the shooting is occurring indoors or out. In the field, cameras are often powered by *batteries* and the most common mounting device is a *tripod.*

VCRs are usually part of the one-piece *camcorder.* However, connections often need to be made to microphones and monitors.

Editing takes on a larger role with single-camera production than with multicamera shooting, because the show is put together in the editing room. The *mixing* of audio is of particular importance.

Graphics are usually a postproduction function not dealt with in the field. Sometimes the location for the taping must be modified to meet the needs of the program, but elaborate sets are not needed.

Producers have a great deal to do during the preproduction stage. Because of the complications of shooting in a number of different places, *breakdown sheets, shooting schedules,* and *stripboards* are useful. Someone must also scout the *location.*

Directors are always on the set, because no control room is available. They must make sure scenes are *slated* and that head and tail *pads* are recorded. They should watch for *continuity* problems and shoot a variety of shots so that they do not run into problems in the editing room, such as those involved with *jump cuts* and *crossing the line.*

A Wrap-up

The traditional *wrap-up* is given to a performer about 15 seconds before he or she has to get off the air. It means that there is very little time left to wrap things up, quickly summarize, and say good-bye. Perhaps it is appropriate that we wrap up quickly at this point.

This text has been concerned with the production *techniques* of production—both for studio productions and for field production. If it has been successful, it has also gotten into the *disciplines* of handling these various elements. Discipline has been defined in several ways throughout this text. As much as anything, it can be considered a matter of attitude.

Attitude toward learning and improving is one major ingredient of discipline. If you truly want to learn as much as you can about the business of television, you will gain quite a bit from this course. You will observe intently. You will try conscientiously. One of the most important secrets of learning in a course such as this is the ability to admit areas of temporary ignorance and then ask questions or seek experiences to fill in those areas. If you are unsure about audio patching, ask to have it explained to you. If you are insecure with the switcher, get all the experience you can as technical director. Do not try to bluff your way through; no one gets very far in that manner.

Attitude toward communication is important. Unless you have a strong feeling for the pursuit of communication—unless you really have a deep desire to succeed in communicating a message—then you are in the wrong field. Television is not just a business of glamour or money or excitement. It is the business of communication. For example, every program starts with a specific purpose—a clear-cut idea of what is to be attained in the production. Until you begin program planning with this attitude, your productions may be slick and polished, but they most certainly will turn out to be meaningless and devoid of any substance.

Finally, *attitude toward a professional obligation* must be considered. The terms *professional attitude* and *professionalism* are bandied about with little thought as to their implications. We use the terms here to imply more than just a means of earning a livelihood. We challenge the student to think of professionalism in the original sense of the three learned professions (law, medicine, and theology), which carry a strong societal obligation. The true professional is one who is dedicated to high principles and a sense of community benefit. If you are committed to this kind of self-giving professionalism, you certainly will be more likely to leave your mark upon the field of video production.

Footnotes

1. There is no information that parallels chapter 9 on the switcher, because a switcher is not used for field production. There is also no section that parallels chapter 13 on interactive production

because, although interactive production often uses the single-camera techniques, it does not feed into field production in the same way that equipment, producing, and directing do.

2. Historically, most of the people given these jobs were female, so the term *script girl* was used in early times. For many years the script supervisor was the only woman on most film and video crews. Although the functions of script supervisor are very important, this is still a low-paying job.

3. Some professional music recording sessions will use in excess of 100 different tracks. Quincy Jones, for example, has used over 200 in some sessions. This involves several *slave* tapes (up to 24 tracks each) that are premixed before the final mixing session. Some audio consoles, however, can handle more than 50 inputs for a single mixing session.

4. These prices were compiled from a number of rental catalogues including those of: Birns and Sawyer (213-466-8211); Ametron (213-466-4321); Bexel (818-841-5051); and Raleigh (213-466-3111).

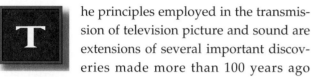

Appendix A

Electromagnetic Waves

The principles employed in the transmission of television picture and sound are extensions of several important discoveries made more than 100 years ago involving the related phenomena of electricity and magnetism. In 1856, James Clerk Maxwell expressed the theory that electrical energy existed within the universe in the form of oscillating waves. He further suggested that not only did these electrical waves travel at the same speed as light but also that they were physically related to light itself.

By 1887, Heinrich Hertz was able to prove the existence of waves of electrical force by developing the equipment with which to generate them. His experiments revealed that the waves had varying lengths and differing rates of oscillation. It was further seen that these two factors interact with each other in a mathematical relationship also involving the wave velocity.

Before proceeding, it should be pointed out that while the vibrations that constitute natural sound in some ways resemble the qualities of the waves of the *electromagnetic spectrum*, present-day scientific thinking considers each of these to be a separate phenomenon, existing side by side within the physical laws of the universe. Pressure sound waves can be transmitted only through the media of the atoms and molecules of solids, liquids, and gases; whereas electromagnetic waves can move also through the vacuum of space.

The analogy to water waves has developed as a convenient way of expressing the very complex properties of both of these forms of energy transmission. While sound pressure waves are relatively well understood, most scientists confess an inability to comprehend totally the nature of electromagnetic energy.

In any case, let us use the water wave analogy as a means of understanding the properties of both types of oscillations. Think of a series of ocean waves as seen from a cutaway side view. In the water, there is a rubber ball that floats up and down with the crests and troughs of the passing waves, but remains stationary in relation to a fixed point on the sand beneath. Riding just in front of a wave crest is a body surfer. If the person moves in a straight line, he or she will indicate the speed at which the wave is traveling relative to the shoreline. In our hypothetical ocean, all the waves come into the shore at the same speed. With this in mind, we can tell several important things by looking at the ball and the surfer. (See figure A.1.)

First, we can measure the distance from crest to crest to determine the *wavelength*. We then notice that this wavelength has a definite relationship to the number of times the ball goes up and down in a certain period of time. This crest-to-trough and back-to-crest rate of oscillation is the measure of *frequency*. If the wavelength were shorter (distance between crests), the ball would go up and down more often in the same period of time. (Do not forget that our waves move through the water at a constant velocity.) This is an important quality of waves of electrical energy—*the greater the frequency, the shorter the wavelength.*

Watching the up-and-down movements of the ball over a long period of time may give us one more important piece of information. The ball may continue its same up-and-down movement at a consistent number of oscillations per minute, but as the hours pass, we may notice that it is not going as far

up and down. As in a real ocean, the height of the wave is often the result of energy expended by a storm out at sea. The height of the wave will decrease as the energy creating it decreases. In electrical energy wave theory, the *amplitude* or amount of oscillation is the result of the amount of energy applied to the wave.

The *velocity* of the wave is simply a measure of how long it takes the crest of a single wave to move from one given point to another. In the case of electromagnetic energy, this speed is constant—the same as the speed of light, roughly 186,000 miles per second. As with light, the direction follows that of a straight line. The complex exceptions to this general rule are such that they need not draw our attention.

The basic wave cycle that measures one complete oscillation from crest to trough and back to crest again is usually called a *hertz* in honor of Heinrich Hertz, who did much of the preliminary research in this scientific area. Because the number of cycles per second

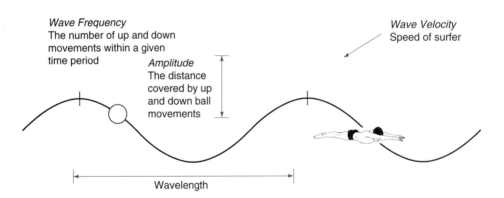

Figure A.1

Relationship of wavelength, frequency, amplitude, and velocity.

is so large in most scientific measurements, figures are usually expressed in *kilohertz,* or thousands of cycles, and *megahertz,* or millions of cycles.

Looking at the AM radio, we see that the carrier frequencies utilized for transmission are those of 540 kilohertz (540,000 cps) to 1,705 kilohertz. Each AM station occupies a band of frequencies 10 kilohertz wide. The station's call letters are identified with the midpoint of these frequencies. For example, KNX in Los Angeles, 1070 on the dial, actually utilizes 1,065 to 1,075 kilohertz for broadcast purposes.

In AM (amplitude modulation) radio, the broadcast signal is, in effect, added onto the carrier fre-

quency and, in the process, variously alters the amplitude of the signal. It is this modulation of the amplitude that the receiver translates back into sound. (See figure A.2.)

FM (frequency modulation) radio uses much higher carrier frequencies, from 88 to 108 megahertz. Here, it is the frequency of the carrier signal that is changed by the modulation process and, in turn, translated or demodulated back into sound. (See figure A.2.)

As shown in figure A.3, radio and television occupy but a small part of the immense range of the known electromagnetic spectrum.

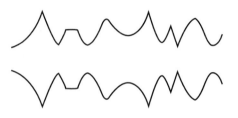

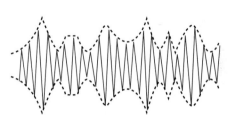

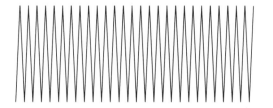

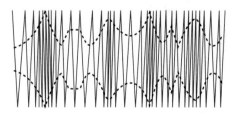

Figure A.2

AM and FM modulation of a carrier wave. *Top,* the electronic signal coming from the microphone or recorder consists of electrical information that carries the original sound waves. *Bottom,* the unmodulated carrier wave is generated at a specific frequency in the electromagnetic spectrum.

Top, **AM Broadcasting.** The electronic signal can be superimposed onto the carrier wave by changing or *modulating the amplitude* of the carrier wave. (The dotted line indicates the original electronic signal.)

Bottom, **FM Broadcasting.** The electronic information also can be combined with the electromagnetic wave by varying or *modulating the frequency* of the carrier wave. Where the original electronic signal is strongest (indicated by the pattern of the dotted lines), the frequencies are relatively compressed.

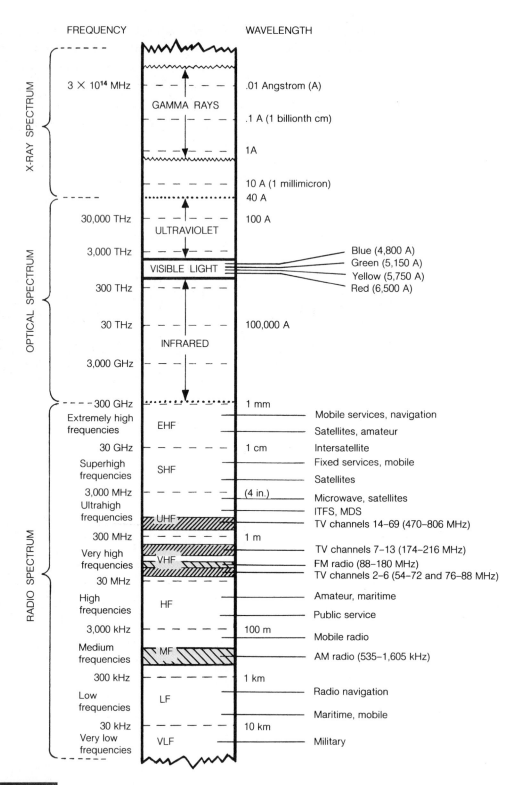

FREQUENCY   WAVELENGTH

X-RAY SPECTRUM

3×10^{14} MHz — .01 Angstrom (A)

GAMMA RAYS

.1 A (1 billionth cm)

1A

10 A (1 millimicron)

40 A

OPTICAL SPECTRUM

30,000 THz — 100 A

ULTRAVIOLET

3,000 THz — Blue (4,800 A)
VISIBLE LIGHT — Green (5,150 A)
— Yellow (5,750 A)
300 THz — Red (6,500 A)

30 THz — 100,000 A

INFRARED

3,000 GHz

RADIO SPECTRUM

300 GHz — 1 mm
Extremely high frequencies — EHF — Mobile services, navigation
— Satellites, amateur
30 GHz — 1 cm — Intersatellite
Superhigh frequencies — SHF — Fixed services, mobile
— Satellites
3,000 MHz — (4 in.) — Microwave, satellites
Ultrahigh frequencies — ITFS, MDS
UHF — TV channels 14–69 (470–806 MHz)
300 MHz — 1 m
Very high frequencies — TV channels 7–13 (174–216 MHz)
VHF — FM radio (88–180 MHz)
30 MHz — TV channels 2–6 (54–72 and 76–88 MHz)
High frequencies — HF — Amateur, maritime
— Public service
3,000 kHz — 100 m — Mobile radio
Medium frequencies — MF — AM radio (535–1,605 kHz)
300 kHz — 1 km
Low frequencies — LF — Radio navigation
— Maritime, mobile
30 kHz — 10 km
Very low frequencies — VLF — Military

Figure A.3

The electromagnetic spectrum. The entire electromagnetic spectrum includes waves that range from infinitesimally short X-rays measured in angstroms (1 angstrom equals 1 ten-millionth of a millimeter) to radio waves that vary in length from 1 millimeter to several miles. Radio and television broadcast services occupy only a very small portion of the radio spectrum. Most of the electromagnetic space is assigned to hundreds of various services—military, navigational, satellite, data transmission, cellular radio, amateur (ham) radio, cable TV distribution, fire and police services, CB radio, microwaves, short wave, mobile paging, and on and on.

Appendix B

The Overtone Series

I n the audio chapters of this text, we explained in rather simple terms the process whereby the waveform of natural sound, known as pressure waves, is transformed for broadcasting purposes into the very different electromagnetic energy wave. The production use of microphones, speakers, and other audio equipment depends largely upon a good understanding of the qualities of sound itself. The water wave analogy used in Appendix A is of considerable help in examining these qualities.

The factor that distinguishes the tone of middle C on a piano from its higher neighbor, D, is its *frequency*. Whether it is the string on a violin, the reed on a clarinet, or the vocal cords of the human voice, each instrument has an element that is able to vibrate at varying rates of cycles per second. The relative size of the vibration is the measure of amplitude. If more force in terms of air pressure is applied to the reed, the vibration is bigger and the tone therefore is louder. The frequency, however, does not change. The pitch of the note stays the same—until the apparatus producing the tone (the clarinet's column of air or a violin string) is altered in shape or length to change the frequency of the vibration.

The *velocity*, or traveling speed, of a sound wave is relative to the density of the form of matter within which it moves. In the air, altitude and temperature can affect this speed. In fairly average conditions, the velocity of sound is 1,120 feet per second. With the increased density of water, the speed is 4,700 feet per second. In solid steel, for example, the velocity is sixteen times that which occurs in the air. Such velocities are a very minor consideration in broadcasting.

Our primary consideration is the effect of a vibrating instrument upon the molecules of the air. Let us take the example of a middle C tone struck on a piano. Actually, three middle C strings are set in motion when struck by the hammer, but let us follow just the action of one. The string is set in motion at the rate of 256 cycles per second. Each oscillation presses against the molecules of the air and creates a moving pressure wave. When 256 of these pressure waves strike the ear every second, we hear its frequency as being the same tone as a middle C on a piano. (See figure B.1.)

This simple example of the back-and-forth movement of the string is not a complete description of what is happening to the agitated string. Actually, a vibrating string further subdivides itself into smaller vibrating lengths that produce additional pitches or *overtones* or *harmonics* at higher frequencies. The main tone we hear is called the *fundamental tone*. As an example, we shall move two octaves down the piano keyboard to the low C that is written on the second

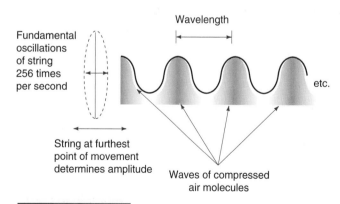

Figure B.1

Sound pressure waves.

line below the musical staff. Being a low fundamental tone, it vibrates at a frequency of only sixty-four times a second. (See figure B.2.)

In addition to this main vibration of the string between its two endpoints, a series of smaller subdivisions occurs, each of which produces its own tone. The first subdivision divides the string in half and produces the first overtone. (See figure B.3.) Each subsequent subdivision separates the vibrating string into quarters, eighths, sixteenths, and so forth. (See figure B.4.)

The series of succeeding overtones are of far less intensity or loudness than the fundamental tone. Only the most discriminating ear even hears them as separate notes. Generally speaking, the lower overtones predominate, with the higher frequencies becoming almost inaudible. It is the resonating quality of each type of instrument that determines the presence or absence of overtones. The fundamental tone of A, at 440 cycles per second, on a violin will resonate and thereby reflect certain overtone frequencies better than others in the series as a result of the very design of the instrument. A metal flute playing the identical tone will resonate an entirely different series of overtones. It is this differing profile of selected overtones from among the entire series that determines the distinctive tonal quality of an instrument. The electronic synthesizer artificially creates tones closely resembling real instruments by manipulating the overtone series. In the same manner, it can create tonal effects previously unattainable on conventional instruments.

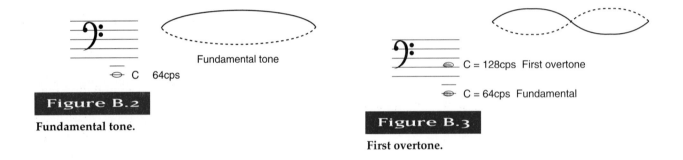

Figure B.2

Fundamental tone.

Figure B.3

First overtone.

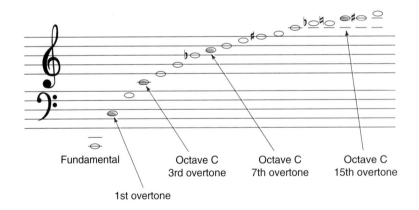

Figure B.4

Overtone series.

Appendix C

Hand and Arm Signals

 n a production situation, the hand and arm signals of the stage manager are simply a visual extension of the director's commands. Most of these gestures were developed during the early days of radio. A few have been altered somewhat for use in television production. The following examples (see figure C.1) show the signals most generally in use today.

CUE		MEANING	DESCRIPTION
STAND BY		Ready to start show Ready to record Quiet on the set	Stage Manager raises hand in air, with fingers pointing upward
YOU'RE ON TAKE YOUR CUE	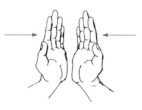	Start talking Talent is on the air	Points to performer or live camera
GET CLOSER TOGETHER	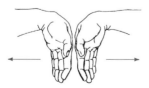	Talent, performers or reporters too far apart Get closer together Get closer to object of interest	Stage Manager plays an invisible accordian, bringing palms together repeatedly
GET FARTHER APART		Talent too close together	Stage Manager moves hands together, back to back, then spreads them sharply apart

Figure C.1

Television hand signals.

CUE	MEANING	DESCRIPTION
TALK TO THIS CAMERA CAMERA CHANGE 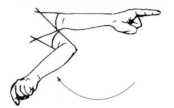	Changing cameras	Stage Manager swings hands through a wide arc from camera that is on the air to the camera that will be on the air
STRETCH IT OUT SLOW DOWN 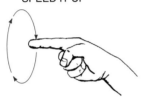	Talking too fast	Move hands as if pulling taffy apart or stretching rubber bands
SPEED IT UP 	Talking too slow Running out of time	Move forefinger in circles
O.K. ALL IS WELL YOUR POSITION IS FINE 	Well done Stay right there	Foam an "O" with thumb and forefinger with other three fingers raised

Figure C.1—Continued

FIVE MINUTES TO GO
TWO MINUTES TO GO
ONE MINUTE TO GO

Time cues to end of show

Raise hand with corresponding number of fingers spread apart or raise flash cards

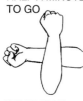

HALF A MINUTE TO GO

Time to end of segment or end of show

Cross forefingers or forearms at midpoint

WRAP IT UP

10 seconds left
Come to a conclusion

Rocking or shaking of clenched fist

CUT
FINISH
OFF THE AIR

Segment or show is over

Stage Manager slashes own throat with fore-finger or edge of hand

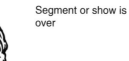

Figure C.1—Continued

Appendix D

Production Projects

Class Audio Production Project

COPY: "INTEGRATED SOUND CORPORATION" COMMERCIAL

MUSIC: UP FULL, 10 SECONDS AND UNDER.

ANNC. #1: THE INTEGRATED SOUND CORPORATION IS PLEASED TO PRESENT ITS HOME STUDIO SOUND SYSTEM, FEATURING A CD PLAYER, DIGITAL TUNER, TURNTABLE, AND CASSETTE DECK, ALL HEARD ON SPEAKERS WITH 120 WATTS OF POWER FOR EACH STEREO CHANNEL. THESE COMPONENTS FEATURE A REMOTE CONTROL OPTION FOR YOUR CONVENIENCE.

MUSIC: UP FULL, 5 SECONDS AND UNDER.

ANNC. #2: DO YOUR OWN HIGH QUALITY DUBBING TO CASSETTE FROM RADIO, CD, OR THE TWO SPEED TURNTABLE. THE FIVE-BAND GRAPHIC EQUALIZER LETS YOU SHAPE THE SOUND TO YOUR TASTE. SPEAKERS EACH HAVE A 12-INCH WOOFER, A 5-INCH MIDRANGE AND A 3-INCH TWEETER.

MUSIC: UP FULL, 5 SECONDS AND UNDER.

ANNC. #1: THE HOME STUDIO SOUND SYSTEM REPRODUCES FREQUENCIES AS LOW AS 20 CYCLES PER SECOND WITH A HIGH END OF 20,000 CYCLES PER SECOND. THIS IS SLIGHTLY GREATER THAN THE RANGE OF HUMAN HEARING. THE RESULT IS A LIFELIKE "OPEN" QUALITY THAT FILLS THE ROOM WITH A SOUND OF UNEQUALLED FIDELITY AND CLARITY.

VIDEO	AUDIO

MUSIC: UP FULL, 5 SECONDS AND UNDER.

ANNC. #2: OTHER FEATURES INCLUDE DIGITAL TUNING THAT LOCKS ANY SELECTED FREQUENCY

TO A PRECISE QUARTZ-CRYSTAL REFERENCE, ELIMINATING DRIFT IN ANY OF THE

TEN AM AND TWELVE FM PRESET STATIONS. THE <u>HOME STUDIO</u> MULTIPLE

FACILITIES UNIT COMES IN EBONY, LIGHT OAK AND MAHOGANY FINISHES. SEE

YOUR <u>INTEGRATED SOUND</u> DEALER TODAY TO EXPERIENCE THE <u>HOME STUDIO</u> FOR

YOURSELF.

MUSIC: UP FULL, 5 SECONDS AND OUT.

 Discussion Program
Opening and Closing Format

VIDEO	AUDIO

**WIDE
ESTAB.
SHOT
CAM 2
CG: TITLE,
KEYED OVER
CAMERA 2**

<u>MUSIC:</u> ESTABLISH 5 SECONDS AND UNDER

<u>ANNC:</u> "Frame of Reference," an information service program designed to explore the multifaceted issues that affect us, both as individuals and as members of an increasingly complex society. Here with our guests is the "Frame of Reference" moderator,_____.

<u>MUSIC:</u> OUT

MCU, CAM 1 <u>MODERATOR:</u> Our area of examination today is _____.
To help us in gaining a greater understanding of the problems that are involved in this issue are three people who hold somewhat differing views on the solutions to those problems. Seated next

CU CAM 3 to me is _____ from _____.

VIDEO	AUDIO

CU CAM 2 Our second guest is _____ who

represents _____.

CAM 3 Our final guest, who is from _____, is _____.

WIDE SHOT As a way of establishing the background to today's issue, I would

like to address my first question to _____.

(BODY OF PROGRAM TO CONCLUSION OF DISCUSSION)

CU MODER-
ATOR
CAM 1 MODERATOR: With that last point we must, for now conclude our

discussion of _____. The issue is a large one and

our program time is, unfortunately, limited. I would like to thank our

guests _____, _____, and

_____ for joining us today and for measurably

adding to our collective knowledge of this controversial issue.

This is _____. Good-bye until next week.

EXTREME MUSIC: ESTABLISH 5 SECONDS AND UNDER
WIDE SHOT
CAM 2
KEY ANNC: As a program, "Frame of Reference" does not attempt to
CREDITS
establish any final solutions to the problems under discussion. Our goal

is that of presenting well-informed opinion leaders to our viewing

public so that each individual can come to his or her own conclusions.

Next week our "Frame of Reference" will encompass the matter of

_____. Be sure to join us then.

FADE TO MUSIC: FADE OUT
BLACK

D.3 Script For Full-Facilities Production Exercise

VIDEO	AUDIO
CG FRAME OF REFERENCE	MUSIC: ESTABLISH 3 SECONDS AND UNDER BOOTH ANNC: SHOULD THE UNITED STATES GOVERNMENT BAN SALE AND MANUFACTURE OF PESTICIDES FOR EXPORT THAT ARE BANNED IN THIS COUNTRY? KENNETH ANDERSON IS JOINED BY EXPERTS ON BOTH SIDES OF THIS IMPORTANT QUESTION ON "FRAME OF REFERENCE," SATURDAY AFTERNOON AT FOUR O'CLOCK ON KCSU-TV.
PUBLIC SERV. VCR: 30	SOUND ON TAPE
STUDIO NEWS ANNOUNCER	ANNC: Tonight on the six o'clock news, we have the latest statement by the president on the new crisis in the Middle East. . . . A report from Washington on new plans for the homeless. . . . Another aftershock hits quake-prone southern California . . . and Sportscaster Stan Dilbeck has a report on the Matadors and their chances for a winning season.
STUDIO PROMO ANNOUNCER COMPUTER GRAPHIC, JOHNSON	ANNC: Tonight at nine o'clock our program series, "The Magnificent Burden" presents an account of the triumphs and defeats of Lyndon B. Johnson. As a man forced to assume power in a time of crisis, he was often admired and criticized for the manner in which he took over the responsibilities of leadership. Many of his proposed social reforms were diminished by the demands of a war that seemingly could not be ended

VIDEO	AUDIO

SECOND GRAPHIC, TIME PROMO ANNOUNCER <u>ANNC</u>: Coming up in just a moment, we have something in a lighter vein on "Campus Rock and Country." Host Charlie "Red" Stewart presents the Grass Valley Boys singing "It's Pure Pleasure," Bonnie Street does her version of "The Sadness of My Life," and that new group, The Electric Car, performs their hit, "Turn on the Lights Again."

STATION ID They get it all together on KCSU-TV here on campus channel 42.

VCR <u>SOUND ON TAPE</u>

Dramatic Production "It's a Date"

In blocking out any studio production that involves considerable movement of people to various parts of the studio, a storyboard (see figure D.1) can be immensely important. This is especially true of any dramatic presentation. The storyboard presented shows the framing of the main shots of the dramatic sequence as the actors assume new positions in relation to each other. A number of other shots should also be planned to adequately follow the flow of conversation.

1	2	3	4	5	6	7
CAMERA ① LONGSHOT HARRY ON COUCH, NANCY ENTERING	CAMERA ② CLOSEUP HARRY ON COUCH	CAMERA ① CLOSEUP NANCY AT FIREPLACE	CAMERA ③ MEDIUM SHOT HARRY ON COUCH, NANCY WALKING UP BESIDE HIM	CAMERA ① LONGSHOT KIM ENTERING ROOM	CAMERA ③ CLOSEUP KIM	CAMERA ③ TWO SHOT KIM & NANCY

8	9	10	11	12	13	14
CAMERA ② WIDE SHOT HARRY, NANCY & KIM	CAMERA ③ MED SHOT HARRY & NANCY AT DOOR	CAMERA ① MED SHOT DEREK JUMPING ON COUCH	CAMERA ③ TWO SHOT HARRY & NANCY ON COUCH	CAMERA ① MED. CLOSEUP DEREK ON COUCH.	CAMERA ② WIDE SHOT HARRY, NANCY & DEREK KIM ENTERING	CAMERA ① MED SHOT DEREK JUMPING OVER COUCH

15	16	17	18	19	20	21
CAMERA ③ CLOSEUP NANCY	CAMERA ① MEDIUM TWO SHOT KIM & DEREK	CAMERA ② WIDE SHOT HARRY, NANCY, KIM & DEREK EXIT	CAMERA ③ MED SHOT NANCY AT DOOR	CAMERA ① CLOSEUP HARDY	CAMERA ② TIGHT TWO SHOT HARRY & NANCY	IT'S A DATE VTR CREDITS

Storyboard for "It's a Date."

HARRY: (TALKING TO NANCY, WHO IS OFFSTAGE) I see where old Harold Osgood is fighting with the university again.

NANCY: (ENTERING FROM DOOR, CENTER) What, dear?

HARRY: Councilman Osgood objects to the fact that taxpayers' money is being spent on a college course called "The Crisis in Human Sexuality." He says that it's part of a plot to destroy the morals of American youth.

NANCY: (WALKS TO FIREPLACE) Oh, it's probably just one of those courses that teach people how to get along with one another.

HARRY: (SARCASTICALLY) YEAH, I'll bet it is. I can just imagine how they're telling them to get along.

NANCY: (WALKING TO SIDE OF COUCH) Oh, Harry, it's not that. Those kind of classes just help people to establish their personal identity . . . you know, who they really are.

HARRY: Well, when I was in college no professor had to tell me who I really was.

NANCY: I remember very well what kind of a guy you were. (KIDDING) You were a big hunk, that's what you were.

HARRY: (SMILING) Oh, come on, Nancy, so I was cool. That's all . . . no big deal.

VIDEO	AUDIO

NANCY: (SITTING NEXT TO HIM) Well, it just might have done <u>you</u> some good to have taken one of those courses. Things are different now with men and women, Harry. We're not living in the 1950s.

HARRY: Yeah, a lot of good it's done . . . a bunch of so-called liberated females running around. . . .

NANCY: (INTERRUPTING) Harry, they don't run around. They do a lot of constructive things. Why only last week. . . .

KIM: (INTERRUPTING FROM OFFSTAGE) Daddy, what time is it? (ENTERING SOMEWHAT BREATHLESSLY) Derek will be here any minute.

HARRY: (STERN BUT FATHERLY) It's seven twenty-five, and who is Derek?

KIM: He's only this really neat guy, that's all. Can't you just <u>chill out</u>, Daddy?

NANCY: Kim, you know that your father always thinks of your dates as being direct descendants of someone out of <u>The Night of The Living Dead</u>.

KIM: Well he's not. He's really nice. He writes on the school newspaper and he's also very into video.

HARRY: Well, if he's somehow made you suddenly aware of the discipline of time, he can't be all bad.

KIM: Well, he's very . . . you know, intellectual. He knows <u>all</u> about music and things.

VIDEO	AUDIO

HARRY: Yeah, I can imagine. I remember that football player friend of yours. From the way he carried on a conversation you felt that his IQ number was about the same as his coat size.

VTR INSERT   MUSIC: HEAVY METAL STYLE AS IF FROM OUTSIDE.

OFF-ROAD   SFX: SQUEALING TIRES COMING TO A STOP.

VEHICLE

PARKS

HARRY: (CONTINUING) Yeah, well at our school football players . . . say, what's that noise?

KIM: Oh, that must be Derek. Will you go to the door? I'm not quite ready yet! (EXITS)

NANCY: Well, we should be thankful that Derek at least comes to the door . . . not like the boy who sat in the driveway and honked. (WALKS TO DOOR)

(HARRY PUTS DOWN THE NEWSPAPER AND SLOWLY STANDS UP SHAKING HIS HEAD.)

NANCY: (OPENING DOOR) Hello, I'm Kim's mother. You must be Derek. Won't you come in? She will be right out. Harry, this is Kim's friend, Derek. I'm afraid that Kim hasn't told us your last name.

DEREK: Uh, Derek's O.K. . . . or, Rick.

(THERE IS AN AWKWARD 3-SECOND PAUSE WHILE ALL TRY TO THINK OF SOMETHING TO SAY.)

NANCY: Well, it's so nice to meet . . . . . .

HARRY: (OVER NANCY'S LINE) Is that coming from your car?

DEREK: That's my van, man, it sleeps two.

(HARRY STARTS TO SAY SOMETHING, THINKS BETTER OF IT, AND QUICKLY TRIES

TO COVER HIS STARTLED EXPRESSION. DEREK WALKS OVER TO CAMERA RIGHT COUCH

AND JUMPS OVER THE BACK TO SIT DOWN.)

DEREK: (CONTINUING) Like, I do a lot of camping. It's really great with

my tape deck out in the woods.

HARRY: (STRAIGHT, BUT WITH A TOUCH OF SARCASM AS HE AND NANCY SIT DOWN)

Yes, I guess you could really get back to nature.

(NANCY GIVES HIS ARM A WARNING SQUEEZE.)

DEREK: That's Wretched Yellow playing "Let's Boogie Till 1999." It's

their big hit. Great guitar. (HE BRIEFLY PANTOMIMES A

GUITAR PLAYER.)

NANCY: Kim tells us that you write for the school newspaper.

DEREK: Yeah, like I write a column called "Makin' It On Disc." They

wanted me to call it "Pickin' the Platters," but I thought it sounded

kinda' corny.

HARRY: You're right, it just doesn't have the same ring to it.

(NANCY GIVES HARRY ANOTHER WARNING SQUEEZE.)

DEREK: What do you do, Mr. Olmstead?

HARRY: Well, I . . . uh . . . I'm a loan officer at First Federal.

DEREK: Oh yeah, Kim told me. Well, I guess everybody has to do something.

HARRY: (REACTING) It may seem sort of quaint, but in today's society. . . .

KIM: (INTERRUPTING AS SHE ENTERS FROM CAMERA LEFT) Hi, Derek. (SHE CROSSES TO HIM AS HE STANDS.) I just love your jacket. It's really neat. Hey, we better go.

NANCY: Wait a minute. Where are you two going?

KIM: To the movies. We can either see a musical, "The Monster on Lead Guitar," or "My Secret Swedish Summer." They say it's a beautiful, artistic movie about this couple in love. . . .

HARRY: I don't think I want to hear . . . I can already guess.

NANCY: Isn't there something else playing?

DEREK: Yeah, but they're just like what's on television. Kim, let's go to the monster movie. They say that Lulu Bash is fantastic in the death scenes. She does karate moves and, like you know, plays the love theme from the movie on her guitar.

KIM: Oh Wow!! Well, we better go. See you later. (EXITING) Everybody at school has seen it by now. We just have to go.

NANCY: Don't be too late, dear.

KIM: I WON'T. (OFFSTAGE) Bye-bye.

(WHEN THEY ARE GONE, THERE IS A PAUSE AS NANCY AND HARRY LOOK AT EACH

OTHER.)

HARRY: (LAUGHING RUEFULLY) Well, what do you think?

NANCY: Oh, he's alright, Harry. He's just at that age. (SHE SITS NEXT TO

HIM.)

HARRY: I guess you're right. I hope so anyway. Say . . . how would you

like to sneak off and see "The Monster On Lead Guitar"?

NANCY: (LAUGHING) How about something really wild, like, "My Secret

Swedish Summer"? (SHE GIVES HIM A HUG.)

MUSIC: BRIEFLY FADE ROCK MUSIC UP FULL AND OUT.

(END)

Field Production Exercise: "The Stolen Item"

This is a generic script—the specifics are to be filled in by the students undertaking the production. The item to be stolen can be anything—a book, a teddy bear, a ball, a girlfriend. Obviously, the dialogue can be changed, and extra dialogue can be added. The basic shot structure should remain the same, because it presents a number of common production problems related to continuity, shooting angles, and pacing. The shots, however, will not be taped in the order listed. The order given is the sequence for the final edited product.

"THE STOLEN ITEM"

EXT. SOMEWHERE—DAY (SCENE 1)

1. LS establishing that the MAIN CHARACTER is doing something with an object.

2. MS of main character continuing to do something with the object.

3. CU of object the main character is working with.

4. MS as main character picks up his belongings, including the item, and exits screen left. The camera follows part of the way with a pan and then stops and allows the main character to exit the frame.

EXT. MAIN LOCATION—DAY (SCENE 2)

5. LS as the main character enters the frame, sits down, and places his belongings, including the item, near him.

6. CU of the item.

7. MCU of the main character as he becomes preoccupied with something.

8. CU of the THIEF looking at the item from behind some cover.

9. CU of the item from the thief's point of view.

10. CU of the thief as he moves toward the item and out of frame.

11. MS (reaction shot, cut-away) of the main character's FRIEND approaching and seeing what is happening and reacting in a startled manner.

12. MS of the thief stealing the item and sneaking off to the right.

13. MS of the friend running toward the main character, alarmed. The friend goes out of frame.

14. MS of the thief running away with the item.

15. Re-establishing shot of the friend joining the main character who stands up.

16. CU (over the shoulder) of the friend:

                            FRIEND

              A thief just stole your item.

17. CU (reverse over the shoulder) of the main character appearing confused and then understanding:

                        MAIN CHARACTER

          What? Oh, no! Someone stole my item.

18. Re-establishing shot as the main character and his friend run out of frame after the thief.

Bibliography

Adams, Michael H. *Single-Camera Video.* Dubuque, IA: Wm. C. Brown, 1992.

Alten, Stanley R. *Audio in Media*, 4th ed. Belmont, CA: Wadsworth, 1994.

Amyes, Tim. *The Technique of Audio Post-Production in Video and Film.* Stoneham, MA: Focal Press, 1990.

Apple Computer. *Multimedia Demystified.* New York: Random House Electronic Publishing, 1994.

Armer, Alan A. *Directing Television and Film.* Belmont, CA: Wadsworth, 1990.

Armer, Alan A. *Writing the Screenplay: TV and Film*, 2nd ed. Belmont, CA: Wadsworth, 1993.

Brown, Blain. *Motion Picture and Video Lighting.* Stoneham, MA: Focal Press, 1993.

Buzzell, Linda. *How to Make It in Hollywood.* New York: Harper Perennial, 1992.

Carlin, Dan, Sr. *Music in Film and Video Productions.* Stoneham, MA: Focal Press, 1991.

Compesi, Ronald J. and Ronald E. Sherriffs. *Video Field Production and Editing*, 3rd ed. Boston: Allyn and Bacon, 1994.

Di Zazzo, Ray. *Corporate Scriptwriting.* Stoneham, MA: Focal Press, 1992.

Di Zazzo, Ray. *Directing Corporate Video.* Stoneham, MA: Focal Press, 1993.

Dyas, Ronald D. *Screenwriting for Television and Film.* Madison, WI: Brown & Benchmark, 1993.

Eargle, John M. *Music, Sound, and Technology.* New York: Van Nostrand Reinhold, 1995.

Farris, Linda Guess. *Television Careers: A Guide to Breaking and Entering.* Fairfax, CA: Buy the Book Enterprises, 1995.

Ferncase, Richard K. *Film and Video Lighting: Terms and Concepts.* Stoneham, MA: Focal Press, 1994.

Gates, Richard. *Production Management for Film and Video.* Newton, MA: Focal Press, 1995.

Graham, Ian S. *HTML Sourcebook.* New York: John Wiley & Sons, 1995.

Grant, August E. *Communication Technology Update.* Boston: Butterworth-Heinemann, 1994.

Gross, Lynne S. *The Internship Experience.* Prospect Heights, IL: Waveland Press, 1993.

Gross, Lynne S., and David E. Reese. *Radio Production Worktext: Studio and Equipment*, 2nd ed. Stoneham, MA: Focal Press, 1993.

Gross, Lynne S., and Larry W. Ward. *Electronic Moviemaking*, 3rd ed. Belmont, CA: Wadsworth, 1997.

Hofstetter, Fred T. *Multimedia Literacy.* New York: McGraw-Hill, 1995.

Hyde, Stuart W. *Television and Radio Announcing*, 7th ed. Boston: Houghton Mifflin, 1995.

Kehoe, Vincent J.R. *The Technique of the Professional Make-Up Artist.* Stoneham, MA: Focal Press, 1995.

Kristof, Ray, and Amy Satran. *Interactivity by Design: Creating and Communicating with New Media.* Mountain View, CA: Adobe Press, 1995.

Maier, Robert G. *Location Scouting and Management Handbook.* Newton, MA: Focal Press, 1994.

Mazda, F. F. *Telecommunications Engineer's Reference Book.* Boston: Focal Press, 1993.

Millerson, Gerald. *Technique of Lighting for Television and Film.* Stoneham, MA: Focal Press, 1991.

O'Donnell, Lewis B., Philip Benoit, and Carl Hausman. *Modern Radio Production*, 4th ed. Belmont, CA: Wadsworth, 1996.

Ohanian, Thomas A. *Digital Nonlinear Editing.* Stoneham, MA: Focal Press, 1992.

Olson, Robert. *Art Direction for Film and Video.* Newton, MA: Focal Press, 1993.

Richards, Ron. *Director's Method for Film and Television.* Stoneham, MA: Focal Press, 1992.

Semrau, Penelope, and Barbara A. Boyer. *Using Interactive Video in Education.* Boston: Allyn and Bacon, 1994.

Stuxal, John G. *The Age of Electronic Messages.* New York: McGraw-Hill, 1990.

Summitt, Paul M., and Mary J. Summitt. *Creating Cool #D Web Worlds with VRML.* Foster City, CA: IDG Books Worldwide, 1995.

Tucker, Patrick. *How to Act for the Camera.* New York: Routledge Press, 1993.

Vane, Edwin T., and Lynne S. Gross. *Programming for TV, Radio, and Cable.* Boston: Focal Press, 1994.

Viera, Dave. *Lighting for Film and Electronic Cinematography.* Belmont, CA: Wadsworth, 1993.

Watkinson, John. *The Art of Digital Audio.* Stoneham, MA: Focal Press, 1992.

Watkinson, John. *An Introduction to Digital Video.* Newton, MA: Focal Press, 1994.

Whittaker, Ron. *Video Field Production*, 2nd ed. Mountain View, CA: Mayfield, 1996.

Wurtzel, Alan, and John Rosenbaum. *Television Production*, 4th ed. New York: McGraw-Hill, 1995.

Zettl, Herbert. *Sight-Sound-Motion: Applied Media Aesthetics.* Belmont, CA: Wadsworth, 1990.

Zettl, Herbert. *Television Production Handbook*, 6th ed. Belmont, CA: Wadsworth, 1997.

Glossary

A

A/B roll editing A videotape editing procedure that uses two source tapes on separate machines. The availability of two simultaneous picture sources allows for dissolves, wipes, and similar transitions through a switcher/controller. In news and similar productions, the primary roll is designated the "A" roll in that it contains interviews and basic expositional material. The "B" roll is a collection of *actuality* visuals, such as fire footage, that can be shown as conversations and interviews continue.

above-the-line Costs for creative and performing personnel (such as the producer, writer, director, musicians, and actors).

acquisition mode The means used to gather material before it is edited; examples of acquisition modes are film, Hi8, and Betacam.

actors TV talent who perform as someone other than themselves.

adapter plugs Connectors that convert from one type of connector to another (e.g. from phone to RCA).

adaptive presentations Interactive media presentations whose content can change in response to information input by the user.

additive A color system that combines two colored lights to form a third.

address system Those editing components with their numerical readout, based on either the SMPTE time code or upon the vertical sync pulse on the control track, that allow for the precise location of each recorded picture on a given reel of videotape.

AD See *associate director.*

ADR See *automatic dialogue replacement.*

ADT See *advanced television.*

advanced television A term for television that will have better resolution than the present NTSC system.

AFM See *audio frequency modulation.*

AGC See *automatic gain control.*

agents People who find work for actors, writers, and others engaged in creative aspects of the media business.

air monitor 1) In video, the TV set that shows what has been transmitted or what is the output of the videotape recorder. 2) In audio, the speaker that allows an operator to hear the transmitted broadcast signal.

amplify To magnify an audio or video electrical signal for mixing, distribution, and transducing purposes.

analog A process in which the electromagnetic output varies as a continuous function of the input creating degradation as the signal is reproduced.

animation A sequence of graphics that rapidly cycles to create the illusion of motion.

aperture The opening in the camera lens that determines how much light will pass through.

arc A combination trucking, panning, and dollying movement in which the camera is moved in a semi-circle around a subject while the camera head is always pointed toward the subject.

arm move To move the boom arm of a crane left or right.

art director A person who deals with the look of sets and other artistic aspects of a television program.

aspect ratio The ratio of the height of a television screen to its width.

assemble An editing mode where various segments are added together sequentially in the final

program order; the control track of the source tape is transferred along with audio and video information to the edit tape.

assistant director See *associate director.*

assistant producer See *associate producer.*

associate director The person who keeps track of timing for a program and assists the director in other ways.

associate producer A person who helps the producer with any of a number of production chores.

asymmetrical balance An informal arrangement in which an important object placed close to the center of the picture is balanced by a lightweight object some distance from the center.

ATV See *advanced television.*

audio console The piece of equipment that is used to gather, mix, and amplify sounds and send them on to their next destination.

audio control booth The room where all audio signals are controlled and mixed.

audio frequency modulation A diagonal method of recording audio on a videotape in which the sound cannot be separated from video for editing; also called hi-fi.

audio operator A person who sets mics in a studio or location setting and/or operates the audio console.

audio track The portion of a videotape or audio tape that holds the sound information.

auto key A special type of key effect in which one source is used to establish the external shape of the key.

auto transition rate The control on a switcher that is used to determine how fast a switch from one picture to another takes place.

automatic dialogue replacement Rerecording dialogue for a production after the principal shooting is over because, for some reason, it was not recorded properly when it was shot.

automatic gain control   An internal control device, for either audio or video signals, that automatically increases or decreases (as needed) the strength of the incoming sound or picture in order to maintain optimum signal strength.

automatic iris control   A setting on a lens that continuously alters the diaphragm to create the best exposure possible.

automatic transition   A feature on many switchers that allows dissolves, wipes, and other transitions to take place for predetermined durations without the use of the fader levers.

auxiliary send   A special audio feed that goes to an earphone worn by a performer in the studio so that he or she can hear the program signal.

axis of action   An imaginary line that extends the path in which a character or object is moving, with the result that if one camera is on one side of the line and another is on the other side, cutting from one camera to another will make the person or object appear to change direction.

axis of conversation   An imaginary line that connects two persons talking to each other with the result that, if one camera is on one side of the line and another is on the other side, cutting from one camera to another will make the person appear to change position.

```
                 B
```

back light   A highly directional light coming from above and behind a subject, adding highlights, shape, and separation from the background.

background light   General lighting on the set behind the talent.

backplate   The part of a condenser mic that is electrically charged.

backtime   The process of timing a piece of audio and/or video so that it can be started at a precise time and end at the properly appointed time.

balance   In audio, the achievement of the correct ratio among several sound sources; in video, a picture composition where the various portions of the screen appear to have equal weight.

balanced line   Audio cables that have three wires, one for positive, one for negative, and one for ground.

ballast   An attachment to an HMI light that protects it from surges in power.

bandwidth   The number of frequencies within given limits that are occupied by a particular transmission.

bank   A row of buttons representing various video inputs on the switcher.

barn doors   Movable metal shutters, attached to the front of a lighting instrument, that are used to limit the area of the projected light.

batch capture   A process through which selected segments of video are digitized onto a hard drive.

batten   A counterweighted lighting grid that can be raised and lowered so that lights can be worked on near the studio floor.

beam splitter   The optical device in a color camera, consisting of a prism and mirrors, that separates the incoming visual image into the primary colors of blue, red, and green.

below-the-line   Costs for technical and production personnel and for equipment, facilities, and services.

Betacam   A broadcast quality ½-inch component camcorder manufactured by Sony.

bit   One on or off digital pulse.

bit rate reduction   Limiting the amount of digital information that must be transmitted by transmitting only that which changes from one element, such as a video frame, to another.

black   Technically, a synchronized video signal that contains no picture information—a blank screen.

blanking pulse   A signal that momentarily turns off the scanning beam in a camera tube or TV set so that the beam can retrace its path before starting to scan another line.

blocking   Careful planning and coordinating of all movement and positioning of talent and production equipment.

blocking diagrams   Drawings made by directors to help them visualize where actors and cameras should be placed.

body time   The length of a program not including closing credits and titles.

boom   1) Any device consisting of a movable base, an adjustable stand, and a long arm for suspending a microphone above and in front of a performer. 2) An arm of a crane that can be used to move a camera up and down or sideways. 3) To move a camera with a boom arm.

breakdown sheets   Different pieces of paper or computer screens that list what will be needed for each shot, such as actors, props, and special effects.

brightness   An indication of where a color would fall on a scale from light (white) to dark (black).

broad   A rectangular-shaped floodlight.

browser   A program that is used to view interactive media presentations on the World Wide Web.

bus   The mixing bar that connects the buttons representing various video inputs on the switcher.

button   See *link*.

byte   A group of digital zeros and ones that have a particular meaning.

```
                 C
```

C-clamp   A metal clamp with a pivot adjustment for attaching lighting instruments to a lighting grid.

call sheet   A posted list that lets cast and crew know when and where they should report.

cam   A type of camera mounting head that consists of a flat plate that rests between the camera and the mount and enables the camera to move various directions.

camcorder   An integrated unit that contains both a camera and videotape recorder in one housing.

cameo lighting   A type of lighting where the performer is lit but the background is not.

camera   A piece of equipment that contains an imaging device that changes light into electromagnetic energy.

camera chain   The electronic camera plus associated equipment such as the sync generator and camera control unit.

camera control unit   Electronic control equipment that is used to regulate all the engineering functions, such as luminance and chrominance, of each camera.

camera mount   The support arrangement that holds the camera mounting head and the camera itself—usually a tripod, pedestal, or crane.

camera operator   The person who frames the shots for a production.

camera rehearsal   The first rehearsal where the camera operators and other technical personnel are operating their equipment.

camera-to-source distance   The space between the camera and what the camera is framing.

Cannon connector   See *XLR connector.*

capacitor   The part of a condenser mic that stores electrical energy and permits the flow of alternating current.

cardioid   A microphone that picks up sound in a heart-shaped pattern.

carrier wave   The specific range of frequencies used to carry an electronic signal from a transmitter to a receiver.

cart machine   Audio or video equipment that records or plays back material on tape that is on a continuous loop in a self-contained unit.

cartridge   An audiotape or videotape recording and/or playback tape container that holds the tape in a continuous loop on a spool.

cassette   An audiotape or videotape container that holds both the supply reel and take-up reel in a self-contained case.

casting   Deciding who will act various roles in a television program.

casting agencies   Companies that can be hired to select people for various roles in a production.

cathode-ray tube   A TV reception device in which an electronic beam can be focused to a small cross section on a luminescent screen and can then be varied in position and density to produce what appears to be a moving picture.

CCD   See *charge-coupled device.*

CCU   See *camera control unit.*

CD player   Equipment that plays back discs on which sound has been recorded digitally.

CD-ROM   Compact disc/read-only memory; a computer input device that can be read but not written to.

central processing unit   The part of a computer that calculates and stores information.

channel   1) The specific pathway used to get a signal from source to destination. 2) To move signals from one place to another.

channel fader   The part of the audio console that controls the volume for one particular input, such as one microphone.

character generator   A special electronic effects device with a typewriter-like keyboard that can produce letters and numerals directly on the television screen.

charge-coupled device   A microchip, consisting of a photodiode and transistor, that is used to pick up picture information.

cheat to camera   Having an actor face slightly toward camera rather then directly toward another actor, in order to get a better camera angle.

chroma key   A special effect whereby a special color (usually green or blue) is used as a key to determine what picture information is to be cut out of the picture with the foreground image.

chroma knob   The control on the switcher that varies the intensity of a color.

chrominance   Information pertaining to the color characteristics of a video signal.

cleats   Pieces of metal on the back of a flat that are used to join two flats together with a rope.

clip knob   A special effects generator adjustment that can set a threshold level for a particular video variable such as luminance value for a key.

clip LED indicator   A light-emitting diode that, when flashing, confirms that the audio levels on an audio console have been properly set.

close-up   A view of a subject from a relatively short distance.

coaxial cable   Standard camera and video cable with a central insulated conducting wire and a concentrically arranged outer wire.

coil   The part of a dynamic microphone that vibrates within the magnet setting up an electrical charge.

color bar generator   The part of the camera or switcher or other piece of equipment that produces the basic colors—red, blue, green, yellow, cyan, and magenta.

color bars   An electronically generated pattern of vertical color strips that can be used to standardize and calibrate the color values of all cameras and monitors.

color temperature   The relative reddish or bluish quality of a light source, as measured in degrees Kelvin.

complementary colors   Yellow, cyan, and magenta.

component   A video system that records chrominance and luminance information separately.

composite   A video system that records chrominance and luminance information together.

compression   A technique for placing more video information in less space by including only elements that change from one frame to another or by reducing the quality of what is shown.

compressor   An electronic device used to lessen the distance between the highest and lowest audio volume levels.

condenser mic   A high quality mic whose transducer consists of a diaphragm, backplate, and capacitor.

continuity   Maintaining a consistent and unobtrusive progression from shot to shot in terms of screen direction, lighting, props, and other production details.

contrast ratio   The relationship of the brightest area to the darkest area in a given camera shot, as determined by reflected light readings.

control room   The area where all video signals are mixed; the director and technical director (and other crew members) control all program elements from this location.

control room rehearsals   A rehearsal with the director seated where he/she will be calling the shots, rather than in the studio.

control track   The portion of a videotape that contains the sync information that keeps all elements in a proper timing relationship.

cookie   See *cucalorus*.

copyright   The exclusive right to a production or publication.

corner insert   A special effect with one input inserted into a specific quadrant of the picture.

cover shot   See *wide shot*.

CPU   See *central processing unit*.

crab dolly   A small studio crane that can move on tracks.

cradle   A type of camera mounting head with a curved bottom that rests on the camera mount and enables the camera to move various directions.

crane   1) A large camera mount with an extended boom arm or tongue for a camera and a seat for a camera operator, all placed on a large, four-wheeled base. 2) To move the boom arm of a crane up and down.

crop   To cut off the edges or border of a picture.

cross-key   A lighting technique that uses multiple key lights aimed onto the set from different directions.

crossed-pairs mics   See *X-Y mics*.

crossing the line   Having one camera shot come from one side of the axis of action/conversation and another camera shot come from the other side.

CU   See *close-up*.

cucalorus   A metal or wooden cutout pattern that is placed in front of a spotlight to produce a shadow effect on a scenic background.

cue   To prepare an audio or video source for a precise start at some predetermined point.

cue button   A control on an audio board that allows an operator to hear a sound without transmitting or taping it.

cue cards   Sheets of cardboard with the script written on them that are held next to the camera lens so that the talent can look at the camera and read the script.

cue channel   A separate route on an audio board through which sound can be heard but not mixed or transmitted; it is used to prepare sound before it is to be aired or taped.

cue track   The part of a video tape on which time code can be laid down.

cut   An instantaneous change from one video source to another.

cutaway   A shot of something that is not directly visible in the shot before it; used to avoid jump cuts.

cuts-only editing   Editing where various shots are butted against each other without any dissolves, wipes, or other special effects.

cyc   A large, continuous, smooth backing, usually made of cloth, that may cover two or three walls of a studio.

cycle per second   A basic unit of frequency measurement for electromagnetic and acoustic waves; now usually referred to as *hertz*.

cyclorama   See *cyc*.

D

DA   See *distribution amplifier*.

DAT   See *digital audiotape*.

daily hire   Employment by the day rather than as a full-time staff member.

dB   See *decibel*.

decibel   1) A unit of measurement of sound that compares the relative intensity of different sound sources. 2) A unit of measurement for video that relates to the output gain of the video imaging device.

defocus   A camera transition in which the picture on the on-air camera becomes fuzzy.

demodulate   To remove a broadcast signal from its carrier wave so that it can be reproduced.

depth of field   The distance between the nearest point at which objects are in focus and the farthest point at which objects are in focus.

desktop video   Editing and graphics equipment that takes up only a small amount of space and can be used in the home or office.

diaphragm   1) The vibrating element in a microphone that responds to the compressed air molecules of sound waves. 2) The adjustable mechanism that controls the size of the lens aperture.

digital   A process that uses discreet on and off steps so that individual elements of picture or sound can be controlled and material can be reproduced without degradation of the signal.

digital audiotape   Tape that gives high quality sound because it records information in numerical data bits and bytes.

digital board   A computer interface card that allows audio and video to be put in and out of a computer and manipulated in the computer.

digital player/recorder   A device that can accept digitized material and enable it to be heard and seen and duplicated.

digital video effects   Special effects accomplished through digital technology whereby discrete elements of the video can be manipulated, resulting in pictures that change size, move across the screen, and so forth.

digitizing   Converting analog information to digital information.

digitizing pen   A hand-held pen-shaped electronic instrument used to draw onto a tablet that translates the image into a computer.

dimmer board   A lighting control unit, operated on the same principle as a rheostat, that determines the intensity of a light by controlling the amount of electric current flowing to the instrument.

dimmer circuit   One fader of a dimmer board that brings up one or several lights.

directional response   In referring to microphones, the sides from which the mic picks up sound effectively.

director The person in charge of everything that takes place in the studio or on a remote and during the editing process.

dirt skin Material used to simulate a patch of natural earth.

dissolve A simultaneous fading out of one picture while fading in to another.

distribution amplifier A power amplifier that increases signal strength as an electronic signal is traveling from one place to another.

dolly To move the camera and its mount closer to (dolly in) or farther from (dolly out) the subject.

double headset system An audio intercom system that provides two earpieces to one person so that a boom operator can hear the director in one earpiece and program audio in the other.

downstream A term used to describe any process that occurs beyond a given point in terms of signal flow; for example, the audio console is downstream of the patch bay and a downstream keyer manipulates the signal after it has left the switcher.

downstream keyer Part of a switcher used to place an image (usually credits or other words) over a picture after it has gone through all other switcher manipulations, such as setting a corner insert.

DPR See *digital player/recorder.*

dress rehearsal The final, full rehearsal before the actual production take—using all sets, props, and costumes—designed to be conducted straight through without interruption.

dry-run A session where the director and talent work together on the basic staging of a program without actually doing a full rehearsal.

dub 1) To make a copy of a tape or disc. 2) A copy of a tape or disc.

DVE See *digital video effects.*

dynamic content A characteristic of interactive media that allows a presentation to change according to a user's wishes.

dynamic mic A rugged microphone whose transducer consists of a diaphragm connected to a movable coil.

E

earphone A small audio speaker that fits in the ear.

echo Sound that has bounced off a surface once.

ECU See *extreme close-up.*

edit controller The electronic editing console that is used to operate both the source deck and edit deck and to execute edits.

edit decision list A log of all recorded segments as they will be assembled during the postproduction editing process.

edit deck The VCR onto which material is transferred from the source deck(s) during the editing process.

edited master tape The final version of a program—the tape that is edited on the record deck.

editing software Computer program material that someone can use to edit.

editor The person who assembles raw footage into a final program.

EDL See *edit decision list.*

EFP See *electronic field production.*

electromagnetic spectrum The continuous frequency range of wavelengths that includes radio waves and light waves.

electron gun The part of a television camera tube or receiver that shoots electrons to the target of the tube or the face of the TV set.

electronic field production The use of a single video camera to record any kind of program on location for later editing in the postproduction process.

electronic news gathering The use of single-camera portable equipment to record news events and other actualities.

electronic still store (ESS) A system of storing video frames in digital form, indexed for each retrieval.

ellipsoidal A spotlight with a reflecting mirror at the back of the housing that enables it to create a very directional, well-defined beam.

ELS See *extreme long shot.*

ENG See *electronic news gathering.*

equalize To emphasize, lessen, or eliminate certain audio frequencies.

ESS See *electronic still store.*

essential area The center portion of a graphics card or screen that contains all the critical information that must be seen on the receiving set.

establishing shot A long shot used at the beginning of a program or segment that relates program elements to each other and orients the audience.

event video The production of tapes dealing with special occasions, such as birthdays and weddings.

executive producer A person who oversees several TV productions.

extender A part of a lens that doubles the focal length.

external reflector A spotlight in a small housing that has no lens.

extreme close-up A shot, usually of a person, that shows less than the person's full face.

extreme long shot A shot in which the characters are so far away that they are not distinguishable as specific individuals.

F

f-stop A notation that indicates the size of the lens opening; the higher the f-stop number the smaller the opening and vice versa.

facilities request form A sheet that someone fills out in order to reserve studio and/or equipment time.

FACS See *facilities request form.*

fade The gradual bringing in or taking out of an audio or video source.

fade time control On cameras that can fade up to or from black, a control that governs the amount of time it takes the camera to get from black to full picture or vice versa.

fader 1) The audio console control that raises and lowers volume by controlling the amount of resistance going through the system. 2) On a switcher, the lever that controls the amount of video signal flowing to a specific bus.

fc See *footcandle.*

feedback 1) In audio, a high-pitched squeal that results from accidentally feeding a program monitor into a live microphone, causing an instantaneous overamplification of the system. 2) A video effect caused by re-entry of a video signal into the switcher with subsequent overamplification that can make the video appear to go to infinity.

fiber optics Glass strands through which large amounts of information can be sent.

field production Television production, usually consisting of single-camera recording and postproduction editing, that takes place outside of the studio.

field One half of a television picture, consisting of alternate scanning lines, lasting one-sixtieth of a second.

field of view The size or scope of a shot, indicating how much is encompassed.

fill light An unfocused and diffused light used to complement the key light, coming from the side opposite the key to fill in dark areas and soften the shadows.

film-style scripts Scripts that are organized by scene with description written the width of the paper and dialogue centered in the middle.

film-style shooting Taping the way movie makers have traditionally filmed by using one camera and resetting the camera and lights for each shot.

filter A glass or gelatin element mounted in front of a light or in front of a camera imaging device that compensates for changes in color temperature, or in other ways, changes the color of the light.

fishpole A small light-weight arm to which a microphone is attached, to be hand held by an audio assistant outside of the picture frame.

fixed-focal-length lens A simple lens that is one specific focal length, such as 25 mm.

flag A rectangular cloth-covered or metal frame placed in front of a lighting instrument to produce a precise shadow on one side of the light beam.

flat A standard staging unit, constructed of a wooden frame covered with cloth or hardboard, often used to represent walls of a room or the exterior of a building.

flip-flop A term to denote the action of certain switchers (with program and preset buses) that, at the conclusion of a dissolve, automatically switch the illuminated buttons on the buses to indicate that the input on the preset bus has now become the program feed.

floodlight A diffused light that covers a wide area.

floor director See *stage manager*.

floor manager See *stage manager*.

floor rehearsals Rehearsals where the director is in the studio rather than in the control room.

focal length The distance from the optical center point of a lens, when it is set at infinity, to a point where the image is in focus on an imaging device such as a CCD.

focal plane The place in a camera where the image is picked up—for example, the CCD chip, the target of a tube, or the frame of film.

focus To make an image look sharp and distinct.

follow shot A camera shot whereby the camera follows the subject, usually keeping the same distance from it.

follow spot A light of high intensity that is most commonly used to follow a performer as he or she moves around a stage area.

font A complete set of type of one style.

footcandle A unit of light measurement equivalent to the amount of light falling upon a surface 1 foot away from a standard candle.

frame One complete television picture, consisting of two fields, lasting one-thirtieth of a second.

frame-accurate editing A method of editing wherein the frame selected as the inpoint for the edit will not slip during the editing process and will actually be the inpoint of the edit; this method uses SMPTE time code.

frame synchronizer The electronic component that takes outside video sources such as satellite feeds, analyzes their sync pulses as compared with studio sync, converts the signals to a digital format, adjusts the differences, and therefore can route all signals through the same switcher.

freelancers People who work by the hour or day on one project at a time and are not employees of any particular organization.

frequency The number of oscillations per second (hertz) of an electromagnetic wave that, in the audio range, determines the pitch of the tone and, in the light range, determines color.

frequency response chart A graph that shows how well a microphone or other piece of audio electronic equipment picks up various different frequencies.

Fresnel A light with a well-defined lens; the beam width is varied as the bulb is moved toward and away from the lens.

front focus The lens focus that is obtained by zooming in tightly on a subject and then focusing.

fundamental The main frequency of a particular sound.

G

gain Volume of an audio signal or amount of amplification of a video signal.

gain knob An adjustment on the special effects generator that is used to determine the sharpness of a key.

gel A thin translucent, colored material such as gelatin or plastic that can be mounted in front of lighting instruments to produce specific color effects.

gigabytes One million groups of digital zeros and ones.

giraffe A small boom that consists of a counter-weighted arm supported by a tripod on casters.

gobo A scenic cutout unit that is positioned several feet in front of a camera to provide foreground design, depth, and framing interest.

graphics generator A computer-based electronic device designed to produce graphics and animations for television use.

graphics operator A person who creates words, drawings, and some visual effects that are incorporated within a production.

graphics tablet A pad used in conjunction with an electronic pen to enter coordinates into a computer to create drawings.

grid Pipes near the studio ceiling from which lamps are hung.

group assign switch A control on each input channel of an audio board that allows the operator to group some audio inputs together so they can be controlled separately from other audio inputs.

group master fader A volume control on an audio board that handles a subgroup of input channels before they are sent to the master fader.

guilds Organizations that set wages and working conditions that producers must adhere to for people (usually above-the-line people) that they hire.

H

hand mic A microphone that a person holds to speak or sing into.

hard drive controller A digital processor that controls the functions of access, playback, and record on digital storage disks within a computer or server.

harmonics See *overtones*.

HDTV See *high definition television*.

head 1) The mechanism that connects the camera itself to the camera mount. 2) The magnetic element in a tape recorder that rearranges iron particles on a tape so that information can be stored. 3) The beginning of a tape.

head pad Material at the beginning of a shot that is not used in the final edit, but that alows edit machines to get up to speed to make an edit.

headroom Space between the top of a subject's head and the upper edge of the camera frame.

headset The apparatus (worn over the head and consisting of an earphone and mouthpiece) that connects all production personnel on the intercom network.

helical scan A videotape recording format that lays down the video information in a slanted pattern on the tape.

hertz A basic unit of frequency measurement for electromagnetic and acoustical waves, named after Heinrich Hertz.

Hi8 A Sony 8mm tape format that is an improvement on the Video 8 format in that it uses metal particle tape and a wider luminance band.

hi-fi A diagonal method of recording audio on a videotape in which the sound cannot be separated from video for editing; also called AFM.

high definition television A television system that uses over 1,000 scanning lines resulting in a sharper picture than the NTSC system; it also involves a wider screen ratio.

high impedance A characteristic of microphones that have a great deal of opposition to the flow of alternating current through them and therefore must have short cables; they are less likely to be used in professional situations than low impedance microphones.

high-key lighting Lighting that is generally bright and even, with a low key-to-fill ratio.

HMI light A hydrogen medium-arc-length iodide lamp that is balanced for daylight and is often used outdoors as a supplement to the light from the sun.

horizontal synchronization pulse The portion of the sync signal that controls the sweep of a scanning beam from left to right.

HTML See *Hypertext Markup Language*.

hue The actual color base, such as red, green, or orange.

hypertext In interactive media, text that is designated as a link.

Hypertext Markup Language (HTML) A text-based computer language used to author interactive media presentations for the World Wide Web.

hyphenate A person who undertakes two jobs, such as producer-director or writer-director.

Hz See *Hertz*.

I

IFB See *interrupted feedback system*.

image map In interactive media, a picture that is designated as a link or series of links; different parts of a picture may trigger different links.

image sensor The part of the camera on which the picture is gathered and focused after it has gone through the lens.

impedance Opposition to the flow of an audio signal in a microphone and its cable.

incident light Light coming directly from the source of illumination.

in-house Producing a program using equipment and facilities that belong to the company desiring the production.

inpoint The precise spot on both the source tape and master tape where an edit is to begin.

input channel On an audio board, the control into which a source such as a microphone or tape recorder is plugged.

insert An editing mode where new material can be placed in previously recorded material, because only the audio and/or video material, not the control track, is transferred.

Instructional Television Fixed Service Television channels, usually used by educational institutions, in the 2,500 megahertz range that need a special receiver to be viewed.

interactive Methodology whereby the person operating a media program has control, to some extent, over the content of the presentation.

interactive multimedia video TV material that uses several media forms, such as graphics and video, and that can be manipulated by the user.

intercom A closed-circuit audio network connecting all production personnel with headsets.

interlace The process of combining two television fields into one frame by first scanning all the odd lines and then scanning all the even lines of the frame; this process has less flicker than would scanning all the lines from top to bottom in one pass.

internal key   See *self key*.

internal reflector spotlight   A bulb with a reflector unit and focusing lens built into it.

Internet   A worldwide computer network over which people can send and receive a vast amount of information.

interrupted feedback system   An audio setup that allows the talent, wearing a small earpiece, to receive instruction from the director or hear program audio.

intranet   A self-contained computer network configured to operate like a smaller version of the Internet.

inverse square law   A principle of physics that states that when the distance between a light (or an audio source) and its point of perception is cut in half, its intensity will be increased fourfold.

iris   The part of the lens that allows light to pass through.

ITFS   See *Instructional Television Fixed Service*.

J

jack   A hinged stage brace attached to the rear of a flat.

jump cutting   Taking between two cameras or editing in such a way that the connecting shots have almost identical views of the same object, and the result is that the object appears to jump slightly for no apparent reason.

K

K   See *Kelvin*.

Kelvin   The scale of measurement used to measure frequencies so that color temperature can be determined.

key   A generic term for any number of special visual effects whereby video signals from two or more sources are electronically combined in such a way that one image looks like it has been cut out and placed on top of the other image.

key light   The primary source of illumination falling upon a subject that is highly directional and produces a definite modeling or shaping effect with well-defined shadows.

key memory   A feature on a switcher that remembers the clip and gain levels that have been set for a particular key so that the next time that key is used the values will be correct.

kicker   Additional light, usually a spotlight, coming from the side and slightly to the rear of the subject.

kinescope   An old-fashioned film recording of a TV program made by adapting a film camera to record from the face of the TV tube.

kook   See *cucalorus*.

L

lapel mic   A small mic that can be clipped inside clothing or to a tie or lapel.

lavaliere   A small mic that can be worn around the neck on a cord.

LCD   See *liquid crystal display*.

LD   See *lighting director*.

lead room   Additional framing space in a camera picture on the side toward which a subject is looking or moving.

LED   See *light emitting diode*.

leko   See *ellipsoidal*.

light emitting diode   An electron tube that puts out light that is used in audio to show the amount of volume a sound has—in this way making it a high tech version of a VU meter.

light meter   A photoelectric device that measures the amount of light falling upon a specific area.

light plot   A floor plan that indicates the lighting requirements—location, type, and function of each instrument—for every staging area in the studio.

lighting director   The person who oversees the lighting of the set and makes lighting changes, if they are needed, during production.

lighting grid   A permanent arrangement of pipes suspended below the studio ceiling on which lighting instruments can be hung.

limbo lighting   A type of lighting where the performer is seen clearly, but the background appears to be vague or nondescriptive.

limiter   An electronic device used to cut off audio levels when the volume is too strong.

line   A general term for a conductor of audio and video signals. It is most often used to denote a specific level of amplification emitting from a component such as a video machine or an audio console.

line level   An audio amplification level for equipment, such as a videotape recorder or an audio tape recorder, that has already been amplified.

line monitor   See *program monitor*.

line producer   A person who is on the production set representing the producer by making sure the program finishes on time and on budget.

linear   1) A type of editing in which the material is put together from beginning to end; if changes are needed, everything after the change must be re-edited. 2) Audio tracks that run horizontally on an audio tape or videotape.

link   In interactive media, an object that—when activated by the user—triggers an event.

liquid crystal display   Chemical elements that display black or a particular color when power is applied.

location scout   Someone who looks for appropriate places to shoot a remote TV production.

logging   Writing down what is on a videotape including the content of each shot, the inpoints and outpoints, and comments about the quality of the shot.

long lens   A long focal-length lens with a narrow viewing angle; it includes relatively little in the picture and tends to compress distance.

long shot   See *wide shot*.

low impedance   A characteristic of microphones that have little opposition to the flow of alternating current through them and therefore can have long cables and be of high professional quality; low impedance mics are generally in the 150- to 350-ohm range.

low-key lighting   Lighting that is dark and shadowy with a high key-to-fill ratio.

low-Z   See *low impedance.*

LS   See *long shot.*

luminance   Information pertaining to the brightness characteristics of a video signal.

lux   A unit of light measurement equivalent to the amount of light falling upon a surface 1 meter away from a standard candle; approximately 10 footcandles.

M

M-II   A broadcast quality component camcorder manufactured by Panasonic and JVC that utilizes two chroma channels and one luminance channel.

M-S mics   A coincidental stereo mic setup that involves three microphones arranged like an inverted T.

macro   A special position on a lens that enables it to focus close-ups of small objects at short distances.

magnet   The part of a microphone that creates a field that produces an electric current.

main menu   The opening screen of an interactive media presentation.

masking plate   Part of the TV set that focuses the electrons as they strike the phosphor coating on the front of the tube.

master control room   The primary engineering control center where all video and audio signals are ultimately channeled; program input, camera controls, video recording, and transmitter distribution often are handled from this location.

master fader   The volume control on an audio board that is located after all the input channel controls and after the submaster controls.

medium shot   A view of the subject from a comfortable distance between a long shot and a close-up.

menu   In interactive media, a screen that allows a user to choose from a series of options.

microphone level   Indicates the relatively low strength of the electronic signal produced by a microphone prior to several stages of later amplification.

MIDI   See *musical instrument digital interface.*

mid-side mics   See *M-S mics.*

minus decibels   Sound levels to the left of the 0 level on a VU meter.

mix   To combine and balance two or more audio signals through an audio console or two or more video sources through a switcher.

mix bus   Audio inputs that can be controlled in such a way that several sounds can be raised and lowered in volume in relation to each other.

M-JPEG   A compression system used for motion.

moiré effect   Distracting visual vibration caused by the interaction of a narrow striped pattern and the television scanning lines.

monitor   1) An audio speaker used to check the actual sounds being mixed. 2) A video display device that features a high quality television picture that has not been modulated to an RF signal. 3) To listen to or view sound or picture as it is being manipulated.

morphing   Gradually transforming one digital image into another by making a series of slight changes in the first image until it takes on the characteristics of the second image.

mount   See *camera mount.*

mouse   A rolling ball or moving instrument that is used to move elements around on a computer screen or to respond to computer questions or instructions.

MPEG-2   A compression system that analyzes frames and uses specially designated frames to predict the degree to which a picture will change.

MS   See *medium shot.*

multimedia authoring program   A computer program that is designed to produce interactive media presentations.

multipin connector   A connector that allows video, audio, power, and remote control to flow through it between a camera and a VCR.

multitrack   Tape or a tape recorder capable of holding a large number of audio signals, such as eight, sixteen, or twenty-four, in parallel with each other.

musical instrument digital interface   A communication methodology that allows musical instruments and other electronic gear, such as computers and tape recorders, to interact.

music licensing company   An organization that collects money from stations or production groups that use music and then distributes that money to composers and record companies.

N

National Television System Committee   A TV industry body that developed the basic technical standards used in American TV today, including the color standards that are usually referred to as NTSC standards.

negative/positive selector   A switch on a video camera that changes a positive picture to its negative.

network   A group of computers linked together so that they can share data.

neutral density   Material in a filter that reduces the amount of light hitting the camera tube or CCD without affecting the quality of the color.

noise   Unwanted sound or static in an audio signal or unwanted electronic disturbance or snow in a video signal.

nondimmer circuit   A switch that turns a light off and on but cannot adjust its brightness.

nonlinear   A type of editing in which the program does not need to be edited from beginning to end; material can be laid down in any order and can be added to, changed, or deleted without having to edit all over again from the point of the change.

normalled   Having a certain output on an audio patch bay permanently wired to a given position on the console so that a patch cord is not needed to make the temporary connection.

NTSC See *National Television System Committee.*

O

off-line A basic electronic editing process whereby original footage is transferred to a workprint that is used for making editing decisions.

off-mic Distorted sound that occurs when noise from outside a mic's pickup area is transduced and amplified.

original master The tape or disc on which footage is first recorded.

omnidirectional A microphone that picks up sound from all directions.

on-line A concluding electronic editing stage in which all editing takes place on the finished master tape.

O/S shot See *over-the-shoulder shot.*

outlines A general listing of what will be included within a program, usually in sentence fragment or paragraph form.

outpoint The precise spot on the source tape and/or edit tape where an edit is to end.

over-the-shoulder shot A camera shot looking at one person framed by the back of the head and shoulder of another person in the foreground.

overtones Acoustical or electrical frequencies that are higher than the fundamental tone.

P

PL See *intercom.*

pad 1) An audio component that can reduce the strength of a preamplified feed so that it does not exceed the volume limits of a control channel. 2) In video, extra material at the beginning or end of the shot that is needed to maintain sync in editing.

pad switch A control on an audio board that selects the proper amplification for certain audio equipment such as a guitar.

paintbox The part of a graphics generator that allows the user to select and use different colors.

pan 1) To turn a camera horizontally by rotating the camera mounting head. 2) A control on the audio board that is used to determine the balance of sound between the left and right channels. 3) A rectangular-shaped floodlight.

pan handle The handle extending toward the rear of the camera with which the camera operator controls movement of the camera.

parabolic dish A large curved surface that collects sound and reflects it to a microphone.

patch bay A board with numerous terminals (inputs and outputs) through which various audio, video, or lighting signals can be connected by patch cords to other channels or circuits.

patch cord A cable with connectors on both ends that is used to go from one connector on a patch bay to another.

pause mode On a VCR, the control that places the head against a stationary piece of tape so that the same frame can be seen for an extended period.

pause/record mode The point on an edit at which the edit deck begins to record.

PCM See *pulse code modulation.*

peak In audio, to reach the highpoint of volume level for a particular sound sequence; the ideal place to peak is at the 0 position on the VU meter.

pedestal 1) A heavy camera mount that facilitates easy raising or lowering of the camera head, usually with a counterweight system or with compressed air. 2) To move the camera head up or down with the pedestal mount. 3) The brightest part of the darkest part of a video signal as seen on a waveform monitor.

perambulator boom A large three-wheeled movable platform that holds a mic operator and a mic in such a way that the mic can follow action throughout a studio.

performance release A form signed by people appearing on video giving the production company the

right to distribute their performances.

performers TV talent who are on as themselves, not acting the part of someone else.

persistence of vision A human phenomenon whereby the brain retains images for a short period of time so that still images that are projected very quickly look like moving images.

perspective In audio, the matching of visual and sound distance.

phantom power Current sent to a condenser mic from the audio console.

phase control A control on a piece of audio or video equipment that changes the positive portion of the sine wave to negative and the negative portion to positive.

phasing The relationship of the positive and negative portions of the sine waves of two different electrical signals to determine to what extent their oscillations are synchronized.

pickup shots Material recorded after an entire program or sequence is recorded so that it can be edited in to correct some element of what was shot.

pickup tube A transducing device within a camera that changes light energy into photoelectrical energy through the use of a target and an electron beam that scans the target.

picon Picture icon; freeze frames of certain points of an edit.

pilot A taped production of one representative program from a proposed series of programs.

pin To focus the rays of a spotlight to a narrow beam of intense light.

pitch A meeting during which people with a program idea try to convince other people to buy their idea.

pixel The computer-derived term for "picture element" that designates the smallest addressable triad of phosphor dots on a picture tube or CCD that can be manipulated and illuminated.

PL See *private line.*

playback To retrieve electronic signals from a tape or disc and turn them into sound and/or images.

plus decibels Sound levels to the right of the 0 level on a VU meter.

polar pickup pattern The directional sensitivity of a microphone as shown in a chart.

pop filter A metal or foam ball placed over the top of a mic to minimize plosive sounds.

position jump A cut between two cameras in which a person or object appears to change position from one side of the screen to the other.

postbox A postproduction system that includes a character generator, a paint system, and other effects.

postproduction A time after TV program material has been shot during which it is edited.

postproduction editing The electronic editing process that takes place after the individual program segments have been produced and recorded.

preamp An electronic device that can magnify the low signal output of microphones and other transducers before the signal is sent to a mixing board or to other amplifiers.

pre-edit roll period The time during which the source and edit decks get up to speed.

pre-edit session A meeting held before editing occurs at which the director, editor, and others involved in the creative aspects of the production meet to discuss what the final edited program will look like.

prepreproduction The period during which preparation and planning are undertaken for a television program.

presence The authenticity of a sound in terms of perceived fidelity and distance.

preset bus The switcher bank that controls the picture that will go on the air after the one that is currently on the air.

preset monitor The monitor that shows the output of the preset bus—the source that will be going on-air next.

pre-studio rehearsals Rehearsals with talent in a rehearsal hall or other location before coming into the studio.

preview To look at an edit before it is actually transferred to make sure it is correct.

preview monitor A large monitor that can be used to look at any camera picture or video effect before putting it on the program line.

primary colors Red, blue, and green.

private line See *intercom*.

proc amp The electronic component that takes the composite video signal from the switcher, stabilizes the levels, and removes unwanted elements.

producer The creator and originator of a television program, usually in charge of elements such as writing, music clearance, financial considerations, and hiring the director.

production The stage during which all the shooting for a TV program is undertaken.

production designer A person in charge of the overall look of a film or video.

production house An organization that produces various types of video material—commercials, corporate videos, broadcast programs, educational programs.

production manager A person who works for an independent production company who determines costs that will be incurred by a particular production.

program bus The switcher bank that controls the actual picture being sent out on the air.

program line out The final output of an audio board or of a switcher that shows what has been mixed through the console or switcher.

program monitor A large monitor that shows what is being sent out over the air or to the videotape recorder.

program speaker The main monitor in an audio booth that outputs what has gone through the audio console.

program time The total length of a show.

proscenium arch In the theater, the arch that separates the stage from the auditorium.

public domain The legal condition covering copyright that says that when material is old enough it can be used without copyright clearance being obtained.

pull focus To change the focus of a camera lens from one extreme to the other in order to shift attention from one object to another (either in the foreground or the background).

pulse code modulation An audio digital signal that is recorded diagonally on videotape separate from the picture information.

PZM mic See *surface-mount mic*.

Q

quad split A special effect in which the TV screen is split into four sections, each showing a different picture.

quadruplex An older videotape recording format that used four rotating heads in a pattern transverse to the movement of the videotape.

quartz light A highly efficient lamp with a high-intensity tungsten-halogen filament in a quartz or silica housing.

R

radio frequency The carrier wave on which radio and television signals are superimposed for transmission.

rain drum A rounded surface on which black paper streaked with white is turned to simulate rain.

random access The ability to bring up video and/or audio information instantly, in any order, from a disc or similar storage device without having to wait for tapes to rewind.

raster The viewing area of a camera picture tube.

rate card A listing of costs for renting equipment or a facility.

reaction shot A shot that shows someone responding to what someone else is saying or doing.

real time Being able to do something, such as show moving video, in the same amount of time as it actually happens; usually used in conjunction with how fast a computer system can show video.

record To use audio and/or video electronic signals to arrange iron-oxide particles on the magnetic recording tape or disc or laser inputs on a disc so that they can be retrieved later.

recording head   See *head*.

reference white   A white object, such as a piece of paper or a T-shirt, that can be used on location to white balance a camera.

reflected light   Light bounced back from the surface of an object.

render   A computer process that allows effects to be built over time.

retrace   The area in the scanning process where the electron beam is turned off so that it can move from the bottom of the screen to the top to begin scanning another field.

reverberation   Sound that has bounced off a surface or various surfaces more than once or sound that has been processed so it sounds like it has bounced off surfaces.

review   To look at an edit after it has been transferred to make sure it was executed correctly.

RF   See *radio frequency*.

RF mic   See *wireless mic*.

riding gain   Adjusting volume through an audio console during a production or taping.

riser   A raised platform, usually made of wood, on which talent can sit or stand.

robotic cameras   Cameras that do not need an operator standing by them because they are controlled remotely.

rough cut   A loose assemblage of video and audio that will eventually become the edited master of a program.

routing switcher   An audio device that allows for two or more inputs to be fed into the input channel of an audio board.

rule of thirds   A principle of composition that divides the TV screen into thirds, horizontally and vertically, and places objects of interest at the points where the lines intersect.

rundown   A list of various segments that will be included in a program.

run-through   A rehearsal of a production that may not involve all cast and crew.

S

SA   See *studio address*.

safety chain   A steel chain on a lamp housing that should always be attached to the lighting grid so that the light will not fall if it comes loose.

sampling   Selecting certain portions of something, such as a large number of small parts of an electromagnetic signal.

sandbag   A heavy weight placed on the brace of a flat to hold the flat in place.

saturation   The strength or intensity of a color—how far removed it is from a neutral or gray shade.

scanner   A computer peripheral that can convert printed material, such as photographs or slides, into digital form.

scanning area   The portion of a graphic card that actually can be seen by the camera imaging device.

scanning beam   The stream of electrons that goes across the camera tube or receiver tube in order to change light energy into electromagnetic energy or vice versa.

scoop   A floodlight that contains a single bulb in a bowl-shaped metal reflector.

screens   In interactive media, the building blocks of interactive presentations; the amount of information that can be displayed on a computer monitor at one time, including various media elements such as video, text, or graphics.

scrim   A translucent filter, often made of fiberglass or fine screening, used in front of either a spotlight or floodlight to soften and diffuse the light quality.

script   The written guideline from which a TV program is produced.

script supervisor   A person who keeps notes during production so that continuity is maintained and the material shot can be edited properly.

search mode   The part of the editing system that enables the operator to move the source deck and edit deck forward or backward at varying speeds to locate the precise point for editing precision.

SEG   See *special effects generator*.

serif   Small extensions on the tips of letters.

segment timing sheet   A form that helps the AD keep track of the running times of various portions of a program so that they add up to the proper overall time required.

selective attention principle   The ability of the human ear to filter out unwanted noise so that a person can concentrate on the particular sound he or she wants to hear.

self key   A key effect in which the dominant brightness level cuts its own pattern over the background.

server   A master recipient of video that can hold the video information and then distribute it to various users.

servo capstan   The part of a recorder that pulls the tape through the machine at the proper speed.

set designer   The person who determines the environment where the production takes place.

set light   General lighting on the scenery or other background behind the talent.

set-up   Getting a studio ready for production.

shader   A person who makes technical adjustments on a camera using a camera control unit located at some distance from the camera.

shape   To alter an audio signal by controlling volume, filtering out certain frequencies, emphasizing upper or lower pitches, creating an echo effect, and so forth.

shift registers   The part of a CCD camera that collects the output of the pixels and transfers it to wire.

shooting schedule   A sheet that lists what is to be accomplished each day of production and the major elements needed in order to accomplish it.

short lens   A short focal-length lens with a wide viewing angle; it includes quite a bit in the picture and tends to exaggerate distance.

shot sheets   Lists that the director makes that can be attached to the back of each camera so that the camera operators know what they will be shooting.

shotgun A highly directional microphone used for picking up sounds from a distance.

silhouette A type of lighting where the background is lit but the performers are not.

skew A VCR control that adjusts the tension on a tape to correct for when the top part of a video picture appears to bend to the right or left.

slant-track See *helical scan*.

slate An identification procedure whereby date, scene, segment, and other information necessary to tape and film editing are recorded at the beginning of a designated camera sequence.

slave To send the output of a camera being used in a multicamera production to its own separate videotape recorder.

SMPTE time code A frame location address system, developed by the Society of Motion Picture and Television Engineers, that can label and find any section of a videotape or disc by hour, minute, second, and frame.

snake A connector box that contains a large number of microphone input receptacles.

softlight A lamp that has the bulb positioned in such a way that the light is reflected on the back of the lamp housing before leaving the fixture.

sound card A board for a computer that enables audio to be heard.

source In electronic editing, the VCR or tape that contains the original raw footage that is to be edited.

spaced mics A stereo mic setup that uses two mics placed parallel to each other facing into the set.

special effects Fancy electronic video transitions and methods of combining video sources such as wipes, keys, page turns, and so on.

special effects generator The part of the video switcher that can be used to create special electronic effects.

specifications Technical facts about electronic equipment such as power consumption, impedance, and frequency response.

specs See *specifications*.

split-pair mics See *spaced mics*.

split screen A special effect with the screen split into two or more sections, with a picture from a different input filling each portion of the screen.

spotlight 1) A concentrated light that covers a narrow area; it usually provides some means for varying the angle of the illumination by moving the bulb within the housing. 2)A special effect in which one part of the picture is lighter than the rest of the picture.

spread To focus the rays of a spotlight to a relatively wide area so that the light is less intense than when the light is in the pinned position.

staff People who are employed by a particular production organization and receive regular weekly wages regardless of what project they are working on.

stage manager The director's key assistant in charge of all production concerns on the studio floor.

start-and-stop rehearsal A full facilities rehearsal with cameras operating, designed to be interrupted to work out problems as the production progresses.

stereophonic sound Audio that is recorded, transmitted, and played back through two separate (left and right) channels to simulate binaural hearing.

stock footage Scenes of various types that can be purchased to insert into a production.

storyboard A series of simple drawings or computer generated frames that lay out visually the content of a commercial or program.

strike Cleaning up a set after a production.

strip lights A series of pan lights or low-wattage bulbs mounted in a row of three to twelve lights in one housing, used as a specialized floodlight for lighting a cyclorama or other large background area.

stripboards Large boards or computer-generated sheets that summarize the scenes, locations, and actors needed for each day of production.

studio The primary room devoted to video production containing all the paraphernalia for sets, lighting, cameras, microphones, and so forth—the space where all acting or performing takes place.

studio address A public-address loudspeaker system, allowing those in the control room to talk directly to the studio floor.

studio talkback See *studio address*.

submaster See *group master fader*.

submastering Controlling groups of sound inputs, such as separate inputs from each percussion instrument in an orchestra, separately from other groups of sound inputs, such as all the strings.

super See *superimposition*.

superimposition A picture resulting from the simultaneous display of two pictures that are half way through a dissolve.

surface-mount mic A flat microphone that consists of a thin pickup plate that, when mounted on a table or ceiling, uses the surface it is mounted on to collect sound waves.

S-VHS A half-inch tape format that is an improvement over VHS, mainly because of the type of tape it uses and its treatment of the chrominance and luminance channels.

sweetening Improving sound and/or video during the editing process.

switcher A video mixing panel, consisting of selection buttons and control levers (fader arms), that permits the selection and combining of incoming video signals to form the final program picture.

symmetrical balance Formal arrangement, usually with the most important element centered in the picture and other equal objects placed equidistant from the center.

sync generator The part of the video system that produces a synchronizing signal (sync pulse) based on the basic 60-cycle alternating current (in the U. S.), which serves as a timing pulse to coordinate the video elements of all components in the video system.

sync pulse A signal that operates in relation to the 60-cycle alternating current that is often placed on videotape as a timing coordinator.

syndication A process by which programs are distributed to individual stations that air them when they wish as opposed to network programs that are generally aired by all network affiliated stations at the same time.

T

tail pad Material after the end of a shot that will not be used in the final edit but will give sync information so that the edit remains stable.

take 1) An instantaneous change from one video source to another. 2) an indication of the number of times a certain shot or scene is recorded—the first time is take 1, the second time is take 2, etc.

tally lights Small red indicators on each camera to let the talent and camera operators know which camera is on the air.

tape switch A control on an audio board that selects proper amplification for the input of a tape recorder.

target The part of a television camera tube that is scanned by the electron beams.

TBC See *time base corrector*.

TD See *technical director*.

technical director The production person who operates the switcher.

telecine The equipment used to transfer film to video.

telephoto lens A lens with a very long focal length, used for close-ups of objects from a great distance.

teleprompter A mechanical device that projects the moving script, via mirrors, directly in front of the camera lens.

3-to-1 cutting ratio A principle that states you should not take to a shot that is three times larger or three times smaller than the preceding shot.

three-to-one rule A microphone placement principle that states that, if two mics must be side by side, there should be three times the distance between them that there is between the mics and the people using them.

three-point lighting The traditional lighting setup that incorporates a key, a fill, and a back light.

tilt To pivot the camera vertically by pointing the camera mounting head up or down.

time base corrector The electronic apparatus that takes the video feed from the video recorder, encodes that signal into a digital form, and then reconstructs an enhanced control track and video signal for distribution and playback.

time code See *SMPTE time code*.

timing Setting electronic parameters so that mic signals or camera signals from a studio go through their cables and reach their destinations at the same relative time.

top hat A circular metal object placed in front of a light in order to pinpoint the light onto a particular area of the set.

tracking The VCR control that adjusts the video head to put it in the optimum position when a tape is played back.

transduce To receive energy in one form (sound waves or light energy) and convert it into another form of energy (electromagnetic signals).

transfer editing The electronic re-recording (or dubbing) of video and audio information from an original videotape to a second tape for assembly in a program sequence.

transitions Methods, such as dissolves and wipes, for getting from one shot to another.

treatment Several written pages that describe the main premise and elements of a series or program.

trim 1) To add a few frames or subtract a few frames from an edit. 2) To make final adjustments on lights.

tripod A three-legged camera mount, sometimes with casters, that facilitates camera movement.

truck To move the camera and its mount laterally to the right or left.

two-column scripts Scripts with video in the left-hand column and audio in the right-hand column.

twofold Two flats hinged together.

U

U-matic The ¾-inch tape format.

unbalanced line Audio cables that have two wires, one for positive, and one for both negative and ground.

undercut To change one video source of a two-camera super or other effect instantaneously while the effect is on the air.

uninterrupted run-through The rehearsal of an entire show without stopping for anything except major problems; minor problems are fixed later.

unions Organizations that set wages and working conditions that producers must adhere to for people (usually below-the-line people) that they hire.

unit manager A person who works for a production facility who draws up a rate card and schedules facilities.

user interaction See *interactive*.

V

VCR See *videocassette recorder*.

vectorscope A specialized electronic monitor that graphically displays the saturation levels for each of the three primary and three complementary colors.

vertical interval The area in the scanning process where the electron beam turns off to retrace from the bottom of the screen to the top so that it can begin to scan another field.

vertical interval time code Information about hours, minutes, seconds, and frames that is placed in the area of a TV signal where the electron beam has turned off so that it can retrace from the bottom to the top of the screen.

vertical synchronization pulse The portion of the sync signal that controls the movement of a scanning beam from top to bottom.

video capture Hardware and software that allows a personal computer to convert video into digital form.

videocassette recorder A magnetic-electronic recording machine that records audio, video, and control track signals on a videotape enclosed within a container.

video disc A round storage device that can hold video and audio signals in such a way that they can be randomly accessed.

video mixer See *switcher.*

video on demand A system, delivered over cable or via satellite or microwave, in which a user can order a specified program at any time.

video operator A person in charge of recording a program.

video output control A control that increases the gain of a video signal so that a camera can obtain a picture in low lighting conditions.

video server See *server.*

video track The part of a videotape that holds the picture information.

virtual reality A computer simulation of a real-life event, such as flying a plane or driving a car.

Virtual Reality Modeling Language (VRML) A computer language that allows the production of interactive media presentations in which users control the presentation by moving through 3D landscapes.

VITC See *vertical interval time code.*

voice levels The talking that studio talent does before taping so that the audio technician can set proper volume controls for the microphones that will be picking up the talent's audio.

volume unit meter A display meter that shows the relative volume of an audio signal.

VRML See *Virtual Reality Modeling Language.*

VTR machines Videotape recorders that place information on tape electronically.

VU meter See *volume unit meter.*

W

walk-through rehearsal An abbreviated rehearsal, conducted from the studio floor, to acquaint the talent and/or crew with the major outline of the production.

warning lights Lights on a camera or within the viewfinder that warn that something is wrong or about to go wrong, such as insufficient lighting or a low battery level.

waveform An electronic representation of a signal.

waveform monitor A type of oscilloscope that displays the brightness of all picture elements and, like a VU meter, allows the operator to keep the elements with highest intensity from exceeding the capabilities of the equipment.

wavelength Measurement of the length of an electromagnetic wave from one theoretical crest to the next.

white balance An adjustment process through which light reflected from a white card in a given lighting situation is used as a reference point; in this setup mode, the camera automatically balances the red and blue intensities with the available light.

wide-angle lens See *short lens.*

wide shot A view of the subject from a relatively great distance.

wildtrack Background noise recorded at a site so that it can be mixed in with other sounds during postproduction.

window 1) A part of a computer screen that is used for a particular application and usually can be expanded and contracted so that the various aspects of that application can be undertaken. 2) A portion of a tape output that shows time code on top of the picture.

wipe A video transition whereby one image is gradually pushed off

---

the screen as another picture replaces it.

wireless mic A microphone with a self-contained miniature FM transmitter built in that can send the audio signal several hundred feet, eliminating the need for mic cables.

workprint A copy of original tape footage that is used for interim editing so that the master does not need to go through the wear and tear of the editing process.

workstation Audio and/or video equipment that can be contained in a small space, such as a table top, to manipulate sound and/or picture with the aid of computer technology.

Worldnet A satellite operation run by the United States Information Agency.

World Wide Web A system that allows interactive media presentations to be delivered over the Internet or an intranet.

WWW See *World Wide Web.*

X

XCU See *extreme close-up.*

XLR connector A professional quality balanced connector with three prongs.

XLS See *extreme long shot.*

X-Y mics A coincidental stereo mic setup that uses two cardioid mics placed like crossed swords.

Z

zoom lens A variable-focal-length lens that, through a complicated optical system, can be smoothly changed from one focal length to another.

zoom ratio The ratio between the widest angle a particular zoom lens is capable of and the narrowest angle it can capture.

Index